The Mac OS 8.6 Book

Mark R. Bell

The Mac OS 8.6 Book
© 1999 The Coriolis Group. All rights reserved.

This book may not be duplicated in any way without the express written consent of the publisher, except in the form of brief excerpts or quotations for the purposes of review. The information contained herein is for the personal use of the reader and may not be incorporated in any commercial programs, other books, databases, or any kind of software without written consent of the publisher. Making copies of this book or any portion for any purpose other than your own is a violation of United States copyright laws.

Limits of Liability and Disclaimer of Warranty

The author and publisher of this book have used their best efforts in preparing the book and the programs contained in it. These efforts include the development, research, and testing of the theories and programs to determine their effectiveness. The author and publisher make no warranty of any kind, expressed or implied, with regard to these programs or the documentation contained in this book.

The author and publisher shall not be liable in the event of incidental or consequential damages in connection with, or arising out of, the furnishing, performance, or use of the programs, associated instructions, and/or claims of productivity gains.

Trademarks

Trademarked names appear throughout this book. Rather than list the names and entities that own the trademarks or insert a trademark symbol with each mention of the trademarked name, the publisher states that it is using the names for editorial purposes only and to the benefit of the trademark owner, with no intention of infringing upon that trademark.

The Coriolis Group, LLC
14455 N. Hayden Road, Suite 220
Scottsdale, Arizona 85260

480/483-0192
FAX 480/483-0193
http://www.coriolis.com

Library of Congress Cataloging-in-Publication Data
Bell, Mark R.
   The Mac OS 8.6 book / by Mark Bell.
     p. cm.
   Includes index.
   ISBN 1-57610-443-5
   1. Mac OS. 2. Operating systems (Computers) 3. Macintosh (Computer) I. Title.
QA76.76.O63B449   1999
005.4'469--DC21   99-18767
                                                                                 CIP

Printed in the United States of America
10 9 8 7 6 5 4 3 2 1

Publisher
Keith Weiskamp

Acquisitions Editor
Stephanie Wall

Marketing Specialist
Diane Enger

Project Editor
Michelle Stroup

Production Coordinator
Jon Gabriel

Cover Design
Jody Winkler

Layout Design
April Nielsen

CD-ROM Developer
Robert Clarfield

*This book is dedicated to my wife Virginia, my own personal Venus.
You are courageous beyond measure.*

—Mark

About The Author

Mark R. Bell is author of more than 20 books, articles, and software manuals about the Mac OS and the World Wide Web, including *The Mac Web Server Book*, *The Mac OS 8 Book*, *BBEdit 4 for Macintosh*, and *The Mac OS 8.5 Black Book*. Mark also serves as a technical editor and speaks at conventions and workshops, including Mactivity/Web and Macworld Expo.

Mark holds a bachelor's degree in English, history, and political science from MTSU, and a master's degree in theology from Duke University. He lives in Chapel Hill, North Carolina with his wife Virginia D. Smith, a network of Macs, and a small herd of Cocker Spaniels.

Acknowledgments

There is one individual and three groups of people who make it possible for books like this to be published. Craig Danuloff wrote the first edition of this book several years ago, and even though it has been revised many time, since, Craig's voice can still be heard. The first group includes all the professionals at Coriolis who know what they are doing and make it look like authors know what they are doing as well! This time around, it includes Michelle Stroup (Project Editor and Principal Bearer of Responsibility), Stephanie Wall (Acquisitions Editor and She Who Gets the Ball Rolling), Virginia D. Smith (Copy Editor and She Who Keeps the Author from Butchering the English Language), Mary Catherine Bunn (Proofreader and Finder of Even the Smallest Mistakes), Jon Gabriel (He Who Oversees Design and Typesetting), Debbie Suggs (Technical Reviewer and Consummate Mac Guru), Robert Clarfield (CD-ROM Developer and Master of Mass Storage), as well as a cast of dozens who make me look good and whom I never get to meet. You *are* appreciated! Last but not least, thanks to Tristan "Mr. Java" Reid, who revised four chapters between teaching assignments across North America.

Next, there are the Macintosh professionals around the world who tolerate our queries for information (obscure and mundane) and provide their software for our CD-ROMs. In return, they ask only for a free copy of the book instead of what their time and effort are really worth. This group includes Rob Terrell (perpetually), Tim Holmes, Keith Hatounian, Gregory D. Landweber, Anita Holmgren, Kenji Takeuchi, Caerwyn Pearce, Bob Fronabarger, Jeremy Hall, Turlough O'Connor, Thorsten Lemke, Mihail Lari and Humayun Lari, to name but a few.

Finally, there are those persons who lend their support on a more personal level. Translation: They put up with my warbling attitudes while writing books, yet encourage me to finish the race! Special thanks to Gregg Johnson and Mary Catherine Bunn; Craig and Angelika Waddell; Bailey and Ruby; Lenora, Andy, Kristi, Kasey, and Hailey Bell; Scott and Marti Fanning; and Ella Lee Kennedy Jones, who contributed to this book in the most unexpected way.

Contents At A Glance

Part I	The Operating System
Chapter 1	Operating System Basics
Chapter 2	The System Folder
Chapter 3	The Finder And Desktop
Chapter 4	Customizing Your Mac
Chapter 5	Managing Your Data
Chapter 6	PowerBook System Software

Part II	Applications
Chapter 7	Mac OS 8.6 And Your Software
Chapter 8	Working With Other Types Of Computers
Chapter 9	Applications And Memory Management
Chapter 10	Working With Multiple Applications
Chapter 11	Fonts And Printing
Chapter 12	Interapplication Communication And OpenDoc
Chapter 13	AppleScript
Chapter 14	Java
Chapter 15	Multimedia
Chapter 16	Troubleshooting

Part III	Networking
Chapter 17	File Sharing
Chapter 18	Working On A Network
Chapter 19	Internet Connectivity
Chapter 20	Personal Web Sharing
Chapter 21	Internet Applications And Utilities

Part IV	Appendixes
Appendix A	Getting Help
Appendix B	Shortcuts
Appendix C	Installing Or Updating Mac OS 8.6
Appendix D	Additional Resources On The Web

Table Of Contents

Part I
The Operating System

Chapter 1
Operating System Basics 3
    What Tasks Does The Mac OS Perform?   3
    Mac OS Components   5
    Using The Mac OS   8
    Basic Mac OS Operations   9
    Transferring Data   21

Chapter 2
The System Folder 31
    Exploring The Mac OS 8.6 System Folder   32
    Modifying The System Folder   56

Chapter 3
The Finder And Desktop 61
    Finder Menus   62
    Finder And Desktop Window Basics   71
    Advanced Finder And Desktop Features   92
    Context-Sensitive Help   101
    The Get Info Dialog Box   107

Chapter 4
Customizing Your Mac 113
    Mac OS Customization Features   113
    Third-Party Utilities   130

Chapter 5
Managing Your Data 139
    Aliasing   139
    The Sherlock Search Engine   153
    Labels   167
    Comments   169

Chapter 6
PowerBook System Software 173
    PowerBook Issues   173
    Power/Performance Management   175
    Display Management   180
    SCSI Disk Mode   182
    Remounting Servers   183
    Apple Remote Access   184
    The PowerBook Control Strip   184
    File Synchronization   187
    Location Manager   189
    Security   191

Part II
Applications

Chapter 7
Mac OS 8.6 And Your Software 197
    Mac OS 8.6 Compatibility   197
    What Is Compatibility?   198
    Launching   200
    Stationery Documents   207
    The Desktop Level   212
    Dialog Box Keyboard Equivalents   214

Chapter 8
Working With Other Types Of Computers 217

Sharing Data   217
SuperDrive   219
File Exchange: PC Exchange   220
File Exchange: File Translation   222
MacLinkPlus   225
Other OS Solutions   229

Chapter 9
Applications And Memory Management 235

Memory Vs. Storage   235
The Memory Control Panel   236
Controlling Memory   245
The Get Info Dialog Box   250
Virtual Memory And Virtual Memory Requirements   255

Chapter 10
Working With Multiple Applications 259

What Is Multitasking?   260
The Old MultiFinder   262
Multitasking In Mac OS 8.6   263
Working With Multiple Applications   264
Multitasking Tips   276
The Memory Implications Of Multitasking   277

Chapter 11
Fonts And Printing 281

Imaging Models   281
Fonts And The Mac OS   288
TrueType Fonts   296
Font Reserve   301
Advanced Typography   304
Installing Fonts   307
Desktop Printing   310
Desktop Printer Utility   315
ColorSync And Color Matching   316

Mac OS 8.6

Chapter 12
Interapplication Communication And OpenDoc 321

    Interapplication Communication (IAC)   322
    The Edition Manager   327
    How Publish/Subscribe Works   327
    Publish/Subscribe Commands   329
    Editing Subscribers   337
    Edition Files In The Finder   338
    Edition Manager Tips   340
    OpenDoc   342

Chapter 13
AppleScript 351

    What Is AppleScript?   352
    The AppleScript Architecture   355
    Scripting Basics   357
    The Script Editor   362
    Scripting Applications   369
    The Scriptable Finder   371
    A Few New Tricks In Mac OS 8.6   371
    Sample Scripts   375
    Learning More About AppleScript   376

Chapter 14
Java 379

    Java On The Macintosh   380
    Mac Runtime For Java   381
    Running Java Applets   383
    Other Java VMs   385
    The "Look" Of Cross Platform Programs   389

Chapter 15
Multimedia 395

    QuickTime   396
    QuickTime VR   407

Mac OS 8.6

QuickDraw 3D   409
Speech   413
Other Multimedia Applications   414

Chapter 16
Troubleshooting 423
Common Problems And Their Solutions   423
Useful Tools   438
Preventing Problems   447

Part III
Networking

Chapter 17
File Sharing 451
What Is File Sharing?   452
Preparing For File Sharing   455
Starting File Sharing   456
Registering Users & Groups   459
Creating New Users   461
Sharing Folders Or Volumes   467
Access Privileges   471
Monitoring File Sharing   476

Chapter 18
Working On A Network 479
Accessing Network Volumes   479
The Network Browser   485
Program Linking   487

Chapter 19
Internet Connectivity 491
Getting Connected: ISP Vs. LAN   491
Internet Assistants   493
Open Transport And Remote Access   497

Mac OS 8.6

Chapter 20
Personal Web Sharing 505
    The Web And HTML   505
    Web Server Configuration   507
    Web Sharing Preferences   514
    Security   516
    Getting Help   519

Chapter 21
Internet Applications And Utilities 521
    Mac OS 8.6 Internet Software   521
    Netscape Communicator   522
    Microsoft Internet Explorer   531
    Microsoft Outlook Express   534
    Mac OS Internet Features And Utilities   537
    Must-Have Internet Utilities   542

Part IV
Appendixes

Appendix A
Getting Help 551

Appendix B
Shortcuts 563

Appendix C
Installing Or Updating Mac OS 8.6 567

Appendix D
Additional Resources On The Web 577

Index 581

PART I

The Operating System

Operating System Basics

Why is the Macintosh so popular? Is it the graphical user interface? Maybe it's because most Macintosh applications use similar menus and commands. Or is it because configuring hardware and peripherals on the Mac is so easy?

The answer, as everyone knows, is all of the above. But while you probably know how easy a Macintosh is to use—it's friendly, consistent, and expandable—you may not know why. The operating system (OS) controls the computer and gives it all of these qualities.

The enhancements in Mac OS 8.6 give the OS even more flexibility than before, especially in the area of user customization. While Mac OS 8 added lots of new features to enable you to customize the aesthetics of your computer, Mac OS 8.6 goes even further with the new Appearance Manager. To understand how to make the most of the expanded capabilities of the OS, we need to look at how the OS works. This chapter introduces and defines the functions of the Mac OS, and offers a quick tour of Macintosh basics as well as some of the more common commands and features provided by the OS.

This tour is designed for readers who are using a Macintosh for the first time and those who'd like a little review before diving into the details of Mac OS 8.6's features. If you're comfortable using your Macintosh, you can probably skip the "Basic Macintosh Operations" section of this chapter and skim "What Does the Operating System Do?" and "Using the Operating System" before moving on to Chapter 2.

What Tasks Does The Mac OS Perform?

What makes the Macintosh smile and chime when you turn it on? Why does the CD-ROM icon appear on the Desktop when you insert an audio CD? How can you access the Internet and check your email? How are fonts shared among all your applications? The answer to these questions is an easy one: the operating system does it for you. The operating system (abbreviated OS, which computer geeks rhyme with boss) has three main responsibilities: it controls the hardware built into your Macintosh or Macintosh clone (and any peripherals you have connected to it), provides common elements and features to all your software applications, and helps you manage your disks, files, and directories. Let's briefly look at each of these areas:

- *Hardware control*—In order for your Mac to work, its RAM, disk drives, video monitor, keyboard, mouse, printer, and DVD drive (or other peripherals) must be collectively managed. Saving files to disk, drawing images on the screen, and printing are examples of hardware control managed by the OS.

- *Common software elements*—Every Macintosh software application has common elements, such as menus, dialog boxes, and support for fonts. These common elements are delivered to software applications from a "software toolbox" in the OS. Apple assures consistency among applications and spares software developers the difficult task of programming these elements by providing them centrally and including conventions for their use as part of the OS.

- *Disk and file management*—The Finder, which is part of the OS, provides the ability to format disks; lets you find, copy, move, rename, and delete files; and displays icon and text-based information about disks and files. The Finder also allows you to launch other applications and acts as the "home base" from which you start up or quit other applications. In other words, it provides a graphical user interface (GUI) using icons and windows to represent complex operations that manage your disks and files.

Another great thing about the Mac OS is its history of backwards compatibility with earlier versions of the OS and older computer hardware. For example, Mac OS 8.6 allows the third generation of PowerPC processors (G3 processors), which are Reduced Instruction Set Computing (RISC) microprocessors, to run programs and software libraries written for the much older Complex Instruction Set Computing (CISC) microprocessors—albeit more slowly than software specially written for the Power Macintosh. (CISC-based Macs are also called 68K Macs after the 680x0 series of Motorola microprocessors.) Much of Mac OS 8.6, including the Finder, is now PowerPC native, making this version of the OS much faster than previous versions. And don't forget, Mac OS 8.6 will not work on non-PowerPC computers anyway.

Without the OS, each application would have to provide its own self-contained operating features for running the hardware and managing your disks and files. There would be no continuity from one application to the next, and software programs would be far more complex, as well as more time-consuming and costly

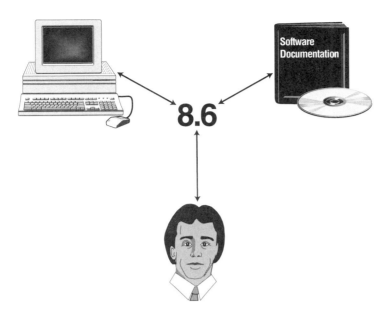

Figure 1.1 The OS provides the link between you, your Macintosh, and your software.

to develop. Fortunately, Mac OS 8.6 performs these tasks well, allowing developers to focus on unique and sophisticated programs while leaving the rest to Apple. Figure 1.1 illustrates the central role of Mac OS 8.6.

Mac OS Components

The most prominent files that make up Mac OS 8.6 are the System suitcase and the Finder. Printer and network drivers, Control Panel devices, Extensions, and resources (fonts, desk accessories, sounds, function keys) are also part of the OS, however. All operating System components are found in the System folder, which is described more fully in Chapter 2. The following list summarizes the functions of these components of the OS:

➤ *System suitcase*—The System suitcase is involved in the most important aspects of the OS (file management, tasking, memory management, and so on). It also acts as the framework to which other parts of the OS can connect. The System suitcase helps the Mac start up and provides many of the dialog boxes, menu bars, commonly used icons, and code that help applications manage memory and other hardware resources. The System suitcase also contains resources, including sounds and keyboard layouts.

➤ *Finder*—The Finder is a program designed to help you control your disks, drives, and files. It puts a "human face" on an otherwise complicated program. The heart of the interface, the Finder makes the Mac OS user-friendly. It provides utility features such as formatting disks, printing disk catalogs, and deleting files; it also serves as a "home base" for sorting and working with files and launching other applications. Starting with Mac OS 8, the Finder is multithreaded, and with Mac OS 8.6 it is also PowerPC native, features which enable you to perform a copy operation while continuing work on other tasks, for example.

➤ *ROM*—A vital part of the Macintosh operating system is stored in a read-only memory (ROM) chip on the computer's logic board. ROM-based software handles start-up and many basic aspects of Mac hardware control, as well as instructions for drawing windows and menus. The OS looks at your computer's ROM and adds or updates missing OS instructions so that only the latest and greatest OS loads in the memory.

➤ *Printer drivers*—Printer drivers are small conversion programs that change data from its original format into a format that a particular printer can process. Printer drivers are selected in the Chooser and "run" with the Print command. QuickDraw significantly improves the Macintosh print architecture by providing third-party developers with a framework in which to write printer drivers. This new feature is described in Chapter 11.

Apple provides printer drivers for most Apple printers and output devices. Other vendors offer printer drivers that allow the Macintosh to be used with output devices that are not necessarily supported by Apple drivers. If you're having printing difficulties, check with your printer vendor to determine if you have the latest version of a printer driver that's compatible with Mac OS 8.6.

➤ *Open Transport*—Open Transport is the name of the networking portion of the OS that allows your computer to communicate with network file servers, printers and print servers, modems, the Internet, and other network services. Apple provides network drivers for AppleTalk, TCP/IP, and Ethernet network communications. Many other network drivers are provided along with third-party Macintosh network hardware. Open Transport drivers are found in the Extensions folder and are often classified as Extensions, but they actually work in conjunction with the TCP/IP and AppleTalk control panels. The network drivers described here are part of Mac OS—other drivers are distributed by third-party software and hardware vendors.

➤ *Extensions*—Because Mac OS is modular, it can be enhanced, modified, or extended by files that temporarily become part of the OS at every start-up. These files are called Extensions (or INITs, in previous versions of the OS). The icons for many Extensions appear across the bottom of your screen at start-up.

Examples of important Extensions in Mac OS 8.6 are the Appearance Extension, AppleScript, AppleShare, AppleTalk, File Sharing Extension, LaserWriter 8,

QuickDraw 3D, QuickTime, and Speech Manager. Most specialized peripheral devices (printers, monitors, CD-ROM players, and networks, for example) normally come with a customized Extension file that must be moved or copied into the Extension folder in order to use the device.

> **Tip**
>
> Apple uses *extensions* to "extend" the OS without having to release a major new OS upgrade. Thus, when QuickTime was first released in 1990, it appeared as an Extension. As Extensions are improved and stabilized over time, they are often added directly to the OS; their functional code is added to the System or Finder file. Finally, when OS code becomes routine and standardized, what initially started out as an Extension may eventually end up encoded in the OS itself.
>
> Extensions sometimes conflict with one another, with your regular applications, or with the OS. As a means of circumventing Extension conflicts, you can control which Extensions load at start-up as well as the order in which they load. The Extension Manager Control Panel, which is described in more detail in Chapter 2, provides a means for doing this.

Many Extensions are provided with the OS, but there are many others created independently by third parties. Most are designed to add some new feature or capability to the OS. For example, the Speed Doubler Extension replaces certain functions of the Mac OS to increase performance, and StuffIt Engine boosts compression and decompression times for the StuffIt program.

➤ *Control Panels*—These are mini-applications that provide additional functionality for some aspect of the OS, an Extension, or a hardware peripheral. Control Panels control your Mac's memory settings, internal clock, colors, file and Web sharing, and many other system attributes. At the system level, Control Panels work much like Extensions, but they utilize a user interface (UI) that offers the user control over certain variables in the device's function. In some cases, a program you purchase (such as Speed Doubler) will ship with both an Extension and a Control Panel.

What's the difference between Extensions and Control Panels? In reality, not much. Often these two types of files perform many of the same tasks. Developers use Control Panels when they want to allow you to make changes; otherwise, they use Extensions. Settings you make to your system with Control Panels are stored until you change them again; if you remove the Control Panels from your System folder, the settings can't be changed.

➤ *Desk Accessories*—Like Extensions and Control Panels, Desk Accessories are independent files that operate just like normal applications. (In previous versions of the OS, Desk Accessories were special files run in their own single layer of

Mac OS 8.6

memory and accessed only from the Apple Menu.) Desk accessories (DAs) provide utility functions that are not built into the OS. DAs provided as part of the OS include the Chooser, Alarm Clock, Calculator, and Key Caps, to name but a few.

Using The Mac OS

The Mac OS is used almost constantly from the moment you turn on your computer. To further help you understand its role, let's take a look at a few of the tasks it controls:

➤ *Start-up*—From just a moment after the power is turned on, your Macintosh's OS controls the start-up process, loading any available Extensions, Control Panels, and fonts and verifying that your hardware is functioning properly and loading the Finder.

Only the System, Finder, and Enabler files are required for your Macintosh to start up. Although the additional components are important, they're not required for minimal operation. If your computer won't start up properly, insert the emergency boot disk or CD-ROM that came with your computer. See your Mac's documentation to learn how to create an emergency boot disk for your specific model of computer.

➤ *File management*—When you manipulate windows and icons in the Finder and on the Desktop, your actions are translated from the onscreen graphical display into actual changes to the files on disk. But files aren't stored on disk as cute little icons; they're simply strings of magnetic 1s and 0s. It's the OS that turns them into meaningful text, beautiful graphics, stirring sounds, and moving images.

➤ *Application launching*—When you run a software program, the OS accesses the computer and ensures that the correct portions of the file are read from disk, that the available memory is properly managed, and that data files (and sometimes temporary work files) are created and maintained on disk.

➤ *Font usage*—Every time a font is used on the Macintosh—whether it's a bitmapped, PostScript, TrueType, or QuickDraw outline font—the OS provides information about the font, including the way it should look in any particular size and style, so it may be displayed on screen or printed properly.

➤ *Windows and dialog boxes*—The OS provides the basic format of almost every window and dialog box used on the Macintosh. For the Open and Save As dialog boxes, the OS also supports the scrolling list of files and the reading or writing of files. Apple publishes a complex set of documentation called the "Apple Human Interface Guidelines" to help software programmers create consistent window elements and dialog boxes.

Mac OS 8.6

➤ *Printing*—An application must pass its data through one of the OS's printer drivers in order to convert it into a format that the printer can understand. After this, the OS communicates the file to the printer and, in some cases, receives feedback from the printer during output.

➤ *Screen display*—The OS is responsible for producing the display that appears on your Macintosh screen. Applications communicate the display information to the OS using something called QuickDraw, which converts this information and draws it on the screen.

➤ *Networking*—Nearly every aspect of communication between the Mac and its peripherals is controlled by the OS. This includes data transfer from the disk to the AppleTalk port (and other ports), the timing of network communications while other software is being run onscreen, cabling, and two-way communications with sophisticated printers, modems, and storage drives.

As you can see, almost every task you perform on your Macintosh—from the smallest mouse click to the largest data transfer—relies on the OS. Fortunately, you don't need to understand the technical intricacies of how the OS performs its tasks in order to use your Macintosh. An appreciation for the range and depth of the OS's functions is useful, nonetheless.

Basic Mac OS Operations

We'll now turn from technical descriptions of the OS to the easiest and most fundamental aspects of using the Macintosh. This section looks at the things you need to know in order to use the Macintosh efficiently, and defines terms you'll encounter throughout the book. This information is intended primarily for readers who are using Mac OS 8.6 in their first experience on the Macintosh.

The Graphical User Interface

The first and most fundamental requirement for using the Mac OS is understanding its graphical user interface. Instead of communicating your commands in words, you select pictures—or icons—that represent Macintosh hardware and software functions and features. The mouse cursor also plays an important role in communicating with the Macintosh. (Yes, you'll use the keyboard too, but we'll assume you've already mastered that device.)

Let's look at each of these elements individually.

Icons

These are small graphics (pictures) that appear on the Macintosh screen; they represent items such as disks and folders (the icons actually look like a hard drive or folder, as shown in Figure 1.2).

Mac OS 8.6

Figure 1.2 Hard drive and folder icons.

Different icons are used to represent the various types of files stored on your disks. An example application icon and document icon for the application BBEdit (a text and HTML editing program) are shown in Figure 1.3.

Figure 1.3 Standard application and document icons.

Most applications and their associated documents use custom icons. A collection of custom application and document icons appears in Figure 1.4.

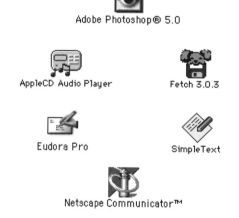

Figure 1.4 Custom application and document icons.

Windows

When a Macintosh file is opened, its contents are displayed in a window. The most common type of window looks like the one shown in Figure 1.5; it includes a title bar at the top and scroll bars on the right and bottom edges. You can move a window around (by dragging its title bar), close a window (by clicking the close box in the upper left corner), and change the size of a window (by dragging the size box located in the lower right corner).

Operating System Basics   11

Figure 1.5   A sample Finder window.

The Mac OS features other types of windows as well, including dialog boxes. A sample dialog box is shown in Figure 1.6. These small specialized windows usually present a set of options that allow you to customize a command or activity.

Figure 1.6   A sample dialog box.

There are four common kinds of dialog box options:

➤ Small round radio buttons present a set of mutually exclusive choices.

➤ Small square check boxes present a set of choices you can select in any combination.

➤ An option box is a small area where you type in your choice. Some option boxes offer a set of alternatives in a pop-up menu; you can click on your choice with the mouse.

➤ Lastly, some dialog boxes don't present options but simply provide information. Usually this information is feedback concerning a command or action you're engaged in or a message from one of your hardware devices. These are called alert dialog boxes, or simply alerts; a sample is displayed in Figure 1.7.

Mac OS 8.6

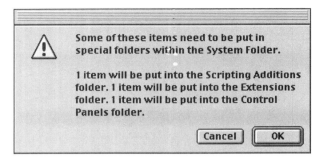

Figure 1.7 An alert dialog box.

A palette is another type of window used in some software applications. It's called a palette because it "floats" on top of the active document windows and the Desktop and can't be obscured by them. Unlike an ordinary dialog box, which disappears after you've selected options or closed it, a palette may remain open for the duration of a work session. A palette provides a collection of icons that represent tools you can work with; sometimes it presents a text list of commands or options for you to choose from. Figure 1.8 shows a palette from the HTML editing portion of the application BBEdit.

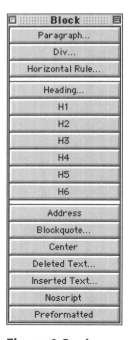

Figure 1.8 A sample palette.

Menus

Most commands in Mac OS applications are presented in menus displayed along the menu bar at the top of the screen. Commands are usually grouped logically, with logical names that provide clues to their functions. The menu bar is the most distinctive element of the Mac OS. The familiar font *Chicago* was specifically designed for the purpose of attractive screen display on the original Macintosh and has since been supplemented by new fonts such as *Charcoal*.

Tip

In Mac OS 8.6, menus drop down and stay open until you make a menu selection or click somewhere else on the screen (they're sometimes referred to as "sticky" menus). This way, you don't need to hold down the mouse button while navigating the menu.

Menus drop down when you click on the menu name and stay down until you make a menu selection or click somewhere else on the screen; this feature was introduced in Mac OS 8, but was previously available using third-party utilities. As you drag the mouse down, each command is highlighted (or "selected," in computer parlance) as the mouse cursor passes over it. Releasing the mouse while the command is selected executes that command; to confirm you have successfully executed a menu item, the selection command flashes two or three times. (Using the mouse will be covered more fully later in this chapter.)

The Mac OS employs four basic types of menu commands, some of which execute as soon as they're selected. Others toggle the status of some features on and off. Command names that end with an ellipsis (…) bring up a dialog box of related options.

A fourth type of menu option offers you a hierarchical submenu of commands. Clicking once with the mouse lets you select one of these normal, toggling, or ellipsis subcommands. Figure 1.9 shows an example of a hierarchical menu.

The Mouse And Cursors

Each of the graphical elements we've discussed so far interacts with your Macintosh via mouse manipulation. Operating the mouse is simple enough: you move the mouse on your desk, and the cursor moves onscreen accordingly. Only the motion of the cursor on your Desktop produces a change in cursor position, making the mouse a relative pointing device. (Some devices like graphics tablets are absolute pointing devices, as each point on their surface maps to a point on your screen.) The type of cursor that appears at any given time depends on many variables: the item you're pointing to, the software you're using, the commands you've chosen, and the keys you've pressed on the keyboard.

Mac OS 8.6

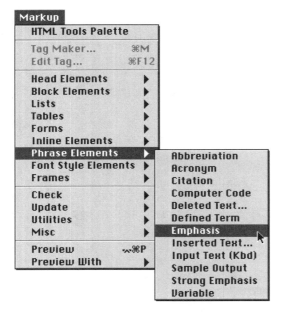

Figure 1.9 A hierarchical menu, one of four basic menu types.

Arrow cursors appear whenever you're pointing to the menu bar, regardless of the application being used. When you're working in the Finder, the mouse cursor will be a left-facing arrow. Macintosh applications also use the arrow cursor to select and manipulate objects. Other common cursors are shown in Figure 1.10.

Figure 1.10 Common types of cursors.

You can perform five common actions with the cursor. These actions manipulate icons, invoke commands, and control application tools:

➤ *Pointing*—Positioning the cursor over a particular icon, object, or window element. When the cursor takes the form of an arrow, the arrow's tip marks the exact spot you're pointing to. Other cursor styles have their own "hot spots," or specific points of action.

➤ *Clicking*—Quickly pressing and releasing the mouse button. In most cases, the click executes when the button is fully released, not while it's pressed. Mouse clicks select objects, including icons, buttons, and dialog box options.

Operating System Basics   15

▶ *Double-clicking*—Pressing and releasing the mouse button twice in rapid succession. Most beginners don't double-click fast enough to prevent the Macintosh from interpreting them as two single clicks instead of one double-click. Double-clicking controls many Macintosh actions, like opening icons to display their windows. The sensitivity with which the operating system responds to double-clicking can be changed using the Mouse Control Panel.

▶ *Pressing*—Holding down the mouse button while a command or action is completed.

▶ *Dragging*—Moving the mouse—and therefore the cursor—while holding down (pressing) the mouse button. This action usually moves an item or employs the active cursor tool (such as when you are drawing a line with a pencil tool).

Files And Folders

Now that you understand icons and windows, and you're comfortable working with your mouse, you're ready to put all that knowledge and skill to work. Manipulating files on the Desktop is one of the most important tasks you'll undertake.

There are many different types of files—applications, data documents, OS files, utilities, fonts, and dictionaries. To keep all these files organized, you'll put them into folders. Using the File menu's New Folder command, you can create new folders to hold any type of file. You can also create folders inside other folders to establish a hierarchical arrangement of files and folders, as shown in Figure 1.11. If you've worked on other types of computer systems, folders are directly analogous to directories or subdirectories.

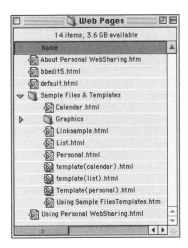

Figure 1.11   A hierarchical view of a collection of related files and folders.

Mac OS 8.6

To reposition files or folders—add them to a folder, or copy them to another disk or hard drive—point to the icon of the file or folder you want to manipulate, click and hold the mouse button, drag the file onto the destination icon, and release the mouse button. If you drag files to a different folder on the same disk, the files are moved (they now appear only in the new location, not in the old location). If you drag files to a different disk, or to a folder on a different disk, they're copied instead of relocated (they exist in both the new location and in the old location).

Floppy Disks

Two types of floppy disks are supported by the Macintosh: 800K floppies (sometimes known as regular or double-density or DD), and 1.44MB floppies (sometimes called high-density or HD). Most Macs can use either disk type, but some older models can only use 800K disks. You can tell the difference between the two by the number of small windows at the top of the floppy disk: 800K floppies have one window; 1.44MB floppies have two. High-density disks usually have a distinctive HD logo stamped on the lower left corner, near the shutter. As older Macintosh models recede into history, 800K floppy disks are used less often. If your Apple Macintosh is capable of running Mac OS 8.6, then you'll have a high-density floppy drive.

Before using a floppy disk for the first time, it must be formatted. This erases the disk and prepares it for use. (If the disk has been used before, formatting erases whatever is on it, making the data unrecoverable.) Formatting creates cylindrical sections (with magnetic lines) on the floppy's surface and writes a directory or table of contents for the disk, thereby decreasing somewhat the actual capacity of the floppy disk.

When you insert a new floppy disk into your computer's internal floppy drive, the Macintosh detects that the disk has never been used and asks if you want to format it. You can reformat a disk at any time, which will delete all its files, by inserting the disk, selecting its icon, and then choosing the Erase Disk command from the Special menu. The Erase Disk dialog box is shown in Figure 1.12.

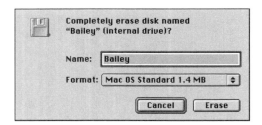

Figure 1.12 The Erase Disk dialog box.

With Mac OS 8.6, you are given the additional options (enabled by the File Exchange Control Panel) of formatting your floppy disk as a DOS disk for an IBM PC or PC clone, or as a Pro-DOS disk for Apple II family computers. A DOS disk icon bearing the letters PC appears on your Desktop. It will operate correctly in an IBM PC. Be careful to format the floppy disk as you intend, as it's easy to forget and use your previous format setting.

Macintosh Utilities

When working with the Macintosh, you'll frequently use several built-in utilities.

The Chooser

The Chooser is an electronic switchbox that lets you select from printers, networks, and file servers that your Macintosh is connected to. The Chooser, shown in Figure 1.13, appears when its name is chosen from the Apple menu. Icons representing the devices that may be available are on the left side of the Chooser window. Selecting an icon brings up a list of available devices on the right side of the dialog box. Selecting the name of the device you want activates your connection to that device.

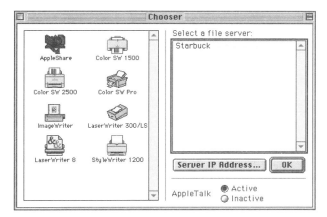

Figure 1.13 The Chooser.

Control Panels

Several of the Control Panels in the Control Panels folder, which is accessed via the Apple menu, are used to specify basic settings and preferences for your Macintosh. Mac OS 8.6 reworks several of the Control Panels, consolidating functions that were previously separate and adding new capabilities.

▶ The General Controls Control Panel is used to change various characteristics of the Desktop. As with earlier versions of this Control Panel, you can change the number of times a menu command blinks when selected and the frequency with which an inserted cursor blinks. It also allows you to indicate whether you want to show the Desktop when in another application, view the Launcher at start-up, or display a warning when the system has been shut down improperly. The settings for system and application folder protection and the default location to which a new document is saved are also found here. The General Controls Control Panel is shown in Figure 1.14.

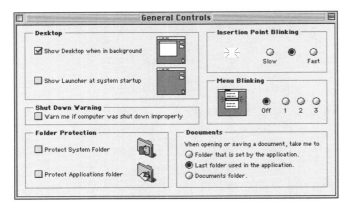

Figure 1.14   The General Controls Control Panel.

▶ The Date & Time Control Panel is used to set the date and time, time zone, and Daylight Savings Time information. This Control Panel allows you to establish the date and time that appear in your menu bar (optionally set here) and provide data for file creation or modification times. It is also used by many applications as part of maintenance and updates (for example, to find "today" in a calendar program). The Date & Time Control Panel, which can also access a time server over the Internet (such as the U.S. Naval Observatory's atomic clock), is shown in Figure 1.15.

Figure 1.15   The Date & Time Control Panel.

Mac OS 8.6

Operating System Basics   19

Dates and times are a central function of your computer's bookkeeping. You normally set these parameters once, and then an internal battery runs the clock under its own power. If your Mac isn't keeping time accurately, your battery may be low.

➤ The Appearance Control Panel, shown in Figure 1.16, is used to select the background pattern or picture for your Desktop, as well as to select a system font, sounds, and other preferences that affect the overall *theme* of your Desktop. Apple has created a new way to draw windows, icons, and all other Finder elements, and software developers are hard at work creating new *appearances* to enhance the look and feel of the Mac OS.

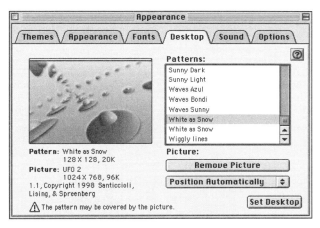

Figure 1.16   The Appearance Control Panel.

➤ The Monitors & Sound Control Panel is used to define your monitor's display of colors or gray values, resolution (if you have a multi-resolution monitor), sound, and preferences. It also lets you set the relative position of each monitor if you have more than one connected to your Macintosh. The Monitors & Sound Control Panel is shown in Figure 1.17.

Changes made to a monitor's color or resolution go into effect immediately. Another feature that PowerBook owners are sure to appreciate is the capability of putting PowerBooks with external monitors to sleep with the external monitor attached.

➤ The Mouse Control Panel is used to define the speed of your onscreen cursor relative to the speed with which you move the mouse and the amount of delay between clicks. The double-click speed setting determines if two clicks will be interpreted as two separate clicks instead of one double-click. A PowerBook-specific Control Panel lets you make similar adjustments to the Track Pad, the PowerBook's equivalent of a mouse. The Mouse Control Panel is shown in Figure 1.18.

Mac OS 8.6

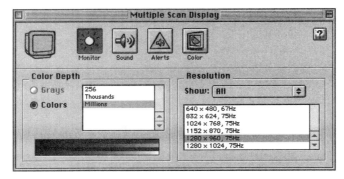

Figure 1.17 The Monitors & Sound Control Panel.

Figure 1.18 The Mouse Control Panel.

➤ The Keyboard Control Panel lets you choose the character set for your keyboard. You can also use this panel to control the repeat rate for keystrokes. A shortcut to the Keyboard Control Panel is shown in Figure 1.19.

Figure 1.19 The Keyboard Control Panel.

The Text Control Panel and the Numbers Control Panel support foreign language text and number formats, respectively. For example, settings on both the Text and Numbers Control Panels enable SimpleText's (the text editor included with the Mac OS) stylized text, graphics, and language scripting support. The Text and Numbers Control Panels include the following features:

➤ The Text Control Panel offers two simple options: Script and Behavior. A script is a method of writing characters, such as left to right for Latin or Roman languages or right to left for Hebrew or Arabic. A script also defines what constitutes a word (delimiting characters). Behavior specifies the character set, which is often country-dependent. In the United States, we use ASCII; England uses a different character set; and so on. Behavior affects sort order and letter case. The Text Control Panel is shown in Figure 1.20.

Figure 1.20 The Text Control Panel.

➤ The Numbers Control Panel lets you specify a format by country. You can also set separators and currency symbols. The Numbers Control Panel is shown in Figure 1.21.

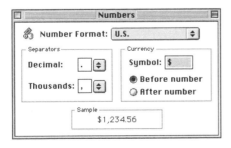

Figure 1.21 The Numbers Control Panel.

Several other important Control Panels affect the way you interact with the Mac OS; we'll discuss them in Chapter 3 and Chapter 4.

Transferring Data

The Clipboard is the Mac OS's simple built-in method for transferring text, sounds, graphical elements, and even movies from one location to another. You can use the

Clipboard to move items within a document or from one document to another—even if the documents were created by different software applications. The metaphor of the Clipboard is continued in the commands used to manipulate it: Cut, Copy, and Paste, each of which can be found in the Edit menu.

Since you never see the information being transferred, it's easy to make mistakes with Clipboard operations. Even when you're careful and check the contents of the Clipboard using the Show Clipboard command, Clipboard transfers are at least a two-step operation; checking the Clipboard for content adds a third step.

Drag and drop is a more direct method for moving information about in Mac OS 8.6. With drag and drop, you click and drag information to other locations on your Desktop, hard drive, or in other applications. Most users will find spring-loaded folders, a new variation of drag and drop, to be one of the best features of Mac OS 8.6. When you drag an item such as a document, folder, or application onto a folder or hard drive containing subfolders, just hold the item over the folder or hard drive until it "springs" open. You may continue to drag the item and hold it over folders that subsequently appear, as well as navigate backward through the hierarchy of subfolders to the point at which you began. Clicking the spacebar while dragging an item onto a folder or disk will cause it to spring open immediately.

Drag and drop can even move data to the Desktop as clipping objects: text as text clippings, graphics as picture clippings, sound as sound clippings, video as video clippings, and Internet addresses and URLs as one of eight different types of Internet clippings. The old Clipping Extension that managed these actions was a separate Extension to the OS; now it's part of the OS itself. Clippings can be created by many types of applications—just drag and drop them to the Desktop or to any open window. Applications that are being upgraded to take advantage of Mac OS 8 or higher will include drag-and-drop capability. In Mac OS 8.6, the Clipboard, Note Pad, Find File, and SimpleText utilize drag and drop. Drag and drop also starts processes like printing (drag and drop a file to a printer icon) or opening files (drag and drop a file onto an application icon). We'll pay particular attention to drag and drop as we proceed through the book, repaying your reading with tremendous time savings.

Cut And Paste: Using The Clipboard And The Scrapbook

You rarely access the Clipboard directly; instead, you manipulate the contents of the Clipboard using the Cut, Copy, and Paste commands. These commands are used so frequently that it's a good idea to remember their keystroke equivalents: Command+X for Cut, Command+C for Copy, and Command+V for Paste. They provide you with the following capabilities:

- *Cut*—Removes the selected objects from their current location and places them on the Clipboard, replacing the previous Clipboard contents. (The Clipboard can contain only the result of the last Cut or Copy command.)
- *Copy*—Places the selected objects on the Clipboard, but leaves them in their current location as well. The copied objects replace the previous contents of the Clipboard.
- *Paste*—Places a copy of the objects currently on the Clipboard into the current document at the cursor location. Using the Paste command does not remove items from the Clipboard; you can paste the same item repeatedly.

There are many ways to use the Clipboard. The most common is to move an element—like a paragraph or graphical item—from one place to another in the same document. To do so, you select the element, choose the Cut command, position the cursor at the new location, and choose the Paste command.

The Clipboard is also used to move elements—even elements created by different applications—between different documents. For example, to move a chart from a file you created with your spreadsheet into a word processor file, follow this procedure:

1. Open the spreadsheet and select the chart. Use the Copy command, since you want to leave the chart in the spreadsheet even after it has been moved to the word processor.
2. Open the word processor, or switch to it if it's already open. Open the document that will receive the copied chart. You can quit the spreadsheet, but it's not necessary. (Details on opening and switching between several applications are presented in Chapter 10.)
3. Position the cursor at the point in the word processor file where you want the chart placed. Choose the Paste command.

Chances are that if you can select some information, you can copy it to the Clipboard and move it about. In addition to simple ASCII text, the Clipboard supports stylized text and various graphics formats. The Clipboard even supports sound and QuickTime video.

If you want to remove selected items without involving the Clipboard, use the Clear command or the Delete key. Since the Clipboard can hold only one item at a time and is not saved out to a file, it is overwritten whenever it is modified. Sometimes when you have a large selection on the Clipboard, you can tie up Macintosh memory needed for other programs. To free up that memory, clear the Clipboard or copy a single character to it.

Mac OS 8.6

It's easy to forget the contents of your Clipboard. Some applications have as a menu item a command called Show Clipboard; its placement varies. In the Finder, this command is found in the Edit menu; Microsoft Word places it in the Window menu; other programs place it on a View menu. In the Finder, the Show Clipboard command is enabled by the Clipboard file placed at the top level of the System folder. Selecting this command opens a window that lets you view the Clipboard's contents and tells you what kind of data it contains. Figure 1.22 shows an example of the contents of the Clipboard (a Photoshop image).

Figure 1.22 The Clipboard window.

The Scrapbook, another related Mac OS tool, is a desk accessory found on the Apple menu that can hold a catalog of text and graphical elements you use frequently or need to move from one document to another. The Scrapbook saves data to a file and thus provides permanent storage (until you modify the data). Elements are moved into or out of the Scrapbook via the Clipboard and the Cut, Copy, and Paste commands previously described. A Scrapbook displaying a single element is shown in Figure 1.23.

For example, if you need to use a set of icons throughout a magazine layout you're creating, you could transfer all of them into the Scrapbook and access them from there as needed. To do so, you would follow these steps:

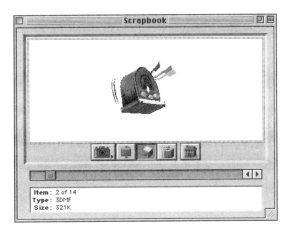

Figure 1.23 The Scrapbook.

1. Open the file containing the icons. Select one icon, and choose the Copy command to move it to the Clipboard.

2. Open the Scrapbook, and choose the Paste command to move the icon on the Clipboard into the Scrapbook. The Scrapbook automatically creates a new page each time you paste in a new element.

3. Go back to the file containing the icons, select another icon, and again use the Copy command to move it to the Clipboard. Access the Scrapbook again, and paste in the new icon. Repeat this process until the Scrapbook contains all the needed icons.

4. Open your page layout program, and as each icon is needed, open the Scrapbook, locate the icon, and use the Copy command to transfer it from the Scrapbook onto the Clipboard. Set the cursor at the location where the icon is needed, and choose the Paste command to transfer the icon into your layout. Repeat this procedure until all icons are in place.

The Scrapbook has been enhanced for Mac OS 8.6, as it has been for most major system upgrades. Now the Scrapbook not only supports new sound, video, and 3D Meta File (3DMF) formats, it also gives you information about the type of item, the size in bytes, and the dimension in pixels. Best of all, the Scrapbook is drag-and-drop enabled. Let's look at this great feature: drag and drop.

Macintosh Drag And Drop

Drag and drop is a technique for sharing data between documents, files, and applications. Various aspects of drag-and-drop behavior have been around for some time now. In versions of System 7, you could drag a file icon onto an application, and if the application could open that file and translate it, it would. For example, when Macintosh drag and drop was used with the System 7 Pro Finder and Macintosh Easy Open (a System Extension), any file dragged onto an application could be automatically translated and opened provided that the capability was set up beforehand.

Mac OS 8.6 uses drag and drop so that you can print files by dragging them to a printer icon on your Desktop (a feature covered in Chapter 11). The most important extension of drag and drop is the ability to transfer data within a file, between files, and even to the Macintosh Desktop. Drag and drop, which was previously monitored by the Drag Manager Extension, is now part of the OS itself.

Macintosh drag and drop is a terrific method for data exchange because it is intuitive. If you've used drag and drop in other applications (like Microsoft Word 5.x), then you're familiar with the basics: Simply select the data and drag it to a new location. This action moves an outline of your selected data to the new location and completes the data move when you release the mouse button. Figure 1.24 shows an example of moving text within a document using Apple's text editor, SimpleText.

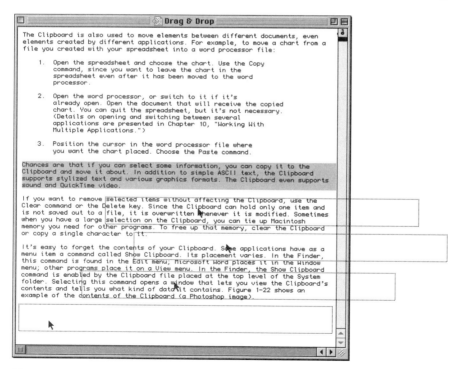

Figure 1.24 Macintosh drag and drop.

SimpleText is a text editor that opens files containing simple ASCII text, stylized text, and graphics in the PICT format. It replaces TeachText and expands upon it by allowing basic text editing as well. You could think of SimpleText as a basic word processor; it even records and plays sounds and speech. SimpleText will open the Read Me files that often accompany new software; these files tell you about late-breaking information that couldn't be included in the manual. Whenever you're trying to open an unknown file on your Macintosh, try SimpleText first.

One very convenient feature of the Mac OS is the ability to drag and drop selections to the Desktop. The resulting objects are called clippings and are given a default filename, such as text clipping, to indicate the data type. You can edit the filename using standard Macintosh editing techniques. Click on the filename, type a new name, and press the Return key to change the name. If an application has been written to take advantage of Mac OS 8.6 or higher, the clipping will be automatically named using the first 18 or so characters of the clipping contents (if it is a text clipping). Some clippings are shown in Figure 1.25, including a clipping from Microsoft Word that uses this feature.

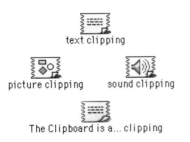

Figure 1.25 Desktop clippings.

To use clippings, simply drag them to the desired location within another file. Clippings are a convenient way to add logos or headers to documents, glossary items, or other items you might have stored in your Scrapbook. You may want to consolidate your clippings within a single folder on your Desktop to reduce clutter.

The Mac OS has a desk accessory called Stickies that you can find on the Apple menu. With Stickies, you can create windows of text that float on your Desktop, as shown in Figure 1.26. They resemble the paper version, found in most offices and homes, that are stuck to desks, lamps, doors, and refrigerators as reminders. You can scroll the text using the arrow keys and collapse the windows to a single bar.

The Stickies accessory supports Cut, Copy, and Paste, and can import and export text; it even supports drag and drop. Stickie notes can be different colors and any rectangular size down to a single line. When you're done with a note, you can close it and save it to a file or simply delete it.

Mac OS 8.6

Figure 1.26 Several Stickies and the Text Style formatting dialog box.

Note Pad is an older desk accessory that can place a single window on your Desktop. You can move from page to page by clicking on the dog-ear of the notepad. Note Pad, an example of which is shown in Figure 1.27, has been part of Mac OS from its inception.

Figure 1.27 Note Pad.

Wrapping Up

The OS is the core of what we think of as the Macintosh. The Mac OS makes it possible for you to interact with the computer, the computer to communicate with your applications, and you and the computer to connect to the Internet and access peripheral hardware such as printers, scanners, and storage devices.

Some of the features the Mac's OS provides to the user are:

➤ Icons, windows, and dialog boxes instead of lines and lines of computer code and obscure syntax.

➤ Mouse controls and menus instead of just keystrokes.

➤ Windows and palettes.

➤ The Clipboard and the Scrapbook.

In Chapter 2, we'll examine the contents of the System Folder. We'll find out just exactly what all those items are and why they shouldn't stray from their homes.

Mac OS 8.6

The System Folder

Every Macintosh hard drive has one folder that's distinct from all the others—the System Folder, home of the operating system and many other important files. The System Folder is given special treatment by the operating system, by other software applications, and by you as a Mac OS user.

While you can arrange most other files and folders on your hard drive to suit your personal needs, you can change the organization of the System Folder only in certain ways. That's because of the fundamental role that software in the System Folder plays in the operation of your computer. However, the Mac OS hasn't always been organized like it is in Mac OS 8.6, which is an important concept to keep in mind as you read through this chapter.

In January 1984, when version 1.0 of the system software was released with the Macintosh 128K, the System Folder contained 22 items that consumed only 225K of disk space. Using System 6 on a Mac with a normal assortment of applications and utilities could easily result in a System Folder containing 100 items or more, easily causing the total size of the System Folder to soar above one megabyte. In System 7, you could barely fit just the System and Finder files and an Enabler file on a single 1.44MB floppy disk. A freshly installed System Folder in Mac OS 8.6 can easily run between 100MB and 150MB in size, and although the PowerPC processor is exponentially faster than the original 68K processor, larger System Folders will almost always result in slower boot-up times and an additional effort towards the care and feeding of your computer. Figure 2.1 shows what the contents of the System Folder looked like in an older version of the OS. Note that everything is just heaped together instead of placed into specific folders.

The level of disorganization seen in Figure 2.1 results in a crowded System Folder that's slow to open on the Desktop. Finding what you want in the maze of files is a slow and tedious process.

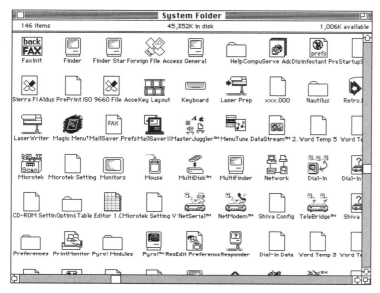

Figure 2.1 A large, messy System 6.x System Folder.

Although increasing complexity has been partially responsible for the growth of the operating system software, the growing number of nonsystem software files, such as third-party fonts, sounds, Control Panels, Extensions, and System Extensions that reside in the System Folder is a more direct cause. Nonsystem software files place obvious demands on disk space and can also result in chaotic System Folder disorganization and some measure of system instability.

System 7 provided new methods of maintaining System Folder organization, but did little to slow the pace of System Folder growth. It also introduced a few basic ways to avoid the instability caused by the old System Folder organization.

In this chapter, we'll look at the System Folder organization under Mac OS 8.6 and offer some suggestions to help you effectively manage this important resource.

Exploring The Mac OS 8.6 System Folder

In Mac OS 8.6, the System Folder includes a number of predefined subfolders designed to hold a specific type of file. This organizational system, which is created when Mac OS 8.6 is installed, greatly reduces the potential for clutter (refer back to Figure 2.1 for a good example of clutter). The actual number of items in the System Folder depends on the components chosen for installation and the type of Mac (desktop versus PowerBook, for example). See Appendix B for exactly what options are available for installation. The System Folder includes many subfolders, including the following (depending on which components you install in addition to the OS):

➤ Appearance
➤ Apple Menu Items
➤ Application Support
➤ Clipboard
➤ ColorSync Profiles
➤ Contextual Menu Items
➤ Control Panels
➤ Control Strip Modules
➤ Extensions
➤ Favorites
➤ Finder
➤ Fonts
➤ Help
➤ Internet Search Sites
➤ Language & Region Support
➤ Launcher Items
➤ MacTCP DNR
➤ MS Preference Panels
➤ Preferences
➤ PrintMonitor Documents
➤ Scrapbook File
➤ Scripting Additions
➤ Scripts
➤ Shutdown Items
➤ Startup Items
➤ System
➤ System Resources
➤ Text Encodings

Mac OS 8.6

Once you launch the Extension Manager Control Panel to turn off or on Extensions, Control Panels, or other System Folder items, you'll see the following folders in the System Folder as well:

➤ Contextual Menu Items (Disabled)

➤ Control Strip Modules (Disabled)

➤ Control Panels (Disabled)

➤ Extensions (Disabled)

➤ Scripting Additions (Disabled)

➤ Shutdown Items (Disabled)

➤ Startup Items (Disabled)

➤ System Extensions (Disabled)

These folders are created "on the fly" (which is computer-speak for automatically) by the Extensions Manager program; the types of folders that are created depend upon what portions of the Mac OS you disable (turn off). A display of the most basic parts of the Mac OS 8.6 System Folder is shown in Figure 2.2.

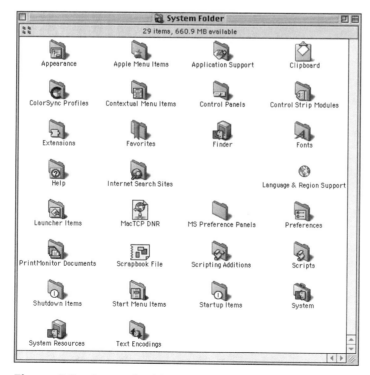

Figure 2.2 A standard Mac OS 8.6 System Folder.

Mac OS 8.6

In some ways, the new System Folder is more complex than the old one. Fortunately, as we'll see, Apple has built in an "invisible hand" to help make sure that System Folder files are always located correctly.

Because the new System Folder and subfolders are so important to the operation of your computer, it's important to understand what type of files should be placed in each subfolder. The following section describes the subfolders and provides some basic tips for organizing and using them.

Appearance

The Appearance folder serves as a storage area for many of the elements used to help you customize the aesthetics of your computer. Desktop pictures, sound sets, and themes are all stored here in individual folders, shown in Figure 2.3.

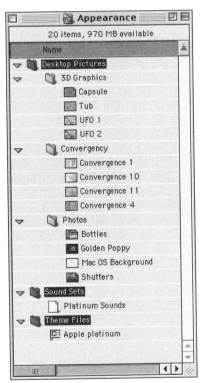

Figure 2.3 The Appearance folder contains elements used by the Appearance Control Panel to customize the look and feel of your computer.

Mac OS 8.6

The Mac OS will automatically direct to this folder images, sound sets, and theme files dropped onto the System Folder, as it does for some other subfolders as well. This feature is designed to help keep files where they belong within the System Folder, which is good for the overall stability of the OS, and helps users by reducing the number of operations needed to store files correctly. Figure 2.4 shows a typical alert dialog box that appears when a JPEG image file is dropped onto the System Folder.

Figure 2.4 The Mac OS is aware that certain files should be stored in specific locations, such as Desktop Pictures.

The Apple Menu Folder

Accessibility—from inside any application via the Apple Menu—is one of the best features of the many utilities and small applications that come with Mac OS 8.6. Many of these programs were known as desk accessories in earlier versions of the Mac OS. In System 7, the convenience of the Apple Menu was extended beyond desk accessories to include access to applications, documents, folders, and even aliases to volumes (hard drives mounted on your desktop). And best of all, this powerful new Apple Menu was completely customizable.

When Mac OS 8.6 is installed, the following items are automatically placed in the Apple Menu folder:

➤ Apple System Profiler

➤ AppleCD Audio Player

➤ Automated Tasks

➤ Calculator

➤ Chooser

➤ Control Panels

➤ Favorites

➤ Graphing Calculator

➤ Internet Access

➤ Jigsaw Puzzle

➤ Key Caps

➤ Network Browser

➤ Note Pad

➤ Scrapbook

➤ Sherlock

➤ SimpleSound

➤ Stickies

Some of these items are applications, such as the Apple System Profiler, but others are desk accessories, folders, or aliases to other files and folders. (An alias is like a shortcut to an original file or folder; you can always tell an alias from the original when viewing it in a Finder window because its name is italicized and often contains the word *alias* at the end.) Figure 2.5 shows the Apple Menu activated using the mouse (left), and the contents of the Apple Menu Items folder viewed by *Kind* to show the types of files contained in the folder.

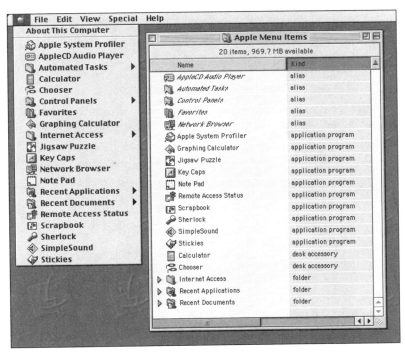

Figure 2.5 The Apple Menu (left) and Apple Menu Items folder.

Long-time Macintosh users will note the loss of the venerable Alarm Clock desk accessory from the Apple menu. It was replaced by the Date & Time Control Panel in Mac OS 8.0, and is now easily accessible through the Control Panels submenu of the Apple Menu. The Alarm Clock was the preferred method for changing the system date and time in several whole-number versions of system software. Prior to System 7.5, you could also change the date and time from within the General Controls Panel.

> **TIP**
>
> Some people prefer to rearrange the Apple Menu items to make them easier to find. To modify the contents of the Apple Menu, add or remove files or aliases to the Apple Menu Items folder. The Apple Menu is updated immediately and alphabetically displays the first 50 items contained in the top level of the Apple Menu Items folder. The only item you can't remove is the About This Computer option, which is always the first choice in the Apple menu when the Finder is the active application.

To make frequently used folders and applications more easily accessible, add their aliases to the Apple Menu Items folder. For example, you can add the aliases of applications, documents, folders, and volumes. Each item will be much easier to access from the Apple Menu than by using traditional double-click methods. Choosing an item from the Apple Menu is equivalent to double-clicking on the item's icon—the selected application or Control Panel will run, or the selected folder or volume will open.

Most of the files added to the Apple Menu Items folder should be aliases rather than original files, so that you avoid moving the file, folder, or volume icon from its original location. In the Apple Menu Items folder, the alias filename is displayed in italics, but it appears in standard font in the Apple Menu—you can't tell by looking at the Apple Menu that the file in the Apple Menu Items folder is an alias.

Because the Apple Menu displays files alphabetically, you can reorder the menu items by modifying their names with numerical or alphabetical prefixes. A list of the available prefixes appears in Figure 2.6, where a blank space ( ) forces an item to be listed first in the Apple menu, and the division symbol (÷) forces an item to be listed last.

The result of using some of the prefixes is shown in the Apple Menu pictured in Figure 2.7, in which applications, folders, desk accessories, Control Panels, documents, and volumes are ordered separately. This easy example shows groups of folders for commonly used applications in the middle, with elements of the OS in the top section, and miscellaneous items in the bottom section of the Apple menu.

Mac OS 8.6

The System Folder   39

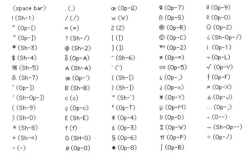

Figure 2.6 This list demonstrates the special characters that can be used to alphabetize files in the Apple Menu and the keys you use to access them.

Figure 2.7 Files are arranged in this Apple Menu using filename prefixes.

To insert dividers:

1. Create an empty folder or SimpleText document.

2. Paste over the preview icon by choosing File|Get Info, selecting the icon with the cursor, and pasting a 32×32 pixel white icon created using GraphicConverter (which is on the companion CD-ROM).

3. Name the empty, iconless folder or document with dashes, underscores, or bullets (Option+8).

To some extent, the inclusion of the Recent Applications, Recent Documents, and Recent Servers folders in the Apple Menu obviates the need to add commonly used items to the Apple Menu. However, if you find that a favorite item disappears every now and then from the submenu of one of these folders (because these folders only

Mac OS 8.6

remember as many items as you specify in the Apple Menu Items Control Panel), then by all means add its alias to the Apple Menu folder for persistent inclusion.

Application Support

The Application Support folder is created by the Mac OS for the benefit of other applications that are designed to store important files and folders for their own use. By default, this folder is empty, and it cannot be renamed.

Clipboard

The Clipboard is a file that holds information (text, pictures, sounds, and so on) that has been cut or copied using the Cut (Command+X) or Copy (Command+C) commands found under the Edit menu of most applications. It can only hold one piece of information at a time, although several utilities that allow users to have multiple clipboards now exist. Figure 2.8 shows the contents of the Clipboard file.

Figure 2.8 The Clipboard file, which contains a QuickTime movie clipping in this example.

ColorSync Profiles

ColorSync is a system created by Apple to assist in the conversion and management of colors used in documents that were created on computers and with printers. Since monitors and printers use different methods of interpreting color values, a standard method of describing color was created to ensure consistency across the board. ColorSync creates profiles for computers, which define colors using red, green, and blue (RGB); and printers, which use cyan, magenta, yellow, and black (CYMK);

and then attaches these profiles to a document. The ColorSync folder in the System Folder, shown in Figure 2.9, stores profiles for most models of Macintosh computers, as well as custom profiles you create with the ColorSync Control Panel.

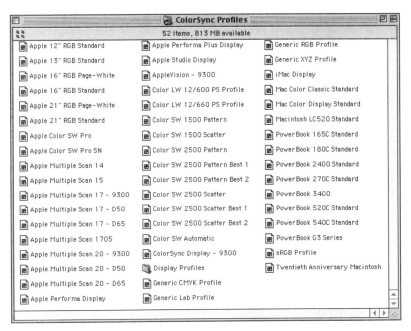

Figure 2.9 ColorSync profiles for most Macintosh computers are stored in the ColorSync folder.

Contextual Menu Items

Contextual menus are accessible in the Finder (and in most Mac OS 8-savvy applications) by clicking the mouse while holding down the Control key. The Contextual Menu Items folder contains two contextual menu plug-ins (Find CM Items, and Folder Actions Menus) that are automatically installed by the Mac OS, as well as any others installed by third-party applications. Figure 2.10 shows an example of a contextual menu in Microsoft Word 98.

The Control Panels Folder

Control Panels are control devices (referred to as "cdevs" in programmer-speak) and applications ("appcs") that used to appear in the System 6.x Control Panel desk accessory. In System 7, Control Panels were small, independent applications launched by double-clicking on their icons. Many Control Panels in Mac OS 8.6 function just like applications in that they are launched, have menu options, and are exited by quitting. Figure 2.11 shows a typical Control Panels folder for a G3 PowerBook.

42 Chapter 2

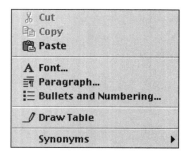

Figure 2.10 The Contextual Menu Items folder contains plug-ins that provide contextual menus for applications such as Microsoft Word 98.

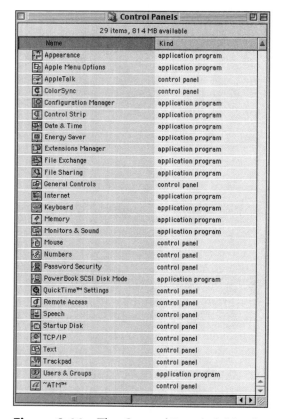

Figure 2.11 The Control Panels folder for a G3 PowerBook.

The individual files for each Control Panel are stored in the Control Panels folder, which is stored inside the System Folder—mainly because Control Panels often contain special resources (like Extensions) that must be run during startup. If the Extensions portion of the Control Panel isn't loaded at startup, the Control Panel may not function properly.

Mac OS 8.6

The contents of your Control Panels folder will depend on the components of the Mac OS that you've installed. Moreover, different models of computers will contain different Control Panels, which is most obvious when you compare the contents of the Control Panels folders of desktop and PowerBook computers. However, most Macs will have the following items in common:

- Appearance
- Apple Menu Options
- AppleTalk
- ColorSync
- Configuration Manager
- Control Strip
- Date & Time
- Energy Saver
- Extensions Manager
- File Exchange
- File Sharing
- General Controls
- Internet
- Keyboard
- Launcher
- Location Manager
- Memory
- Monitors & Sound
- Mouse
- Numbers
- QuickTime Settings
- Remote Access
- Speech
- Startup Disk
- TCP/IP

Mac OS 8.6

➤ Text

➤ Users & Groups

➤ ~ATM

If you want to keep a copy of any Control Panel in another location, create an alias and move the alias to your preferred location. You could, for example, store aliases of frequently used Control Panels in the Apple Menu Items folder or in a folder containing other utility applications. Figure 2.12 shows several Control Panels.

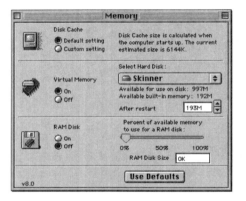
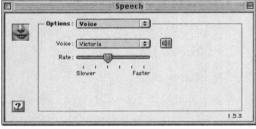
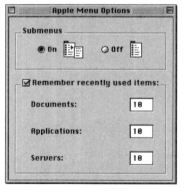
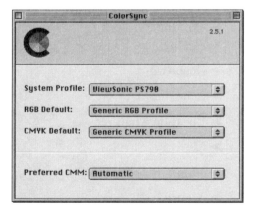

Figure 2.12   A few of the many Control Panels in Mac OS 8.6.

Control Strip Modules

The Control Strip was originally designed to provide easy access to frequently used commands for PowerBook users, who until recently had small displays and limited processing power. The Control Strip Modules folder is similar to the Contextual Menu Items folder in that it contains items installed by the Mac OS, as well as modules installed by other applications. Figure 2.13 shows the contents of the

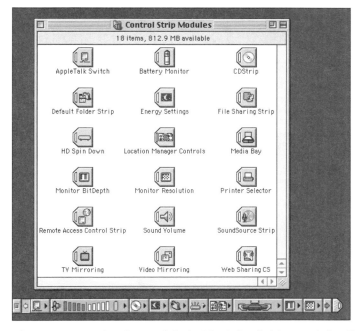

Figure 2.13 The Control Strip Modules folder and the Control Strip.

Control Strip Modules folder, most of whose modules are visible in the Control Strip below.

The Extensions Folder

As mentioned previously, Extensions (referred to as *INITs*), printer drivers, and network drivers are major contributors to System Folder overcrowding. Beginning with System 7, these files, which invaded System Folders in epidemic proportions since the introduction of System 6.0, have a home in the Extensions folder. Your Extensions folder may become quite crowded, as exemplified by Figure 2.14, but at least you can find your more important system files without having to wade through all of your Extensions by sorting the Extensions folder by *Name* or by *Kind* while viewing the folder as a list.

Most INITs add features to the Mac OS, thereby extending its capabilities—hence the name Extensions. Drivers extend system software capabilities in a less dramatic but important way.

TIP
The Extensions folder can become quite crowded in Mac OS 8.6, inviting the View as List option instead of View as icons.

Mac OS 8.6

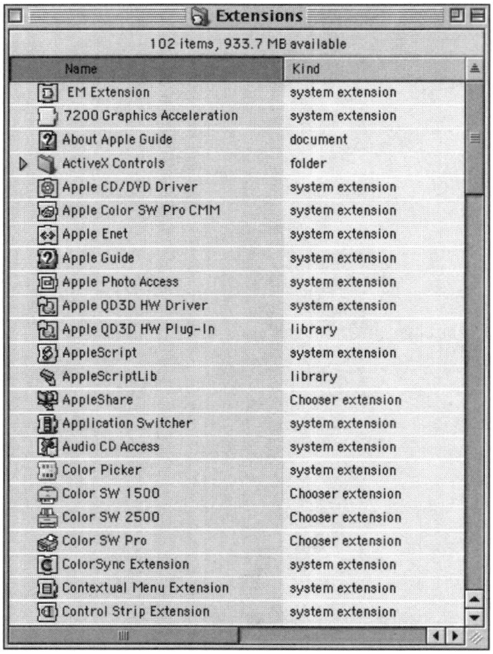

Figure 2.14 The Extensions folder holds Extensions, printer drivers, and network drivers.

During startup, the Mac OS looks in the Extensions folder and loads all its contents. Extensions and Control Panels that aren't stored in the Extensions or Control Panels folders won't execute at startup and won't operate properly until they're correctly positioned and the computer is restarted. The icons of some, but not all, Extensions will appear at the bottom of your screen during startup, as will the icons of some Control Panels.

Because Extensions and Control Panels modify or enhance the Mac OS at startup, a newly installed Extension or Control Panel may cause your Macintosh to crash. Crashes can occur if the item is incompatible with the system software, another Extension or Control Panel, a certain combination of Extensions and Control Panels, or even an application.

If you experience a compatibility problem, such as sudden or unexplained freezes or crashes, suspect an Extension conflict first. To test the theory, try turning off your Extensions: Hold down the Shift key while restarting your Macintosh. This will disable all but the most essential system Extensions and allow you to remove the incompatible file from the System Folder.

When you restart or start up with the Shift key held down, the words "Extensions Off" will appear under "Welcome to Mac OS" during startup. As soon as these

Mac OS 8.6

words appear, you can release the Shift key, and the computer will start up without executing any of the items in the Extensions or Control Panels folders.

In the good old days of System 6, you could resolve Extension conflicts by adding or removing Extensions one at a time from your System Folder until the offending Extension (or combination) was found. Often, you could avoid conflicts by changing the loading order with a simple renaming of the Extension (changing ATM to ~ATM, for example).

Various third-party utilities were introduced to automate the process of turning Extensions on and off, changing the loading order, or creating Extension worksets. The best-known of these products is Cassidy & Green's Conflict Catcher, which you should purchase if you are having a significant startup problem or otherwise suspect an Extension conflict.

TIP
The Mac OS loads Extensions first, then Control Panels, then the contents (if any) of the Startup Items folder. All items are loaded alphabetically.

In Mac OS 8.6, the number of Extensions is so overwhelming that Apple has expanded the capabilities of the Extensions Manager Control Panel shown in Figure 2.15. Click the checkmark off to remove an Extension, System Extension

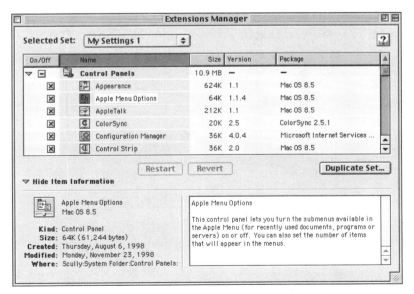

Figure 2.15 The Extensions Manager Control Panel.

(one found in the System Folder, not the Extension folder), Control Panel, or Startup item. Disabled items are placed into one of the following folders:

➤ Control Panels (Disabled)

➤ Control Strip Modules (Disabled)

➤ Extensions (Disabled)

➤ Shutdown Items (Disabled)

➤ Startup Items (Disabled)

➤ System Extensions (Disabled)

You can create sets of enabled and disabled Extensions, or get information about a particular item, by clicking on it once, as in the following example, which shows a set called *My Settings 1* with the Apple Menu Options item selected to display more information. You will still need to reboot your Macintosh to effect the new system configuration.

Favorites

The Favorites folder serves as a storage bin for shortcuts to your favorite documents, applications, folders, disks, file servers, and Internet URLs. You can add items to the Favorites folder from within Mac OS 8.6-savvy applications such as the Network Browser, by selecting an item in the Finder and choosing File|Add To Favorites or by activating the contextual menu (Control+click) and choosing Add To Favorites. The contents of the Favorites folder are either aliases or Internet Location documents, but you can manually add subfolders as well, such as *URLs* in Figure 2.16.

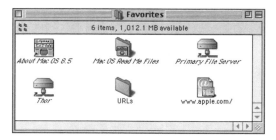

Figure 2.16 The Favorites folder contains shortcuts to frequently accessed files and other resources.

Finder

The Finder is the most frequently used feature of the Mac OS, and one of the two most critical components of the System Folder. The Finder is actually an application that allows you to manipulate files, folders, and applications using a graphical user interface (GUI). The Finder isn't a traditional application in that it can be easily launched and quit, nor can you change the memory allocation for the Finder as you can with most all other applications. Figure 2.17 shows the general information window for the Finder.

We'll look at the role of the Finder in much more detail in the Chapter 3.

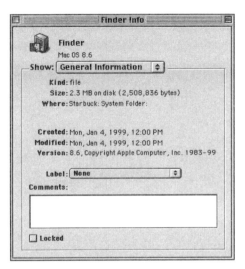

Figure 2.17 The Get Info dialog window for the Finder.

Fonts

Support for a wide range of typefaces has always been an important characteristic of the Macintosh, and Apple has finally figured out an efficient way of handling fonts in its system software. The Fonts folder, introduced in System 7.1, holds PostScript screen fonts and printer fonts as well as TrueType and QuickDraw GX fonts. After screen fonts or TrueType fonts are added to the Fonts folder, they become available to all applications. Fonts moved out of the Fonts folder, or into subfolders of the Fonts folder, are no longer available to applications. All aspects of working with Fonts in System 7.0 through Mac OS 8.6, including the Fonts folder, are described in detail in Chapter 11. Figure 2.18 shows the font suitcases installed as part of Mac OS 8.6.

Help

The Help folder is new to Mac OS 8.6 and contains the new Help Viewer application and its associated HTML-style Help documents. The Help folder also contains sample AppleScripts and Balloon Help files, all of which you'll probably never need to access except through the Help Viewer application. Refer to Appendix A for a detailed explanation of how to use the new Help Viewer application.

Mac OS 8.6

Figure 2.18 Fonts installed by Mac OS 8.6.

Internet Search Sites

Mac OS 8.6 includes a new search engine called Sherlock that takes the place of the old Find command, both of which are activated by selecting File|Find… or by pressing Command+F. It allows you to search the Internet as well as your hard drive. The Internet Search Sites folder, shown in Figure 2.19, is used to store the resources needed by Sherlock to search particular Internet sites, such as AltaVista or Apple's Tech Info Library.

Launcher Items

The Launcher Items folder contains aliases and folders used by the Launcher Control Panel to assist with the organization of frequently used items. The Launcher, described later in Chapter 4, is a holdover from previous versions of the Mac OS, but is still utilized by many users. Figure 2.20 shows the contents of a customized Launcher Items Folder as well as the Launcher itself. Note that items beginning with a bullet (Option+8) become subcategories in the Launcher window.

The System Folder   51

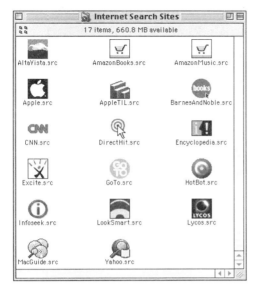

Figure 2.19   Some of Sherlock's search resources are stored in the Internet Search Sites folder.

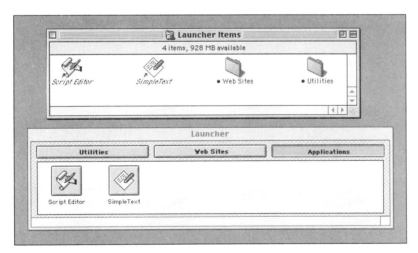

Figure 2.20   The Launcher Items Folder may be customized to suit your needs.

MacTCP DNR

The MacTCP DNR file is a holdover from the days when MacTCP (instead of Open Transport) was the primary networking software on the Mac. Its presence ensures backward compatibility with applications that require MacTCP. You'll never need to worry about what it does or the fact that you'll never need to use it, but don't delete it—that could cause problems down the road.

Mac OS 8.6

MS Preferences Panels

Microsoft Internet Explorer (IE) is installed as part of the default installation of Mac OS 8.6. The MS Preferences Panels folder contains twenty or so files that are used by IE to configure such things as downloading options, security, and user passwords.

The Preferences Folder

Under System 6.x, preferences files created by applications became important contributors to System Folder growth. Starting with System 7, these files are stored in the Preferences folder, shown in Figure 2.21.

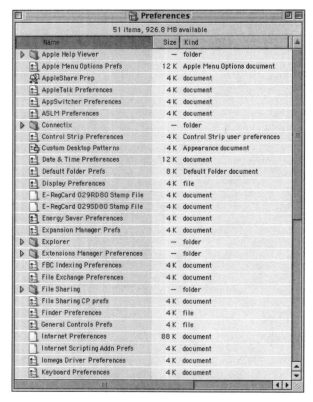

Figure 2.21 The Preferences folder.

As a user, you shouldn't have to do anything to the Preferences folder or its files (except in certain troubleshooting situations, as described in Chapter 16). Your applications should create and maintain these files automatically. However, you might want to check this folder occasionally and delete the preferences files of unwanted applications or utilities that you've deleted from your drives. This will reduce the time it takes for your computer to start up, and free up some space on your hard drive.

Mac OS 8.6

PrintMonitor Documents

The PrintMonitor application is used to handle printing tasks in the background; the PrintMonitor Documents folder serves as a temporary storage area for documents that are to be printed. Once a document has been printed by the PrintMonitor, it will be deleted from this folder.

Scrapbook File

The Scrapbook File is a file that may contain various types of data, including text, images (such as the one seen in Figure 2.22), and sounds, that are accessible via the Scrapbook utility. Mac OS 8.6 installs samples of the various types of data that may be stored in the Scrapbook. You can easily modify the contents of the Scrapbook File using the Cut and Paste commands.

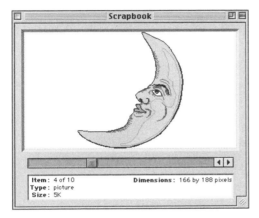

Figure 2.22 The Scrapbook File may contain many types of data, including images, but only one at a time.

Scripting Additions

The Scripting Additions folder contains several files that AppleScript uses to enable certain operations, such as providing scripting for File Sharing. Figure 2.23 shows the items installed in the Scripting Additions folder by Mac OS 8.6. Other applications may install items in this folder in order to enable close collaboration with AppleScript.

As with other special folders in the System Folder, a scripting addition that is dropped onto the closed System Folder will be automatically placed in the Scripting Additions folder by the Mac OS.

Scripts

The Scripts folder, a relatively new addition to the Mac OS, stores AppleScripts in a central location. In earlier versions of the Mac OS, scripts could be stored wherever

Mac OS 8.6

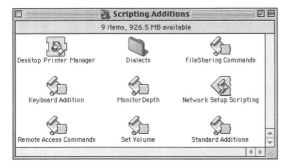

Figure 2.23 The Scripting Additions folder.

you liked. The addition of the Scripts folder has proved to be a great help in organizing various scripts. See Chapter 13 for more information about AppleScript and how to use the Scripts folder.

Shutdown And Startup Items

The contents of the Shutdown Items folder are executed as the last step when you request that the Mac OS restart or shut down the computer. This is especially helpful if you want to sweep your hard drive for viruses prior to restarting or shutting down. For example, if you have an application that can quickly scan your hard drive for viruses, just make an alias to that application and place it in the Shutdown Items folder.

Applications, documents, folders, and volumes in the Startup Items folder automatically run (or open) each time your Macintosh is started or restarted. This folder takes the place of the Set Startup command found in the Special menu in previous versions of the system software. As with the Apple Menu Items folder, most of the icons in the Startup Items folder will probably be aliases, as shown in Figure 2.24.

Figure 2.24 The Startup Items folder with alias icons that will be launched or mounted at startup.

Mac OS 8.6

While the Startup Items folder's main purpose is to open applications and documents, it's also a good place to put folder and volume aliases. These aliases will be opened, or mounted, at startup—a simple but important function. Of course, before mounting a networked volume, your system may ask you to supply a password.

System Suitcase And System Resources

The System file (technically it's a suitcase) is the second of the two most critical elements in the System Folder, along with the Finder. The System suitcase oversees all basic Mac OS activities and assists every application and utility that runs on the Macintosh. The System Resources file contains data that is utilized by various elements of the Finder, System suitcase, and the Mac OS in general. As a user, you can remain blissfully ignorant of most of the work performed by the System suitcase. However, you should understand the System suitcase's traditional role as home to sounds and keyboard resources, some of which are shown in Figure 2.25, does require user interaction. Most other types of data stored in the System suitcase are hidden from view and are inaccessible to the user.

When stuffed with these items, a single System file in the days before System 7 could grow to 600K or larger—often much larger. This overload often resulted in

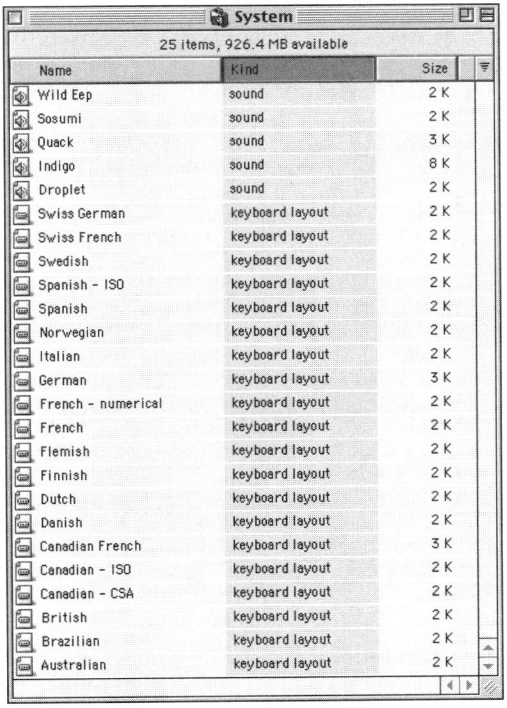

Name	Kind	Size
Wild Eep	sound	2 K
Sosumi	sound	2 K
Quack	sound	3 K
Indigo	sound	8 K
Droplet	sound	2 K
Swiss German	keyboard layout	2 K
Swiss French	keyboard layout	2 K
Swedish	keyboard layout	2 K
Spanish - ISO	keyboard layout	2 K
Spanish	keyboard layout	2 K
Norwegian	keyboard layout	2 K
Italian	keyboard layout	2 K
German	keyboard layout	3 K
French - numerical	keyboard layout	2 K
French	keyboard layout	2 K
Flemish	keyboard layout	2 K
Finnish	keyboard layout	2 K
Dutch	keyboard layout	2 K
Danish	keyboard layout	2 K
Canadian French	keyboard layout	3 K
Canadian - ISO	keyboard layout	2 K
Canadian - CSA	keyboard layout	2 K
British	keyboard layout	2 K
Brazilian	keyboard layout	2 K
Australian	keyboard layout	2 K

Figure 2.25 The System suitcase is very important to the Mac OS.

an unstable System file that would easily and frequently become corrupt, necessitating the annoying and time-consuming effort of deleting and rebuilding the System file. In Mac OS 8.6, the System file is between 8MB and 10MB in size. We'll look at several aspects of the System suitcase, including adding sounds and keyboard layouts, in several upcoming chapters.

Text Encodings

The Text Encodings folder stores conversion files used by the Mac OS to translate data between languages, such as Chinese, Hebrew, and Korean. You won't need to interact with the contents of this folder yourself, but certain applications may not work if the proper translator isn't located in this folder.

Modifying The System Folder

The System Folder and its subfolders are created by the Installer when you first install Mac OS 8.6. At that time, all system software files are placed in their proper locations. The System Folder is constantly modified, however, as you install other software applications or perform other common tasks on your Macintosh.

Several types of files are added to the System Folder after the initial installation—fonts and sounds, system Extensions (which add functionality to the Mac OS, applications, and utilities), and miscellaneous files that enable other software applications to function properly.

You can modify the way the system software works and extend the features provided by the system software via several features, including Extensions, Control Panels, and printer or network drivers. Ram Doubler, Speed Doubler, Default Folder, and GoMac are among the most popular of the hundreds of examples of Extensions and drivers that modify your system software. You've probably already added files of this type to your System Folder.

Many applications store miscellaneous files—files that don't interact directly with the system software—in the System Folder. They're placed in the System Folder for these reasons:

➤ *Safety*—The System Folder is the only "common ground" on a Mac hard drive that applications can rely on in every configuration.

➤ *Simplicity*—The Macintosh operating system can easily find the System Folder, regardless of what it's called and where it's located. This allows applications quick access to files stored in the System Folder.

➤ *Security*—The System Folder is a safe place for applications to add files because most users are not likely to disturb files in their System Folder.

To further improve upon the safety factor of placing files in your System Folder, you can enable the Protect System Folder option found in the General Controls Control Panel. This feature essentially locks the folder so that changes can't be made to it. If you create a folder called the Applications folder, then you can use the Protect Applications Folder option in the same Control Panel. Files in a protected folder cannot be removed or renamed. Changes to files (such as Preference files) can occur, however.

Some of the many application-related files (or folders) that use your System Folder as a safe storage place are Microsoft Word's Word Temp files (later versions of Word store temp files in the Word folder), PageMaker and StuffIt's encryption engines, Translators, Claris translators, and Viewers.

Printer font files are also in this category. Printer fonts are placed in the Fonts folder so they'll be available when needed for automatic downloading to a PostScript printer, and so they can be found by Adobe Type Manager. They can be in the System file as well, but you should try to keep them in the Fonts folder. Printer font files are usually the most space-consuming files—30K to 50K each—in the System Folder (when loading in the System file). Although utilities like Suitcase II and MasterJuggler make it possible to store printer and screen fonts in other locations, many people choose to keep them in the System Folder anyway. It's the preferred location when you have a static set of fonts that you normally work with.

Adding Files To The System Folder

After Mac OS 8.6 has been installed or upgraded, files may be added to the System Folder in several ways:

- ➤ *By the Mac OS Installer*—To add additional printer drivers, network drivers, or keyboards, you can run the Mac OS Installer application at any time. The Installer adds the selected files to your System Folder, placing them in the proper subfolders. You don't have to use the Installer to add drivers or files from the system software disks; you can drag-copy files (by holding down the Option key while dragging a file) directly from these disks into your System Folder.

  - ➤ *By application software installers*—Many software applications use installation programs that copy the software and its associated files to your hard drive. Installers that have been specifically written or updated for compatibility with Mac OS 8.6 can place files correctly into the System Folder or subfolders.

    Older installer applications often place all files directly in the System Folder, ignoring the subfolder structure. In these cases, the application may require that the files remain as positioned by the installer. However, most Extensions should be moved to the Extensions folder, and Control Panels should be moved to the

Mac OS 8.6

Control Panels folder—regardless of how they were originally positioned. Although all Extensions should be placed in the Extensions folder or Control Panels folder, most items of this nature located directly in the System Folder will be executed at startup.

➤ *By software applications*—Historically, many software applications read and write temporary and preferences files to the System Folder. Others use the System Folder for dictionaries and other ancillary files. Older applications not rewritten for Mac OS 8.6 may not use the proper subfolders found in the System Folder, such as the Scripting Additions and Scripts folders. Files placed directly in the System Folder may not be accessed properly and may cause problems for your system software or other programs.

➤ *By you, the Macintosh user*—Since some programs and utilities don't use installer applications, many files must be placed into the System Folder manually. These files can be dragged onto the System Folder icon or dragged into an open System Folder window.

When files are dragged onto the System Folder icon, the Mac OS automatically places many of them in the System Folder or correct subfolder. This helps you add files to the System Folder correctly, even if you know nothing about the System Folder structure.

Before positioning files, the OS informs you that it's at work and tells you how it's positioning your files, as shown in Figure 2.26. This works only when files are dragged onto the System Folder icon.

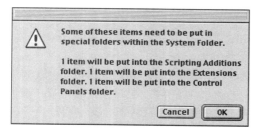

Figure 2.26 The Mac OS ensures that files are positioned properly.

Once files are in the System Folder, you can reposition them freely. The Helping Hand will not affect the movement of files moved from within the System Folder.

You can also keep the Mac OS from performing this task by dragging files directly onto the System Folder and navigating the subfolders using the spring-loaded folder feature. When you drag files this way, you can place them in any System Folder subfolder, or into the System Folder itself, without interference.

Deleting Files From The System Folder

For the most part, files in the System Folder can be deleted just like any other file—by dragging them into the Trash. However, some files cannot be deleted because they're "in use." "In-use" files include the System file, the Finder, any Extensions or Control Panels with code that ran at startup, fonts, open Control Panels, and any temporary or preferences files used by open applications.

To delete the System file or Finder (but you wouldn't ever want to do this, would you?), you must restart the Macintosh using another boot disk. To delete an "in-use" Extension or Control Panel, move the file out of the Extensions or Control Panels folder, restart the Mac, and then delete the file. To delete open Control Panels or temporary or Preferences files of open applications, simply close the Control Panel or application and drag the file to the Trash.

Wrapping Up

Working in the System Folder used to be like playing with a house of cards, but as we've seen, Mac OS 8.6 brings new order and stability to this important part of your computer. The items contained in the System Folder that are especially useful include:

➤ The Apple Menu Items folder, which lets you customize your Apple Menu.

➤ The Control Panels folder, which holds special "mini-applications" that set preferences for system software features, utilities, and even hardware peripherals.

➤ The Extensions folder, which contains all the Extensions and drivers that add features to your Mac and the system software.

➤ The Favorites folder, which holds shortcuts and aliases to your favorite files, folders, applications, file servers, and Internet addresses.

➤ The Extensions folder, which contains all the Extensions and drivers that add features to your Mac and the system software.

➤ The System suitcase, which holds keyboard mappings and sounds, which are visible, and critical portions of the Mac OS that are responsible for a wide variety of functions, which are invisible to the user.

➤ The Startup and Shutdown Items folders, which let you determine which files and applications are opened or launched each time your Mac is started, restarted, or shut down.

In Chapter 3 we'll examine two important aspects of the operating system, the Finder and the Desktop, both of which provide the interface and tools that help control the disks and files you use on the Macintosh.

Mac OS 8.6

The Finder And Desktop

Just like your word processor, spreadsheet, or Web browser, the Finder is an application—even though most people don't think of it that way. Whereas each of those other applications is dedicated to creating and manipulating one specific type of data, the Finder focuses on helping you manage your disks and files.

The Finder provides you with the distinctive Macintosh Desktop, where icons represent each disk, drive, folder, and file, as well as the Finder menus and the Trash. Through the Finder, you can view and modify the contents of your disks and drives in many different ways, and launch other applications or Control Panels. Although most people equate the Desktop with the Finder, the Desktop is really just a window used to view the contents of the Finder.

In Mac OS 8.6, the Finder has been enhanced to give you more information about your disks and files, more consistency in commands and features, and additional customizing capabilities. Fortunately, these benefits come without significant changes in the Finder's familiar interface—if you were comfortable working in System 7.x or earlier versions of Mac OS 8, you'll have no problem adjusting to the new Finder and taking advantage of its expanded capabilities.

This chapter starts by examining the Finder's menu commands and then looks at Finder windows. Features new to Mac OS 8.6, including customizable list views and icon proxies, are covered, along with other familiar features in the Finder, such as Apple Help Viewer, Balloon Help, the Trash, and the Get Info dialog box.

This chapter is not, however, the only place in this book where you'll read about new Finder capabilities. Many Finder features are introduced in this chapter and then elaborated on in other chapters where the context is more appropriate. For example, aliasing, Sherlock (the old Find command), and the Label menu are discussed in Chapter 5. The About This Computer command is described in detail in Chapter 9, and the Sharing command is explained in Chapter 17.

Finder Menus

Since System 7.x, a lot has changed in the Finder and Desktop—but it's all for the best! Take a quick look at Figure 3.1, which shows a few Finder windows in System 7.0.1.

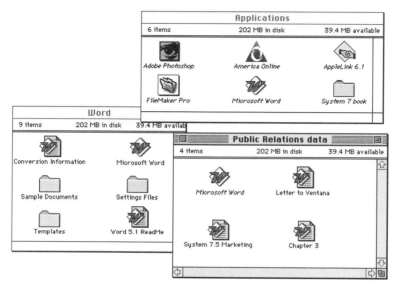

Figure 3.1   Finder windows in System 7.0.1.

Now look at Figure 3.2, which shows the new Finder and Desktop in Mac OS 8.6. You may notice a few new elements, including:

➤ A revised Help menu.

➤ The removal of the Label menu.

➤ Tabbed folders (an example of which can be seen at the bottom of the screen).

Of course, the most obvious change is in the overall appearance of the interface. The OS now draws windows to offer a more appealing 3D look called the Apple Platinum appearance.

You can familiarize yourself with any new or upgraded application by taking a quick tour through its menu bar and menu commands; we'll use this approach to start learning about the Finder. Figure 3.3 shows the Finder menus and commands as they appear on most systems when Mac OS 8.6 is first installed. Your menus may vary slightly depending on your hardware configuration and option settings.

Mac OS 8.6 enhances a few of the Finder menus, but most of the Finder commands have retained the same name or position from System 7.x and function in

Mac OS 8.6

The Finder And Desktop 63

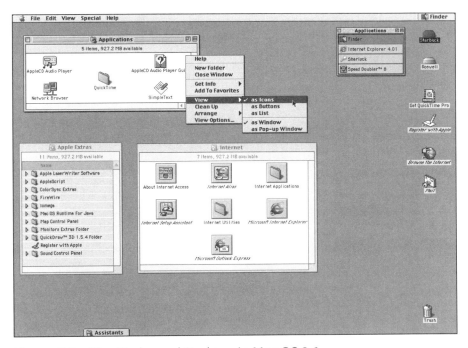

Figure 3.2 The Finder and Desktop in Mac OS 8.6.

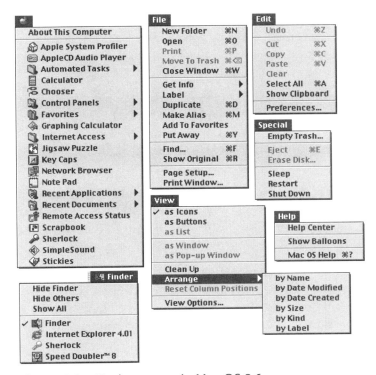

Figure 3.3 Finder menus in Mac OS 8.6.

Mac OS 8.6

the same way today as they did then. To save space (and avoid boring you), this section focuses on the most popular commands, or those new or enhanced under Mac OS 8.6. They are listed on the following pages in the order they appear in the menus, from left to right on the menu bar, starting with the Apple Menu:

- *About This Computer (Apple Menu)*—This command opens a dialog box that displays information about your computer, such as available physical memory, virtual memory, and open applications (more information about this dialog box appears in Chapter 9.) This menu choice was previously called About This Macintosh.

- *Apple System Profiler*—This command launches a small application that inventories your computer's hardware and software, in case you want to know what's going on "under the hood," or if requested by an Apple tech support representative or "help desk" staff member trying to help you with a problem.

- *Favorites*—The Favorites folder contains aliases to your favorite folders, applications, volumes, file servers, or Internet URLs (discussed in the previous chapter). Items may be placed in or retrieved from the Favorites folder with any Mac OS 8.6-savvy application that uses the new Navigational Services for Open and Save dialog windows, such as the Appearance window used to select a Desktop picture.

- *Recent Documents, Recent Applications, and Recent Servers submenus (Apple Menu)*—Selecting one of these commands displays a list of your most recently used files, applications, or servers, allowing you to launch a file or application or mount a server. This is a tremendous time-saver that you're likely to use frequently in your daily work.

- *Sherlock*—Sherlock is the replacement to the old Find command from previous versions of the Mac OS. Like the Find command, Sherlock can search for files by filename, size, creation date, label, and so on. When files matching your search criteria are located, the Finder opens a window containing the file (or files) and selects the file's icon. We'll cover Sherlock in great detail in Chapter 5.

If you haven't taken Sherlock for a test drive yet, go ahead and give it a try. As you can see in Figure 3.4, Sherlock adds two powerful features to the Mac OS (Find by Content, and Search Internet) and is probably the best feature in Mac OS 8.6.

Prior to OS 7.5, finding a number of items that matched the search criteria with the Find command was a time-consuming procedure with Find and Find Again. In Mac OS 8.6, the Sherlock application concludes a search by displaying the Items Found window showing *all* of the documents, applications, or disks that match the search criteria.

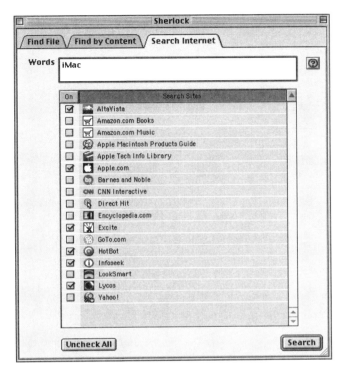

Figure 3.4 The new Sherlock application replaces the old Find command and adds several valuable features, including the ability to search the Internet.

Note that the Items Found dialog box is Macintosh Drag-and-Drop enabled; this means you can drag a file onto your Desktop or into a window to move it, onto an application icon to open it, to a printer icon to print it, and so on. Figure 3.5 shows an example of the Items Found window.

➤ *Move To Trash (File menu)*—This command allows you to throw a selected item into the Trash without dragging it there. To use this command, select an item to delete by clicking on it once; then choose the Move To Trash command or use the keyboard equivalent (Command+Delete).

➤ *Label (File menu)*—The Label menu has moved from being a menu unto itself under System 7.x to being a submenu under the File menu. It works just as it has in previous versions of the OS; only its location has changed. See the Edit|Preferences option later in this list for more information on how to configure the names and colors of the labels.

➤ *Show Original (File menu)*—The Show Original menu option is identical to the Reveal Original option of System 7.x., which allows you to select an alias and then find its original file, folder, or application. In older versions of the OS, you

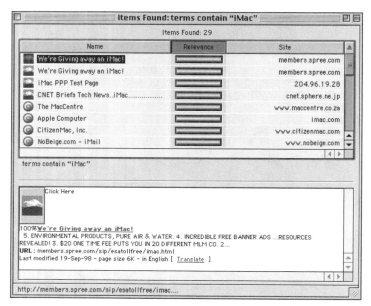

Figure 3.5 A successful search using the new Sherlock application.

could also click once on an alias, choose Get Info from the File menu, and then click a button entitled Find Original. In Mac OS 8.6, this option is no longer available when you select Get Info on an alias.

➤ *Preferences (Edit menu)*—Under the Edit menu, the Show Clipboard menu choice has been moved up one notch to make room for the Preferences menu options, which have also been changed in Mac OS 8.6. Shown in Figure 3.6, the Preferences option takes the place of System 7.x's Views Control Panel and Label menu. It also incorporates new configuration options into three tabs—General, Views, and Labels. The Preferences|Views dialog window now allows you to configure default preferences for each type of window view (icon, list, or button).

➤ *View menu*—The View menu allows you to change how you view the contents of a folder to an icon, button, or list view. Each view has its own set of preferences, as shown in Figure 3.7. Mac OS 8.5 introduced the ability to revert the view of a particular window using a predefined set of options, which are configured in the Edit|Views menu.

➤ *Pop-up window*—In addition to viewing the contents of a folder or hard drive as icons, buttons, or lists, Mac OS 8.6 allows you to view folders and their contents in a pop-up window, three of which are shown in Figure 3.8 (two minimized and one opened). When a folder is dragged to the bottom of the screen, it turns into a tabbed pop-up window, only one of which can "pop up" at a time. You can resize the window or "bring it back" as a normal window by lifting it up or out with the resizing corners on either side.

The Finder And Desktop 67

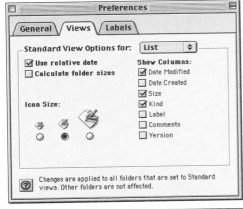

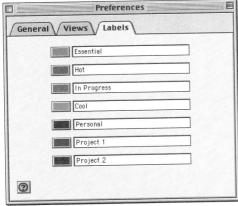

Figure 3.6 The Edit|Preferences menu takes the place of several other menus and adds new features.

68   Chapter 3

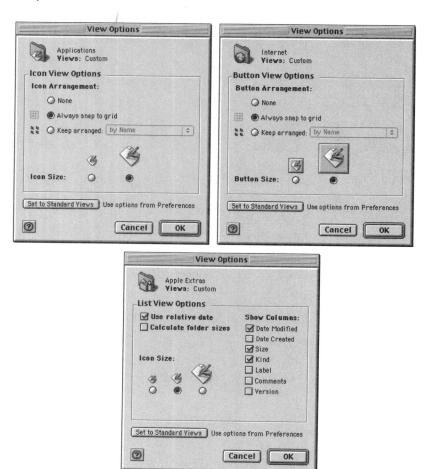

Figure 3.7   The View menu provides several new ways to display the contents of a folder or hard drive.

- *Clean Up (View menu)*—The Clean Up menu option was moved from the Special menu starting with Mac OS 8, where it was called Clean Up Window. This option performs the same task as before—uncluttering your window by aligning icons.

- *Arrange/Sort List (View menu)*—The Arrange menu option is available when viewing the contents of a folder or hard drive by Icons or by List, and in the latter case, the menu option is called Sort List. If viewed by Icons, the options are to Arrange By Name, Date Modified, Date Created, Size, Kind, or Label. If viewed by List, the Sort List options are by Name, Date Modified, Size, and Kind.

- *Special*—The Special menu is pretty much the same as in earlier versions of the Mac OS and System 7.x versions of the OS, but with two minor exceptions. First, the Clean Up Window option found in earlier versions of the Mac OS has been moved to the View menu and is now called Clean Up. Second, the remaining

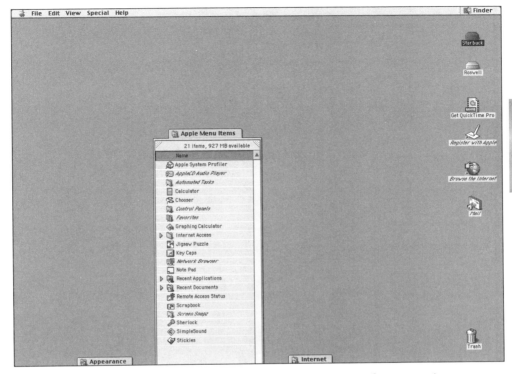

Figure 3.8 Pop-up windows offer you another alternative for managing your Desktop.

items in the Special menu have been regrouped so that Sleep, Restart, and Shut Down all appear at the bottom of the menu in a single grouping.

➤ *Help menu*—Another big change in Mac OS 8.6 from System 7.x is the removal of the Balloon Help icon from its old position next to the Application menu. You may select Show Balloons to activate Balloon Help, or select Mac OS Help (or press Command+?) to open the Mac OS Help document in the new Apple Help Viewer. Mac OS Help is the OS's main method of providing help to users, and sports an HTML-like interface that should be very familiar to anyone who has ever surfed the Web. Figure 3.9 shows the new Help Center and Mac OS Help document.

The Apple Help Viewer, Apple Guide, and Balloon Help are available at all times in all applications, not just in the Finder. No matter what help system you choose, the quality and quantity of help are determined by how well the developers of your software chose to implement it.

➤ *Application menu and Application Switcher*—The Application menu is located in the upper right corner of your screen and is the primary method of switching between open applications. It's available at all times, not just when you're using

Mac OS 8.6

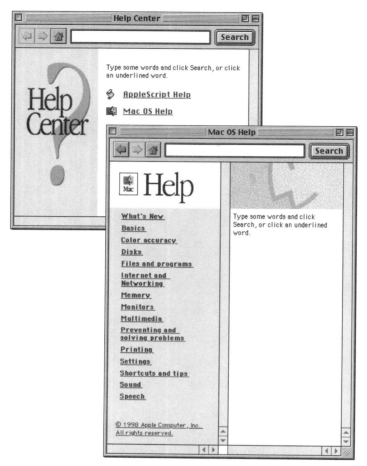

Figure 3.9 You can still choose Apple Guide and Balloon Help from the newly named Help menu.

the Finder. Mac OS 8.6 also makes it possible to "tear off" the Application menu and move it about the Desktop as a type of window known as a "floating palette" (see Figure 3.10), a feature of the new Application Switcher.

Figure 3.10 Two views of the Application menu, the normal pull-down view (left) and the new tear-off menu (right) that is part of the new Application Switcher.

Mac OS 8.6

The name of every open application will automatically appear in this menu. To switch from one application to another, choose the name you want from the Application menu; that application and its windows will immediately appear. You may also press Command+Tab to cycle through all the open applications, including the Finder.

Note that in most cases only your current application, the one selected with a check mark in the Application menu, is actually running and processing. Only a few active processes, like printing and communications, can efficiently run in the background.

While you're running one application in the foreground, the Mac OS saves the status of your other applications and processes in memory. This feature is called multithreading; moving between applications (and threads) is called context switching. Running application sessions concurrently, or multitasking, is being written into Mac OS gradually but is not available with all applications. We'll have more to say about this in subsequent chapters, particularly in Chapter 7, Chapter 9, and Chapter 10.

Using the Hide command under the Application menu, you can temporarily hide all windows relating to the current application, or hide all windows *except* those of the current application, thus reducing the onscreen clutter that can result from running multiple applications at once.

TIP
If you've lost your place on the Desktop and menus have changed, check the Application menu to see what program is active in the foreground.

You may also hide the Finder. In the General Controls Control Panel, the default condition is to show the Desktop in the background. Just click off the Show Desktop When in Background check box (found in the Desktop section) to hide the Finder, and consequently prevent losing your place when working in an application. When the Finder is hidden, you don't see any icons on the Desktop like the Trash, disk or drive icons, or folders.

Finder And Desktop Window Basics

Menu commands are only a small segment of the Finder's overall function as a disk and file management tool. Most of the time, you move, copy, delete, arrange, and open files by using the mouse to directly manipulate icons on the Desktop and in Finder windows. In Mac OS 8.6, your ability to see and manipulate files and folders in windows has been dramatically improved compared to the capabilities you had before System 7. The basic attributes of Finder windows, however, have not changed:

Mac OS 8.6

- ➤ Windows are created each time a volume or folder is opened.
- ➤ Each window has a title bar, zoom box, and close box.
- ➤ Windows can be freely positioned by dragging their title bars.
- ➤ Windows can be resized by dragging on the resize box.
- ➤ Windows display the files and folders contained in a single volume or folder.
- ➤ The window display is controlled via the View menu.

The improvements to the Finder in Mac OS 8.6, however, give you more control over windows, a more consistent user interface, and a wider range of display options:

- ➤ The font, icon size, and information displayed in Finder windows are customizable.
- ➤ Keyboard commands let you navigate windows and select files without using the mouse.
- ➤ Smart zooming opens windows only enough to display their content, or to the maximum available display area.
- ➤ The contents of any folder or subfolder can be displayed in hierarchical format in any window.
- ➤ Hierarchical levels allow files in different folders to be manipulated simultaneously.
- ➤ Icon proxies (in the title bar) allow you to move, copy, or alias Finder windows.
- ➤ List view columns may be resized and reordered.

It's easy to get lost when you have a number of windows open on your screen—particularly a problem on PowerBooks or Macs with very small displays. Most applications have a Window menu for just such occasions, but the Finder does not. Two features in Mac OS 8.6 offer some help with the problems presented by window clutter. System 7.5.x included a version of WindowShade, formerly a shareware program which is now also referred to as *collapsible windows*. WindowShade is now built into the Mac OS. Using WindowShade is easy; just click twice on the title bar to reduce the window to its title bar only. Or, click once on what is known as the WindowShade widget (see Figure 3.11). Double-click again on the "minimized" window's title bar or click once on the widget to return the window to its full size. An example of a minimized window created by WindowShade is shown in Figure 3.11 along with the maximized window.

You can disable the collapsing window feature in the Options tab of the Appearance Control Panel, which we'll cover in the next chapter.

Figure 3.11 Using the WindowShade feature can help clean up a cluttered Desktop.

Another improvement in Mac OS 8.6 (which we've already seen) is the pop-up, or tabbed, folder feature. This very handy feature, which allows you to minimize a folder or hard drive at the bottom of the screen (see Figure 3.8 for an example), has been available to Mac OS users through commercial and shareware utilities for some time. Apple has finally gotten around to including it in the OS itself, starting with Mac OS 8.0. To open a pop-up window once it has been minimized, click on the title bar area once. Click on it again to minimize it.

These and other new features and refinements in the operation of Finder windows are discussed in detail later in this chapter.

Finder Preferences

In older versions of the Finder, the presentation of text and icons in Finder windows was preset and could not be modified. Text was always shown in Geneva 9 point, and icons in preset sizes appeared in each icon view. In System 7, the Views Control Panel provided a variety of options that enabled you to control the information and the way it was displayed in Finder windows. In Mac OS 8.0, the options relating to viewing the contents of a folder or hard drive became even more flexible and customizable, as well as more a part of the core OS rather than a branch of it, such as a Control Panel or Extension add-on. Mac OS 8.6 goes even further to allow users to customize more Finder elements—which is what the Mac OS is all about anyway, right?

Several elements of the Finder are configurable in the Edit|Preferences menu, as we've already seen in Figure 3.6. Mac OS 8.6 breaks the configuration of the Finder's preferences into three categories:

Mac OS 8.6

➤ General

➤ Views

➤ Labels

The trend in Mac OS 8.6 is to centralize the configuration options once provided by multiple Control Panels into the Finder itself. This centralization makes it easier to find all the various configuration choices, makes the Mac OS less prone to Control Panel conflicts, and makes it easier for software developers to write new utilities that can help you customize your Mac. Let's take a look at the three tabs in the Preferences configuration window.

General Preferences

The General tab in the Preferences window provides options that affect three features in the Finder (see Figure 3.12). Checking the Simple Finder option will remove many of the menu options and their keyboard equivalents, as in Figure 3.13. This feature may be useful in certain settings such as learning situations like teaching labs or elementary schools, or if you want to let your children have a go at your computer. It simplifies the Finder by temporarily limiting the Finder menu choices. You can restore all the complex features of the Finder by simply unchecking this menu choice.

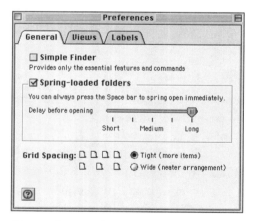

Figure 3.12 The General tab of the Finder Preferences.

The spring-loaded folder option (not to be confused with the pop-up folder feature) is a variation on the drag-and-drop capability of the Mac OS. With the sliding rule, you can set the amount of time the OS will wait to spring open a folder onto which you have dragged an item (such as a file, folder, or document). Once the folder springs open, you can drop the item into place. If you hold an item over a subfolder, that folder will spring open as well. To navigate backward, drag the folder

The Finder And Desktop   75

Figure 3.13   The Simple Finder option (right) temporarily removes all but the most basic menu options to help younger users operate the Mac OS, or to help keep adults out of trouble!

you want to relocate outside the highlighted folder where it's currently located and drop it in its new home. To start completely over, drag the item to the Desktop without letting go and hold it over the hard drive's icon. For example, Figure 3.14 shows a file being moved two levels deeper from the Desktop, into the hard drive named Starbuck, and into a folder entitled QuickTime.

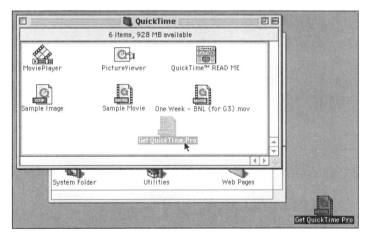

Figure 3.14   Use spring-loaded folders to make relocating or copying items much easier.

TIP

A new feature in Mac OS 8.6 is the ability to tap the space bar to immediately open a folder or volume onto which you are dragging a selected item. In effect, tapping the space bar overrides the spring-loaded folder delay setting.

Mac OS 8.6

The final Finder Preference under the General tab lets you determine the amount of space between items when viewed by icon or by button (but not by list), and when the "Keep arranged by" options is also selected in the View|View Options menu (described below). This feature is very handy if you like to view folders containing dozens or hundreds of items but are concerned with how much space is available on your monitor to display these items. If desktop "real estate" is limited, you should choose Tight Grid Spacing. This will instruct the Mac OS to leave as little space between icons as possible when you choose the Clean Up command from the View menu. Conversely, selecting the Wide Grid Spacing option will allow the OS to space icons further apart and prevent them from overlapping, which looks neater. Figure 3.15 shows an example of wide-versus-narrow spacing. Note that the windows are the same size, and when the spacing is set to Wide, the icons will not all fit in the window; you'll have to scroll down to see all of them.

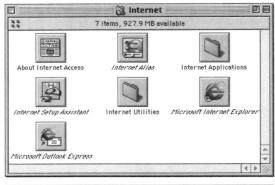

Figure 3.15 Grid spacing affects the way the Mac OS places icons and buttons on the Desktop.

Views Preferences

The Views tab controls the default, or Standard, viewing options for the three types of window views in the Mac OS—icons, buttons, or lists. Mac OS 8.0 introduced the option of viewing icons as buttons. Buttons differ from icons in that they require only a single click to open or activate. A single click on a button name will select the item the button represents. Mac OS 8.6 gives you the ability to define a default, or Standard, view, for all windows. However, you can selectively override the default view and customize each folder as you like. We'll look at all the details associated with window views later in this chapter, but for now, here's an overview of the settings that you can choose as the defaults for icon, button, and list views.

Figure 3.16 shows the defaults for windows viewed by icons, traditionally the preferred view of most Mac OS users. Icons may be arranged in several ways and displayed in two sizes—small and large.

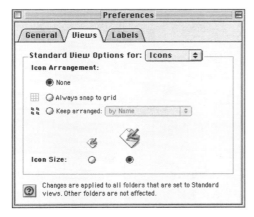

Figure 3.16 Default settings for windows viewed as icons.

Figure 3.17 shows the defaults for windows viewed as buttons, a new feature beginning with Mac OS 8.0. Buttons have the same view options as icons.

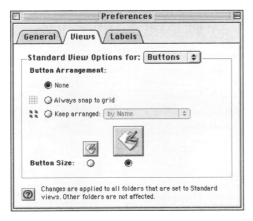

Figure 3.17 Default settings for windows viewed as buttons.

Finally, Figure 3.18 shows the defaults for windows viewed as lists. List windows have more options than icon and button windows, and are probably the preferred viewing method these days because users often have tens of thousands of files instead of just a few thousand. List views are easier to manage and quicker to open than icon or button views.

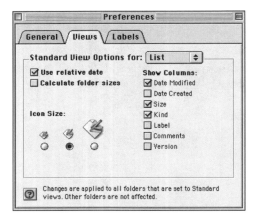

Figure 3.18   Default settings for windows viewed as lists.

Labels Preferences

The Labels tab is the last Finder Preferences tab you need to configure. The Label options are fundamentally similar to the Colors menu used in System 6.x in that they allow you to specify colors for file and folder icons. A few important improvements have been added to the colorization process since then, however. You can now color-code your files by specifying a classification title for each color. In addition, color labels are supported by the View menu and Find command, so you can use label categories as part of your hard disk organization and management strategy. We'll look at an example of this in just a few minutes, but for now go ahead and type in a few meaningful (or non-meaningful!) phrases in the spaces provided.

Apple provides examples that might be useful for project management (Essential, Hot, In Progress) or for home use (Cool, Personal, Project 1, Project 2). Figure 3.19 shows these default labels, as well as another approach to making labels. This second example takes advantage of the fact that labeled Finder elements (files, folders, volumes, etc.) are also sorted in alphabetical order, which we'll elaborate on in Chapter 4.

Window Viewing Options

The Finder's View menu, like View menus in past Finder versions, determines how information is displayed in the active window. Previous versions of the View menu let you display files and folders by icon, small icon, name, date, size, kind, and color. In

The Finder And Desktop   79

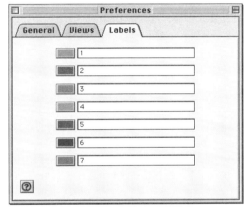

Figure 3.19 The default label colors and names, as well as a customized set of label preferences.

System 7, the View menu provided all these view methods (except for color), and added View by label, version, and comment. Mac OS 8.0 and 8.6 go even further and add two new viewing features—buttons and pop-up windows. Many of the options formerly found in the Views Control Panel are now found in the Finder's View menu.

There are two types of windows in Mac OS 8.6:

➤ Normal windows

➤ Pop-up windows

And as we've seen earlier, there are three types of normal window viewing options as well:

➤ As Icons

➤ As Buttons

➤ As Lists

Mac OS 8.6

Before you customize the way in which a window is viewed, the default settings, based on the settings in the Edit|Preferences|Views menu, are used. Each time you apply a View menu command to a particular window, that window's display is arranged according to the selected format (by icon, button, or list), and it retains that view format until a different View menu command is applied, or until the Set To Standard Views button is selected. When a window is closed and later reopened, it always appears in the same display view it had before it was closed. Under Mac OS 8.0 and 8.1, however, you couldn't change the View option for all open or closed windows because the View menu controlled each window independently. No default viewing options were configurable.

View As Pop-up Window

Pop-up windows are very cool—not to mention extremely useful—because they provide easy access to frequently used files, folders, volumes, and applications without cluttering up the Desktop. Once you've selected a window on the Desktop (i.e., made it the front-most window), you can make it into a pop-up window using one of three ways:

➤ Select View|as Pop-up Window.

➤ Activate the contextual menu while clicking on the window's title bar and select View|as Pop-up Window, as in Figure 3.20. We'll look at how to use contextual menus later in this chapter.

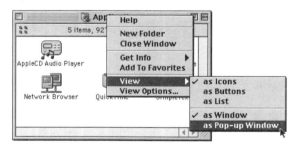

Figure 3.20 Use the contextual menu feature to create a pop-up window.

➤ Drag the window to the bottom of the screen until it turns into a pop-up window, as in Figure 3.21, which illustrates how the Applications folder looks as it goes from being a normal window to a pop-up window.

If you like pop-up windows as much as some of us do (ahem), consider using them to organize your recently used documents, servers (see Figure 3.22), and applications, as well as items in the Favorites folder. A good rule of thumb is that you can never have too many shortcuts, and because you're using a Mac, you can arrange these shortcuts just about any way you like!

The Finder And Desktop   81

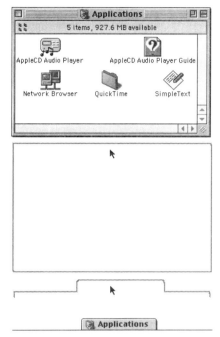

Figure 3.21   To change a normal window into a pop-up window, just drag it to the bottom of your screen until the tab pops up.

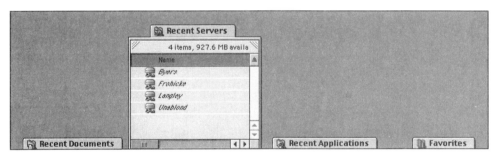

Figure 3.22   Use pop-up windows in conjunction with other shortcuts like these to make the Mac OS even more user friendly.

View As Icons

In Mac OS 8.6, you can no longer view the contents of a folder by name only, as you could in pre-Mac OS 8 versions of the operating system. An icon of some type (either large, medium, or small) will always be associated with an item. The particular View Options that you select determine what a particular window looks like, as shown in Figure 3.23.

Mac OS 8.6

82   Chapter 3

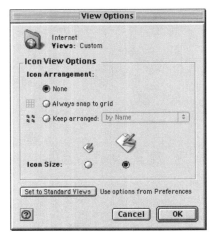

Figure 3.23 When viewing a window using icons, change the View Options settings for a folder or the Desktop to suit your preferences.

The following options may be found in the Icon View Options configuration window:

➤ *Icon Arrangement: None*—This option tells the Finder that items in a particular folder are not to be arranged in any predetermined way.

➤ *Icon Arrangement: Always Snap to Grid*—The Always Snap to Grid option forces any repositioned icons or buttons to automatically snap to the nearest point on an invisible grid. This is the same invisible grid used by the Clean Up command and will result in either tight or wide baseline alignment, depending on whether the Tight Grid or the Wide Grid option is chosen in the General preferences tab of the Finder Preferences (described earlier). The concept of always keeping files grid-aligned in this way may sound appealing, but it can be disconcerting when the Finder grabs and relocates files while you're trying to position them precisely. In most cases, it's probably better to leave this option off and use the Clean Up command to correct any icon alignment problems in Finder windows.

➤ *Icon Arrangement: Keep Arranged*—This option tells the Finder that items in a particular folder are to be arranged according to either Name, Date Created,

Mac OS 8.6

Date Modified, Size, Kind, or Label (see below). This may seem a bit odd at first because you can tell the Finder to arrange a group—not a list—of items by a criteria such as name or date created. The result is that the icons or buttons are listed in a particular order, left to right or top to bottom, like a list.

➤ *Set to Standard Views*—Clicking this option will cause the selected window to revert to the default, or Standard, view as defined in the Icons section of the Edit|Preferences|Views configuration window. Otherwise, the window will retain any custom options you apply to it.

For example, Figure 3.24 shows the contents of a hard disk viewed as small icons ordered by the date their contents were last modified, instead of by larger icons ordered by name. The result looks like a combination of list and icon views.

Figure 3.24 Viewing the contents of a hard drive by small icons and date modified.

When viewing by icon, the following options are available under the Keep Arranged option under the View|View Options menu:

➤ *By Name*—This command sorts files and folders alphabetically (A through Z), from top to bottom.

➤ *By Date Modified*—This command sorts files by the date they were last modified, with the most recently updated files at the top of the list. This view is useful when you're looking for files that are much older or much newer than most of the other files in a certain folder.

➤ *By Date Created*—This command sorts files by the date they were created, with the most recently created files at the top of the list. When you copy a file or folder from another source, it will retain its original creation date.

➤ *By Size*—This command sorts files in descending size order. Otherwise, folders are grouped alphabetically at the end of the list. Commonly, the By Size command is used to find files known to be either very large or very small or to locate large files that could be deleted to free up space.

- *By Kind*—This command sorts files alphabetically by a short description based on the file type, a designation assigned by the creator of the application. Files associated with a particular application often include the name of that application as the kind. Common kinds of files include alias, application program, Chooser Extension, Desk Accessory, document, folder, and System Extension. Common kinds of application files include BBEdit text file, SimpleText read-only document, GraphicConverter PICT Picture, and Photoshop PICT file. Viewing files by kind is useful if you know the kind of file you're looking for, and if the window containing that file has many different files in it.

- *By Label*—This command sorts by the label name given to the file with the Label command. Labels are used to group files according to some user-defined scheme, as we've seen earlier in this chapter. For example, you might have a group of files that all relate to personal (non-business) issues, a group relating to one project you're working on, and so on. In any case, this command lets you sort the files in the current window according to labels previously applied. Files are arranged as they appear in the Label submenu, and when viewed in the Finder, the labeled files, folders, and volumes will also have their icons colored accordingly. Unlabeled files appear at the bottom of the listing.

View As Buttons

The View as Buttons option has exactly the same viewing options as the View as Icons option—except that you may choose to view the contents of a window by small or large buttons instead of small or large icons. Figure 3.25 shows the View as Buttons|View Options configuration window and an example folder viewed with these settings.

TIP
When viewing items such as buttons, you only have to single-click them to open or launch them.

Even when viewing the contents of a folder or hard drive as buttons, you can still arrange them by date created, size, label, and so on. In Figure 3.26, the contents of the hard drive named Starbuck are viewed as small buttons and arranged by name; the names are listed alphabetically from left to right and top to bottom.

View As List

Finally, a different set of View options becomes available when you are viewing the contents of a folder or hard drive as a list. These options, shown in Figure 3.27, are similar to those found on previous versions of the Mac OS, especially System 7.5.

Mac OS 8.6

The Finder And Desktop   85

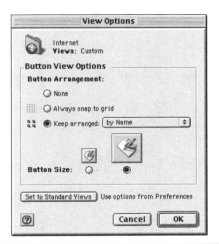

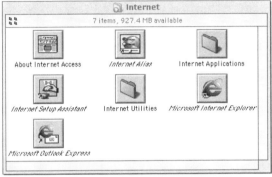

Figure 3.25 The View as Buttons options work exactly like the View as Icons options—but with buttons instead of icons.

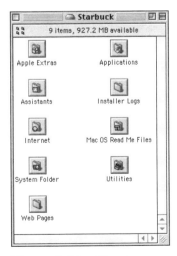

Figure 3.26 Viewing as small buttons, arranged by name.

Mac OS 8.6

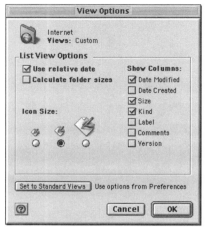

Figure 3.27 Viewing the contents of a folder as a list.

List view options are significantly different from icon and button options. Because lists always include the names of items in the window, you can't eliminate the ability to arrange the window by name. Other differences include the following:

➤ *Use Relative Dates*—Documents created or modified recently will be listed as Today (time) and Yesterday (time), and all others will be listed as Date (time). This is helpful when you have a long list of documents and you want to quickly find the ones you've recently modified.

➤ *Calculate Folder Sizes*—Checking this option will cause the total number of items in a window's subfolders to be calculated and displayed in the list view. Don't check this option unless you absolutely have to— it may dramatically slow down the performance of your computer.

➤ *Show Columns: By Date Modified, Date Created, Size, Kind, Label*—These options work just like they do when viewing the contents of a window by icons or buttons.

➤ *Show Columns: By Comment*—This command sorts files alphabetically by the text contained in their Get Info dialog box comment fields. Displaying comment text in Finder windows is a major new file management feature, but it's useful only if the first characters of the comment are significant or if you just want to separate all files that have comments from those that don't. Files without comments are placed at the top of any windows using the View menu's By Comment command.

- *Show Columns: By Version*—Useful only for application files, this command sorts by the software developer's assigned version number. Ancillary application files (e.g., dictionaries and references) and data files you create do not have this type of version number.
- *Icon Sizes*—In addition to the small and large icon and button sizes, when you select View as List, you can also select a medium-sized icon.

Figure 3.28 shows the System Folder viewed with small icons, sorted by name, and all the List View Options checked.

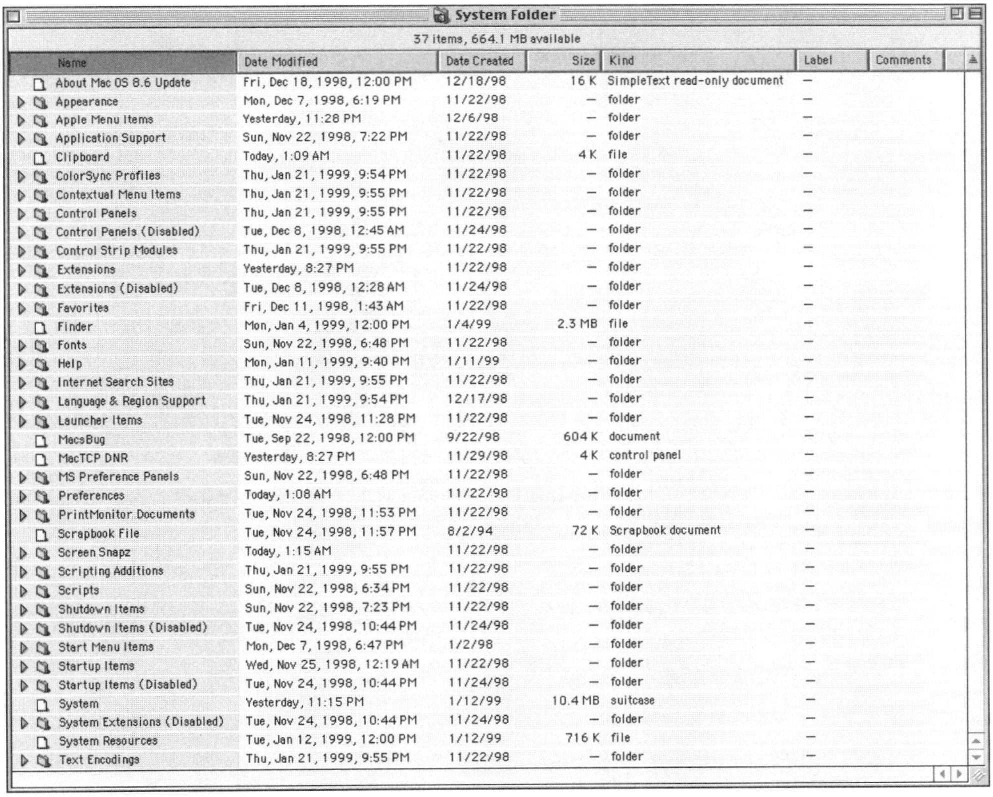

System Folder

37 items, 664.1 MB available

Name	Date Modified	Date Created	Size	Kind	Label	Comments
About Mac OS 8.6 Update	Fri, Dec 18, 1998, 12:00 PM	12/18/98	16 K	SimpleText read-only document	–	
Appearance	Mon, Dec 7, 1998, 6:19 PM	11/22/98	–	folder	–	
Apple Menu Items	Yesterday, 11:28 PM	12/6/98	–	folder	–	
Application Support	Sun, Nov 22, 1998, 7:22 PM	11/22/98	–	folder	–	
Clipboard	Today, 1:09 AM	11/22/98	4 K	file	–	
ColorSync Profiles	Thu, Jan 21, 1999, 9:54 PM	11/22/98	–	folder	–	
Contextual Menu Items	Thu, Jan 21, 1999, 9:55 PM	11/22/98	–	folder	–	
Control Panels	Thu, Jan 21, 1999, 9:55 PM	11/22/98	–	folder	–	
Control Panels (Disabled)	Tue, Dec 8, 1998, 12:45 AM	11/24/98	–	folder	–	
Control Strip Modules	Thu, Jan 21, 1999, 9:55 PM	11/22/98	–	folder	–	
Extensions	Yesterday, 8:27 PM	11/22/98	–	folder	–	
Extensions (Disabled)	Tue, Dec 8, 1998, 12:28 AM	11/24/98	–	folder	–	
Favorites	Fri, Dec 11, 1998, 1:43 AM	11/22/98	–	folder	–	
Finder	Mon, Jan 4, 1999, 12:00 PM	1/4/99	2.3 MB	file	–	
Fonts	Sun, Nov 22, 1998, 6:48 PM	11/22/98	–	folder	–	
Help	Mon, Jan 11, 1999, 9:40 PM	1/11/99	–	folder	–	
Internet Search Sites	Thu, Jan 21, 1999, 9:55 PM	11/22/98	–	folder	–	
Language & Region Support	Thu, Jan 21, 1999, 9:54 PM	12/17/98	–	folder	–	
Launcher Items	Tue, Nov 24, 1998, 11:28 PM	11/22/98	–	folder	–	
MacsBug	Tue, Sep 22, 1998, 12:00 PM	9/22/98	604 K	document	–	
MacTCP DNR	Yesterday, 8:27 PM	11/29/98	4 K	control panel	–	
MS Preference Panels	Sun, Nov 22, 1998, 6:48 PM	11/22/98	–	folder	–	
Preferences	Today, 1:08 AM	11/22/98	–	folder	–	
PrintMonitor Documents	Tue, Nov 24, 1998, 11:53 PM	11/22/98	–	folder	–	
Scrapbook File	Tue, Nov 24, 1998, 11:57 PM	8/2/94	72 K	Scrapbook document	–	
Screen Snapz	Today, 1:15 AM	11/22/98	–	folder	–	
Scripting Additions	Thu, Jan 21, 1999, 9:55 PM	11/22/98	–	folder	–	
Scripts	Sun, Nov 22, 1998, 6:34 PM	11/22/98	–	folder	–	
Shutdown Items	Sun, Nov 22, 1998, 7:23 PM	11/22/98	–	folder	–	
Shutdown Items (Disabled)	Tue, Nov 24, 1998, 10:44 PM	11/24/98	–	folder	–	
Start Menu Items	Mon, Dec 7, 1998, 6:47 PM	1/2/98	–	folder	–	
Startup Items	Wed, Nov 25, 1998, 12:19 AM	11/22/98	–	folder	–	
Startup Items (Disabled)	Tue, Nov 24, 1998, 10:44 PM	11/24/98	–	folder	–	
System	Yesterday, 11:15 PM	1/12/99	10.4 MB	suitcase	–	
System Extensions (Disabled)	Tue, Nov 24, 1998, 10:44 PM	11/24/98	–	folder	–	
System Resources	Tue, Jan 12, 1999, 12:00 PM	1/12/99	716 K	file	–	
Text Encodings	Thu, Jan 21, 1999, 9:55 PM	11/22/98	–	folder	–	

Figure 3.28 Viewing the contents of folder with all possible viewing options activated.

Desktop Views

Like most button- or icon-view windows, the Desktop is configurable. It is not viewable as a list, however, and it may be hidden when not in the foreground. Many people like being able to view windows and the Desktop using buttons instead of icons because it only requires a single-click, rather than a double-click, to open an item. Figure 3.29 shows the Desktop viewed as buttons.

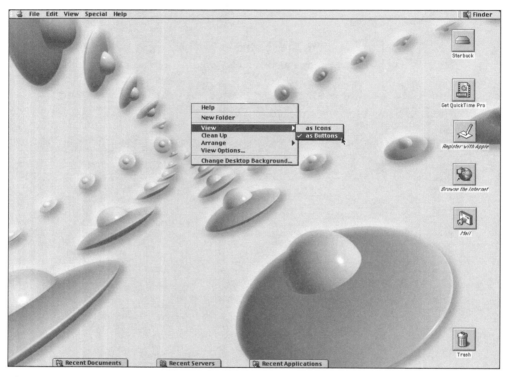

Figure 3.29 The Desktop viewed using buttons (and a fancy Desktop graphic).

In the section entitled "Advanced Finder And Desktop Features," we'll look at how to hide the Desktop—and why you'd want to do such a thing in the first place.

Viewing Hierarchical Lists

List views may not be the most aesthetically appealing way to look at your files and folders, but most people have so much data on their hard drives that viewing them as lists is the most practical way to find things. List views can also be manipulated more easily than icon or button views, which makes this method of viewing even more pragmatic. List views are more versatile because they can be expanded hierarchically or collapsed back into a single list with great ease. This important feature lets you display as a list the contents of any folder without opening a new folder window. In older versions of the operating system, the only way to view and manipulate folder contents was to open the folder, thereby creating a new window.

Expanding And Collapsing Lists

In System 7 and all subsequent versions of the operating system, the contents of any folder can be displayed by clicking on the small triangle that appears to the left of the folder icon. For example, Figure 3.30 shows the folder entitled AppleScript expanded within the Apple Extras folder, which is shown as a list view. The contents of the expanded folder appear indented slightly beneath the preceding folder.

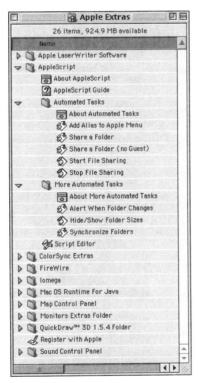

Figure 3.30 A Finder window with hierarchical display.

A hierarchical view allows you to see the contents of several levels of nested folders (folders inside of folders) at one time simply by clicking on the triangle next to the appropriate folder. (Alias folder icons, which are discussed in Chapter 5, appear without a triangle and cannot be displayed hierarchically.) Figure 3.31 shows a window in which the aliased folders are not displayed hierarchically; the folder entitled Apple LaserWriter Software is displayed hierarchically.

Mac OS 8.6

Figure 3.31 A Finder window with an open folder displayed hierarchically.

If you drag hierarchically displayed folders from one list view window to another, they will retain their hierarchical (open) status. You may drag files or folders from a list window to other volumes (copying the files), to other open Finder windows (moving the files), to the Desktop, or to the Trash (deleting the files), just as you would with icons or buttons. Eliminating Desktop clutter is the primary benefit of hierarchical view—there's no need to open a new Finder window for every folder you want to open. In addition, hierarchical views allow you to simultaneously select and manipulate files and folders from different hierarchical levels; this was impossible in previous Finder versions because each time you clicked the mouse in a new window, the selection in the previous window was released.

Figure 3.32 illustrates this capability, showing the selection of three different files, each on a different hierarchical level. The files in this selection can now be copied, moved, deleted, or manipulated as easily as a single file. To select files and folders at multiple levels of the hierarchy at the same time, hold down the Shift key while clicking on the filenames or icons.

To collapse a folder's hierarchical display, click the downward pointing triangle next to the folder icon; the enclosed files and folder listing will disappear. When you close a window, the OS remembers the hierarchical display settings and will restore them the next time the window is opened.

Of course, you can still open a completely new window for any folder rather than display its contents hierarchically. Simply double-click on the folder icon rather than on the triangle, or select the folder icon and then choose the Open command from the File menu.

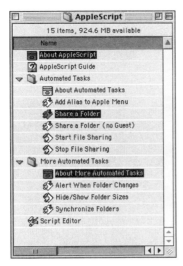

Figure 3.32 The Finder window showing multiple nested folders open with three files selected.

Resizing List Columns

A new feature in Mac OS 8.6 is the ability to resize the width of a column in a list view. Because the Mac OS still limits the length of filenames to 32 characters, a practical limit on the width of a column remains a good idea. The lack of space on your display is just one of many possible reasons to want to shrink a column's width. Figure 3.33 shows an example of a list view after the column widths have been manipulated.

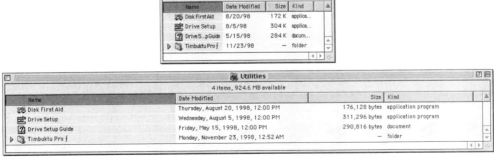

Figure 3.33 Column widths may be expanded or compressed in Mac OS 8.6.

To manipulate a column's width, follow these steps:

1. Open a window to a list view.

2. Place the cursor between two column headings, such as Name and Date Modified, until the cursor changes to one of three shown in Figure 3.34. The type of cursor indicates whether a column may be expanded (left and middle), expanded or contracted (middle), or contracted (middle and right).

Figure 3.34 When resizing a column in a list view, the cursor will indicate whether the column may be expanded, contracted, or both.

The OS limits the maximum and minimum sizes for columns. Watch for the cursor to change as a visual clue as to how far you are allowed to resize a column.

Reordering List Columns

In Mac OS 8.6, you can reorder any visible column except the Name column, which cannot be reordered or removed from view in the List View Options configuration window. This capability is useful for anyone who wants to sort a list without having to scroll horizontally to bring a particular column into view. Now you can just drag that column closer to the Name column on the left side of the window, as in Figure 3.35.

To manipulate a column's position in a list window, follow these steps:

1. Open a window to a list view.
2. Place the cursor in the center of a column heading, such as Date Modified, and drag it horizontally to a column occupied by another heading, then release it. Figure 3.36 shows a column (which is translucent) as it is being repositioned.

Advanced Finder And Desktop Features

Now that we've covered the basics of how windows work and how they can be configured and customized, let's look at a few advanced features for working with windows and the Desktop.

Navigating From The Keyboard

Even though the Mac OS relies primarily on its graphical interface and the mouse, there are many instances when you need keyboard control. A variety of keyboard shortcuts can now be used to select files, move between file windows, and manipu-

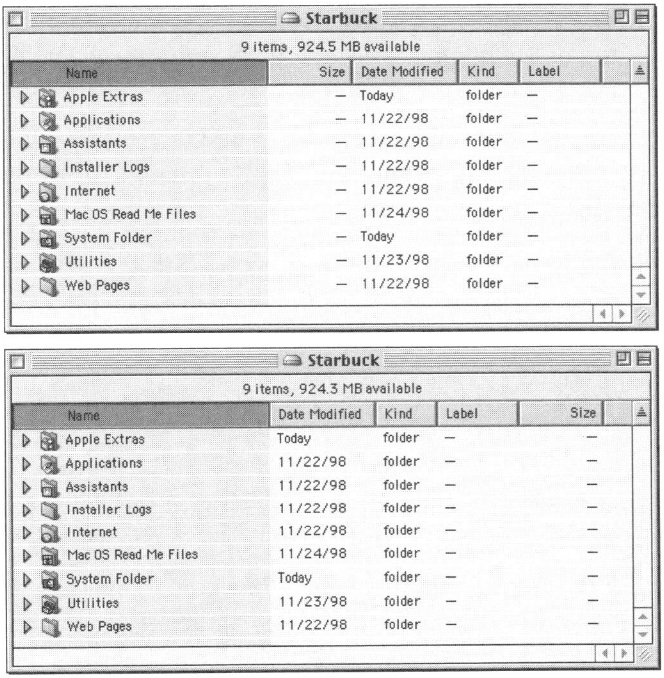

Figure 3.35 Reordering a column's position gives you greater control over how a list is viewed.

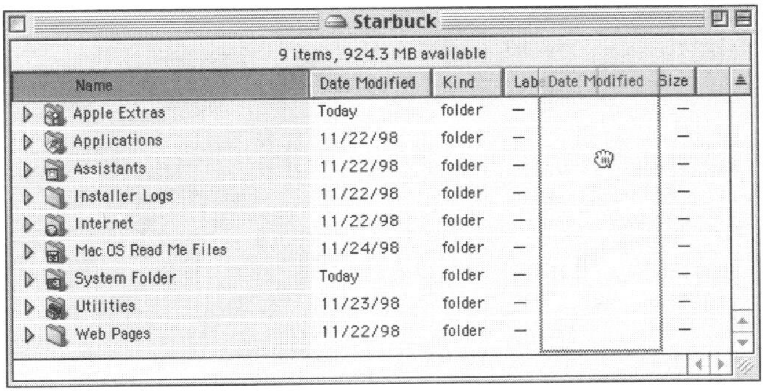

Figure 3.36 Moving a column from one position to another.

late icons. The keyboard commands that follow are available in all Finder windows and on the Desktop; for a complete list of keyboard shortcuts, see Appendix B.

➤ *Jump to filename*—Typing the first few letters in a filename selects that file. For example, if you want to select a file named Budget, when you type *B*, the first filename starting with a *B* is selected. When the *u* is typed after the *B*, the selection will be the first filename starting with *Bu*, and so on. Don't pause between letters, or the Mac will interpret each additional letter as the first letter of a new search. If you don't know an exact filename, type an *A* to cause the display to scroll to the top of the list, an *L* to scroll to the middle, or a *Z* to scroll to the end.

➤ *Select next alphabetical filename*—This is done by pressing the Tab key. All files visible in the current window, including those displayed in hierarchically open folders, are included in this shortcut.

➤ *Select previous alphabetical filename*—Press Shift+Tab. This is useful when you press the Tab key one time too many and need to back up one step in reverse alphabetical order.

➤ *Select next file*—Down, Left, and Right arrow keys select the next file or folder icon in the respective direction.

➤ *Open selected folder*—Command+Down arrow opens the selected file or folder unless the selected file or folder is already open, in which case this key combination brings its window to the front. Command+O will also open your selection.

➤ *Open selected file or folder and close current window*—Press Command+Option+Down arrow. If the selected file or folder is already open, this key combination brings its window to the front and closes the current folder or volume window. Command+Option+O performs the same function.

➤ *Open parent folder window*—Press Command+Up arrow. If the selected file or folder is already open, this key combination brings its window to the front.

➤ *Open parent folder window, close current window*—Pressing Command+Option+Up arrow closes the current window.

➤ *Edit filename*—Press Return. (Filenames can also be opened for editing by clicking the cursor once on the text of the filename.) You can tell the name has been selected for editing when its display is highlighted and a box is drawn around the filename. Once the filename is open for editing, the backspace key deletes characters and the Right and Left arrow keys position the cursor. Pressing Return again saves the filename changes and returns the name to an inverted display. Note that you cannot rename folders or volumes that are currently being shared; you must first turn off File Sharing to edit the filename. Items that are locked or whose names are reserved by the Mac OS, such as Apple Menu Items, Desktop, or Trash, may not be edited.

➤ *Make Desktop active*—Command+Shift+Up arrow makes the current window inactive and the Finder Desktop active.

➤ *Throw item into the Trash*—Pressing Command+Delete will move the selected item to the Trash.

Mac OS 8.6

The following keyboard commands are available only when working in Finder windows viewed as lists (By Name, Size, Kind, Version, Label, or Comment):

➤ *Expand hierarchical display*—Command+Right arrow hierarchically displays the folder contents.

➤ *Expand all hierarchical displays*—Command+Option+Right arrow hierarchically displays the contents of the current folder and all of its enclosed folders.

➤ *Collapse hierarchical display*—Command+Left arrow collapses the hierarchical display of the current folder.

➤ *Collapse all hierarchical displays*—Command+Option+Left arrow collapses the hierarchical display of the current folder and all enclosed folders.

Dragging Files Between Inactive Windows

Mac OS 8.6 allows you to select and move a file from one window to another—even from one inactive window to another. This is a big improvement over Finder versions previous to System 7. Back then, as soon as an icon was selected, the window containing that icon became the active (and, consequently, the foremost) window. This created a problem when that window overlapped and obscured other folder icons. Now, in the OS 8.6 Finder, any visible icon in any window can be selected and dragged to a new location without the source file window becoming active. Figure 3.37 shows this improvement in action.

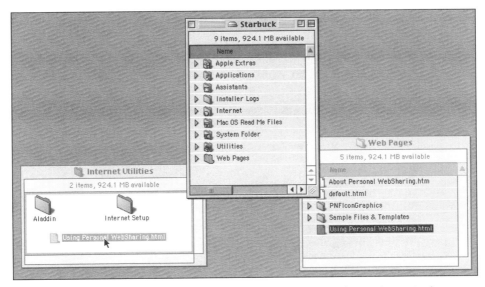

Figure 3.37 Dragging a file between overlapping, and inactive, windows.

This feature is more clearly described by an example. Suppose we want to drag an item from the Web Pages window into a folder called Internet Utilities. This would have been impossible in Finder versions older than System 7 without first repositioning the windows. As soon as the item was selected in the Web Pages window, that window would become active, thereby adding a step to the process.

> **TIP**
> To move a Finder window without making it active, hold down the Command key while dragging the window's title bar.

In Mac OS 8.6's Finder, however, we can simply point the mouse to the item to be moved from the Web Pages window and, while holding the mouse button down, drag the icon over the Starbuck window on its way into the Internet Applications window. As long as the mouse button is not released, only a single mouse movement is required to move the file.

This method cannot be used to move more than one file at a time, however. To move multiple files from one inactive window to another, the window containing the files must be made active.

When you drag items over and into a window, the inside of the window that will contain the item becomes outlined. This feature first appeared in System 7.1 and System 7 Pro and is preserved in Mac OS 8.6.

Working With Multiple Files

Selecting one item in a Finder window or on the Desktop is easy enough, but you'll often want to select more than one item at a time to duplicate, alias, or move to the Trash. To perform any operation on one or more items in a window or on the Desktop, first select the file or group of files. Most aspects of selecting files in Mac OS 8.6 are the same as in previous versions of the Mac OS:

➤ *Immediate marquee selection*—The marquee (selection rectangle), created by clicking the mouse button and dragging with the button pressed, now selects files as soon as any part of the filename or icon is inside the selection rectangle. In previous versions, files were not selected until the mouse button was released, and only files completely contained in the selection rectangle were selected.

➤ *Marquee selection in all views*—Previously, the marquee could be used only in By Icon or By Small Icon views or on the Desktop. In System 7.5, marquee selection is supported in all Finder windows; for example, you can drag-select in the

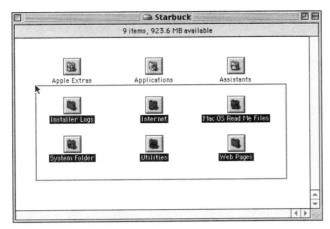

Figure 3.38 Multiple files can be selected using the marquee, even when files are listed as buttons.

By Name or By Date views. In Mac OS 8.6, you can use the marquee selection when windows are viewed as icons, lists, and buttons, as shown in Figure 3.38.

➤ *Shift select*—Use the Shift key while drawing a marquee to select noncontiguous sections of any Finder window.

➤ *File dragging*—It's still possible to drag files by clicking on their names. To open a filename for editing, click on the filename and wait a few seconds for a box to appear around it. To move a button, you must drag it by the title, not the actual button.

➤ *Finder scrolling*—When dragging with a marquee, the Finder window scrolls automatically as soon as the cursor hits one of its edges. For example, Figure 3.39 shows the folder entitled Sound Control Panel scrolling from bottom to top when an item is dragged from the bottom of the window (which you can no longer see) to the top. This is very useful when selecting in Finder windows that display icons.

Figure 3.39 Finder windows scroll automatically when items are dragged past their edges.

Mac OS 8.6

Title Bar Pop-up Menu

Hierarchical window views make it easy to move down the folder hierarchy—and now with the new title bar pop-up menu, you can move up the folder hierarchy just as easily. You'll find a pop-up menu in the title bar of any window when you hold down the Command key and click on the folder's name in the title bar.

Figure 3.40 shows two views of the pop-up menu for the folder named Recent Applications, which is inside the Apple Menu Items folder, which is inside the System Folder on the hard drive named Starbuck. In the top portion of the figure, the Recent Applications folder is a regular window; the bottom portion of the figure shows how pop-up menus work with pop-up windows. Note that you must Command+click on the icon proxy, described next, rather than on the name of the pop-up window.

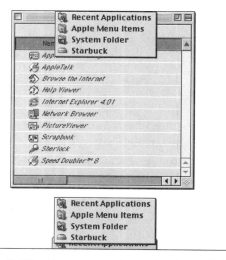

Figure 3.40 You can navigate backward through your hard drive by holding down the Option key while clicking the mouse on the title bar.

Selecting a folder or volume name from this pop-up menu opens a new Finder window that displays the folder or volume contents. If a window for the selected folder or volume is already open, that window is brought forward and made active. This feature is a real time-saver when hunting down folders in the Finder.

Holding down the Option and Command keys while selecting a folder or volume name from the title bar pop-up menu closes the current window as the new folder or volume is opened. This helps you avoid a cluttered Desktop by automating the process of closing windows that aren't being used.

Mac OS 8.6

Icon Proxies

A great new feature in Mac OS 8.6 is the addition of icon proxies. Each window and pop-up window now has a small icon before the name of the window, which serves as a proxy for the folder itself in the Finder. So, you can now move, copy, alias, or delete a folder by manipulating its icon proxy as follows:

1. Click once and hold on the icon proxy until it becomes highlighted.
2. Drag the icon proxy to the Desktop, Trash, or anywhere else.
3. Hold down a modifying key to invoke the command to copy the item (Option+drag), or to make an alias of the item (Option+Command+drag). Figure 3.41 demonstrates how to copy the Applications folder to the Desktop by dragging the icon proxy.

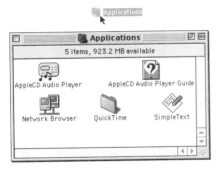

Figure 3.41 Use a window's icon proxy to manipulate folders.

Option Key Options

The Option key performs more functions than just working with title bar navigation. Holding down the Option key also closes windows in several other situations:

▶ *Folders*—While opening a folder by double-clicking on its icon at the Finder, the current folder will close as the new one is opened.

▶ *Windows*—While clicking the zoom box in any Finder window, the active window will be opened to its maximum size.

▶ *Multiple Windows*—Click the close box to close all open windows.

▶ *Applications*—While launching an application, the window in which the application icon appears closes.

Resizing Windows

Windows don't always open up to the size you need, but you can resize them using one of several methods. To resize an open window, you can either drag the size box in the lower right corner of a window, or click in the zoom box in the upper right corner of the window's title bar (to the left of the WindowShade widget). The zoom box expands the window size just enough to display the complete file list or all file and folder icons; it no longer opens the window to the full size of the screen unless you hold down the Option key.

Pop-up windows also have a size box, but it appears in both the left and right corners when the window is in a popped-up position. The WindowShade feature can also be thought of as a means of resizing a window. Figure 3.42 shows an example of all these methods of resizing an active window in the Finder.

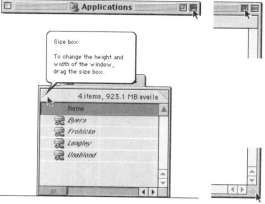

Figure 3.42 Resize your windows using the size box, the WindowShade function, or the zoom button.

Cleaning Up Windows And Icons

As in previous system software versions, the Clean Up command rearranges icons in Finder windows or on the Desktop to make them more orderly and visible. Several new Clean Up options were added in System 7 to help arrange icons in specific situations or to create custom icon arrangements. These commands included Clean Up Desktop, Clean Up All, and Clean Up Window, and they were continued under Mac OS 8. Although they have been removed under Mac OS 8.6, you can still activate the Clean Up command in several ways:

➤ *Clean Up Desktop*—When you're working with icons or buttons on the Desktop (but not in a Finder window), the View|Clean Up command will align icons to the nearest grid position.

➤ *Clean Up Window*—When you're working in a Finder window, the Clean Up command is dimmed when the window is set to view by anything other than icons or buttons. When selected, the Clean Up command arranges all icons in the current window into either aligned or staggered rows, depending on the settings in View|View Options. Figure 3.43 shows the contents of a hard drive before (top) and after (bottom) the Clean Up command was utilized.

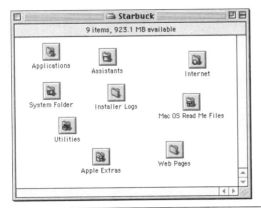

Figure 3.43 A Finder window before and after using the Clean Up command.

➤ *Clean Up Selection*—While a specific file or group of files is selected, holding down the Shift key activates Clean Up Selection, which will reposition only the selected files. Again, this only works with the icon or button views, not a list view.

Context-Sensitive Help

When System 7 was introduced, it included several features that were often touted by Apple as primary benefits of their new system software but that have in fact turned out to be either impractical, poorly implemented, or just plain useless. The new Help menu and Balloon Help, for example, were major disappointments. Although some novice users seemed to actually like Balloon Help, the great majority of Macintosh users actively hated it. Balloons are passive and don't lead you through complex tasks, they argued.

Mac OS 8.6

Apple took so much heat regarding Balloon Help that they rethought the entire issue. In System 7.5, Apple's solution to increasingly difficult software was to create the Apple Guide, an active context-sensitive help system that was the result of several years of work. In Mac OS 8, the help system that used Apple Guide was renamed Mac OS Help (formerly Mac OS Guide); it functioned just as it did under System 7.5. It was accessible under the new Help menu, which replaced the old Apple Guide menu.

With the introduction of context-sensitive (or contextual) help in Mac OS 8, Apple eliminated the necessity of searching for help on a topic. Instead, you could Control+click on an item and choose Help from a pop-up menu. Contextual help was such a big hit that Apple kept not only preserved it in Mac OS 8.6, but went on to tune up the help system again by adding the new Apple Help Viewer. By retaining this feature while touting the advantages of the newest form of help, Apple has also ensured backward compatibility with Mac OS Guide documents. Figure 3.44 shows the three latest versions of the Help menu under the Mac OS.

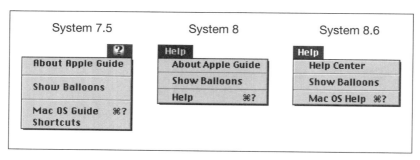

Figure 3.44 The old and new Help menus.

Balloon Help

Balloon Help makes it possible for Macintosh software applications to provide onscreen context-sensitive information. It works by selecting the Show Balloons command under the Help menu, which causes a help balloon to be displayed when the arrow cursor is positioned over any menu command, window element, dialog box option, tool, or icon. This help balloon provides a brief description of that command, element, or icon function, a few examples of which are shown in Figure 3.45.

After the Show Balloons command has been chosen under the Help menu, it changes to the Hide Balloons command, which can be used to turn off the display of help balloons.

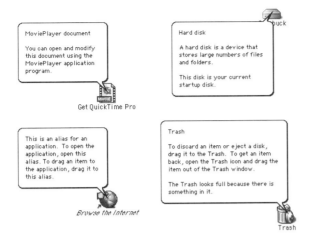

Figure 3.45 A sampling of the Finder's help balloons.

Balloon Help Limitations

In theory, Balloon Help makes it easier to learn new applications and refresh your memory when accessing infrequently used commands or dialog box options. However, these balloons appear only in applications that have been written or upgraded to take advantage of Balloon Help.

In programs that do offer Balloon Help, the information provided may be too limited or generic to be truly helpful. This may be the result of the limited amount of space available for balloon text as well as limited efforts from developers. Always check with the documentation that comes with your software for more information and help.

A bigger problem is the annoying way that help balloons pop up from every element your cursor points to once the Show Balloons command has been chosen. A user who wishes to take advantage of Balloon Help is unlikely to need assistance on every single object, command, and element. Most users would like to read the one or two help balloons relevant to a single, specific problem. Unfortunately, Apple's current "all-or-nothing" implementation of Balloon Help leads to a very distracting display that tends to encourage many users who might occasionally benefit from Balloon Help to stay away from it completely.

Contextual Menus

Mac OS 8 introduced contextual menus, a new way to get help on a specific item. Instead of opening Mac OS Help or the Apple Guide, contextual menus offer help for a particular object such as an application, document, alias, or hard drive when you Control+click on the object. Mac OS 8.6 expands the number of options available in a contextual help menu. Figure 3.46 shows examples of getting contextual help on a variety of objects.

Mac OS 8.6

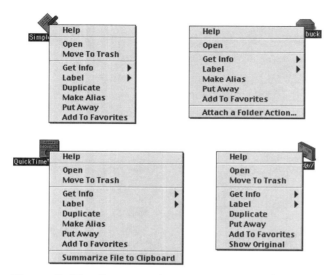

Figure 3.46 Contextual menus are great shortcuts to getting help while working with the Finder and on the Desktop.

Many of your favorite software titles may not yet be programmed to take advantage of this type of help, but look for them to include it in the near future. When they do, you'll be able to click in many locations within an application or one of its documents and get more information on the selected item.

Contextual help is also available from within many programs, but not all. Under System 7, the Apple Guide menu provided access to help that may or may not have been provided as part of the program. In Mac OS 8, however, this menu has been moved to the Help menu, although it provides the same information. Figure 3.47 shows some of the contextual help menu options available for the popular text and HTML editor BBEdit.

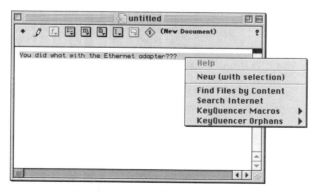

Figure 3.47 Contextual help for a document in BBEdit.

Mac OS 8.6

Trash And Empty Trash

The big news in System 7 was that the garbage collector no longer came without being invited—the Trash was emptied only when the Empty Trash command was chosen from the Special menu. In previous versions of the system software, the Trash was automatically emptied when any application was launched or when the Macintosh Restart or Shut Down commands were selected. In Mac OS 8.6, items remain in the Trash until Empty Trash is selected, even if your computer is shut down or restarted. Figure 3.48 shows the Trash icon when empty (left) and when it contains one or more items (right).

Figure 3.48 The Trash icon changes to let you know whether or not it's empty.

The Empty Trash command is accessed from the Special menu or by Control+clicking on the Trash icon and selecting Empty Trash from the contextual menu. When you execute the Empty Trash command, a dialog box asks you to confirm that you want to delete the current Trash files. Regardless of what files the Trash contains, this dialog box appears and tells you how much disk space will be freed by emptying the Trash, as shown in Figure 3.49.

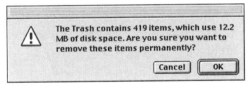

Figure 3.49 The Empty Trash warning dialog box.

TIP
Warning dialog windows are tinted in red to help draw your attention.

Although using the Trash is straightforward, you'll want to know about several less obvious aspects of this process:

➤ *Avoid Trash warnings*—If you hold down the Option key while choosing Empty Trash, the confirmation dialog box will not appear and the Trash will be emptied immediately.

► *Disable Trash warnings*—You can also disable the warning dialog box by selecting the Trash, choosing the Get Info command, and deselecting the Warn Before Emptying option, shown in Figure 3.50. Of course, this will make it easier to delete application and system software files accidentally, so this option should be deselected with caution.

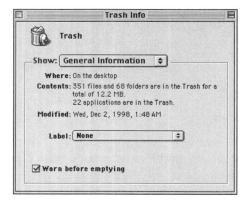

Figure 3.50 The Trash Info dialog box.

► *Retrieving Trashed items*—Any time *before* the Empty Trash command is chosen, items inside the Trash may be recovered and saved from deletion. This is done by double-clicking on the Trash icon and dragging the file icons you want to recover out of the Trash window and back onto the Desktop or onto any volume or folder icon.

► *Freeing disk space*—Only when the Trash has been emptied is disk space released. In previous systems, dragging items to the Trash alone was sufficient to free disk space—although not always immediately.

► *Repositioning the Trash*—You can reposition the Trash on your Desktop and it will stay there, even if you reboot. It's no longer automatically returned to the lower right Desktop corner each time you reboot. This is helpful if you use a large monitor or multiple monitors.

► *Trash for removable media*—Items on removable media such as Zip or Jaz cartridges that are placed in the Trash will not be deleted once the cartridge is ejected, although the Trash icon will appear empty. You must Empty the Trash.

TIP

Don't be in too much of a hurry to empty the Trash. Do it every so often when you need to recover disk space, but be sure to give yourself a chance to retrieve mistakenly trashed items first. Once the Trash is emptied, deleted files can still often be recovered. You will need to use a third-party undelete utility such as Symantec's Norton Utilities or MicroMat's Tech Tool Pro, among others.

The Get Info Dialog Box

As in previous Finder versions, selecting any file, folder, or drive icon and choosing the Get Info command from the File menu or the contextual pop-up menu brings up an Info dialog box (usually called a Get Info dialog box). Basic information and related options are displayed here. The Mac OS 8.6 Get Info dialog box for the text editing program BBEdit, as shown in Figure 3.51, is very different from those in previous Finder versions in that it now has up to three levels of information: General, Memory, and Sharing.

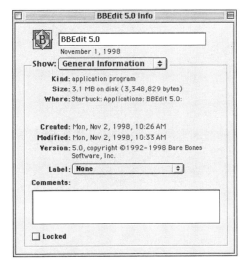

Figure 3.51 The Get Info dialog box for the BBEdit application.

The Get Info dialog box is now available in five different versions—one each for files, folders, applications, volumes, and alias icons. Options may differ among versions, but the basic information is the same for the three levels of information.

General Information

The General Information section of the Get Info dialog box, shown in the above figure, reveals some basic information about the selected item:

➤ *Icon*—A small (32×32-pixel) version of the icon associated with the item appears to the left of the filename, providing a visual reference for the file. You can customize the icon of almost any data file, application, or volume by pasting a new icon on top of the existing icon in the Get Info dialog box. To change an icon, copy any PICT graphic into the Clipboard, select the icon you want to replace in the Get Info dialog box (a box will appear around the icon, indicating its selection), and choose the Paste command from the Edit menu. If the picture is too large to fit into the icon frame, it will automatically be scaled down. Close the Get Info dialog box and the new icon will appear in the Finder window or on the Desktop. Likewise, you can copy and paste any icon between Get Info boxes. For example, you can copy a custom icon from one folder to a folder that uses a standard icon using this cut and paste method.

- *Filename*—This is the filename that appears on the Desktop or in a Finder window. It can now be changed from within the Get Info dialog box.
- *Kind*—Provides a brief description of the selected file. For data files, this usually includes the name of the application that created the file.
- *Size*—The amount of disk space the item and its contents (if it's a folder) consumes on a volume.
- *Where*—The location of the selected file, including all folders enclosing it and the volume it's stored on.
- *Created*—The date and time the file was created. The date is reset when a file is copied from one volume to another, or if a new copy is created by holding down the Option key while moving the file into a new folder.
- *Modified*—The date and time the contents of the file were last changed.
- *Version*—Lists the software application's version number. No information on data files, folders, or volumes is provided.
- *Label*—None, or one of the seven labels you've assigned in the Labels tab of the Edit|Preferences configuration menu.
- *Comments*—Starting in System 7.5, comments about an item could be displayed in Finder windows, and you could use the Find command to locate files by the comment text. A complete discussion of comments is provided in Chapter 5.

Several other options appear in certain Get Info dialog boxes:

- *Locked*—Makes it more difficult to change or delete the selected file. The Locked option appears for data files, applications, and aliases. Locking ensures that unwanted changes are not accidentally made to data files that should not be altered. In most applications, locked data files can be opened, but changes cannot be saved unless you use Save As to create a new file.

    Locked files are protected from accidental deletion because they must be unlocked before they can be emptied from the Trash. If you try to delete a locked file, the dialog box shown in Figure 3.52 appears. It's important to note, however, that locked files will be deleted from the Trash without notice or warning if you hold down the Option key while you choose Empty Trash from the Finder's Special menu.

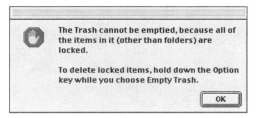

Figure 3.52 The warning that appears when locked items are placed in the Trash.

➤ *Stationery Pad*—Available for data files only, this turns the selected document into a template. (A template is a master document on which new documents are based.) With this option, each time the selected document is opened, a copy of the file is created; any changes or customizations are made to this copy, leaving the original Stationery Pad document available as a master at all times. (A complete discussion of Stationery Pads is provided in Chapter 7.)

Sharing Information

One of the three new portions of the Get Info dialog box is the Sharing section, shown for the BBEdit application in Figure 3.53.

Figure 3.53 The new Sharing section of the revised Get Info dialog box in Mac OS 8.6.

The Sharing section will contain some of the data found in the General Information section, such as icon and name, as well as the following information:

➤ *Program Linking*—Allows an application to be launched from another computer and used by others. This feature will only work, however, if the Program Linking option is enabled in the File Sharing Control Panel, and if all other requirements that enable file sharing have been fulfilled. Even if File Sharing is enabled, each application must have the Program Linking option enabled specifically.

Memory Information

The third portion of the Get Info dialog box that is new in Mac OS 8.6 is the Memory section, shown for the BBEdit application in Figure 3.54. Only applications will have this option.

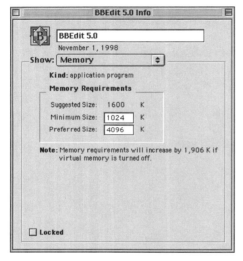

Figure 3.54 The new Memory section of the Get Info dialog box.

This section will also contain some of the data found in the General Information section, as well as the following information:

➤ *Suggested Size*—Suggested Size specifies the application developer's recommendations for the amount of memory that should be allocated to the program when it's opened.

➤ *Minimum Size*—This setting represents the least amount of RAM required to open the application.

➤ *Preferred Size*—Preferred Size indicates the amount of RAM the user wishes to allot the application. (A discussion of these options is presented in Chapter 9.)

➤ *Note*—This section is just a reminder from the Mac OS on how much memory you are saving (or not saving) by using virtual memory.

Get Info For The Trash

The Trash Info dialog box, shown in Figure 3.50, contains two important pieces of information and one useful option. The dialog box lists the number of files and the amount of disk space they consume, which lets you know how much space will be freed by executing the Empty Trash command. It also lists the most recent date on which an item was placed in the Trash.

The Warn Before Emptying option, which is a default, causes a confirmation dialog box to display when the Empty Trash command is selected (shown in Figure 3.49). If you don't want the dialog box to display each time the Empty Trash command is chosen, deselect the Warn Before Emptying option. Just remember—without this warning dialog box, you increase the risk of permanently deleting files you may want later.

Get Info For Aliases

In several ways, the Get Info dialog box for aliases is a little different from the dialog box used by standard files. First, the version information normally displayed beneath the dates is replaced with the path and filename of the original file, as in Figure 3.55.

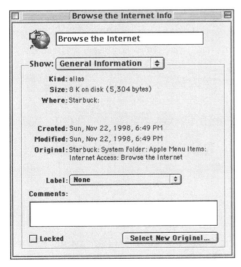

Figure 3.55 The Get Info dialog box for an alias icon.

Also, the Get Info dialog box no longer includes the Find Original button that locates the disk or folder containing the original file from which the alias was made. Mac OS 8 and later versions include what was formerly known as "secret Finder features," which enable the Finder to reveal the source of the original file that the alias was created from. Although this feature had been present in the Finder for some time, it was not made an active feature until Mac OS 8. To find the parent item of an alias, press Command+R (for *reveal*), or choose File|Show Original. This command opens the disk or folder window and selects the original file icon. If the disk or volume containing the original file is not available, a dialog box will ask you to insert the disk containing the original file, or to fix the "broken" alias. If the original is located on a network volume, the volume will be mounted once you have entered your username and password. The contextual pop-up command (Control+click) for this feature is named Show Original.

> **TIP**
> The Comments and Locked options are available for aliases, and they behave exactly as they do for any other files. The Stationery Pad option, however, is not available for alias icons.

To locate a new parent for an alias, you may click on the Select New Original button to invoke the Fix Alias option. We'll look at this option in detail in Chapter 5.

Wrapping Up

The Finder is the most visible part of the Mac OS; as we've seen in this chapter, it gives you powerful and intuitive tools to manage the disks and files you're using with your computer, including:

- The new Finder menus
- The many ways you can see and manipulate data in Finder windows
- The new Help menu
- The Trash and Empty Trash commands
- The new Get Info dialog box

Next, in Chapter 4, we'll look at the various elements in Mac OS 8.6 that you can use to customize your computer to give it a more personal look and feel, as well as a few third-party utilities that are very inexpensive and can add a lot of cool features to the Mac OS.

Customizing Your Mac

Without a doubt, the fierce loyalty among Mac users is primarily due to the Mac OS's capacity for customization. Mac OS 8.6 makes it easier than ever to change the way you interact with your software. With so many ways to personalize your Mac, you'll never feel like you're locked in to using the same computer day after day.

In this chapter, we'll look at some elements of the Mac OS that are easily customized, as well as a few popular utilities that significantly enhance your ability to use the OS.

Mac OS Customization Features

Numerous features, Control Panels, and Extensions in Mac OS 8.6 allow you to customize the way your Mac looks and functions. You'll probably do a lot of experimenting with the options that affect the way your computer looks. Why not treat yourself to a different interface every day?

Setting Appearance Preferences

The Appearance Control Panel takes the place of several Control Panels, including Color and WindowShade panels, in previous versions of the Mac OS, plus adds a host of new features. Shown in Figure 4.1, the Appearance Control Panel has six configuration tabs.

To change the appearance of windows, the Desktop, fonts, and to customize sounds, open the Appearance control panel and select from the following options:

➤ *Default and custom themes*—The Themes tab contains a collection of options for overall appearance, font, Desktop pattern or picture, and sound that can be saved and reloaded. To select a theme, scroll through the list of available themes and click on the theme you want to activate. To save your own theme, choose from the available appearances, fonts, Desktop patterns and pictures, and sounds. Then come back to the Themes tab, choose the Save Theme button, and assign a name to your theme.

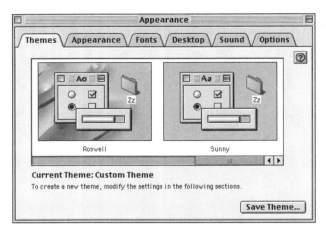

Figure 4.1 The new Appearance Control Panel consolidates most of the features that affect the look and feel of the Mac OS.

➤ *Appearance settings*—The Appearance tab allows you to choose an appearance that comes with the Mac OS, which forms the basis upon which a theme is created. Currently, only the Apple Platinum appearance is available, but more will become available shortly. Figure 4.2 shows an example of the Apple Platinum appearance.

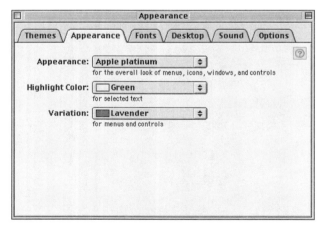

Figure 4.2 Choose an Appearance as the basis of a theme.

➤ *Font options*—In the Fonts tab, choose options (large or small fonts) for system menus, and for viewing window lists and icon titles. Also, Mac OS 8.6 utilizes a font smoothing option that allows fonts over 12 points in size to be anti-aliased for a smooth appearance onscreen (see Figure 4.3).

Customizing Your Mac   115

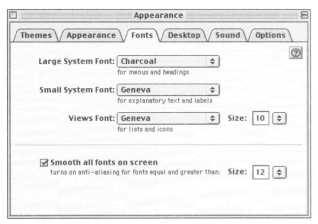

Figure 4.3   The Fonts configuration tab of the Appearance Control Panel.

➤ *Desktop patterns and pictures*—In the Desktop tab, choose a Desktop pattern or picture to replace the default Mac OS pattern. To create your own pattern, drag an image or image clipping to the Desktop preview area, then choose Edit+Pattern Name to assign a name to the pattern. To place a picture on the Desktop, repeat this step, or select the Place Picture button and locate a picture. Figure 4.4 is an example of a picture chosen from the Desktop Pictures folder, which is found in the Appearance folder within the System Folder.

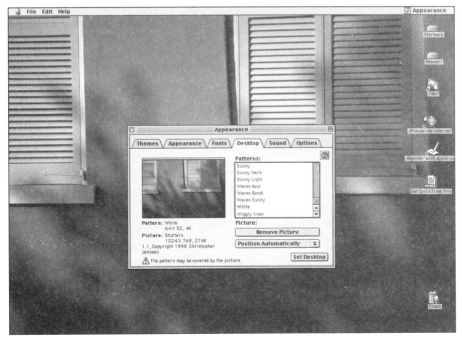

Figure 4.4   The Desktop configuration tab of the Appearance Control Panel.

Mac OS 8.6

To place a different picture on the Desktop every time your Mac is restarted, drag and drop a folder of images in the JPEG format onto the Desktop preview area.

➤ *Sound sets*—Choose a *sound track* from the Sounds tab, a collection of optional sound effects that play in conjunction with changes to the user environment, including:

➤ Opening and selecting menu items

➤ Dragging and resizing windows

➤ Clicking buttons, checkboxes, or scrollbars

➤ Finder actions such as clicking, dragging, and dropping

Mac OS 8.6 includes a sound track for the Apple Platinum appearance, but there are hundreds of "home-made" sets that you may download for free, such as John Rowe's "Evangelist Hardaway" sound set, shown in Figure 4.5.

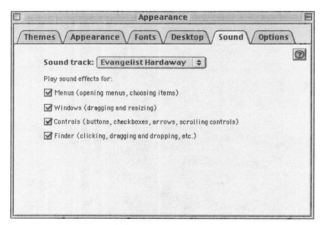

Figure 4.5 The Sound configuration tab of the Appearance Control Panel.

➤ *Other options*—The Options tab, shown in Figure 4.6, provides miscellaneous options that control scrolling and collapsible windows (the old WindowShade feature).

The Smart Scrolling feature has been around for some time, thanks to several third-party utilities, but this marks the first time it has been a part of the Mac OS. The Smart Scrolling feature places vertical and horizontal scroll arrows in both the bottom and right corners of a window, and uses *proportional thumbs* to indicate how much of a window's vertical and horizontal areas are visible. For example, Figure 4.7 shows two views of the same window with Smart Scrolling off (top) and Smart Scrolling on (bottom). A large proportional thumb indicates that more of a window's contents is visible than not.

Mac OS 8.6

Customizing Your Mac   117

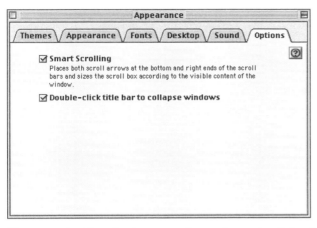

Figure 4.6   The Options configuration tab of the Appearance Control Panel.

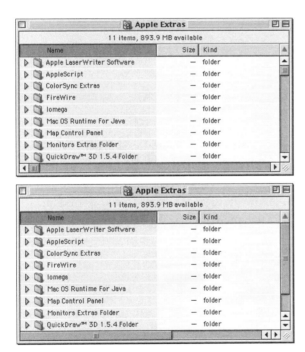

Figure 4.7   The Smart Scrolling option provides more scrolling options and visual clues as to the size of a window.

TIP
Visit Bryan Boyer and Emory Lundberg's "Mac OS 8.6 Themes" Web site at www.themes.hellyeah.com to download the latest themes and sound sets, as well as Chris Gervais's Soundset Constructor application, which you can use to make your own sound sets!

Mac OS 8.6

Apple Menu Options

The Apple Menu Options Control Panel provides a couple of cool time-savers. First, it makes the Apple Menu hierarchical, allowing you to select an item, such as a document or application, that is nested several layers deep with the single click of the mouse. This popular feature of the Mac OS has been mimicked in many other operating systems. The Apple Menu Items Control Panel is shown in Figure 4.8.

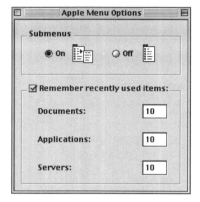

Figure 4.8 The Apple Menu Options Control Panel gives you two ways to customize your Mac.

You can set the number of remembered documents, applications, and servers up to 99, but a high number has a few drawbacks—a slower response to the hierarchical menu feature as well as more system RAM required by the OS to store information about these items. If your system is low on memory or is slow in general, try not using this feature to see if your performance improves.

Configuring The Applications Switcher

The Application Switcher is a relatively new feature to the Mac OS. It allows you to switch between applications using a keyboard shortcut (Command+Tab) and provides the ability to "tear off" the Application menu and place it on the Desktop in one of several orientations. Tearing off the Application menu is an easy task, as shown in Figure 4.9.

To tear off the Application menu:

1. Activate the Application menu.

2. Hold down the mouse and drag the cursor down through the list of active applications.

3. The menu will turn into a dragable silhouette that you can drop anywhere on the Desktop.

Mac OS 8.6

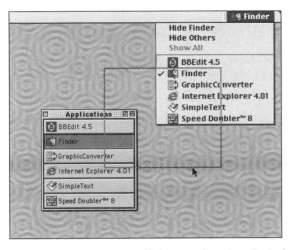

Figure 4.9 Tearing off the Application Switcher.

Once it has been torn off and is in the default position, you can change the configuration of the Application Switcher using one of several configuration methods. First, you may manipulate the Application Switcher by clicking the Zoombox as follows, after tearing off the menu:

➤ View by small icon and name—(This is the default).

➤ View by small icon—Click the Zoombox.

➤ View by large icon and name—Option+click the Zoombox.

➤ View by large icon—Click the Zoombox, then Option+click the Zoombox.

➤ View horizontally by small icon and name—Shift+Option+click the Zoombox.

➤ View horizontally by small icon—Shift+Option+click the Zoombox, then click the Zoombox.

➤ View horizontally by large icon and name—Shift+Option+click the Zoombox, then Option+click the Zoombox.

➤ View horizontally by large icon—Shift+Option+click the Zoombox, click the Zoombox, then Option+click the Zoombox.

This may be a bit confusing, but just remember that you can view the Application Switcher by name and icon, large or small, and vertically or horizontally. You can also hold down the Option key and resize the width (but not height) of the menu of applications. Figure 4.10 shows all the viewing options listed above.

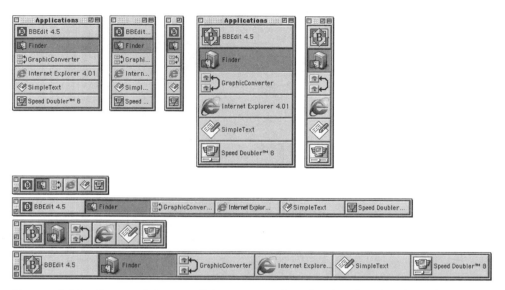

Figure 4.10 Some of the possible ways to view the Application Switcher.

You may also write an AppleScript to perform these configuration tasks. Most people who use the Mac OS rely on AppleScript, an object-oriented programming language, every day without even knowing it. We'll explore AppleScript in Chapter 13.

You may also use AppleScript to hide the title bar, display items in the order they were launched rather than alphabetically, or position the Application menu in a specific location on the screen, such as the lower-left. You can also Command+drag the Application Switcher anywhere on the screen when the title bar portion of the Application Switcher is not visible to use to drag it to another location.

Finally, you can use one of many third-party utilities that perform the same tasks but provide a nice graphical unit interface (GUI) in place of cryptic keystrokes or obtuse scripting commands. One example of such a utility is AppSwitcher Control by Pascal Balthrop (www.pascal.com/software), shown in Figure 4.11. AppSwitcher Control puts a very usable interface on the Application Switcher.

General Controls

Another way to customize your Mac is to hide the Desktop when it is not active by using the General Controls Control Panel. This option is especially helpful if you tend to have multiple applications active at the same time and lots of clutter on the Desktop, creating an unruly scene, as in Figure 4.12.

Notice how hard it is to see what's going on with the applications because of all the windows and Desktop action going on? To clear things up, open General Controls

Customizing Your Mac   121

Figure 4.11   AppSwitcher Control is a great way to configure the Application Switcher.

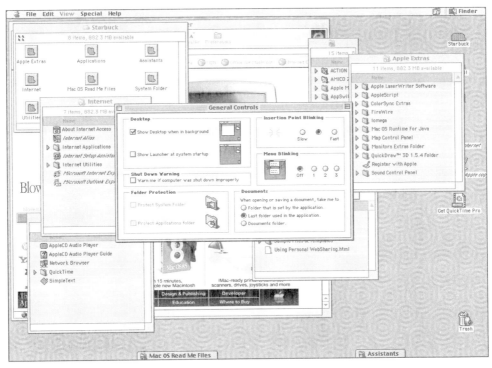

Figure 4.12   You can use General Controls to clean up your Desktop.

and *deselect* the Show Desktop When in Background option. This action will cause the Desktop to be invisible until reselected, as in Figure 4.13, which shows the exact same information as in Figure 4.12 above except that the Desktop is hidden.

Mac OS 8.6

Figure 4.13 Hiding the Desktop can help unclutter your screen.

Several other elements of the Mac OS user interface are configurable through the General Controls, which are as follows:

➤ *Show Launcher at system startup*—Opens the Launcher (described later in this chapter) when the computer is started up without placing an alias to the Launcher in the Startup Items folder.

➤ *Warn me if computer was shut down improperly*—When checked, the OS will warn you with a dialog window and verify the integrity of the startup disk when the computer is restarted following a crash.

➤ *Protect System Folder*—When checked, the Mac OS will lock down critical areas of the System Folder to prevent unwanted items from being installed into the folder, and to prevent critical items from being deleted. This option is only available when File Sharing is turned off.

➤ *Protect Applications folder*—Similar to the Protect System Folder option, but for the Applications folder instead.

➤ *Insertion Point blinking*—Choose to have the insertion point (where you may enter text in a window or document) blink at a slow, medium, or fast rate.

Customizing Your Mac

▶ *Menu Blinking*—Controls whether or not an item in the Apple Menu blinks when selected, and if so, how many times it should blink before opening the selected item. This is a cosmetic feature and should be turned off to enable the fastest response time when you select an item in the Apple Menu.

▶ *When opening or saving a document, take me to*—Select the location where the OS will open automatically. If you select Documents folder, a folder will be created at the root level of the startup disk called *Documents*.

Displaying The Date & Time

Your Mac has a clock built into the OS that is powered by a small battery on the logic board (for times when it is unplugged or if the power is disconnected). Configuring the computer's date, time, and time zone settings is important because documents may be tracked according to the date and time they were created or last modified. Therefore, a file with an incorrect date and time stamp may very well elude you in a search for a file created on an particular date. The Mac OS can display the time and date in the menu bar as well, once the following configuration options have been reviewed:

1. Open the Date & Time Control Panel (see Figure 4.14).

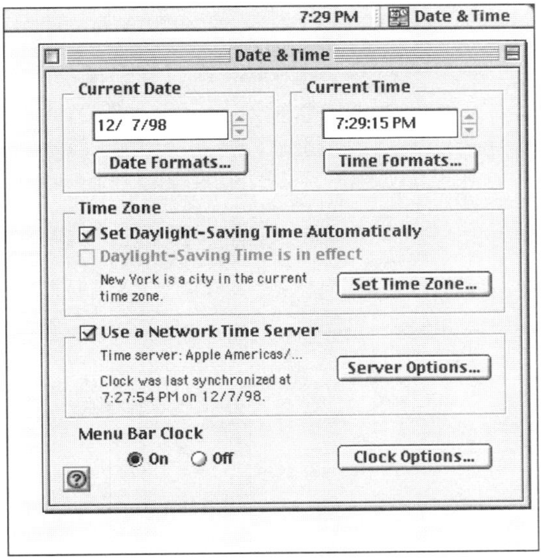

Figure 4.14 The Date & Time Control Panel in Mac OS 8.6.

2. Enter the current date and time.

3. Mark the appropriate Daylight-Saving Time option and select a time zone.

Mac OS 8.6

4. To use a network time server to automatically set the time on your computer, select the checkbox and click the Server Options button (see Figure 4.15).

Figure 4.15 The time server option allows the computer's time to be set automatically by any time server on the Internet.

5. Select a time server from the list, such as Apple's time server (www.time.apple.com), or choose Edit list from the menu and enter another selection.

6. You may choose to display the time and date in the menu bar, as well as several clock display options, by selecting the Clock Options button and making any appropriate configuration options.

Setting Monitors & Sound Preferences

You can go beyond customizing how your Mac looks by individualizing how it displays information on your monitor and how it sounds. This capacity is another of the many features that make the Mac OS so popular with users. The Monitors & Sound Control Panel is where you go to customize several important features of the Mac OS, and depending on what type of monitor you have, your options may look slightly different from the examples that follow. In general, however, you should have at least four main sections—Monitor, Sound, Alerts, and Color.

Monitor

You can customize how your computer displays the information it receives from the Mac OS in the Monitor section of the Monitors & Sounds Control Panel, two different examples of which are shown in Figure 4.16. Apple-manufactured monitors such as the AV, AppleVision, and ColorSync models will typically have more options to choose from, especially if the monitor has built-in speakers.

The color depth, or the number of colors your monitor can display, will depend on the amount of video RAM (also called VRAM) and the type of display. Most monitors that ship with new computers are capable of displaying millions of colors, but if you don't have enough VRAM, you might only be able to display thousands,

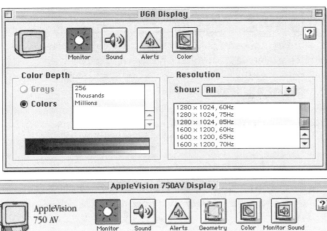

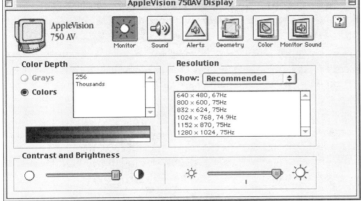

Figure 4.16 Choose the Monitors & Sound Control Panel to customize sound and display features.

or 256, colors. And that's sometimes OK because many games require only 256 colors, but a good rule of thumb is to set your monitor to display thousands or millions of colors if it is capable of doing so, but not 256 unless you must (refer back to Figure 4.16). If you have a PowerBook, which we'll talk about more in Chapter 6, you can reduce the number of colors in order to save battery consumption.

The amount of VRAM also affects the ability of multi-resolution monitors to display multiple resolutions. For example, if your Mac has a monitor that is capable of displaying a maximum resolution of 1024×768 pixels, you will need 2MB of VRAM. If you only have 1MB of VRAM, however, the higher resolution setting will not be available in the Monitors & Sound Control Panel. A variation on this theme goes like this: If you are able to select a higher resolution, the number of colors available to be displayed will decrease. So, to set your monitor's colors and resolution, you'll need to strike a balance between the abilities of your system and the task you're performing.

Mac OS 8.6

What's A Good Monitor?

A good CRT (cathode ray tube) monitor is one that is 17 inches or larger and is capable of displaying at multiple resolutions with a good refresh rate and acceptable dot-pitch. An LCD (liquid crystal display) monitor should be 15 inches or larger, but usually doesn't have as fine a dot-pitch as does a CRT-based monitor. But what does all this mean and why should you care?

➤ The size of a monitor is measured diagonally from the top-left of the viewable area to the lower-right, and not from the outside of the monitor's plastic casing. Early Apple monitors were as small as 8 inches on the diagonal, but the emerging standard these days is 19 inches. A 17-inch monitor is the current standard.

➤ Resolution refers to the width and height of your display, measured in pixels. For example, 1024x768 pixels is a standard resolution for contemporary monitors, whereas first-generation monitors usually displayed at a fixed resolution of 640x480. A good monitor will display multiple resolutions of 1600x1200 and higher.

➤ The refresh rate refers to the frequency at which the image displayed on your screen is refreshed or redrawn per second, which is measured in Hertz (abbreviated as Hz). So, a 75Hz refresh rate means the image is refreshed 75 times per second. The human eye can't detect refresh rates higher than 75Hz or so, but if the rate is any lower the image will appear to flicker. Make sure your monitor can display at your desired resolution with a refresh rate of 75Hz or faster.

➤ Dot pitch refers to the size of the tiny elements in a monitor that pass light to the eye, measured in millimeters. Several different technologies, such as shadow-mask and invar mask, are used to create these elements, but just remember that smaller is better. Look for a monitor with a dot pitch of .26 or smaller. The typical range will be from .30 (unacceptable) to .22 (excellent).

Sound

The Sound portion of Monitors & Sound allows you to customize how your Mac plays and records sound. As you can see in Figure 4.17, you can select many different options, including:

➤ *Computer System Volume*—Sets the volume of sound that is produced by the Mac's internal speaker.

➤ *Sound Output*—Identifies the hardware source to which audio signals are sent. All Macs have internal speakers, so the default is built-in unless you've added hardware to perform this function.

➤ *Sound Output Quality*—Sets the rate of output to the selected sound output device.

➤ *Computer System Balance*—Adjusts the balance between right and left speakers, if attached. If not, this option is not functional.

➤ *Sound Monitoring Source*—Identifies either the internal CD player or the microphone (internal or external) as the source for incoming sound.

Customizing Your Mac   **127**

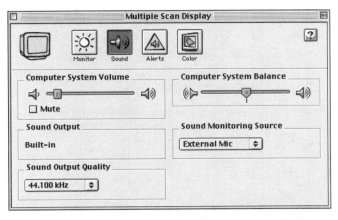

Figure 4.17   Explore the Sound settings available to your Mac.

As with displays, you should customize your sound settings as necessary, and don't be afraid to tinker and explore your computer's options. It's a Mac, after all!

Alerts

The Alerts section, shown in Figure 4.18, is probably the single most familiar, customizable element of your Mac's interface (except perhaps the ability to change Desktop patterns). Longtime Mac users will remember this feature as what made us say to our friends, "Hey, come look at this. My Mac thinks it's a duck!" Now, of course, you can purchase sample sounds or download them from the Web, so instead of just quacking at you, your computer might have Bart Simpson talk back to you or Captain Picard beam you aboard. To record your own alert sounds, all you need is a PlainTalk microphone or another source for sound input, such as a CD-ROM or DVD. Be sure to record sounds that result in small file sizes because large sound files take much longer to replay and thereby slow down the system every time the alert is triggered.

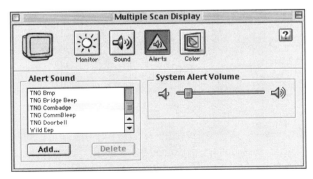

Figure 4.18   Choose a custom alert message to make getting your attention a bit more interesting.

Mac OS 8.6

Color

The Color section may be new to many users, and we'll cover it in more detail in Chapter 15 when we talk more about the multimedia capabilities of the Mac OS. Shown in Figure 4.19, the Color section is where you go to customize how the Mac OS configures its ColorSync capabilities; this affects how colors are displayed on your screen, as well as how they are transmitted to color printers. In short, ColorSync and the Color section of the Monitors & Sounds Control Panel assist in the color management capabilities of your computer.

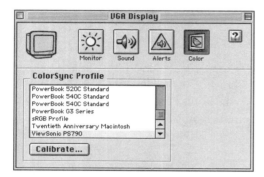

Figure 4.19 The Color section helps you calibrate your monitor to work with ColorSync and the Mac OS's color management capabilities.

Customizing Energy Saver Preferences

You can customize your Mac with the Energy Saver Control Panel. Although you may not think of this Control Panel as a customization feature, it has two elements that can actually be quite useful. First, the Sleep Setup portion of the Energy Saver Control Panel, accessible through the Sleep Setup button shown in Figure 4.20, lets you tell the Mac OS when the computer should revert to a power-saving mode, or tell it to shut itself down after a specified period of inactivity. You can stipulate that the entire computer be shut down or that the display and/or hard drive go into sleep mode.

Finally, you can customize your Mac to automatically start up or shut down at designated times in the Scheduled Startup & Shutdown portion of the Energy Saver Control Panel, shown in Figure 4.21.

You can use this feature to have your computer automatically shut down if you've left it on unintentionally. You can also have it start up automatically to perform a task in conjunction with an item in your Startup Items folder, such as checking your e-mail every morning of the work week.

Mac OS 8.6

Customizing Your Mac 129

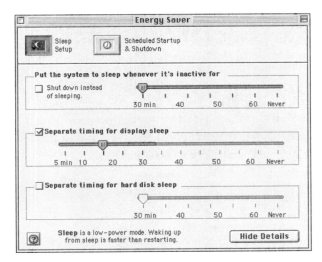

Figure 4.20 Use the Energy Saver Control Panel to configure your Mac to sleep or shut down.

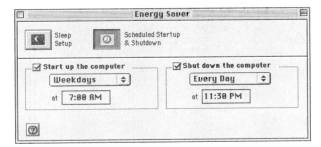

Figure 4.21 Schedule your Mac to start up or shut down automatically using the Energy Saver Control Panel.

You can control the exact hour and minute of an operation, as well as configure it for the following days:

➤ Weekdays

➤ Weekends

➤ Every day

➤ Monday

➤ Tuesday

➤ Wednesday

➤ Thursday

➤ Friday

Mac OS 8.6

These are the major customization features that are part of Mac OS 8.6, but thousands more are available to help with just about every task you can imagine—and then some.

Third-Party Utilities

So many freeware and shareware utilities are available for the Mac OS that it's hard to keep track of them. Fortunately, several enterprising individuals and companies have created Web sites to track these software titles and make them available for downloading. The best places to find software include:

➤ *Yahoo*—www.yahoo.com/Computers_and_Internet/Software/Operating_Systems/Macintosh_OS/

➤ *The MIT HyperArchive*—hyperarchive.lcs.mit.edu/HyperArchive.html

➤ *Shareware.com*—www.shareware/com/SW/Selections/Index/

➤ *Download.com*—www.download.com

➤ *ZDNet's Macdownload.com*—www.macdownload.com

➤ *Apple Software Updates*—http://til.info.apple.com/swupdates.nsf/search

Here are a few programs to help customize your Mac that are very useful, very cool, and very cheap.

Kaleidoscope

By Greg Landweber and Arlo Rose
www.kaleidoscope.net
Shareware

If you haven't already seen Kaleidoscope, you're in for a big surprise. Kaleidoscope can give the Mac OS any number of appearances in much the same way as the Appearance Control Panel. Kaleidoscope consists of a Control Panel (shown in Figure 4.22), an Extension, and a collection of Kaleidoscope themes that contain the resources for changing the appearance of the Mac OS.

To change the appearance of your Mac, just select one of the six or so themes that comes with Kaleidoscope, or any that you may have downloaded from the Web. The theme goes into effect immediately, although some icons may not appear correctly until you have restarted your computer. In addition to selecting a theme, you can select from these options:

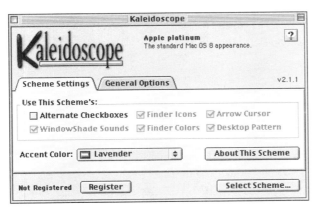

Figure 4.22 Open Kaleidoscope to change your Mac's appearance.

▶ *Scheme Settings*—The Scheme Settings tab offers options that are incorporated into a particular Kaleidoscope scheme. Some of these options may not be available for all schemes.

▶ *General Options*—The General Options tab provides access to features that should be available for all schemes.

Kaleidoscope can really enhance the overall aesthetics of your Mac, and the great thing about it is that people are creating new themes every week. Figure 4.23 shows six of the eight themes that come with Kaleidoscope: Apple Platinum, System 7, Antique, BeBox, Onyx, and Scherzo!.

Of course, you can always switch back to the traditional Mac OS theme by choosing the Apple Platinum theme, but you'll no doubt find one that you'll like better. For a list of links to vast collections of Kaleidoscope themes on the Web, visit the Kaleidoscope home page and link to the themes archive.

ACTION Utilities

ACTION Now Utilities
www.actionutilities.com
Commercial

ACTION Utilities provides many additional features to the Open and Save dialog boxes commonly used by the Mac OS and most applications. Mac OS 8.6 incorporates new improvements, called Navigation Services, to these kinds of dialog windows. ACTION Utilities, however, goes far beyond these improvements to provide a Finder-like interface that, like Navigation Services, is characterized by a non-modal window. This means that with ACTION Utilities

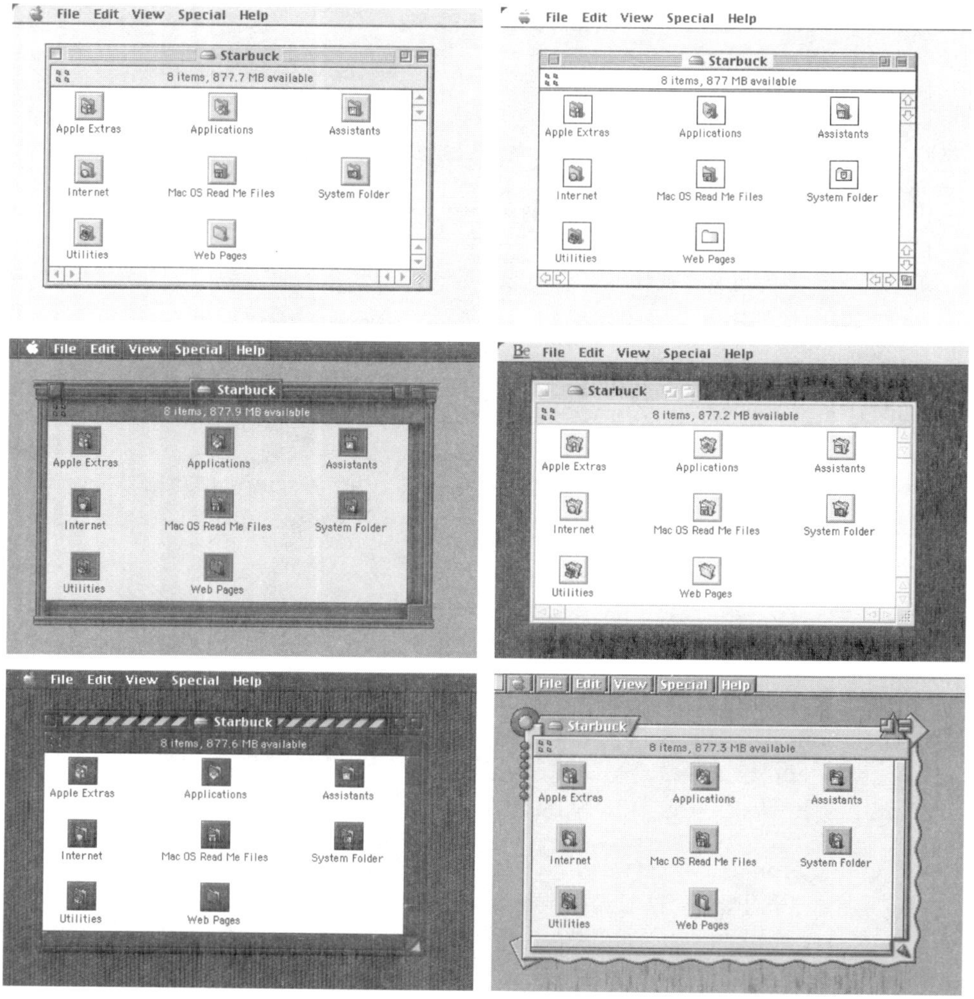

Figure 4.23 Customize your Mac with one of these very distinctive Kaleidoscope themes.

installed, you can return to the Desktop or another application while an Open or Save dialog box is active.

For example, take a look at Figure 4.24, which shows three versions of a standard Open dialog window with a traditional Open dialog box (top), an Open dialog window with a Navigational Services-aware application (middle), and a window using ACTION Utilities (bottom).

ACTION Utilities provides almost all the features available while in the Finder, such as the ability to search for a document, move an item to the Trash, and sort

Mac OS 8.6

Customizing Your Mac 133

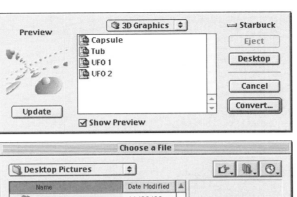

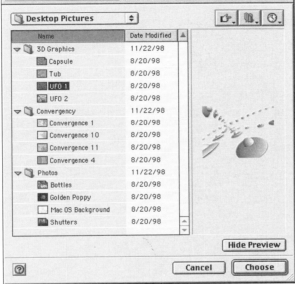

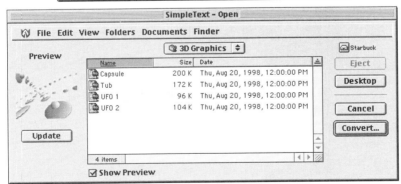

Figure 4.24 ACTION Utilities provides many improvements over traditional and Navigational Services-aware Open dialog windows.

the contents of the Open window by name, size, kind, label, and date. But with a dialog window open using ACTION Utilities, you can also:

➤ Create a new folder

Mac OS 8.6

➤ Get Info

➤ Change the label

➤ Rename an item

➤ Make an alias

➤ Empty the Trash

➤ Add the current folder to a list of favorite or recently used folders

➤ Move to a folder that is already open in the Finder

➤ Use one of several custom keyboard shortcuts to easily navigate among drives, folders, favorites, and recently used folders

ACTION Utilities consists of an Extension and a Control Panel where its many preferences are configured (see Figure 4.25). Even though you'll need to consider several dozen features when configuring ACTION Utilities, you'll no doubt find this is a must-have utility.

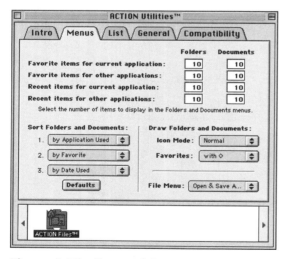

Figure 4.25 Some of the many ACTION Utilities Control Panel options.

GoMac

ACTION Now Utilities
www.actionutilities.com
Commercial

GoMac adds a program bar at the bottom of the screen to provide easy access to your open applications, as well as a hierarchical menu like the Apple Menu. It also provides a calendar, access to your favorite Control Strip modules, and a more user-friendly interface when switching between applications using Alt+Tab. Figure 4.26 shows what GoMac looks like under Mac OS 8.6, including the Task Bar, the Start Menu Items folder, and the GoMac Control Panel.

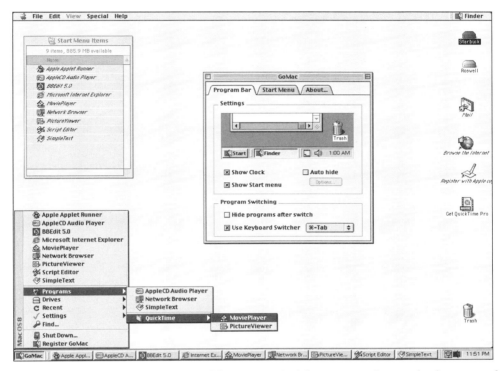

Figure 4.26 Install GoMac to add a customizable program bar at the bottom of your screen.

In addition to the program bar, GoMac adds several configurable options that make the process of accessing applications and data more flexible. GoMac uses a highly customizable menu in the lower-left corner of your screen to store aliases to your most recently accessed applications, documents, and servers, and to your hard drive(s).

GoMac works like an upside-down Apple menu, but with many more options. For example, Figure 4.27 shows the second of two main configuration tabs in the GoMac Control Panel, where you'll choose most of your configuration options.

In addition to providing easy access to files and folders, GoMac can hide itself until you drag your mouse over it, thereby taking up less space on your Desktop. You can also display a clock and pop-up calendar in the program bar by selecting the Show Clock check box. On the Start Menu tab, you can configure GoMac to store aliases

Figure 4.27 Customize GoMac's program bar to optimize access to your computer.

of your favorite applications, documents, and folders. The Start menu contains much of the same information found in the Apple menu, including recently accessed applications, documents, and servers; it also allows you to access your hard drive(s) and the find-file utility of your choice. Once you've configured it to your liking, the Start Menu tab can be a real time-saver.

AMICO

By Dennis Chronopoulos
www.shareware.com
Shareware

AMICO, which stands for Apple Menu Items Custom Order, is a great utility that lets you create customized groups within the Apple menu. The Apple menu normally displays the contents of the Apple Menu Items folder (located in the System folder) in alphanumeric order. You can do a small amount of customization by inserting a blank space (to force an item to go to the top of the Apple Menu when you click on the Apple icon) or a bullet (Option+8) (to make it last in the list).

AMICO is an Extension that tells the Mac OS to look for certain characters in the Apple Menu Items folder and to change how items in that folder are displayed when the Apple Menu is activated. For example, you can reorganize the items under the Apple Menu so that they are no longer listed alphanumerically, insert dividers between groups of items, and change the format of dividers in the Apple Menu. Figure 4.28 shows an Apple Menu and an Apple Menu Items folder that have been customized to display groups of folders in distinctive sections of the Apple Menu.

Customizing Your Mac   137

Figure 4.28 AMICO allows you to customize the Apple menu in several very useful ways.

AMICO looks at how the Apple Menu Items folder is displayed in the Finder and then applies the appropriate changes to the Apple Menu.

The Apple Menu that comes with a new installation of the Mac OS is a bit cluttered, and AMICO is just one way of customizing it to your liking.

BeHierarchic

By Fabian Octave
www.octave.net/BeHierarchic/
Shareware

BeHierarchic is a venerable utility that allows you to customize the Apple Menu in several ways. The BeHierarchic Control Panel, shown in Figure 4.29, allows you to select from more than 30 options that affect the way the Apple Menu sorts the contents of the Apple Menu Items folder, what font is used to list its contents, and what style of icon is used. Figure 4.29 shows just one of many ways you can transform your Apple Menu into a more useful part of the Mac OS.

Wrapping Up

Using the Mac OS for the first time is kind of like driving someone else's car—when you get behind the wheel, the first thing you do is adjust the mirrors and seat so that you're comfortable. The Mac OS is an outstanding operating system in this respect because of the many opportunities it offers for customizing the interface.

Mac OS 8.6

Figure 4.29 BeHierarchic allows you to organize and display the Apple Menu to better suit your needs.

Apple builds much of this capacity right into the interface, but even greater customization is possible through the thousands of third-party utilities, most of which are available on the Internet.

In the next chapter, we'll look at the commands and options that are available through the Mac OS to help you manage your hard drive.

5

Managing Your Data

As we've seen in Chapter 3, the Finder provides a comprehensive set of commands and features that help you manage disks and files. The Finder does not, however, require that you organize your data in any particular way; it's still up to you to decide the best way to arrange your files, folders, and applications. File management is an interesting challenge; you must design a logical arrangement that will allow you to quickly locate the files you need, while balancing your available storage space with the quantity and size of files you need to keep available on your hard drive(s).

Fortunately, Mac OS 8.6 provides several data management tools, including the Make Alias command, the Sherlock search engine, the Label command, and the ability to append comments to items in the Finder. These features affect the ways in which you manage data on your computer—and on floppy disks, cartridges, network file servers, or any other removable or remote storage devices. In this chapter, we'll take a look at these features and how they can help you efficiently organize your data.

Aliasing

Wouldn't it be nice to be in several places at one time? Imagine, for example, that while you are hard at work earning your paycheck, you could also be lying on a beach enjoying the sun. And if being in two places at once sounds appealing, how would you like to be in any number of places at one time? For example, you could be at work earning a living, at the beach getting a tan, at the library reading a book, and on a plane bound for an exotic destination—all at the same time.

Mac OS 8.6 extends this convenience to your electronic files through a feature called aliasing. Aliasing removes the single largest constraint—space limitation—from the task of organizing files and thereby makes it easier to take full advantage of your software applications and data files. In fact, the Mac OS 8.6 takes advantage of aliasing in conjunction with the Favorites folder under the Apple Menu, as we've seen in earlier chapters. Whenever you add a file, folder, or application to the Favorites menu, you're really just adding an alias for that item to the Favorites folder.

Basic Aliasing Concepts

In simple terms, an alias is a special kind of copy of a file, folder, or volume. Unlike copies you might create with the Duplicate command, an alias is only a copy of the icon that represents the file, folder, or volume, and not of the item itself.

To understand this distinction, think of an icon as a door; the file represented by the icon is the room behind the door. As you would expect, each room normally has just one door (just as each file has one icon), and opening that door (the icon) is the only way to enter the room. Creating an alias is like adding an additional door to a room; it presents another entrance to the same place.

Aliases are not new, however. On Unix computers, they are called symbolic links. Microsoft recently implemented aliases, called shortcuts, in post-Windows 3.1 operating systems. Figure 5.1 shows two folders that contain the same aliased file, default.html. The original folder resides in the Web pages folder, and the aliases reside in the Favorites folder and on the Desktop.

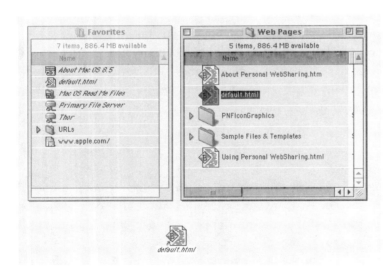

Figure 5.1 Each alias points to the original file that was used to create it.

An alias can be moved to any folder on any volume without affecting the relationship between the alias and its original file. In fact, the link between an alias and its original file is maintained even if both files are moved.

Regardless of the size of the original file, an alias requires only about 1K or 2K of disk space. That's because the alias is a copy of the icon, not of the file itself.

Mac OS 8.6

Details about these and other aspects of aliases are provided later in this chapter, but before getting too far into the technical aspects, let's take a quick look at a few practical ways to use aliases:

➤ *To make applications easier to launch*—Aliases make applications easily accessible by allowing you to launch an application simply by double-clicking on its alias. For example, you can keep one alias of your word processor on the Desktop, another in a folder full of word processing data files, and yet another alias in the Apple Menu Items folder. You could then launch this application using the icon that is most convenient at the moment. Figure 5.2 shows a folder containing aliases to some popular applications.

Figure 5.2 Aliasing an application makes it more convenient to launch when grouped with other applications.

➤ *To organize data files more effectively*—A data file may contain information that's relevant to several different areas of interest. For example, if you keep a spreadsheet file with information on your income taxes in a folder along with all the spreadsheets you've created during that year, you may also want to keep an alias copy of that same spreadsheet in a personal finances folder, in another tax file folder, and in a general accounting folder.

Storing alias copies in multiple locations, as shown in Figure 5.3, makes it easier to locate a file quickly because there are several places to find it. Placing alias files near other files of related content also increases efficiency. Finally, archival storage lets you move the originals off the hard drive, saving disk space while still allowing access to the file via aliases.

➤ *To simplify access to files stored on removable media*—Keeping aliases of files from removable storage media, such as floppy disks, removable hard drives, and CD-ROMs, on your local hard drive allows you to locate those files quickly and easily.

When an alias of a file stored on removable media is opened, the Mac OS prompts you to insert the disk (or cartridge) that contains the original file, if it isn't already available.

Mac OS 8.6

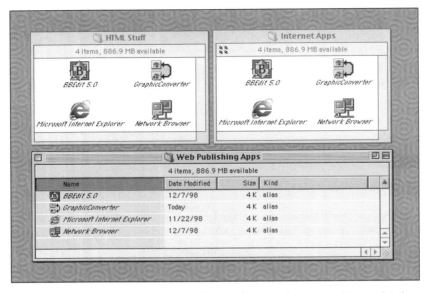

Figure 5.3 Aliasing data files allows them to be stored in multiple, convenient locations.

➤ *To simplify access to files stored on network servers*—Placing aliases of files from network file servers on your local hard drive is another way to promptly locate the files, no matter where they're stored.

When an alias of a file stored on the network server is opened, the Macintosh automatically connects to the server and asks you for necessary passwords.

Creating And Using Aliases

To create an alias, select the file, folder, or volume icon and choose from one of the following methods:

➤ Choose the Make Alias command from the File menu

➤ Press Command+M

➤ Press Control while clicking the mouse on the file to activate the contextual menu, then select Make Alias

➤ Option+Command+drag the icon anywhere—even to the same folder or the Desktop

If the alias is created in the same folder as the original, its icon will appear with the same filename and icon as the original followed by the word *alias*, as shown in Figure 5.4. If the alias is made in a location other than the original, it will have exactly the same filename.

Managing Your Data   143

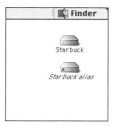

Figure 5.4   Creating an alias of a hard drive named Starbuck.

For the most part, alias icons look and act just like other files, folders, or volumes. You can change the filename of an alias at any time without breaking the link between the alias and its original file (see Figure 5.5). Changing a filename is like changing the sign on a door; it doesn't change the contents of the room behind the door.

Figure 5.5   Renaming an alias doesn't break the link to the original item.

You've probably noticed the small arrow pointing up and to the right on alias icons, and that filenames appear in italics. This is usually the case when aliased files and folders are viewed in dialog boxes, but not when aliases are listed under the Apple Menu. The italic type helps you distinguish the alias files from the original files, as in Figure 5.6.

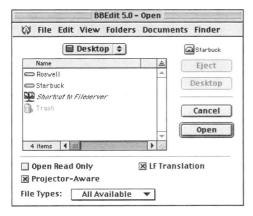

Figure 5.6   When viewed in dialog boxes, alias filenames appear in italics.

Mac OS 8.6

As mentioned earlier, alias icons can be moved to any available folder or volume without losing the link they maintain to the original file. This is the magic of aliases and the key to their utility. No matter how files are moved, the links are maintained.

Original files can also be moved, as long as they remain on the same volume, and they can be renamed without breaking the link with their aliases. When the alias icon is opened, the Mac OS finds and opens the original file.

To illustrate how this automatic linkage is maintained, let's assume you have a file called 1999 Trustee Schedule, which is stored in a folder named Foundation Documents. You create an alias of this file, move the alias into a folder called 1999 Personnel Accounting, and rename the alias 1999 Trustees (see Figure 5.7).

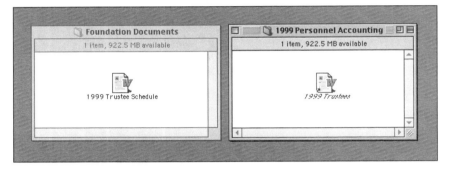

Figure 5.7 Files and aliases as originally named and positioned.

Later, you decide that this file will contain only data for the first six months of 1999, so you rename the original file (1999 Trustees, which was previously called 1999 Trustee Schedule) 1999 Part I and put it in a new folder named Jan-June Stuff within the Foundation Documents folder (see Figure 5.8).

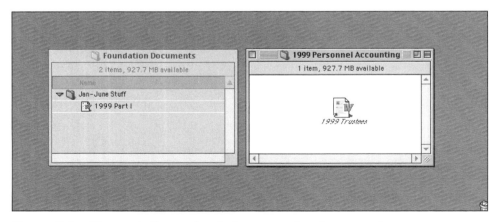

Figure 5.8 Files and aliases after being moved and renamed.

Mac OS 8.6

Even though both the original file *and* the alias have been moved and renamed since they were created, double-clicking on the 1999 Trustees file (the alias) will open the 1999 Part I file.

Advanced Aliasing Concepts

Once you understand the basic concepts of aliases and begin using them, you may have questions, such as: How many aliases can one file have? Is it possible to alias an alias? What happens when an alias's original file is deleted? The answers to these and other questions are as follows:

➤ *Multiple aliases*—There is no limit to the number of aliases you can create from a single file, folder, or volume.

When multiple aliases are created, alias names are designated by numbers to distinguish them from existing alias names. The first alias of a file named Acceptance Letter is named Acceptance Letter alias; the second, Acceptance Letter alias 1; the third, Acceptance Letter alias 2; and so on until the earlier aliases are renamed or moved to different locations. These alias numbers have no significance beyond serving to avoid filename duplication.

➤ *Aliasing aliases*—You can create an alias of an alias, but this causes a chain of pointing references: the second alias points to the first, which points to the original. In most cases, it's better to create an alias directly from the original file or copy the first alias.

If you do create a chain and any one of the aliases in the chain is later deleted, none of the subsequent aliases will be linked to the original file. To illustrate this problem, assume an alias named New Specs alias was created from an original document named New Specs, and then New Specs alias alias was created from the first New Specs alias (see Figure 5.9).

Figure 5.9 Creating an alias of an alias creates a chain that can be broken if one of the aliases is deleted.

At this point, each of these files can be repositioned and renamed and the alias links will be automatically maintained. However, if the "New Specs alias" file is deleted, "New Specs alias alias" will no longer be linked to "New Specs." If you move the parent alias to the Trash, the child alias will continue to work until the Trash is emptied. You can reestablish the link by creating a new alias of "New Specs" named "New Specs alias" or by fixing the alias, a process we'll explore in a moment.

Mac OS 8.6

- *Deleting aliases*—Deleting an alias has no effect on the original file, folder, or volume. It simply means that in order to access the original item that was the parent of the deleted alias, you'll have to locate it manually or create another alias.

  You can delete aliases in any of the ways you delete normal files—by dragging the alias to the Trash, or selecting the alias and pressing Command+Delete, and then choosing the Empty Trash command.

- *Moving original files*—The link between an alias and its original file is maintained regardless of how the original is moved within a single volume, but links are not maintained when you copy the original file to a new volume and then delete the original file. In other words, you can't transfer the alias link from an original file to a copy of that original file.

  If you move a parent file from one volume to another and must delete the original file, all existing aliases created from that file will be unlinked and therefore useless. You can create new aliases from the original file in its new location and replace the existing aliases with the new ones, but you'll have to perform this process manually.

- *Deleting original files*—Deleting a file from which aliases have been made has no immediate effect; no warning is posted when the file is deleted. But when you try to open an alias of a file that's been deleted, a dialog box appears informing you that the original file cannot be found. In previous versions of the Mac OS, it wasn't possible to salvage a deleted file in order to relink with its alias; in most cases, you had to delete the orphaned alias. The exception to this rule was when the original file was still in the Trash. In this case, if you tried to open a trashed alias, a dialog box would inform you that the file could not be opened because it was in the Trash. If you dragged the original from the Trash, it became available to the alias.

- *Finding original files*—Although an alias is, in many ways, a perfect proxy for a file, occasionally you'll need to locate the alias's original file—for example, if you want to delete the original file or copy the original onto a removable disk or cartridge.

  To locate the original file for any alias, simply select the alias icon in the Finder and choose one of the following options:

  - Show Original from the Finder's File menu
  - Press Command+R
  - Choose Show Original from the contextual pop-up menu
  - Press Command+I or File|Get Info and click the Select New Original button

  The original file, folder, or volume is selected and displayed on the Desktop. If the original file is located on a removable volume that's not currently available, a dialog box appears prompting you to insert the disk or cartridge containing that

Mac OS 8.6

file. If the original file is located on a network file server, the Macintosh attempts to log on to the server to locate the file, and asks you for any necessary passwords. Figure 5.10 shows the path information for an original item, not the alias itself, as seen through the alias's Get Info command.

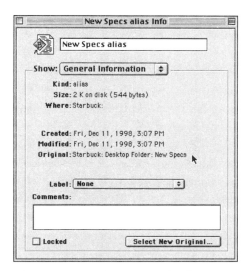

Figure 5.10   The General Information section of the Get Info dialog box reveals the path to the original of an alias.

If the selected alias is an alias of an alias, the Mac OS will find the original file, not the alias used to create the current alias.

➤ *Replacing alias icons*—As introduced in Chapter 3, new icons can be pasted into the Get Info dialog box for any file. This is also true of alias icons. Replacing the icon of an alias has no effect on the icon of the original file.

Aliasing Folders Or Volumes

So far, we've focused on aliasing in relation to application and data files. But almost without exception, aliasing works the same way for folders and volumes. Folder aliases are created, renamed, repositioned, deleted, and linked to their originals in exactly the same way as the file aliases previously described:

➤ Aliasing a folder creates a new folder icon with the same name as the original, plus the word alias.

➤ The name of an aliased folder appears in italics when viewed on the Desktop, in a Finder window, or in a dialog box.

➤ Folder aliases can be renamed at any time. Of course, an alias cannot have the same name as an original or another alias while in the same folder or on the Desktop.

➤ Folder aliases can be located inside any other folder or folder alias, or moved to any volume. However, no two items can reside in the same folder or on the Desktop if they have the exact same name.

➤ When an aliased folder is opened, the window of the original folder is opened. Aliasing a folder does not alias the folder's content. For this reason, the original folder must be available whenever the folder alias is opened. If the original folder is located on a volume that's not currently mounted, you'll be prompted to insert the volume, or the Macintosh will attempt to mount the volume if it's on the network.

➤ Deleting a folder alias does not delete the original folder or any of its contents.

Folder aliases have a few unique aspects, however:

➤ When a folder alias is displayed hierarchically in a Finder list window or in the Apple Menu (see Figure 5.11), it cannot be opened hierarchically (no triangle appears to its left) because the folder alias has no content to display, strictly speaking. You can open the folder alias by double-clicking on it to open a new Finder window.

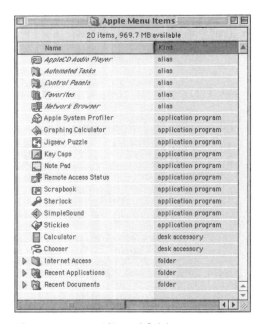

Figure 5.11 Aliased folders are commonly used in the Apple Menu, including the Favorites folder and the Control Panels folder.

➤ Anything put into a folder alias—including files, folders, and other aliases—is actually placed in the original folder. The folder alias has no real contents; it's just another "door" to the original folder.

Volume aliases are similar to file aliases, but have some of the same characteristics as folder aliases:

➤ Opening a volume alias mounts the original volume if it's not already available. If the original volume is not currently mounted, you'll be prompted to insert the volume, or the Mac OS will attempt to mount the volume if it's on the network.

➤ Opening a volume alias displays the Finder window of the actual volume and the contents of this window.

➤ Aliasing a volume aliases the icon of the volume itself—not the contents of the volume.

Figure 5.12 shows a collection of aliased volumes.

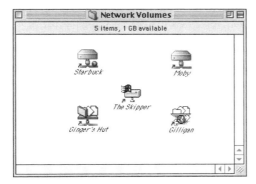

Figure 5.12 Aliased volumes stored in a folder.

Using Aliases

Aliases have a multitude of uses. The following are some of the more interesting possibilities:

➤ *Alias applications*—The easiest way to launch an application is to double-click on its icon. Many applications are stored in folders containing a morass of ancillary files, such as dictionaries, color palettes, Help files, and printer descriptions. Amid all this clutter, it's difficult to locate the application icon in order to launch it. Aliasing allows easier access, as shown in Figure 5.13.

The most straightforward way to simplify application launching is to alias each of your applications inside the Apple Menu Items folder, a subfolder within the Apple Menu Items folder, or as a pop-up folder. You can then launch the applications by simply choosing them from the Apple Menu or the pop-up window.

Alternatively, you might group your application aliases into folders and then alias these folders and place them in the Apple Menu. Doing it this way takes two steps instead of one, but this method leaves room in your Apple Menu for other

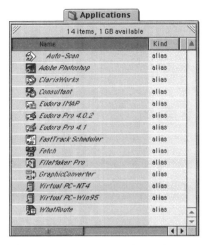

Figure 5.13 Grouping aliases together facilitates access to your frequently used applications.

folder, volume, and file aliases. Of course, you could leave a few applications that you use extensively directly in the Apple Menu, but because the Mac OS shows hierarchical menus for any folder in the Apple Menu folder, the former approach is preferable.

You can also put application aliases, along with groups of documents created with the application, on your Desktop. But since double-clicking on any document will launch the application anyway, this is not really very useful.

➤ *Multiple data file aliases*—To avoid having to remember all the places where a frequently used file is stored every time you want to use it, you can use aliases to store each data file in as many places as it logically fits—anywhere you might look for the file when you need it later.

Suppose, for example, you write a letter to your boss about a new idea for serving your company's big client, Clampdown, Inc. Depending on your personal scheme, you might store this letter, along with other general business correspondence, in a folder pertaining to Clampdown, Inc., or you might even have a file where you keep everything that has to do with your boss. Using aliases, you can store the file in all these locations and in a folder containing all work you've done in the current week, as illustrated in Figure 5.14.

➤ *Aliases of data files from remote or removable volumes*—You can store dozens of gigabytes worth of files on your hard drive, regardless of its size, by using aliases. Keeping aliases of files you normally store on removable disks or drives, and of files from network file servers that you occasionally need, allows you to access the files by simply searching your hard drive—without the cost of hard-drive space.

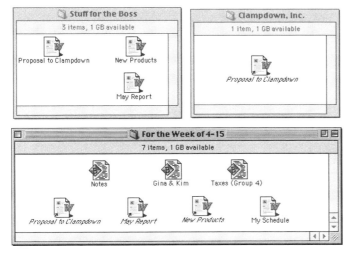

Figure 5.14 Aliasing a file into multiple locations.

This is a perfect method for storing libraries of clip-art files, downloadable fonts, corporate templates, or other infrequently used file groups. If these aliased files are stored on your hard drive, as shown in Figure 5.15, you can browse through them whenever necessary. The hard drive will automatically mount the required volumes or prompt you for them when they're needed.

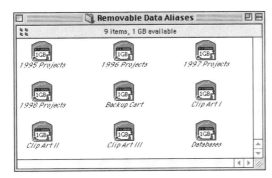

Figure 5.15 A folder full of aliased utility files stored on a removable volume.

➤ *Trash alias*—You can alias the Finder's Trash and store copies of it in any folder. Dragging folder files to the Trash alias is the same as dragging them to the actual Trash. Files trashed in this way will not be removed until you choose Empty Trash from the Special menu, and they can be retrieved by simply opening the Trash (or an alias of it) and dragging the file back onto a volume or folder.

➤ *Removable cartridge maps*—Create a folder for each removable cartridge, drive, or floppy disk. Alias the entire contents of these volumes and store the aliases in the volume's folder. Then you can "browse" these volumes without mounting them.

Mac OS 8.6

You may also want to keep other aliases of files from these volumes in other locations on your drive.

➤ *Network file server volume maps*—Create a folder called Network and place an alias of each remote volume in it. You can then log on to any remote volume by simply double-clicking on the volume alias. This eliminates the need to access the Chooser, locate the file server, and locate the volume every time you want to use the volume. Of course, you'll be prompted for any required passwords. The Network Browser helps simplify this task, which we'll see in Chapter 18.

➤ *Hard drive alias*—If you work on a large AppleTalk network, put an alias icon of your hard drive on a floppy disk and carry it with you. If you need to access your hard drive from another location, all you have to do is insert the floppy disk containing your hard drive alias into any Macintosh on the network, double-click on the alias icon, and your hard drive will be mounted via AppleTalk.

Aliasing Summary

Aliases have many uses and can provide valuable shortcuts, including the following:

➤ You can alias any file, folder, volume, or the Trash.

➤ To create an alias, select the desired icon and choose Make Alias from the Finder's File menu, press Command+M, choose Make Alias from the contextual pop-up menu, or drag and drop an icon while holding down the Option and Command keys.

➤ An alias takes the same name as its original file with the word *alias* appended, unless it is made in another window, in which case the filename is identical to the original.

➤ Alias names always appear in italics, except in the Apple Menu.

➤ Aliases can be renamed at any time. The standard Macintosh 32-character name limit applies.

➤ Aliases can be moved to any location on the current volume or on any other volume.

➤ An alias is initially given the same icon as its original. The icon can be changed in the Get Info dialog box.

➤ An alias requires only a very small amount of storage space.

➤ The link between an alias and its original is maintained even when the originals are renamed or repositioned, but not when moved to another volume themselves.

➤ Deleting an alias icon has no effect on its original file, folder, or volume.

➤ Copying an alias to a new location on the current drive (hold down the Option key while dragging) is the same as creating a new alias of the original file—it does not create an alias of an alias.

➤ Press Command+R after selecting an alias to locate its original, or choose Show Original from the contextual pop-up menu.

➤ Opening a folder alias opens the window of the original folder.

➤ Opening a volume alias opens the window of the original volume.

The Sherlock Search Engine

Regardless of how well organized your electronic filing system is, it's sometimes impossible to remember where specific files are located because many Macs have tens of thousands of files. To solve this problem in the past, Apple provided the Find File desk accessory (DA) to enable you to search for files—by filename—on any mounted volume. Find File located the files and listed them in a section of its window. Once a file was found, selecting the filename revealed the path of the file along with other basic file information, as shown in Figure 5.16. Using this information, you could then quit the Find File DA and locate the file yourself, or Find File would move the file to the Desktop where it was easily accessed.

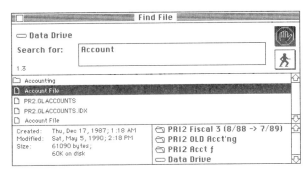

Figure 5.16 The old Find File desk accessory.

Besides Find File, other file-finding utilities have also been available for quite some time. Most of them let you search for files not only by filename but also by creation date, file type, creator, date modified, file size, and other file attributes. Norton Utility's Fast Find is one example of a helpful utility (see Figure 5.17). Like Find File, most of these utilities locate matching files, display the path information, and let you return to the Finder and use or modify the file as required. (Utilities such as Retrieve It!, GOFer, and OnLocation, to name but a few, search inside files to find matches to text strings.)

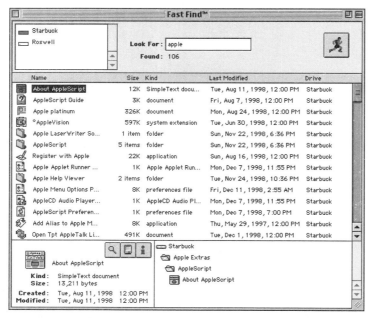

Figure 5.17 The Find File component of Symantec's Norton Utilities.

In System 7, a new Find command was added to the Finder. This command and its companion command, Find Again, significantly improved on the Find File desk accessory. System 7.5 significantly improved on the Find command by returning all matches to a search in a new Found Items dialog box, thereby eliminating repetitive Find Again searches. Because these new commands were built into the Finder, they offered important advantages over other file-finding utilities.

In Mac OS 8.5, a totally new search facility was introduced, and Mac OS 8.6 makes it even better. It's called Sherlock, and it's more than just a utility to help find files and folders. Sherlock is more of a search engine than a utility because it allows you to perform complex searches not only on your Mac, but over the Internet as well.

Sherlock Basics

Just as Find File was, the Sherlock search engine is located in the Finder's File menu; the program itself is in the Apple Menu. In previous versions of the Mac OS, the Find command consisted of both a program named Find File and an Extension named Find File Extension, which worked together to search for items on your, and other, hard drives. In Mac OS 8.6, however, the Find File Extension has been replaced by a number of Extensions and the Sherlock application. These components allow Sherlock to perform three types of searches:

➤ Finding files on local or networked volumes

➤ Finding words and phrases in locally indexed volumes (commonly referred to as a *full-text* search)

➤ Searches of popular Web sites over the Internet

The Sherlock program is actually an application. If you have numerous files or large hard drives and are getting "not enough memory" errors when executing a search, you may find it necessary to increase the amount of memory dedicated to Sherlock. More memory is required to search large numbers of files. Figure 5.18 shows the Memory tab of Sherlock's Get Info window; notice that the default memory allocation has been bumped up from 1926K to 2402K. We'll talk more about memory requirements for applications, such as Sherlock, in Chapter 9.

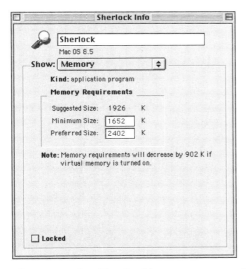

Figure 5.18 Sherlock's memory requirements as seen in the Get Info window.

Sherlock is launched by selecting Sherlock from the Apple Menu, by selecting File|Find, or pressing Command+F; all three options present the window shown in Figure 5.19.

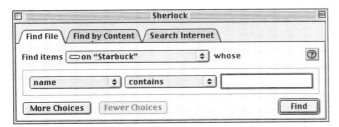

Figure 5.19 Sherlock's default window.

Mac OS 8.6

Sherlock's default search is the traditional Find File window, which we'll discuss in detail a little later.

TIP

Sherlock opens the results of each search in a new results window entitled Items Found.

Searching For Files

When the Find File tab is selected, Sherlock defaults to a "simple search" window, which allows you to search for files whose names contain the characters in the Find File text entry field. You can ask Sherlock to do a very complex search as well. We'll get into that in just a moment, but for now let's start with the basics. Using the basic Find File tab to locate files or folders by name, you can enter the complete name or any portion of the name of the item you're looking for:

➤ *Enter a complete name*—If you know the complete name of the item you're looking for, enter it into the search field. Bear in mind that the correct file may not be found if you make even a slight error in spelling the filename. This is not the most efficient way to execute a file search.

➤ *Enter only the first portion of a name*—Entering the first few characters of the title you're searching for is the most common—and usually the most efficient— filename search method. This locates all files whose names contain the characters you've specified. The exact number of characters you should enter will depend on the circumstances; the goal is to enter enough characters to narrow the search, but not so many that you risk a spelling error and therefore risk missing the file.

For example, if the file you wanted to locate is named Archaeology Report, specifying only the letter *A* would yield a huge number of files to sort through. On the other hand, entering six or seven characters could allow filenames with spelling errors, such as Archio or Arhcae, to escape the search. Decide on the number of characters according to how common the first few characters are among your files, and how well you remember the filename. In this example, searching for files starting with Arc would probably be the best strategy.

After specifying the search criteria, click the Find button to start the search. The search begins with the startup drive and proceeds to search any other volumes you specify (more on that in a minute). If the search seems likely to take more than a few seconds, an animated circular icon will appear to let you know that Sherlock is working on the search. When a file matching the search criteria was located in versions of the system software prior to System 7.5, a Finder window was opened and the file was displayed. In Mac OS 8.6, however, the entire search results are displayed in a second window, as in Figure 5.20, which shows a search for any item on the boot drive Starbuck that contains the word *apple*.

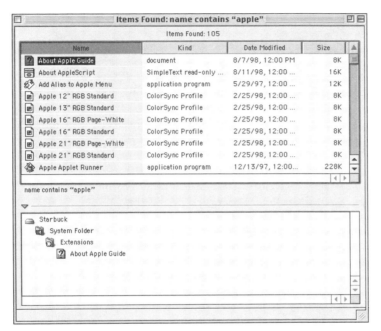

Figure 5.20 The results of a simple search.

Note that the Items Found window is divided into two parts. The upper part lists the search results, which may be viewed by name, kind, date modified (but not created), or size. To change the view, just click on Name, Kind, Last Modified, or Size to re-sort the search results. You may also resize the columns to make them wider or narrower. To open an item after it has been found by Sherlock, just double-click on it in either the upper or lower portion of the Items Found window, or press Command+O. To open the item's enclosing folder or volume, press Command+E. See the File menu for additional options.

The path to an item is displayed in the lower half of the Items Found window. For example, the first item displayed in Figure 5.20 is named About Apple Guide—which is an Apple Guide document located in the Extensions folder, which is inside the System Folder, which in turn is on the hard drive named Starbuck. At this point, you can use or modify the found file as required. Figure 5.21 shows an example of the File menu once a search has been successfully executed.

Figure 5.21 Look in the File menu to see what options are available for a selected item, or to save the search criteria.

The drag and drop capabilities of the Mac OS enable you to do a number of things with selections in the Found Items dialog box after you've executed a search, including:

▶ *Open the item's window*—Press Command+E to open the item's enclosing folder, or select the Open Enclosing Folder command from the File menu.

▶ *Move the file*—Drag the file or folder name to a new location. The item actually moves to where you've dragged it. When you drag the item to another disk, however, it is only copied.

▶ *Open the file*—Double-clicking on a folder, or pressing Command+O with a folder selected, will open the folder. The same actions will open a selected file if the application that created the file is available. You can also drag the filename to an application. If it's not already running—and if it can open this type of file—the application will launch itself. Then the application will open the file (and translate it, if necessary).

▶ *Print the file*—Drag the file onto a Desktop printer icon in the Finder (if you have one).

If the selected file is not the one you wanted, or if after modifying the selected file you want to continue searching for the next file that matches the search criteria, choose Command+F to return to the Find File window.

> **TIP**
> Once you have completed a search, the Items Found window will remain open until you quit Sherlock, even if you perform an additional search or close the main Sherlock window.

You can search more than your startup volume. Sherlock offers the following options in the "Find Items" section of the main Sherlock window:

Mac OS 8.6

- *On All Disks*—Searches all mounted volumes, including all folders and items that appear on the Finder Desktop.

- *On Local Disks*—Limits the search to local disks only, such as internal and external hard drives, floppy drives, and removable media such as Zip drives. Local disks are physically connected to your Mac.

- *On Local Disks, Except CD-ROMs*—Excludes CD-ROMs from local volume searches. This is a feature added in Mac OS 8.5.

- *On Mounted Servers*—Mounted servers are network-connected volumes. These volumes are listed by their volume names.

- *On the Desktop*—Limits the search to the Desktop if no volume or folder is selected. If you have multiple hard drives, the Desktop file of each hard drive will be searched.

- *In the Finder Selection*—Confines the search to the item or items currently selected in the Finder. Clicking a folder in the Finder and then choosing this option will allow you to search only in that item, whether it's a folder, a hard drive, or a mounted server volume.

- *On <hard drive>*—Confines the search to a particular hard drive or mounted volume.

Advanced File Searches

In addition to the search options mentioned above, Sherlock provides three additional options that are only revealed when you hold down the Option key while selecting one of the search criteria pop-up menus:

- *Name/Icon Lock*—Looks for file, folder, or volume names that have their names or icons locked, such as the Apple Menu Items folder or the Clipboard.

- *Custom Icon*—Searches for items with customized icons.

- *Visibility*—Enables Sherlock to search for items marked as invisible by the Mac OS, such as the VM Storage or Desktop DB files.

Many items on your hard drive are marked as locked, have custom icons, or are invisible to the user in the Finder or to most applications because the creators of the Mac OS or other programmers intend them to be that way. To find any of these items on your hard drive, just hold down the Option key to reveal the additional search options, which are shown in Figure 5.22. It's a good idea to leave them alone once you find them because things might go terribly wrong if you decide to experiment with moving or altering these types of files.

Mac OS 8.6

160   Chapter 5

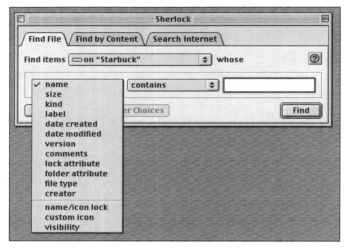

Figure 5.22   Additional search options are revealed by holding down the Option key while selecting a search criteria.

On the most basic level, Sherlock searches for items whose names contain the characters you specify in the search field. But you can also construct highly specific searches with Sherlock. To see additional Sherlock search options, click the More Choices button in the Find File tab, or press Command+M. A single additional criterion appears. Continue to click the More Choices button to fully expose the dialog box and have it look like the one shown in Figure 5.23. Click the Find button to initiate the search, or click Fewer Choices (or press Command+L) to narrow your search options.

Finding By Content

In Mac OS 8.6, you can search a volume for specific words within documents—not just the name of a document itself. This is commonly referred to as a full-text search, and it's helpful in more ways than you might think. For example, how else could you find a specific piece of information without opening every document on your computer? In order to perform a full-text search, you must first index the contents of the volumes you want to search. This can take a long time on the initial indexing session. Subsequent sessions are fairly quick because Sherlock only reads and indexes documents whose modification dates have changed since the last index was processed. Figure 5.24 shows an example of a search for the word *Macintosh*.

To search for a word or phrase by content, follow these steps:

1. Launch Sherlock from the Apple Menu, or by pressing Command+F.

2. Select the Find By Content tab, or press Command+G.

Managing Your Data 161

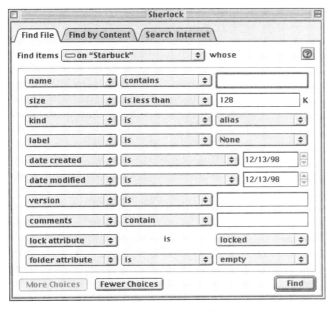

Figure 5.23 The full Find dialog box.

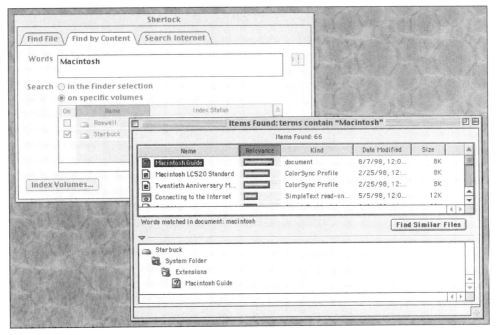

Figure 5.24 An example of a full-text search.

Mac OS 8.6

3. Enter a word or phrase in the Words field.

4. Select a location to search—either the item selected in the Finder or a volume that has already been indexed (more on that next).

5. Press the Find button.

The search results are displayed in the Items Found window, which is similar to that of the Find File search, but with two additional features:

➤ *Relevance*—The Relevance column ranks the search results in descending order of relevance based on what the Mac OS thinks you were searching for.

➤ *Find Similar Files*—The Find Similar Files button will perform a secondary search and look for files whose contents contain some of the key words found in the documents from the original search.

However, you must first index your volumes before you can perform this type of search. Indexing is very easy:

1. Open Sherlock's Find By Content tab.

2. Select the Index Volumes button to reveal your indexing options, as in Figure 5.25.

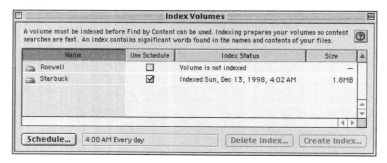

Figure 5.25 Select a volume for indexing before you attempt a Find by Content search.

3. Choose one or more volumes to index.

4. Select the Schedule button to determine how often the selected volumes should be reindexed (see Figure 5.26). You may select the days of the week and the time at which indexing will begin.

The initial indexing could take quite some time, depending on how much data is stored on your drives. Reindexing is usually very quick.

Managing Your Data   163

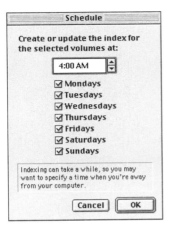

Figure 5.26 Select a schedule for the reindexing of your volumes.

Searching The Internet

The beauty of Sherlock is that it allows you to search multiple Web sites at the same time—directly from your Desktop. You'll still need a Web browser to open any found items, however. Mac OS 8.6 comes with the ability to search several Web sites, including AltaVista, Infoseek, and Lycos. But as the Internet searching capability of Sherlock continues to gain speed, more sites will create the necessary plug-in for Sherlock that enables this type of search. We'll see how this works in just a minute, but for now take a quick look at Figure 5.27, which shows a sample search of several sites for the phrase *PowerMacintosh G3*.

To perform an Internet search:

1. Launch Sherlock and select the Search Internet tab (or press Command+H).
2. Enter some search terms in the Words field.
3. Click the checkbox beside the name and icon of the Web sites you want to search, such as AltaVista or Apple.com.
4. Click the Search button.

Although the Items Found window is similar to those resulting from Sherlock's other search methods, it lists only the name of the site where the document resides, the relevance of each item returned by the search, and the URL of the site containing the document. When you single-click on one of the items, Sherlock will load some basic information about it, such as a banner ad from the site (if it has one), the URL, and the relevance of the item. To go to a particular item using a Web browser, double-click on the item in the Items Found window, or single-click on the item in the preview area of the Items Found window.

Mac OS 8.6

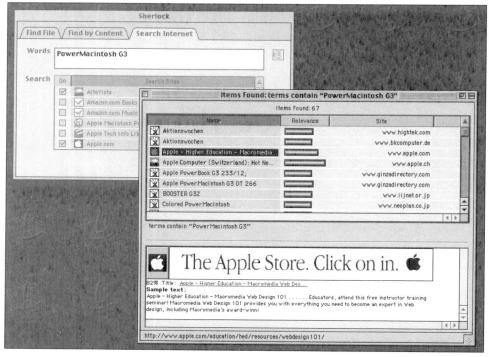

Figure 5.27 Sherlock's Internet search feature is as powerful as it is easy to use.

More and more Internet search sites are becoming available, and existing sites are being updated to make them more compatible and to allow for speedier searches. The Mac OS will automatically alert you if a new search set is available; however, you can command Sherlock to look for newer versions of the search sets it uses by following these steps:

1. Launch Sherlock and select the Search Internet tab (or press Command+H).
2. Choose Update Search Sites from the Find menu.
3. Sherlock will look for newer versions of the existing search sets, which are stored in the Internet Search Sites folder in the System Folder.
4. If new versions are available, a dialog window like the one shown in Figure 5.28 will appear.
5. Select the Update button to download the new version. It will become available after you quit and restart Sherlock.

Configuring Preferences And Saving Searches

Sherlock has a few small configuration preferences that you may adjust by going to the Edit menu and choosing the Preferences option, which is shown in Figure 5.29.

Managing Your Data   165

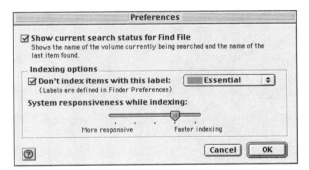

Figure 5.28   Sherlock can update its set of search sites.

Figure 5.29   Configuring Sherlock's preferences.

Sherlock's configuration preference options are:

➤ *Show current search status for Find File*—Displays the item last found for a search and the volume being searched.

➤ *Don't index items with this label*—If this item is checked, Sherlock will not index folders or files matching the label.

➤ *System responsiveness while indexing*—Your Mac may become very sluggish if you're using it to perform other functions while Sherlock is indexing the hard drive. Because Sherlock requires a large amount of the Mac's system resources to complete its task, you'll have to choose between a more responsive system and faster indexing speed.

Finally, Sherlock allows you to save a set of search criteria as a document that you can open again at a later time. This is very handy if you perform the same search on a frequent basis, if you want to be able to recreate a specific search again at a later time, or if you want to automate a search using AppleScript. To save a set of search criteria, just choose File|Save Search Criteria. An example of this process is shown in Figure 5.30.

Mac OS 8.6

166 Chapter 5

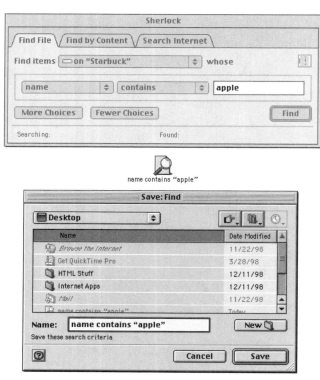

Figure 5.30 Save a search's criteria for later use with Sherlock or an AppleScript.

To recall a saved search, double-click on a saved search criteria, or choose File|Open Search Criteria. Sherlock will automatically execute the search and display the results in a new window.

Tips For Effective Searches

Here are a few tips to help you create effective searches using Sherlock:

➤ You can locate aliases as well as original items using Find. Aliases will appear in italic text in the Found Items window.

➤ Find also locates folders and volumes. Like any other file, any folder or volume matching the specified search criteria will be found.

➤ Use the Search by Kind option to locate all data files created by one specific application. To use the by-kind search criterion, specify the file kind (for example, all HTML documents) that the application assigns to its data files. To see a listing of these additional search types, click the pop-up menu. Items like Folder Type, File Type, and Creator Type appear at the bottom.

➤ Use Find to do quick backups. After you've used the Sherlock search engine to locate all files modified after a certain date, you can drag those files to a removable

Mac OS 8.6

Managing Your Data   167

volume for a "quick-and-dirty" backup. Of course, this procedure shouldn't replace a reliable backup utility—but you can never have too many backups.

➤ Use the selected item's search range to perform multiple-criteria searches. For example, the Sherlock search engine can locate all filenames beginning with *S* that are less than 32K in size and have the Microsoft Word creator type (or any other set of multiple criteria). The first criterion is searched for using the *<on any one volume>* range; then you search for each additional criterion using the selected items range.

➤ Use the Find By Content feature to search your computer for detailed information, such as names and addresses of friends or business contacts sent to you by e-mail. Sherlock will index the data of almost all the popular e-mail clients, such as Eudora, Emailer, and Outlook Express.

➤ Use Sherlock to search the Internet instead of opening up a connection to a specific Web search engine site and therefore limiting your search to only that engine. Leverage the power of Sherlock's ability to search multiple sites simultaneously.

Labels

The Label feature of the Mac OS helps you categorize your files, identify and locate certain types of files, and in some cases, manipulate them as a group. You can name your labels anything you want and change them as often as you like.

Configuring Labels

The Labels menu is no longer located in the Finder menu bar; it's configured using the Finder Preferences option under the Edit menu. Figure 5.31 shows the Labels tab of the Finder Preferences. The text and color of your labels are configured in this area.

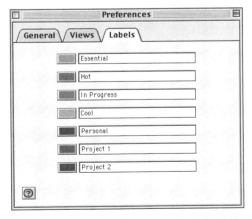

Figure 5.31   Configuring the labels in the Finder Preferences.

Mac OS 8.6

To set label text, click in each label text block and enter the name of the label category you want to define. With label assignments, form must follow function; label assignments that don't help you use and manipulate your data more efficiently offer no advantage. Remember that label names are not sorted alphanumerically by the Finder; instead, labels are sorted as they appear in the Labels Preferences window.

Using Label Categories

There are many ways to use labels:

➤ *To categorize files*—Labels provide an additional level of categorization for files. Files are already categorized by type, creation and modification dates, and related folders, but with labels you can also classify them by topic, importance, or any other way you choose.

➤ *For visual distinction*—Color-coding icons helps you quickly distinguish one type of file from another. For example, all applications can be labeled red, making them easier to spot in a folder full of dictionaries, Help instructions, and other files. In Finder windows, you can also use the Labels column to list label names next to filenames.

➤ *To facilitate data backup*—You can find all files assigned to a specific label and then copy them to another disk or volume for backup purposes.

➤ *To indicate security requirements*—When using File Sharing, you can create labels that remind you of the security level of specific folders, files, and volumes.

➤ *Categories for logical subdivisions of data files*—If your work is project-based, you can specify large projects by individual labels and use one miscellaneous label for smaller projects. You could also have Long-Term Projects, Short-Term Projects, and Permanent Projects labels.

➤ *Categories for software applications*—You can differentiate launchable applications, or label applications and their ancillary files. You may want a separate label for utility programs, including third-party extensions, control panels, desk accessories, and utilities that are launchable applications.

Once labels are defined, you can modify label colors. Click on any color in the Labels control panel to bring up the color picker dialog box, shown in Figure 5.32. Specify the color you want for the selected label using one of the several color picker tools, such as the Crayon Picker, HTML Picker, or the good ol' RGB Picker. Because label colors are applied over existing icon colors, weaker colors with lower hue and saturation values work best.

Managing Your Data 169

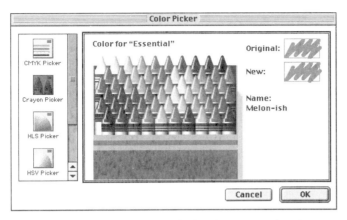

Figure 5.32 Changing a label color using the Crayon color picker.

After you've modified the label names and colors, close the Finder Preferences. The labels and any files or folders affected will then be updated. You can reopen the Label Preferences menu whenever you need to reset the text or colors.

Assigning Labels

Use one of three basic methods to assign a label to an item in the Finder; these methods are equally effective. To assign a label, select an item and perform one of the three following actions:

➤ Choose File|Label.

➤ Activate the contextual menu (Control+Click) and select Label.

➤ Choose File|Get Info and select a label.

Each method, all of which are shown in Figure 5.33, results in the same action.

Comments

In the past, adding lengthy comments to Mac OS files was an inefficient process, to say the least. Comments were likely to disappear every time the invisible Desktop file was replaced or rebuilt, and any comments that survived could only be seen by opening the Get Info dialog box—a major inconvenience. Eventually most Mac users stopped using comments altogether.

System 7 attempted to breathe new life into file comments, correcting some of their former shortcomings and adding some interesting possibilities. In the Finder, comments have been improved in three important ways:

Mac OS 8.6

170 Chapter 5

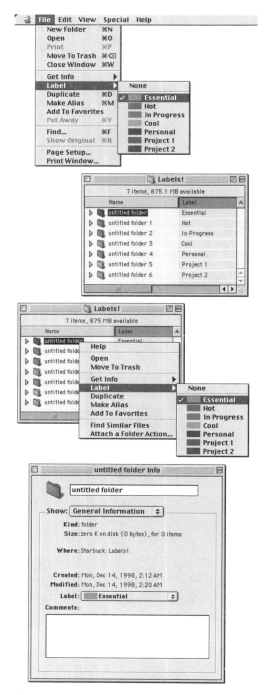

Figure 5.33 The three ways to set a label in Mac OS 8.6.

Mac OS 8.6

- *Visibility*—You can now see comments in Finder windows. When the Show Comments column option in the Views|View Options preferences is selected, comments will display in Finder windows that are viewed as lists.

- *Searchability*—Sherlock allows you to search for text in file comments, making it possible to locate files by comment entries.

- *Permanence*—When the Desktop is rebuilt, hold down the Option and Command keys on start-up to retain comments.

Users will find other productive ways to apply these new comment features. Using comments as cues is one possibility: keywords or phrases can provide information (such as client names, project titles, and related document names) beyond what is already included in the filename, date, kind, or other file information. Many shareware developers make it so files created with their programs automatically add a comment including the author's URL. This additional information would be displayed in Finder windows via the Sherlock search engine.

Figure 5.34 shows some files with comments added. When browsing Finder windows, comments tell you at a glance what the files contain. They also make it easy to retrieve files with the Sherlock search engine.

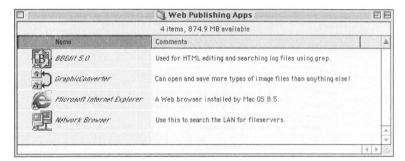

Figure 5.34 A Finder window as it appears when using the Show Comments option.

Wrapping Up

We all suffer from info-glut. With so many files, folders, and applications crowding our hard drives, we need all the help we can get. To help us make shortcuts and to search and organize our data, Mac OS 8.6 has more options than ever before:

- Aliases help you locate and launch files, and allow you to access network data quickly and easily.

- The Sherlock search engine will solve your "where is that file?" problem.

➤ Labels make it easier to organize important files.

➤ Comments remind you of details about the contents of a particular file or folder.

Next, we'll look at the special software and features in the Mac OS 8.6 for PowerBook and mobile users.

PowerBook System Software

With the debut of OS 8.6, many PowerBook users will notice fewer changes when compared to the same version of the Mac OS running on a desktop or server because the hardware used by PowerBooks is more similar to these types of Macs. Of course, PowerBook hardware remains considerably different from desktop hardware in certain respects, such as its use of batteries, hot-swappable expansion bays, and PCMCIA cards; the components of the OS itself are not much different at all, however.

PowerBook system software support began with System 7.0.1. A suite of simple utilities for controlling the PowerBook's basic functions, such as controlling screen display, measuring battery lifetimes, and performing processor cycling, was included. Sensing an opportunity, many vendors rushed in and substantially improved upon Apple's meager offerings with packages like Claris's Power To Go, Connectix's CPU, Norton's Essentials for the PowerBook, and Inline Design's PBTools, to name a few. Several million PowerBooks later, Apple substantially improved the support that PowerBook owners had been seeking elsewhere. Some of these improvements, such as the Control Strip, were eventually incorporated and live on in the latest version of the Mac OS.

PowerBook Issues

Beginning with the Apple PowerBook 100 series—the most successful introduction of any family of portable computers of its time—Apple has had a string of successes with virtually all of its PowerBooks, especially with the G3 line. Millions of Macintosh users have gone beyond using their PowerBooks as supplementary computers and have altogether replaced their desktop machines with them. System software support for the PowerBook series—initially minimal with System 7.0.1—has been fortified over the years. Now, with the 300-MHz G3 PowerBook, you can run Mac OS 8.6 and benefit from its enhancements, just as desktop users do.

PowerBook users have several unique needs, including the following:

▶ *Battery recharging*—PowerBooks can use AC power or run off rechargeable batteries. To reduce power consumption and thereby extend use, Mac OS 8.6 supports capabilities such as slowing down the processor, reducing screen brightness, spinning down hard drives, reducing hard disk input and output (I/O) using a RAM disk, and putting the system to sleep.

▶ *Easy connection*—PowerBook users require remote access, automatic remounting of hard drives and network servers upon wake-up, and other connection features for which the OS provides system support. You can use the Control Panel named PowerBook SCSI Disk Mode (rather than the old PowerBook Setup Control Panel) shown in Figure 6.1 to connect your PowerBook to another Macintosh as if it were an external hard drive.

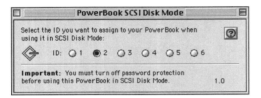

Figure 6.1 With the PowerBook SCSI Disk Mode Control Panel, you can use your PowerBook as an external hard drive on another Mac.

▶ *Presentation services*—PowerBooks can easily connect to external displays, ranging from monitors to a variety of projectors or presentation devices. Video-out is a standard feature of many models, as is video mirroring.

▶ *Spooling of print documents for later printing*—You can send documents to a printer with a Print Later feature, which is enabled by the Assistant toolbox extension (downloadable from the Apple Tech Info Library at http://til.info.apple.com). When you try to print to a printer that isn't connected, you will get a dialog box asking if you want the document stored. Printing occurs automatically the next time you connect to that printer.

▶ *Input support*—Keyboards, trackballs, trackpads, and other ADB devices are supported, as with any desktop Mac. Figure 6.2 shows the two Trackpad settings that are available to allow you to customize your mouse movements.

▶ *File synchronization*—To synchronize files, folders, and disks on a PowerBook with your other Macintosh computers, you can use the File Synchronization Control Panel (in place of the Macintosh File Assistant, used in earlier versions of the Mac OS for synchronizing files).

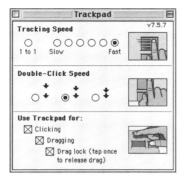

Figure 6.2 Set cursor speed and double-click speed in the Trackpad Control Panel.

Mac OS 8.6 includes a number of features that PowerBook users will appreciate, notably the always-convenient Control Strip and the Location Manager. Many other PowerBook utilities have been reworked to a small extent in Mac OS 8.6, but the changes are generally insignificant.

There is much to know about PowerBooks and not enough space in this book to cover it. Unfortunately, very few up-to-date books about PowerBooks exist, but you can always find plenty of information on the Web at the following URLs:

➤ *Apple Computer's PowerBook site*—www.apple.com/powerbook

➤ *O'Grady's PowerPage*—www.ogrady.com

➤ *The PowerBook Guy*—www.powerbookguy.com

➤ *PowerBook Army*—www.powerbook.org

➤ *PowerBook Owners Club (Italian)*—www.powerclub.org

➤ *The PowerBook Source*—www.pbsource.com

➤ *PowerBook Avenue (Italian)*—www.macity.it/powerbook/

Jason O'Grady's site, shown in Figure 6.3, really stands out. Visit his site frequently for the latest scoop on PowerBooks, software, and hardware.

Power/Performance Management

Some models of PowerPC-based PowerBooks consume more power than others. The power consumption of PowerBooks is a major portability issue, particularly for users with CD-ROM and Zip drives (which consume more battery power). Luckily, Mac OS 8.6 employs a number of techniques to reduce power consumption through the Energy Saver Control Panel. Its basic view is shown in Figure 6.4.

Mac OS 8.6

Figure 6.3 O'Grady's PowerPage is one of the best Web sites for PowerBook enthusiasts.

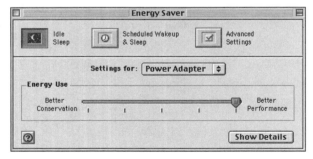

Figure 6.4 The Energy Saver Control Panel.

You want easy? Move the Battery Conservation slider to the Better Conservation side to increase battery longevity when you aren't plugged in. Move the setting to Better Performance when you are plugged in. Your PowerBook translates your settings into the time it takes to dim your screen, spin down your hard drive, and go to system sleep, among other things. As a rule of thumb, use Better Conservation when you are on the road until you notice performance differences that bother you.

To fine-tune your power consumption, click the Show Details button to reveal more configuration options. The Energy Saver on the PowerBook looks much like that on a desktop Mac, but with two important additions:

➤ Different settings for when the PowerBook is running on the power adapter or off the battery, as in Figure 6.5.

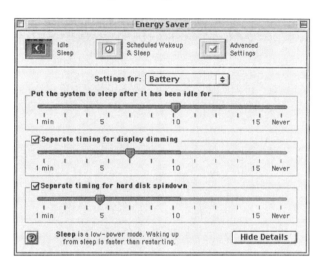

Figure 6.5 PowerBooks have different settings for the two types of power sources, the AC power adapter and internal batteries.

➤ A new Advanced Settings section, which provides additional configuration options for network connectivity issues and for additional ways to conserve power, as in Figure 6.6.

Experiment with the various options in the Energy Saver to determine the settings that are best for you. To help gauge your power consumption, you can monitor your battery's performance by viewing the Battery menu bar icon (top) or the Battery Monitor Control Strip module (bottom); both are shown in Figure 6.7. This battery meter has 10 levels that change color as a function of your battery's voltage level. When all eight bars are colored, your battery is fully recharged. Bars fade to white from top to bottom as the battery is depleted. You'll be given more than one warning about power depletion before the final warning, which is 10 seconds before your PowerBook is sent to sleep.

This system of measuring voltage levels is accurate and reliable—as far as it goes. What voltage measurements don't tell you, though, is how much time your battery

Mac OS 8.6

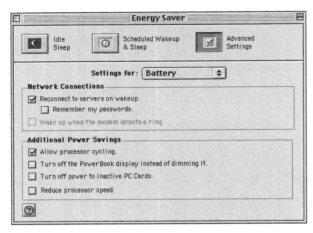

Figure 6.6 The Energy Saver provides new features in Mac OS 8.6 to help you extend the life of your battery's charge.

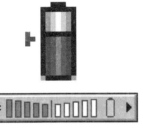

Figure 6.7 The Battery menu (top) and the Battery Monitor (bottom).

has left. For that indicator, you need to know the lowest voltage level your battery will drop to, your instantaneous power consumption, and your history of power consumption. Variables such as which battery you're using, memory effects, and unusual power consumption activities make learning about your battery's life a difficult proposition. So bear in mind that the power warnings only tell you voltage levels, not how much energy remains in a battery.

Accurate measurement of battery life is so valuable that some batteries contain microprocessors to help calculate performance. These batteries give more accurate measurements in the Battery Monitor section of the PowerBook Control Strip, and an estimated time is given in hours.

The microprocessor itself is a major energy draw, using about 25 percent of your battery's current. The display is another major power draw; depending on its type, it can consume anywhere from 20 percent (gray scale) to 50 percent (color) of your power supply. Display issues are covered in the next section of this chapter.

Most current-model PowerBooks contain a microprocessor capable of lower energy consumption states. In one state, the CPU goes down to a lower clock rate. This feature, called processor *cycling*, can save energy when you use it. This state is different from the processor *sleep state*, in which only CPU memory is preserved.

To turn on processor cycling, go to the Advanced Settings section of the Energy Saver Control Panel, and click the Allow Processor Cycling check box in the Additional Power Savings section. Because it allows your processor to fire up instantaneously, processor cycling is preferable to hard drive spindown when you're on battery power.

During sleep, your hard drive spins down, your screen is powered off, and your microprocessor is in a comatose-like state. Each component can be put to sleep separately. You can safely transport your PowerBook, or store it for short periods of time, while it is asleep. Depending on the model, your PowerBook can retain contents of memory for two weeks in this state. However, the amount of memory that needs to be refreshed is a major variable in this equation; larger amounts of RAM require additional battery power to maintain contents during sleep.

In Mac OS 8.6, you have several ways of putting your PowerBook to sleep:

➤ Choose the Sleep command from the Special menu.

➤ Press the Command+Shift+Zero keystroke (added by the Assistant toolbox).

➤ Set the period of inactivity for automatic sleep in the Energy Saver Control Panel.

➤ Choose Sleep Now in the Energy Saver Control Strip module.

➤ Press the Power key on the keyboard and click the Sleep button (or press the letter S on the keyboard).

To wake up your Macintosh, press any key other than the Caps Lock key.

Your hard drive consumes, on average, about 15 percent of your battery power. You can improve the power consumption of this element with any of the following methods:

➤ Use memory-resident (RAM) applications that don't require much I/O.

➤ Press the Command+Shift+Control+Zero keystroke to spin down your hard drive instantly (added by the Assistant toolbox).

➤ Set the period of inactivity necessary for automatic hard drive spindown in the Energy Saver Control Panel.

Mac OS 8.6

➤ Click the HD Spin Down icon in the Control Strip.

➤ Choose Spin Down Hard Disk from the Energy Saver Control Strip.

➤ Use a RAM disk to limit disk access. (This feature is covered in Chapter 9 and is part of the Memory Control Panel.)

Don't get too carried away with keeping your hard drive spun down. The energy expended in spinning up a hard drive is equivalent to something like 30 to 60 seconds of the hard drive spinning at its rated speed. For this feature to be valuable, you would need to be in situations in which you don't access the disk more often than every two or three minutes.

Keeping AppleTalk active draws a noticeable amount of power as well. It perpetually polls the serial port for activity. You can turn AppleTalk on and off using the AppleTalk Control Panel or the Control Strip. File Sharing, which makes the disk less apt to spin down, is another variable to consider; you can also turn it on and off from the File Sharing icon in the Control Strip.

Display Management

You can achieve substantial battery savings by simply turning down your display screen. This savings is particularly true for PowerBooks with large (greater than 12 inches) active-matrix screens. The Energy Saver will make your screen blank (not dim) after some period of inactivity. You can manually dim your screen using the slider or button on your PowerBook (you may be surprised by the substantial amount of dimming possible in low-light conditions). If you want finer control, however, you should purchase a third-party utility such as KeyQuencer (www.binarysoft.com).

The capacity for connecting an external monitor is one of the best features of a PowerBook. Most models have built-in video support and video-out ports, signified by the TV-like icon on the back of the PowerBook; other models can be supplemented by adding video-out through external devices. You can also buy adapters to run a monitor from your SCSI chain or PC card slot with somewhat lower performance quality. The latest PowerBooks utilize an SVGA (36-pin) video-out, which is the standard for Windows-based PCs. An SVGA-to-Mac video adapter that will enable you to connect the video-out port to an external Apple-style monitor should be supplied with your PowerBook.

You can plug in a monitor during sleep or at shutdown. When you start up your PowerBook, make sure the external monitor is already powered up. After the startup icons appear on your PowerBook, the desktop should appear on the external monitor. If the desktop does not appear, open the Monitors & Sound Control

Panel and make the appropriate selections. Also, note the difference in the Monitors & Sound Control Panel before and after an external monitor is connected. Figure 6.8 reveals the differences in the Monitors & Sound Control Panel before (top) and after a generic 17-inch multiscan display has been connected, including the change in the name of the window from Color LCD to Display, and the additional resolutions that are enabled. The three resolution options at the bottom of the list (the ones including the words "built-in") are the same as those in the Color LCD window.

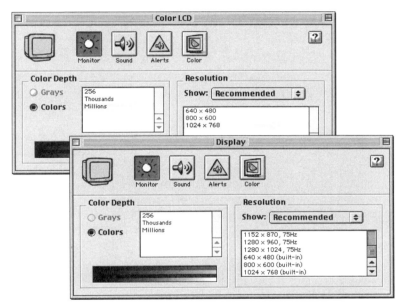

Figure 6.8 The Monitors & Sound Control Panel before (top) and after (bottom) connecting an external display.

You can put your PowerBook into sleep mode when an external monitor is in use only if the monitor is Energy Star compliant. Monitors that are not compliant will not power down, although the PowerBook's processor and hard drive will. For larger external displays, it is recommended that you leave processor cycling turned on so that your battery can recharge and doesn't get too hot. External screen blanking will occur based on your setting in the Energy Saver Control Panel. You can also turn down your PowerBook screen manually. Almost any activity will turn your screen back on; including keystrokes or tapping the trackpad.

When working in presentation mode, you may find it convenient to have the display on your external monitor match the one that appears on your PowerBook. This process is called video mirroring. To turn on video mirroring, open the Monitors &

Sound Control Panel and click the Arrange button, or activate the Video Mirroring module from the Control Strip. If these options are not available, then your PowerBook (or desktop Mac) doesn't support video mirroring.

SCSI Disk Mode

Mac OS 8.6 makes connecting your PowerBook to other Macs and file servers easier than ever before. Most of these features are similar for desktop Macs and PowerBooks; the features that are different for PowerBooks are discussed here.

The so-called *SCSI disk mode*—the ability to mount a PowerBook as an external SCSI hard drive—is enabled using the PowerBook SCSI Disk Mode Control Panel, shown in Figure 6.1. SCSI (small computer serial interface) is a high-speed, directly connected data bus. Mounting a PowerBook as an external hard drive to another Mac via SCSI can be convenient for file synchronization or copying large amounts of data. See "File Synchronization" later in this chapter for more information on maintaining groups of files in two locations.

> **TIP**
> You need to pay special attention to SCSI termination for PowerBook chains; otherwise, you can run into trouble with the SCSI disk mode. Refer to your PowerBook manual or third-party books for more details. Also, you should always shut down your PowerBook before making or breaking SCSI connections.

To connect a PowerBook using PowerBook SCSI Disk Mode, follow these steps:

1. Open the PowerBook SCSI Disk Mode Control Panel and select an SCSI ID number that doesn't conflict with another device on the other Mac.
2. Turn off password protection in the PowerBook Security Control Panel.
3. Shut off both the PowerBook and the other Mac.
4. Connect the two computers using a SCSI Disk Adapter and the proper SCSI cable.
5. Turn on the PowerBook and then the other Mac.

The only catch to all this is that if your PowerBook's hard drive is formatted using HFS+ (a.k.a. extended format), the other Mac must be using Mac OS 8.1 or higher in order to read the file system.

Remounting Servers

In earlier versions of the Mac OS, it was possible to reconnect to a file server after waking up from sleep using the AutoRemounter Control Panel. When your PowerBook went to sleep or disconnected from a network server, volumes were dismounted. AutoRemounter remembered these connections and automatically remounted disks when waking by requiring that a password be entered or by entering it for you.

TIP
It's safer to have a password requested automatically when you are connected to a network and are leaving your PowerBook on.

AutoRemounter, which first shipped in System 7.1, did not work with early PowerBooks (100, 140, 145, and 170); you had to mount your volumes manually and reestablish network connections. Under Mac OS 8.6, the features of AutoRemounter have been incorporated into the Network Connections section of the Energy Saver Control Panel. Figure 6.9 shows these options in the old AutoRemounter (top) and in the Energy Saver Control Panel (bottom).

Figure 6.9   The Network Connections section of the Energy Saver Control Panel replaces the AutoRemounter as a way to reconnect to shared servers after waking up from sleep.

In addition to reconnecting to servers after waking up and automatically entering the appropriate password, the Energy Saver Control Panel can also wake up a PowerBook if the modem detects an incoming call. This feature is useful if you have Apple Remote Access installed, fax software, or other telecommunications software. Not all modems support this capability, however.

Mac OS 8.6

Apple Remote Access

Apple Remote Access (ARA) is a telecommunications application that allows two or more Macs to communicate via modem as if they were on the same network. ARA, which began as a PowerBook-specific application, is mentioned here in passing because it is a terrific product that can connect you to remote servers via modem while you are on the road. Apple Remote Access is also sold in various server configurations to allow multiple users to connect to a network server; the ARA client, shown in Figure 6.10, is now a standard component of the Mac OS.

Figure 6.10 The Apple Remote Access Control Panel.

You can set up your desktop Mac to receive incoming calls and then dial into it using ARA. Using the Apple Remote Access MultiPort Server, you can configure a Macintosh to accept several incoming ARA sessions. Some companies also sell dedicated multiline ARA servers that replace a Macintosh and a set of modems.

Once you supply a password or have ARA supply it automatically, you will be connected to the Mac or the server just as you would be in an office. Modem connections are a slow data exchange medium, so without fast modems, ARA is best used as a message exchange medium. For high-speed modems (56k), you can use ARA to do large file exchanges using File Sharing, remote database work with serious data manipulation, and other tasks. We'll look more at ARA as a networking tool in Part III.

The PowerBook Control Strip

Because third parties expressed so much interest in PowerBook utilities and the class of application has been so popular, Apple decided to include the Control Strip with all versions of the Mac OS. By default it's turned on and visible on your screen. To turn off the Control Strip, use the Control Strip Control Panel shown in Figure 6.11 and choose Hide Control Strip.

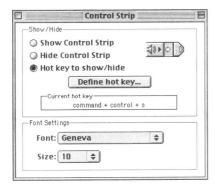

Figure 6.11 The PowerBook Control Strip Control Panel.

The Control Strip, shown in Figure 6.12 along with the Control Strip Modules folder, is a floating palette that appears as the topmost window on your PowerBook screen, regardless of your current application. It's one of Mac OS's best small features.

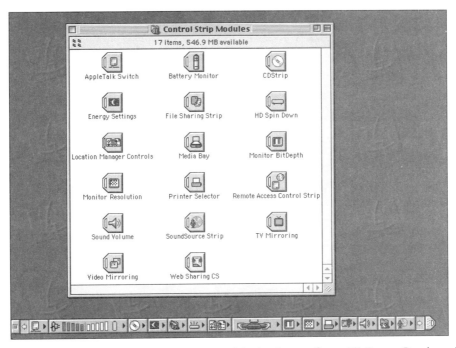

Figure 6.12 The PowerBook Control Strip shown for a G3 PowerBook series computer running Mac OS 8.6.

On a PowerBook, the Control Strip works just as it does on a desktop or server Macintosh. It also contains several additional modules that are unique to Power-Books. Each icon contains a pop-up menu that enables you to select from a set of options. Most are simple on and off settings, but more commands may be added over time. Many additional Control Strip modules are available from software developers. It is now par for the course for these developers to create modules along with their applications and utilities.

The Control Strip has the following features (from left to right):

- *Close box*—Click to compress the strip down to just the Control Tab. To remove the Control Strip, use the Control Strip Control Panel shown in Figure 6.12.

- *Scroll arrows*—Use these arrows (on both ends of the strip) to view additional modules that may be hidden.

- *AppleTalk switch*—By turning AppleTalk off, you can save power. This switch duplicates the function found in the AppleTalk Control Panel.

- *Battery Monitor*—The monitor indicates both voltage and estimated battery lifetime. Icons indicate if the battery is full, discharging, or charging.

- *CDStrip*—If your PowerBook sports a CD-ROM drive, you can control the playing of audio CDs from here.

- *Energy Settings*—This feature provides quick access to the main features of the Energy Saver Control Panel.

- *File Sharing*—You can manually turn File Sharing on and off using this module. You can also check to see who's connected. This panel duplicates functions found in the File Sharing Control Panel.

- *HD Spin Down*—This feature spins down your drive.

- *Location Manager*—This lets you quickly switch between location settings using the Location Manager (see the section in this chapter entitled "Location Manager" for more information).

- *Media Bay*—This module identifies what devices occupy each of your PowerBook's media bays, such as a floppy drive, CD-ROM, Zip drive, or battery.

- *Monitor BitDepth*—This feature lets you change the bit depth of your display, which controls the number of colors or shades of gray.

- *Monitor Resolution*—This feature lets you change the resolution of your display (for PowerBooks that support this feature, such as the G3 models).

- *Printer Selector*—This module allows you to choose between different desktop printers.

- *ARA*—This module provides access to the main components of the Apple Remote Access Control Panel, such as Connect and Disconnect.
- *Sound Volume*—Drag to the sound level you desire. This feature re-creates the sound slider in the Sound Control Panel.
- *Web Sharing*—This module allows you to turn on and off the Mac OS's personal Web server.
- *SoundSource*—The SoundSource module allows you to easily select the sound-in source for recording sounds, such as the CD-ROM or an external microphone.
- *Tab*—Drag the Tab to resize the Control Strip. Click the Tab to shrink the strip to just the Tab. When you are viewing just the Tab, click the Tab to view the Control Strip again.

You will note some differences between Control Strips installed on different models of PowerBooks, and between the modules installed in the Control Strip Modules folder. For example, only intelligent batteries give time estimates, and only models with video-out capabilities support the video mirroring panel. Although a module may be present, it will not appear in the Control Strip itself unless it is supported by your particular model of PowerBook (or desktop).

Here are some tips to help you customize the Control Strip:

- To shorten the Control Strip, drag the Tab to the left.
- You can view modules in the shortened strip by clicking the left- and right-facing arrows at the end of the Control Strip.
- To collapse the Control Strip to just a Tab, click the Close box at the left of the strip (or on the right, if you have the Control strip on the right side of the screen).
- Don't like the order of the icons? It's easy to customize the Control Strip. To reorder the modules as they appear in the strip, Option+click on the item and drag it to where you'd like it to be.
- To move the entire Control Strip, Option+click the end tab and move it up, down, left, or right. The Control Strip may only be in a horizontal position, however.
- To remove an icon from the strip, remove it from the Control Strip Items folder inside your System folder.

File Synchronization

When you use two or more computers for your work, you always want to be sure that you're working with the most current versions of your files. A procedure called *file synchronization* makes it easy to keep track of your file changes. With this utility,

Mac OS 8.6

you can designate files and folders that you want updated. File synchronization is basic and easy to learn—you only need to connect your two computers directly via a network or with modems to use, or you can practice by synchronizing the contents of two folders on your PowerBook.

In the File Synchronization dialog box that appears when you launch the program (see Figure 6.13), you can simply drag and drop files and folders that you want synchronized. You designate pairs of items on either side of the arrow as linked sets. You can create as many pairs as you wish and scroll the window to review them. Using the Preferences command from the File menu, you can also link nonmatching folders.

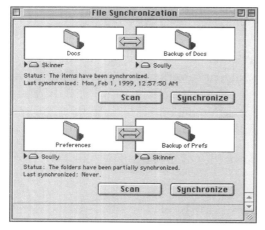

Figure 6.13 The File Synchronization Setup dialog box.

You can specify whether synchronization is manual or automatic via commands on the Synchronize menu shown in Figure 6.14. Other options allow you to choose the direction of the updating. A double-headed arrow will update either file whenever changes are made. Single-headed arrows are most useful when you want to use the server to update a file on your hard disk.

Figure 6.14 The File menu in the File Synchronization Control Panel.

Mac OS 8.6

After you've set up File Synchronization, connect the two computers and run it. The Synchronize command (Command+G) begins the process. If you select a manual synchronization, you'll need to click the arrow outline to synchronize each pair.

For automatic synchronization (selected in the Synchronize menu), you can use the Energy Saver to reconnect shared disks and then place an alias of the File Synchronization in your Startup Items folder. Whenever you start up your PowerBook or remount drives after waking up from sleep mode, your files are automatically updated.

Three types of actions are monitored by the File Synchronization: modifications of files and folders, deletions of missing and moved files and folders, and the replacement of a file with another of the same name. Table 6.1 summarizes the results based on your settings.

Location Manager

As you've noticed, there's a plethora of controls on your Mac, and many of them change depending on where you are. For instance, maybe the printer you use at the office is different from the printer you use at home. Perhaps your office uses an Ethernet-based TCP/IP connection, while at home you use PPP and a dial-up account.

Changing all of these settings just to go home can be a major pain, so Apple devised the Location Manager. The Location Manager lets you create a snapshot of the settings you use at particular locations and switch between them. For PowerBook owners, this is one of the coolest features of the Mac OS. In the old days, you would have to spend 15 minutes fighting with various Control Panels every time you moved to a new place. Now, you can set the Location Manager once and use different configurations of preferences as you move about.

Table 6.1 Actions monitored by File Synchronization.

Left File	Right File	Result
Changes	Doesn't Change	The right file is updated.
Doesn't Change	Changes	For a two-way update, the left file is updated. For a left-to-right update, there are no changes.
Doesn't Change	Deleted	For a two-way update, you get a message asking you whether you want to delete the left file. For a left-to-right update, the right file is updated.
Deleted	Unchanged	You get a message asking you whether you wish to delete the right file.

Mac OS 8.6

To create a set of preferences, first you must create a new location by choosing New Location from the File menu in the Location Manager. Give the location a name, such as Home Office, shown in Figure 6.15.

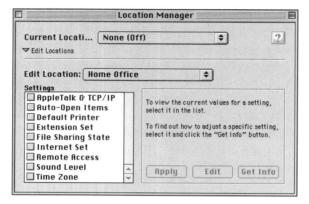

Figure 6.15 The Location Manager lets you pick your current location and resets all of your PowerBook's important settings to match.

It takes a while to set everything up, but the task is made easier by the fact that you don't have to set up items you don't care about. For instance, if you don't want to have your AppleTalk settings change, you can skip over that item. This can save loads of time up front. You may activate, edit, and deactivate settings for each of the following:

➤ AppleTalk & TCP/IP

➤ Auto-Open Items

➤ Default Printer

➤ Extension Set

➤ File Sharing State

➤ Internet Set

➤ Remote Access

➤ Sound Level

➤ Time Zone

Figure 6.16 shows a customized location for a sample home office with all unused settings hidden from view (Command+T). If you need more information about a particular setting category, highlight it and click the Get Info button.

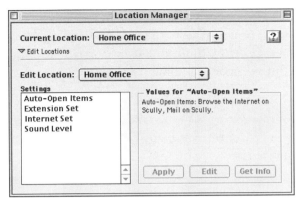

Figure 6.16 You can add nearly any kind of setting to a location. Here, I'm making sure the speaker volume is at a low setting when I'm in the office.

Security

If there's a downside to PowerBook ownership, it's that everyone wants to get their grubby paws on yours. PowerBooks are so fun and cool that sometimes it seems that everyone wants to borrow yours—sometimes without asking!

In the event that someone tries to boot your PowerBook and poke around, you can protect it with a password of your choosing using the Password Security Control Panel shown in Figure 6.17. Just enter a password in this dialog box, confirm it, and the next time you boot the machine, it'll demand a password before anything will load.

Figure 6.17 You can password-protect your main PowerBook volume with this Control Panel.

TIP

Be very careful with the password feature—it's easy to forget a password, and if that were to happen, you'd be out of luck. The only ways to recover from a forgotten password is to reformat the hard drive or to pay a visit to your nearest Apple-authorized repair center. They can recover your data, but it won't be free!

Also, if you partition your drive into multiple volumes, keep in mind that only the boot volume is password-protected. A user without the password could hook your PowerBook up to another Mac using the SCSI disk mode and mount any other nonboot volumes. Keep all sensitive data on your boot volume.

The Password Security Control Panel has a few features to help protect your PowerBook and to keep you from forgetting your password. To configure these features, open the Password Security Control Panel and click the Setup button, the result of which is shown in Figure 6.18.

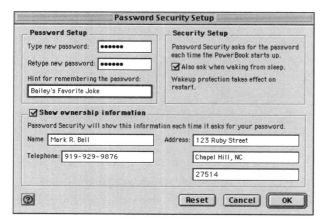

Figure 6.18 Configure several helpful features in the Setup section of the Password Security Control Panel.

For starters, enter a hint to remind you of your password, and as much personal contact information as you're willing to reveal to potential viewers. However, you shouldn't use anything like your Social Security number or anything else that could compromise your personal or financial security. You never know when your Power-Book will be lost or stolen, and this information might make the difference between having it returned or buying a new PowerBook. When started up, the new dialog box looks like the one shown in Figure 6.19.

Figure 6.19 Enter additional information in the Setup portion of the Password Security Control Panel to provide password hints and contact information.

Mac OS 8.6

Finally, you can add an additional layer of security by requiring a password whenever your PowerBook wakes from sleep mode. This could be irritating for some users depending on the frequency with which the PowerBook sleeps. On the other hand, it could help keep prying eyes away from sensitive data.

Wrapping Up

Mobile computing offers different ways of computing, and the freedom comes with a few limitations and risks. In this chapter, you learned:

➤ How to make your PowerBook last longer on a battery charge

➤ How to connect an external monitor and how to synchronize files and folders

➤ How to connect your PowerBook locally or remotely

➤ How to utilize the Control Strip

➤ How to synchronize sets of files and folders

➤ How to create sets of preferences for using your PowerBook in multiple locations

➤ How to make your PowerBook secure

This chapter concludes the first part of this book. In the next section we'll look at applications and using them under Mac OS 8.6. In the first chapter in this section, we'll examine how the Mac OS works with various applications and the Stationery Documents feature.

PART II

Applications

Mac OS 8.6 And Your Software

Thus far, we've discussed the Mac OS 8.6 features that change the way you organize and manipulate data files at the OS level. But as important as the OS is, it's not the reason you use a Macintosh. You use the Mac because its software applications—word processors, spreadsheets, databases, graphics programs, and the rest—help you accomplish your work effectively.

In this chapter, we'll look at some of the ways Mac OS 8.6 affects software applications, beginning with the important issue of compatibility. Then we'll see the expanded launching methods, new stationery documents, and Desktop-level enhancements Mac OS 8.6 provides. Other major enhancements that affect software applications, including data sharing, program-to-program communication, and support for TrueType and PostScript fonts, are discussed in Chapters 10 and 11.

Mac OS 8.6 Compatibility

A new software upgrade is always exciting—it means more features, better performance, and an easier-to-use interface. As seasoned computer users know, however, software upgrades often introduce bugs and incompatibilities along with improvements and solutions. Every Macintosh application is heavily dependent on the operating system, which makes applications particularly susceptible to upgrade-compatibility problems. Each application must be fine-tuned and coordinated to function smoothly with the OS. The relationship between the Mac OS and an application is like that of two juggling partners, each throwing balls into the air that the other is expected to catch. When the OS is upgraded, a new partner replaces a familiar one; the routine may stay the same, but there's no time to practice, and no room for error.

During the development of System 7, Apple worked hard to ensure that it was compatible with as many existing applications as possible. (The beta version of System 7 was distributed to many thousands of people using a variety of applications and Macintosh models.) In fact, Apple claimed that any application running under System 6.0.x would operate under System 7 without alteration, as long as the application was programmed according to System 7's widely published programming rules. Most major applications, as well as a great many utility programs, were compatible with System 7's initial release. Many utility programs whose functions were to modify or extend the system software itself were not initially compatible.

Now, many years after the introduction of System 7, it's almost impossible to find an application or utility that isn't compatible with it. Most programs written or updated in that time period have been created or modified with System 7 (or later) in mind. Mac OS 8.6 continues this trend of extending operating system capabilities while maintaining a high level of backward compatibility with the existing third-party software library.

The introduction of Mac OS 8.6 brings additional changes and more capabilities to the Mac OS, yielding yet another set of potential problems. Very few programs—again, usually utilities that modify or extend the system—have proven incompatible, however. It's more likely that the new capabilities of the OS make many programs you currently use in your working environment obsolete.

What Is Compatibility?

Generally speaking, an application must run under Mac OS 8.0 or higher and provide the same features with the same degree of reliability to be considered *compatible* with Mac OS 8.6. Compatibility can exist in varying degrees in different applications, however. Most compatible applications will launch and provide basic operations under Mac OS 8.6 and operate correctly in Mac OS 8.6's multitasking, multithreaded, and PowerPC-native environment.

Applications that are System 7-compatible will probably survive under Mac OS 8.6, but applications that are Mac OS 8-savvy will thrive. These applications are specifically written to take full advantage of Mac OS 8.6, and must do the following:

▶ *Support multitasking*—Mac OS 8.6 lets your Mac open multiple applications and process data simultaneously. Applications should be able to operate in both the foreground and the background and should support background processing to the greatest degree possible.

▶ *Be 32-bit clean*—Mac OS 8.6 uses a 32-bit memory addressing scheme, but many older applications were written to use the Mac OS when it supported a 24-bit memory addressing scheme that limited computers to only 8MB of RAM. The Memory Control Panel in older versions of the OS allowed users to turn 32-bit addressing on or off, increasing software compatibility. In Mac OS 8.6, however, applications may not run if they are not 32-bit clean.

▶ *Support the Edition Manager's Publish and Subscribe features*—The Edition Manager, described in Chapter 12, allows data to be transferred from one application to another while maintaining a link to the original file. Applications must include the basic Publish and Subscribe commands.

▶ *Support AppleEvents and Core events*—Mac OS 8.6's Inter-Application Communication (IAC), also described in Chapter 12, defines a basic set of AppleEvents that allow one application to communicate with another.

▶ *Impose no limit on font sizes*—Applications should support all font sizes, from 1 to 32,000 in single-point increments, and others should support fonts up to 127 points.

▶ *Provide Balloon Help*—As described in Chapter 3, Balloon Help offers quick pop-up summaries of an application's menu commands, dialog box options, and graphic elements.

▶ *Mac OS Help and Apple Guide support*—The ability to work with a customized Mac OS Help and Apple Guide help system is universal for Macintosh applications. All Macintosh applications are intrinsically "Apple Guide aware," but only newer applications have been revised to take advantage of the new Mac OS Help format. Mac OS Help support is therefore really dependent on whether developers have added this technology to their products.

▶ *Be AppleShare-compliant*—Mac OS 8.6 allows any user to access files shared on AppleShare servers or files from other Macintoshes using File Sharing. Applications should operate correctly when launched over an AppleTalk network or when reading or writing data stored on personal File Sharing or AppleShare volumes.

▶ *Support stationery documents*—Applications should be able to take full advantage of stationery documents, a type of document template featured in System 7.x and later. (See the section entitled "Stationery Documents," later in this chapter.)

Mac OS 8.6 uses other technologies that "savvy" applications should utilize in order to be truly compatible. These technologies include the following:

▶ *AppleScript*—Two levels of AppleScript awareness are recognized. An application is called *scriptable* if it can be controlled by an external AppleScript. A scriptable application contains a dictionary of AppleScript programming verbs and objects supported by the application.

The second level of AppleScript awareness is called *recordable* if the application allows the user to record actions and compose a script reflecting that action using the AppleScript recorder function. Recordable is a lower level of compatibility—it's more like being "aware" than being scriptable. Refer to Chapter 13 for a discussion of AppleScript.

- *Macintosh Drag and Drop*—Drag-and-drop actions can be data transfers within a file, between files, and to the Desktop as clippings, or between applications and the Mac OS, such as Internet clippings that open in the correct application when clicked, such as an Internet URL clipping opening in a Web browser. Additional drag-and-drop techniques let the user initiate processes such as opening a file, printing data, and others. No standard for "full" support exists, but programs such as SimpleText, the Scrapbook, Find File, and other system software come closest. Applications may implement any subset of these features.

- *Navigational Services*—Mac OS 8.5 introduced a new way to navigate Open and Save dialog boxes, and more applications are being written or revised to take advantage of these new features in Mac OS 8.6 as well.

- PowerPC-native code—Since Mac OS 8.5 and later only runs on Macs with a PowerPC processor, a truly optimized and Mac OS 8.6-compliant program will not contain code written for the old Motorola 68000-series of processors.

Whew! That's quite a list. Of course, you have to be careful not to take the "savvy" label too seriously. Many great applications have been upgraded to take full advantage of Mac OS 8.6 but cannot be officially categorized as "savvy." The usual reason is that the programs' developers intentionally decided not to implement one or more of the required items because such features were either unimportant or inapplicable for that application. Sometimes developers use different programming and interface models in their applications, especially when Microsoft Windows applications are converted into applications for the Mac OS. In these cases, windows and dialog boxes often appear very differently than when an application has been written for the Mac from the ground up.

For instance, many applications don't support Balloon Help or Mac OS Help. Some vendors will undoubtedly choose to promote their own online help system in place of Apple Guide. Microsoft is also implementing Object Linking & Embedding (OLE), a compound document technology that competes with Publish and Subscribe. Finally, some of the core system software technologies are complex, multifaceted, and still developing—which will make their adoption slow in coming.

Launching

Double-click, double-click, double-click. That's how most Macintosh users launch their software applications. Two clicks to open the drive or volume, two to open the application folder, and two on the application icon to launch the software.

This method can quickly grow wearisome when it means clicking through many volumes and folder layers to reach the icon you want. As alternatives, a wide range of application launching utilities—including GoMac, Drag Thing, and The Tilery—have emerged. With these utilities, you can launch by selecting application names from a list or button instead of searching through folders for icons. Two- and four-button mice, now available for the Mac OS, allow you to assign button combinations so that a function normally commanded by a double-click can be activated by a single click. And as we've seen, Mac OS 8.6 will allow you to view an item as a button, which is opened using a single click, instead of an icon.

Mac OS 8.6 offers several ways to launch files or applications. You can use the Recent Documents or Recent Applications submenu off the Apple menu (discussed in previous chapters). With the File Exchange Control Panel, applications can do transparent file translation, enabling a drag-and-drop-type process. Lastly, the Launcher Control Panel allows you to group applications and documents for easy launching. Any object that can have an alias—a file, application, AppleScript, server, and so on—can be added to the Launcher window. Activating that object is then just a click away in the Launcher window. We'll look at File Exchange and the Launcher in more detail in this section.

You can now launch applications in each of the following ways:

➤ *Double-click an application icon*—You can double-click an application icon, or its alias, to launch that application.

➤ *Double-click a document icon or its alias*—If the application that created a document is unavailable, the new "file not found" dialog box, shown in Figure 7.1, will appear. If you encounter this dialog box when trying to open a document, you must either locate the original application or use another application that can open that type of document.

Figure 7.1 This error message indicates that the original file could not be found.

For example, suppose a WordPerfect file displays this error when double-clicked. You could open Microsoft Word and then access the file using the Open command under Word's File menu. Similarly, GraphicConverter can open Photoshop files, and many applications can open TIFF or EPS files. Most applications can open documents of several different file types. The Control Panel called File Exchange, which is discussed in the next chapter, addresses this situation.

➤ *Double-click a stationery document or its alias*—Stationery documents are template documents that create untitled new documents automatically when opened. (More about stationery documents appears in the section entitled "Stationery Documents," later in this chapter.)

➤ *Drag a document icon onto an application icon*—This method of launching will work only when the document is dragged onto the icon of the application that created it.

You'll know whether an application is going to launch; its icon will be highlighted when the document icon is dragged above it. Application icons will highlight only when appropriate documents are positioned above them, as shown in Figure 7.2.

Figure 7.2 Application icons are highlighted when you drag documents over them that they're capable of launching.

➤ *Add applications or documents to the Startup Items folder inside the System folder*—To automatically launch an application or open a document and its application at startup, add the application or document icon, or an alias of the icon, to the Startup Items folder inside the System folder. The application or document will be launched automatically at startup.

➤ *Choose an application or document name from the Apple menu*—After you place an application or document in the Apple Menu Items folder (located within the System folder), the name of the application or document will appear in the Apple menu. The object can then be launched by choosing its name from the Apple menu.

➤ *Choose an application or document name from the Recent Document or Recent Application submenus of the Apple menu*—If you've enabled this option in the Apple Menu Options Control Panel in Mac OS 8.6, a variable number of your most recently accessed files or applications is added to these submenus, as shown in Figure 7.3.

➤ *Choose an item from the Favorites menu*—Choose an item (file, folder, volume, or application) from the Favorites folder under the Apple Menu or within an application that uses the revised Navigational Services dialog boxes for opening and saving documents.

Mac OS 8.6

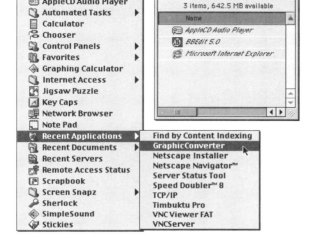

Figure 7.3 Items are launched at startup after you add them to the Startup Items folder, or you can select them from the Apple menu to launch them one at a time.

Launching Methods

There's no one best way to launch applications; choose the method that works best for you. You'll probably find that a combination approach is the most efficient. Keep the following launching tips in mind:

> *The Apple menu*—Add the applications and documents you use most frequently to the Apple menu. If you use a document or program daily, it will probably stay in the Recent Applications or Recent Documents submenu, so you may not need to put it in the Apple menu. Consider your work patterns and personal preferences when organizing your own Apple menu.

> *Alias folders*—Assemble groups of application aliases into folders according to application type, then place these folders in the Apple menu. Alternatively, create a pop-up folder at the bottom of the screen. You can choose the item from the folder in the Apple menu or from the pop-up folder. Figure 7.4 shows a pop-up folder configured using this method.

These methods may be less convenient than relying on the Recent Applications submenu or the Launcher window. There's virtually no setup time involved in configuring the Recent Applications submenu, and it's equally convenient. For the same amount of work as adding a folder of aliases, you can configure the Launcher. In fact, if you've already created a folder of aliases or added aliases to the Apple menu, just copy those aliases to the Launcher Items folder found in your System folder.

Figure 7.4 Application aliases are easy to access when they've been organized in a pop-up folder.

> *Double-click icons*—When you're browsing in Finder windows to locate specific files, use the tried-and-true double-click method to launch applications, aliases, documents, or stationery icons.

> *Drag icons onto applications*—If you store documents and applications or their aliases in the same folder, or if you place application icons or aliases on the Desktop, dragging icons onto applications (or *drop-launching*) may prove useful, although double-clicking the document is often easier. Drop launching is especially useful to open multiple documents by a single application by dragging a group of documents onto an application.

> *Favorites folder*—You can add applications, as well as URLs, documents, and volumes, to the Favorites folder in the Apple Menu, and in Open and Save dialog windows, by selecting Add to Favorites from the Favorites button, shown in Figure 7.5. Once added, you can select them again from the Apple Menu or via an Open or Save dialog window.

The Launcher

The Launcher Control Panel is a way for novice users to launch files, applications, or any other item for which you can create an alias in the Finder. You'll recognize this feature if you've ever worked with Apple's At Ease utility. It's a great time-saver and an absolute boon for novice users, including small children. The features provided by the new Navigational Services (Open and Save dialog windows) might just make the Launcher superfluous at some point in the future of the Mac OS, however.

Mac OS 8.6

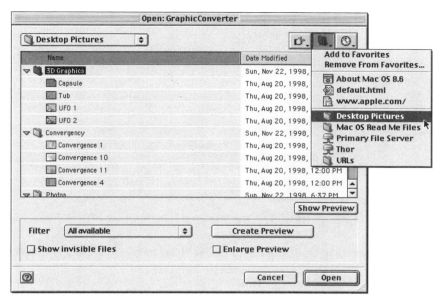

Figure 7.5 Use the Favorites menu to store shortcuts to your favorite applications.

When you use the Launcher and uncheck the Show Desktop When in Background option (found in the General Controls Control Panel), you can prevent users from inadvertently switching to the Finder with a misplaced click, a misstep that can be very confusing to novice users. The combination works well, but it doesn't completely shield the novice user from the Finder because the Launcher itself will be hidden from view when the Finder isn't the front-most application.

To open the Launcher, double-click on the Launcher Control Panel or choose its name from the Control Panel submenu under the Apple menu. You can choose to always show the Launcher upon startup by turning on that option in the Desktop section of the General Controls Control Panel, as shown in Figure 7.6. In this same section, you can turn on Desktop Hiding.

You add items to the Launcher by copying or moving aliases of files, applications, AppleScripts, servers, Control Panels, folders—literally anything you can alias in the Finder—to the Launcher Items folder. This folder is located at the top level of your System folder. You may also create groups within the Launcher by following these steps:

1. Open the Launcher Items folder.
2. Create a new folder by choosing File|New Folder or by pressing Command+N.

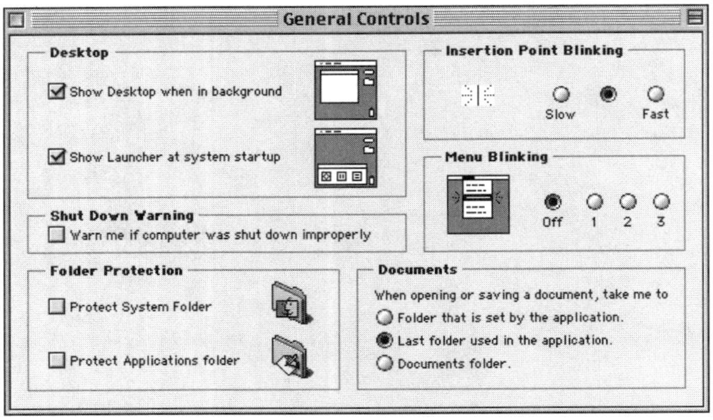

Figure 7.6 The Desktop section of the General Controls Control Panel.

3. Rename the folder with a bullet as the first character (press Option+8 to create a bullet) and a blank space as the second character.

4. Add any items you wish to the new folder. Figure 7.7 shows one additional group in the Launcher Items folder named Utilities. The group named Applications is the default name of the contents of the Launcher Items folder itself and cannot be modified or deleted.

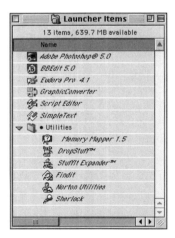

Figure 7.7 The contents of the Launcher Items folder.

If you have a folder of aliases for applications or have added aliases to your Apple Menu Items folder, you may want to copy or move those aliases to the Launcher Items folder to get started. Figure 7.8 shows what the Launcher looks like using the contents of the Launcher Items folder shown in Figure 7.7. You delete items from the Launcher by removing their aliases from that folder.

Figure 7.8 The Launcher with several groups.

Although there isn't much to the Launcher, it's definitely a tremendous time-saver. Click once on an icon to open an object or start a process. The current Launcher is Macintosh Drag and Drop enabled; that is, you can drag a document onto an application icon in the Launcher to have that particular application open it. Remember—you can use the WindowShade feature to minimize the Launcher window when it's not in use.

Stationery Documents

Another useful feature in Mac OS 8.6 is the stationery document. A stationery document is a document that is used as the framework for quickly making an existing document into a template. Templates, as you may know, give you a head start in creating new documents by saving you the time otherwise spent creating the basic features of the document from scratch.

For example, the documents in your word processor probably fall into a handful of specific formats—letters, reports, memos, and so on. Rather than start each new document with a blank, unformatted file, you can use, for example, the stationery document for a letter, which provides the date, salutation, body copy, closing character, paragraph formatting, correct margins, and other basic formatting.

Template support has been available in several Macintosh applications for some time. By adding the stationery documents feature, however, Apple makes templates available in every software package you use to create documents.

Creating A Stationery Document

A stationery document is usually created in three steps:

1. Find an existing example of a document you commonly create.
2. Modify the example document to make it a good generic representation.

3. Save the document as stationery if possible, or select the Stationery Pad option in the file's Get Info dialog box if not.

For example, to create a letter stationery document, open an existing representative document, like the one shown in Figure 7.9. Although this letter is typical, it does have one unusual element—the embedded graphic. Remove that element because most letters do not call for such graphic elements. The remaining letter elements are left to serve as placeholders.

Figure 7.9 A letter that will become a stationery document.

Before you save the letter stationery document, it's a good idea to edit the text in all placeholders so that they're appropriate to use in final documents. Replace placeholder text with nonsensical data (*greeking*), which helps ensure that no placeholder elements are accidentally used in finished documents. For the letter's date, for example, use 00/00/00, and the letter salutation can read Dear Recipient.

You might overlook a date such as 5/1/99 and use it instead of the current date each time you use the stationery document. On the other hand, you're almost certain to notice the 00/00/00 date when you proofread the document. Figure 7.10 shows our sample letter with generic placeholders inserted.

Figure 7.10 After being edited, the stationery document contains placeholders.

After you edit the letter, use the Save As command to save the template document to disk. Use names that are easily identified in Finder windows and dialog box listings: for example, add the letters *stny* to the end of each document name. Although the Mac doesn't require you to use naming conventions (you'll be able to distinguish stationery documents by their icons alone), using distinct filenames will give you an extra advantage when scanning large collections of files for a particular document. See Figure 7.11.

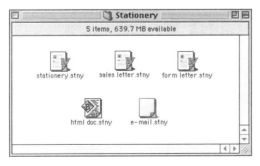

Figure 7.11 A folder containing stationery documents.

One final, critical step remains in the process of creating a stationery document. After you've edited and saved your document, go to the Finder and select the document's icon. Then choose the Get Info command from the File menu. Click in the Stationery check box in the lower right corner of the General Information section of the Get Info dialog box. The icon inside the Get Info dialog box changes to show that the document is now a stationery document. After you close the Get Info dialog box, the conversion is complete.

TIP
Some applications, such as SimpleText and Microsoft Word, give you the option of saving your documents in stationery documents format. Saving this way may be simpler than digging up the Get Info box, particularly if your document is buried several folders deep on your hard drive.

The document's icon in the Finder will also be updated to reflect its new status, but the type of icon that appears depends on the application you used to create the document.

Using Stationery

After you've created a stationery document, you can either launch it from the Desktop by double-clicking its icon or you can open it with the Open command under an application's File menu.

When you launch a stationery document from the Desktop, the document will open in a window that appears to be the original document—in reality, however, it's actually a copy of the stationery. You can see this by looking at the title bar area of the window, which will show the document name as Untitled. Because the stationery document file is duplicated and renamed as Untitled when it's opened, you'll have to manually delete it from your disk if you later decide you don't need this new document. To save the document as a stationery document, choose the appropriate options in the Save As dialog box. For example, Figure 7.12 shows the options available for a SimpleText document being saved as a stationery document.

Note the two document icons in the lower right-hand corner of this figure. The document icon on the left represents a regular SimpleText document, which has one page. The icon on the right, however, appears to have two pages (see the dog-ear tab on the lower-right hand side of the icon). This is a visual signal that the document will be saved as stationery. Once you've opened a copy of a stationery document, you can customize it as needed. Be sure to edit all the placeholders that

Mac OS 8.6 And Your Software   211

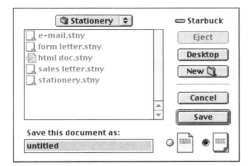

Figure 7.12 A Save dialog box with stationery documents visible.

you set when creating the stationery document. You can delete unnecessary elements, add new ones, and edit the document in any other way you choose.

Stationery Document Tips

Using stationery documents may be a new concept to some, so let's review several tips that might be useful:

➤ *Stationery documents aliases*—Whether they were created before or after the Stationery Documents option was set, aliases of stationery documents will access the stationery documents normally. The alias icon displays the stationery documents icon.

➤ *Stationery documents folder*—Create a stationery or templates folder and keep aliases of all your stationery documents in this folder. Keep the original documents organized as they were originally. This allows easy access to stationery documents when you need them. If you use them frequently, you may want to also put an alias of this folder in your Apple Menu Items folder.

➤ *Application support for multiple documents*—If an application does not support more than one open document at a time, opening a stationery document from the Finder when the application and a document are already open may not work. In this case, close the open document and then reopen the stationery document using the Open command.

➤ *Opening stationery documents with the Open command*—Opening a stationery document from inside an application that isn't "stationery documents aware" may cause problems. The application may open the stationery document itself rather than create a new Untitled copy. When you open stationery documents using the Open command, be sure to assign a new filename using the Save As command so that you don't accidentally overwrite your stationery document.

➤ *Editing stationery documents*—Unselecting the Stationery Documents option in the General Information section of the Get Info dialog box will turn any stationery document back into a "normal" document—it will lose its stationery document properties. You can then edit the stationery document by making changes to your master template. After editing and saving this document, reselect the Stationery Documents option in the Get Info dialog box to turn the file back into a stationery document.

The Desktop Level

It is impossible to work on the Macintosh and not hear—and use—the word *Desktop*, as we've seen in Chapter 3. In Macintosh terminology, *Desktop* usually refers to the onscreen area where volume icons, windows, and the Trash appear. Also, files and folders can be dragged from any mounted volume or folder and placed directly on the Desktop. Access to the Desktop via Open and Save dialog windows has changed over the years, however.

In system software versions prior to System 7, the Desktop was ignored by the Open and Save dialog boxes. In these dialog boxes, each mounted volume was discrete; all files were on disks or in folders, unlike Mac OS 8.6's Desktop, shown in Figure 7.13.

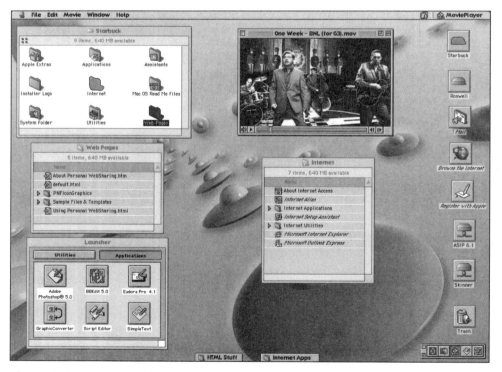

Figure 7.13 The Desktop.

Mac OS 8.6

In System 7, dialog boxes provided access to the Desktop and all volumes, files, and folders that reside on the computer. The Drive button was replaced by a Desktop button that allowed the Desktop view to appear in the scrolling file listing. This Desk-top view displayed the name and icon of each volume, file, and folder that existed on the Desktop. In Figure 7.14 you can see the Open File dialog boxes of Systems 6.0.x and 7.

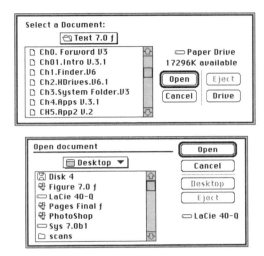

Figure 7.14 A sample dialog box from System 6.0.x (top) and one from System 7 (bottom).

From the Desktop view in these dialog boxes, you could move into any volume, folder, or file on the Desktop by double-clicking a name in the scrolling list, or you could save files directly onto the Desktop. Once any volume or folder was open, the list of files and folders at that location was displayed, and the dialog box operated normally. Saving a file onto the Desktop causes its icon to appear on your Desktop and leaves you free to later drag it onto any volume or folder. Figure 7.15 shows some of the possible volumes that are available when opening a document on the

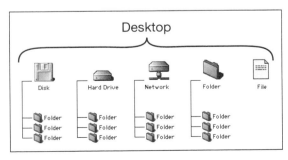

Figure 7.15 The Desktop level offers a bird's-eye view of the available volumes, files, and folders.

Desktop. Note the different icons used by the Mac OS to differentiate between hard drives, floppy drives, and network volumes.

TIP

Saving files to your Desktop writes the actual data to your boot drive (the drive with your System folder on it). Be careful—saving to the Desktop can get confusing if you use multiple drives or volumes.

Figure 7.16 shows the volumes that are available to the application BBEdit when choosing File|Open on the computer whose Desktop is shown in Figure 7.16.

Figure 7.16 The Desktop as seen through the application BBEdit.

Dialog Box Keyboard Equivalents

In addition to having the new Desktop button, all Mac OS 8.6-savvy Open and Save dialog boxes now support a number of keyboard equivalents that make it faster and easier to find and create files. Many of these keyboard commands are also available in applications that support Mac OS 8.x, but are not Mac OS 8.6-savvy:

➤ *Previous or next folder*—To navigate up the folder hierarchy, press the Up arrow key. You can also navigate downward once a subfolder has been highlighted by pressing the Down arrow key.

➤ *Expand and collapse a folder hierarchy*—To expand a highlighted folder within an Open or Save window, press the Right arrow key. To collapse a folder, press the Left arrow key.

➤ *File listing/filename options*—In Save As dialog boxes, pressing the Tab key toggles back and forth between the scrolling file listing and the filename option. You can tell which is activated by the presence of an extra black border, and you can also control the active window from the keyboard. (In earlier

Mac OS 8.6 And Your Software   215

versions of the system software, pressing the Tab key was the equivalent of pressing the Drive button).

When the filename option is active, you can control the cursor position with the arrow keys and, of course, enter any valid filename. When the scrolling file listing is active, use the following keyboard equivalents to locate, select, and manipulate files and folders (see Figure 7.17):

➤ *Jump alphabetically*—Typing any single letter causes the first filename starting with that letter, or the letter closest to it, to be selected.

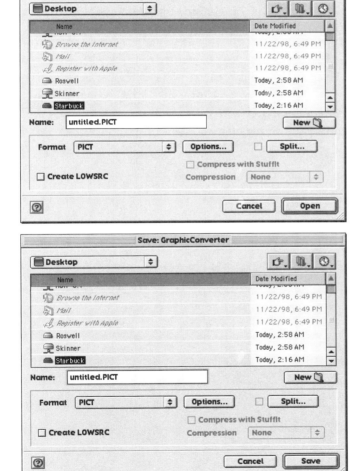

Figure 7.17 A dialog box in which the scrolling list (top) and the Name option box are active (bottom).

➤ *Jump alphabetically and then some*—If you quickly type more than one letter, the Mac OS will continue to narrow down the available filenames accordingly. In other words, typing only the letter *F* will jump you to the first filename that starts with an *F*; typing *FUL* will pass by the file *Finder 8.6 Facts* and select the file named *Fulfillment Info*. When typing multiple characters to find files, you must not pause between characters; otherwise, the Mac will think you're starting a new search. Instead of interpreting your second character as the second letter of a filename, it will treat it as the first letter of a new search.

Wrapping Up

Even the performance of the oldest Macintosh programs improves when used with Mac OS 8.6, as we've seen throughout this chapter. Some improvements are dramatic and substantial, whereas others are more subtle or incidental.

Many people take for granted the Mac OS 8.6's ability to work with other types of computers. In fact, the Mac OS is arguably the most flexible operating system on the market due in part to its minority status. To survive, it has had to be compatible with several different types of computers. As we'll see in the next chapter, the Mac OS gets an A+ on its report card for playing well with others.

Working With Other Types Of Computers

Another of the many great things about using the Mac OS is how well it works with other types of computers: the Mac OS is a good network citizen. When the Macintosh was introduced in 1984, basically only one other type of computer, the IBM PC, was available. Although dozens of others are on the market today, Macs and PC clones account for about 98 percent of the computers in the world. I'd love to be able to tell you that most people use Macs, but that wouldn't be true. The Mac OS is, however, indisputably the easiest operating system in the world to install, maintain, and use in conjunction with other computers—and you can take that to the bank. In this chapter, you'll learn about the software and hardware extensions that allow the Mac to be the best possible corporate citizen.

Sharing Data

Sharing data is one of the most essential tasks that a computer can perform. Applications share data internally (between themselves and the operating system), and they also share data with other computers. You can share data between different computers via three methods:

➤ Physical network (AppleTalk, Ethernet, Token Ring, and so on)

➤ Wireless network (infrared, radio waves, satellite, and so on)

➤ Removable media (floppy, Zip, Jaz, CD-ROM, and so on)

In the early days, when Macs were networked together using AppleTalk and File Sharing (see Part III of this book for all the details), PCs were connected via Sneakernet. To transfer data from one PC to another, you had to put the data onto a big floppy (remember those?), put on your Converse or Adidas sneakers, and walk it on over to the other computer—not very high-tech.

Networked computers of the same type can directly transfer and share data with ease. However, different types of computers often cannot successfully share data because of the many different ways in which they communicate. Unix computers, for example, use different types of communication methods, called *protocols*, but despite the computers' sophistication, they sometimes can't agree on the protocols necessary for effective communication with the various types of Unix operating systems, such as Solaris, IRIX, VMS, and LinuxPPC, for example. Sharing and transferring data gets even more difficult when you try to get varying types of computers together. Computers that use Microsoft Windows, for example, are even more difficult to connect to Unix computers.

The Transmission Control Protocol/Internet Protocol (TCP/IP) suite has made the Internet the great equalizer among different types of computers. As you'll learn when we'll discuss this more in Part III, any computer that can use TCP/IP is potentially easier to connect to over the Internet because the Internet uses TCP/IP as the common protocol for all types of computers to connect. Without TCP/IP, the Internet would probably not be nearly as successful.

Today's computing environment also uses a good deal of removable media to store and transfer large amounts of data. We all know about CD-ROM drives, of course, but Macs also use other types of removable media such as CD-R (recordable), CD-RW (rewritable), Zip and Jaz drives from Iomega, 120MB SuperDrive from Imation, EZ drives from SyQuest, and now DVD-RAM drives. These drives are capable of holding between 100MB and 6GB of data. The hardware required to access these forms of removable media is very easy to install and use. In most cases, removable media use the Small Computer Serial Interface (SCSI), and since most Macs use SCSI, it's usually just a matter of plugging in the drive. The iMacs use the new Universal Serial Bus (USB), however, and some high-end Macs are starting to use FireWire in place of SCSI. It is believed that FireWire will eventually replace SCSI because of its increased speed and other improvements in virtually all areas of comparison.

The good people at Apple decided to make the Macintosh accessible in as many ways as possible, running the gamut from Sneakernet to AppleTalk and Ethernet networking. To work well with other types of computers via Sneakernet, the Mac had to be capable of reading floppies formatted by different operating systems—thus the SuperDrive was born.

This abundance of data is often transferred among various types of computers running several different versions of operating systems. Fortunately, the Mac speaks the languages of many computers, including those that run various versions of Microsoft Windows. Mac OS 8.6 utilizes several features that allow Mac users to read Windows disks or translate common file types into the appropriate format; and if all else fails, it allows you to run the other operating system itself, assuming you have the appropriate software.

SuperDrive

In the early days of desktop computing, the only real way to share data—unless you had a Macintosh—was with a floppy disk. The first disks were almost the size of a Frisbee, but by the early 1980s, when Apple shipped the first Macintosh with a SuperDrive, they were small enough to fit in a shirt pocket.

The SuperDrive, standard equipment on all Macs except certain PowerBooks (in which it is optional) and the iMac, is capable of reading, writing to, and/or formatting four types of disk formats:

➤ Mac OS Standard (also known as HFS, or hierarchical file system) 1.4MB

➤ Mac OS Standard 800K

➤ DOS 1.4MB

➤ ProDOS 1.4MB

These file formats cover about 99 percent of all operating systems that are now on the market or still in use. Transferring data via floppy isn't exactly low-tech or extinct. You can always use a floppy if your network is down. If you receive a floppy that has been formatted by one of the methods just mentioned, you can pop it into the disk drive and a piece of software called File Exchange, which assists the Mac OS in talking to the SuperDrive, will take care of the rest.

TIP
If Apple co-founder Steve Jobs has his way, the computer of the future will not need a floppy drive, an idea that has been incorporated into the iMac design.

When you insert a floppy disk formatted for a PC, it mounts on the Desktop like a Mac floppy but with a distinctive icon that tells you that it's in a PC, rather than Macintosh, format. On the other hand, CDs formatted for PCs look just like Mac CDs, but they often have long or unusual file names. Figure 8.1 shows two Desktop icons for PC-based disks: a CD and a diskette.

Figure 8.1 Desktop icons for PC-formatted disks.

With the aid of a program called File Exchange, the SuperDrive is capable of formatting diskettes for use on a PC as well.

Mac OS 8.6

File Exchange: PC Exchange

File Exchange is a Control Panel that provides two basic functions: mapping PC-based filename extensions to their Mac equivalents (PC Exchange) and translating PC-based documents into Mac documents (File Translation). Although Mac hardware has had the capability to read PC disks for many years, Apple's only software support for this feature was Apple File Exchange, a Font/DA-Mover-like utility that made it possible to copy files from PC disks onto Mac disks or hard drives.

But while everyone else was wondering why PC disks couldn't just mount at the desktop so files could be dragged to and from disks directly, Apple finally released PC Exchange, a $79 addition to the Mac OS, around the time System 7.1 was released. Beginning with Mac OS 8.5, PC Exchange was incorporated into a more powerful version of translation software called File Exchange.

> **TIP**
> PC Exchange was also shipped as part of the Macintosh PowerBook/DOS Companion package. The Macintosh File Assistant, used for synchronizing files between drives, was also part of the Companion package. It is discussed in Chapter 6.

When File Exchange is installed, you can specify which Macintosh application you want to use to open files from PCs when you double-click on the file or application icon. When you open a PC file from within an application using the File|Open command, you apply the translators that are part of that program without using File Exchange in the conversion. For example, if you use File|Open to open a Microsoft Word document created on a PC, Word for Macintosh will usually open that file without the assistance of File Exchange.

Files dragged to PC disks will automatically have their names changed to comply with PC file-naming conventions (eight characters and a three-character extension, also known as the 8.3 rule). Conversely, long filenames under Windows 95, 98, NT, and 2000 will be truncated to 32 characters when copied to a Mac diskette or hard drive.

Setting up the PC Exchange portion of the File Exchange Control Panel requires only a few steps. Once you have opened File Exchange, select from the following three checkboxes (see Figure 8.2):

➤ *Map PC extensions to Mac OS file types on PC disks*—Selecting this option will cause documents on PC disks to assume the appropriate file creator type, which will in turn cause them to be opened by the Mac OS using the appropriate Mac-based application when double-clicked or opened using File|Open.

Mac OS 8.6

Working With Other Types Of Computers   221

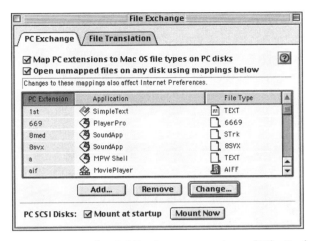

Figure 8.2   The PC Exchange portion of File Exchange.

➤ *Open unmapped files on any disk using mappings below*—This option will perform a similar task as the previous option, but for all disks, Mac and PC, and without translating the file type.

➤ *PC SCSI Disks*—If checked, entire PC-formatted SCSI disks will be mounted when the computer is started up. You can also mount such a disk manually by clicking on the Mount Now button.

You may add a new mapping, remove an existing mapping, or change a mapping by selecting the appropriate button. For example, Figure 8.3 shows how MPEG movies (with the extension .mpg) are mapped to be viewed using the MoviePlayer application.

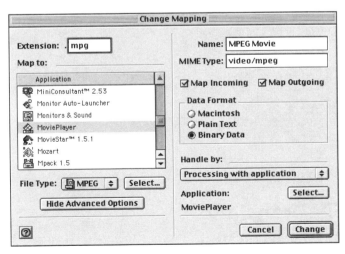

Figure 8.3   Changing a File Exchange mapping.

Mac OS 8.6

You can add conversions of DOS files to the list by clicking the Add button. Enter the three-letter extension, select a Macintosh application that you would like to use to open that file, and then select the type of document you want that application to translate the DOS file into. Any translators are shown in the pop-up menu for the document type.

Here are some of the more common translations:

➤ Lotus 1-2-3 .wks files to Lotus 1-2-3 (Mac) and MS Excel TEXT files.

➤ Excel .xls files to Lotus 1-2-3 (Mac) and Excel (Mac) TEXT files.

➤ Microsoft Word for Windows .doc files to Word 98 (Mac) W8BN files.

➤ PageMaker .pm5 files to PageMaker (Mac) ALB5 files.

➤ Quattro (DOS) .wk1 files to Lotus 1-2-3 (Mac) and Excel TEXT files.

➤ Ventura Publisher .chp files to Ventura Publisher VCHP files.

Use the Open command from within an application to open WordPerfect (DOS) files, since no suffix is assigned to those files.

File Exchange also enables you to format a floppy disk as a PC disk using the same Erase Disk command on the Special menu that you use to format a floppy disk or erase a hard drive. To format a floppy disk for use with a PC:

1. Select the disk icon on the Desktop.
2. Select Erase Disk from the Special menu.
3. Choose the DOS or ProDOS format.

An example of the Erase Disk dialog box is shown in Figure 8.4.

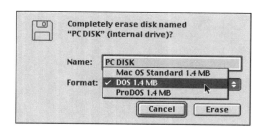

Figure 8.4 Formatting a floppy disk for a PC.

File Exchange: File Translation

The File Translation tab of the File Exchange Control Panel, which incorporates the old Macintosh Easy Open utility, allows your Mac to better communicate with other types of computers by helping you open a file created by one application with another when the original application is not available. A set of "translator" files is used to convert the file, which can be Macintosh, MS-DOS, Windows, or OS/2 in origin, and you are prompted to select an appropriate application from a list of possible choices. If you have DataViz translators installed (part of the MacLinkPlus PC package, described next), then File Translation will work with them as well.

Some Macs may have Insignia Solutions's SoftWindows or Connectix Corporation's VirtualPC, which are applications that emulate the Intel 80x86 and Pentium microprocessors. Using Easy Open and SoftWindows, you can specify documents to open inside other Windows applications rather than in Macintosh applications.

To turn File Translation on or off, open the File Exchange Control Panel and select the File Translation tab, shown in Figure 8.5.

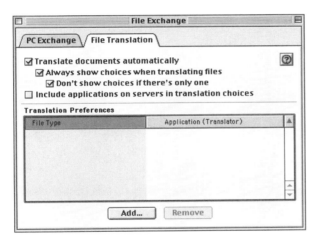

Figure 8.5 The File Translation tab of the File Exchange Control Panel, which replaces Macintosh Easy Open in earlier versions of the Mac OS.

You can select from the following configuration options to control how files are automatically translated:

> *Translate documents automatically*—This option enables or disables files to be translated.

> *Always show choices when translating files*—Check this box to display the list of compatible applications; otherwise, File Translation will make a selection for you.

> *Don't show choices if there's only one*—If only one choice is available, then no dialog box will be displayed and the translation will be automatic.

> *Include applications on servers in translation choices*—This option looks to any mounted server for the appropriate application when translating a document.

Mac OS 8.6

Deselecting this option will increase the speed of translations, but limit the options to those applications located on the local file system.

An example of the File Translation dialog box is shown in Figure 8.6.

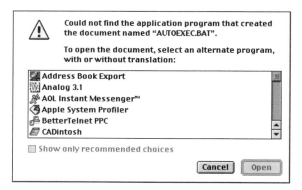

Figure 8.6 The File Translation dialog box.

Adding a translation mapping is very similar to adding a file extension in the PC Exchange tab of File Exchange. To add a mapping for the ubiquitous PC file named AUTOEXEC.BAT, you would follow these steps:

1. Click the Add button.

2. Find an example of the type of file in question.

3. Select an application with which the document may be opened, such as SimpleText (see Figure 8.7).

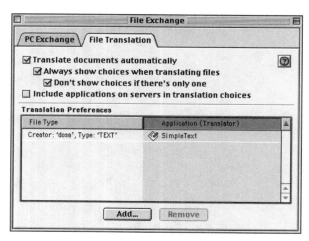

Figure 8.7 Adding a File Translation mapping.

Mac OS 8.6

File Exchange can use the same application to translate different types of PC documents. For example, SimpleText can be used to open AUTOEXEC.BAT documents as well as generic PC documents (see Figure 8.8).

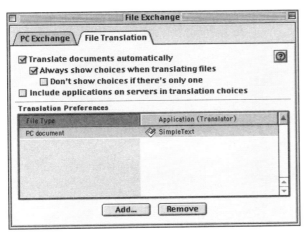

Figure 8.8 Use File Exchange to open generic PC documents.

If you are not presented with the Mac application you'd like to use to open a specific type of application, try this to trick File Exchange into offering the missing application as a choice. Go back to the PC Exchange tab and add that application as the preferred application to open documents with the same file extension instead, if it has an extension. For instance, in the previous example I was unable to open files like AUTOEXEC.BAT using BBEdit, so I had to choose SimpleText instead. So, I went back to the PC Exchange tab and just added BBEdit as the application mapped to files ending in .BAT instead. For some reason, not all applications are offered as choices to which PC document types may be mapped.

MacLinkPlus

Another extension to the Mac OS that helps your Mac live in a Windows world is MacLinkPlus from DataViz. MacLinkPlus, a companion product to File Exchange, helps you open documents created on Microsoft Windows-based computers—even if you don't have the Mac OS version of the application that was used to create the document. MacLinkPlus is available for around $99 and can be ordered from the company's Web site at www.dataviz.com. The following list shows most of the 100+ file types MacLinkPlus is capable of opening:

➤ Ami Pro 1.2, 2.0, 3.x

➤ AppleWorks (Apple II) 2.1, 3.0, GS 1.1

- AutoCAD.DXF through v.9 (read only)
- ClarisWorks 1.0 - 4.0
- ClarisWorks v.4 WP, SS, DB (Mac and Windows)
- Comma Separated Values.CSV
- Corel Quattro Pro 7 (Windows 95)
- Corel Quattro Pro 8 (Windows 95)
- DCA-RFT
- DIF
- EPS Mac (convert to EPS PC only)
- EPS PC (convert to EPS Mac only)
- Excel 2.0 - 8.0
- FoxBASE/FoxPro
- FrameMaker MIF 2.0, 3.0
- GIF
- HTML
- HTML (read only)
- Harvard Graphics.CGM (read only)
- JPEG
- Lotus 1-2-3 WKS, WK1, WK3, WK4
- Lotus Freelance.CGM (read only)
- Lotus.PIC (read only)
- MIF (NeXT/Sun) v. 2, 3
- MS Works (DOS) 2.0, 3.0
- MS Works 2.0, 3.0, 4.0
- MS Works for Windows 2.0, 3.0, 4.0
- MacWrite 4.5, 5.0
- MacWrite II
- MacWrite Pro 1.0, 1.5
- Microsoft Excel 97

- Microsoft Excel 98
- Microsoft Word 97
- Microsoft Word 98
- MultiMate through v.4
- Nisus 3.0, 3.4
- Nisus Writer 4.0
- Nisus Writer v. 4
- OfficeWriter 5.0, 6.0
- PC Paintbrush.PCX
- PICT/PICT2
- Professional Write 2.0
- Quattro Pro (DOS) 4.0
- Quattro Pro for Windows 1.0 - 8.0
- RTF
- SYLK
- SunWrite v. 1.1 (write only)
- Symphony WRK, WR1
- TIFF
- Tab Text
- Tab Values
- Text
- Ventura Publisher.IMG (read only)
- WKS
- Windows Bitmap.BMP
- Windows Metafile.WMF
- Word (DOS) through v.6
- Word 3.0, 4.0, 5.x, 6.0, 8.0 (98)
- Word for Windows 1.0 - 8.0 (97)
- WordPerfect (DOS) 4.2, 5.x, 6.0

Chapter 8

- WordPerfect 1.0, 2.x, 3.x
- WordPerfect Mac 3.5
- WordPerfect Works for Windows 2.0
- WordPerfect Works v. 2
- WordPerfect for Windows 5.x - 8.0
- WordPerfect for Windows 6.1
- WordPerfect.WPG/WPG2
- WordStar 3.0, 4.0, 5.0, 6.0, 7.0
- WriteNow 2.0, 3.0, 4.0
- WriteNow NeXT v. 1, 2
- XYWrite III
- dBase (DBF) II, III, IV

MacLinkPlus is easily configured through MacLinkPlus Setup in the Control Panels, shown in Figure 8.9. In fact, all you need to do is confirm that the default settings are accurate (which they usually are).

Figure 8.9 Configure MacLinkPlus through the Control Panels.

Approximately 10 categories need to be reviewed; configuration selections are made in the Preferences menu. The categories in version MacLinkPlus 9.7.1 are shown in Figure 8.10.

Next, locate the MacLinkPlus folder on your hard drive. To convert a document, you can take one of the following two approaches:

Working With Other Types Of Computers   229

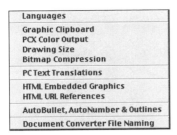

Figure 8.10 Review these categories when configuring MacLinkPlus.

➤ Double-click the document and wait a few seconds for the translation dialog window to open. It will list the applications that are available to successfully translate your document into the appropriate Mac OS application. Make a choice from the scrolling menu and MacLinkPlus will translate the document and launch the appropriate application.

➤ Drag and drop a document onto a translator, an example of which is shown in Figure 8.11.

Figure 8.11 MacLinkPlus, translating a Rich Text Format document created on a PC for use on the Mac OS as a Microsoft Word 6.0 document.

Not all translations go as smoothly as you'd like, so don't be too surprised if a translated document's line spacing or font choices are not the same as in the original document.

Other OS Solutions

Since the majority of computers use operating systems other than the Mac OS, several companies have been making alternative hardware and software solutions for many years. These solutions allow other operating systems to run in place of, or alongside of, the Mac OS, including:

➤ MS-DOS

Mac OS 8.6

- Windows 3.x
- Windows 95
- Windows 98
- Windows NT
- Windows 2000
- MkLinux
- LinuxPPC
- MachTen
- BeOS

And since the release of Virtual PC from the Connectix Corporation in 1997, your Mac can run any operating system that can run on the x86 (Intel) platform, which opens an entirely new level of cross-platform compatibility. The first major application to run another operating system was SoftPC from Insignia Solutions, which later created various versions of SoftWindows (95, 98, etc.). Insignia's approach has been to create an environment within the Mac OS environment that emulates Windows operating systems. These programs run collaboratively and are launched as applications, which means you can run the Mac OS and all its applications at the same time—provided you have the necessary RAM and other hardware requirements. For example, Figure 8.12 shows SoftWindows 95 running as an application under Mac OS 8.6.

Having an application like SoftWindows or SoftWindows 95 gives you the ultimate in compatibility with other computers—you can run not only all your favorite Macintosh applications, but almost any Microsoft Windows application as well, giving you access to about 99 percent of all applications. Not bad, eh?

Because SoftWindows 95 works like many other applications on the Mac OS in terms of installation and configuration, you have the standard pull-down menus that you would have in most other Mac applications. The Setup menu, shown in Figure 8.13, is where you'll configure elements of SoftWindows that emulate various aspects of a PC.

SoftWindows and SoftWindows 95 emulate various elements of PC hardware and software, matching the printer selected in the Chooser, for example, to the PC equivalent, usually the LPT1 port.

SoftWindows runs neck and neck with Virtual PC from Connectix, makers of Speed Doubler and Ram Doubler. Virtual PC is different from SoftWindows in

Working With Other Types Of Computers   231

Figure 8.12   Insignia Solutions' SoftWindows 95 running under Mac OS 8.6.

Figure 8.13   Use the Setup menu to configure SoftWindows 95.

that it emulates the entire PC, not just a particular version of a Microsoft operating system such as Windows 95 or 98. Virtual PC serves as a hardware abstraction layer that emulates a Pentium MMX-based PC and allows you to install any operating system that will run on a PC onto your Mac.

The configuration of Virtual PC, shown in Figure 8.14, allows you to easily configure all the elements of a PC as they should be configured on a PowerMac. You can select what hardware devices to use, such as hard drives, CD-ROM players, a floppy drive, sound support, and the like. The options are self-explanatory.

Mac OS 8.6

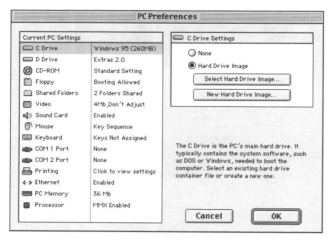

Figure 8.14 Use the Preferences menu to configure Virtual PC to emulate the hardware of a Pentium-based PC.

When installed, Virtual PC boots without an operating system, so the first thing you'll need to do is install one, such as MS-DOS. Figure 8.15 shows a Virtual PC

Figure 8.15 Virtual PC running MS-DOS version 6.22.

Working With Other Types Of Computers 233

session when running MS-DOS, which takes just a few megabytes of hard drive space to install.

Many older network and business environments still rely on older versions of the Windows operating system, such as Windows 3.1, shown in Figure 8.16 running on a PowerMac under Virtual PC.

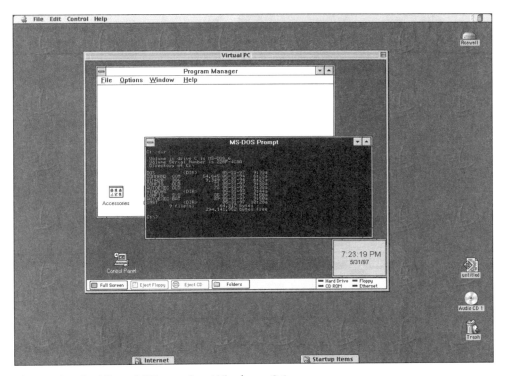

Figure 8.16 Virtual PC running Windows 3.1.

However, because Virtual PC can run any operating system that a Pentium-based PC can run, you can install a more modern operating system such as Windows 95, shown in Figure 8.17. You can even run Virtual Game Station from Connectix as well, for all you gaming fans out there.

If you have a very fast PowerMac, you should give one of the software emulation packages such as SoftWindows or Virtual PC a chance. However, if you need more speed, you can always purchase a hardware solution in the form of a DOS card from Orange Micro (www.orangemicro.com). For well under $1,000, you can get a fast DOS card that includes a Pentium processor running up to 350 MHz, 64MB of RAM, an L2 cache, MS-DOS, and your choice of Windows operating systems. You can also get DOS cards with Intel, Cyrix, or AMD chips; and, if you want to

Mac OS 8.6

Figure 8.17 Virtual PC running Windows 95 is an excellent tool for cross-platform Web developers to test their work.

pay the price, you can get a Pentium Pro 400 MHz and Windows NT. Expect to pay at least $2,000 for a system like that, however.

Wrapping Up

You'll want to choose the road to compatibility that's best for your Mac and your environment. All Mac OS 8.6 owners will have the benefits of Apple's SuperDrive, File Exchange, File Translation, and MacLinkPlus. These tools can help your Mac be a better neighbor to other computers. However, if you need more compatibility, you can always run other operating systems, such as Windows and Windows 98, on your PowerMac. If your computer is in a network environment dominated by Unix computers, you can install one of several Unix-on-Mac solutions, such as MachTen from Tenon Intersystems (www.tenon.com), MkLinux (mklinux.apple.com), or LinuxPPC (www.linuxppc.org). The latter two are free Unix operating systems that replace the Mac OS. Whatever your needs, you'll find a good solution to help your Mac better communicate with other computers in your environment.

In the next chapter, we'll look at ways in which your Mac uses memory to operate applications and how you can tweak the Mac OS to help your applications run peacefully on your computer.

Applications And Memory Management

When someone asks you about your Macintosh, you probably say something like, "I've got a G3/266 with 64 megs of memory and a 2-gig hard drive." It's no accident that the three variables you use to describe your computer are its model name, the amount of installed memory, or random access memory (RAM), and its hard disk size. These are the factors that determine the speed and range of activities you can perform with your computer.

With Mac OS 8.6, the amount of RAM installed in your Mac is still important, but it's no longer the total measure of memory or the only important memory issue. In this chapter, we'll look at the overall picture of Macintosh memory, including the new Memory Control Panel options, the About This Computer dialog box, ways you can configure applications to use memory most efficiently, and a few tools to help you better monitor your Mac's memory usage.

Memory Vs. Storage

Before we jump into the Mac OS 8.6's new memory options and their implications, let's clarify the difference between memory (RAM) and storage (disk space). This distinction may be clear to experienced Macintosh users; however, if you're not certain you understand the difference, please read this section carefully.

In the simplest terms, memory consists of the chips in your computer where data is temporarily stored while it is being used by the Macintosh. This is in contrast to your hard disk, floppy disks, and other storage devices where data is permanently stored when it's not being used by your Macintosh.

The differences between RAM and storage (hard drives, floppies, and other media) are very important. Both RAM and storage hold data—application programs, system software, and data files—but the similarities end there. RAM stores data electronically on a set of chips, and as a result, these chips "forget" their contents as soon as the power is turned off or the Mac is restarted. Storage devices

RAM And You

If we compare the way your Mac uses memory and storage with the way you work and think, perhaps the difference will become more apparent and easier to remember. In this analogy, the computer (and its processor) plays the part of the human brain, memory (RAM) is equated with our own memory, and floppy and hard disk storage is equated with written or typed notes.

As you know, no information can gain access to your brain without also entering your memory; regardless of whether information originates from your eyes, ears, or other senses, it is immediately put into memory (RAM) so that your brain (the Macintosh processor) can access it. But what do we do with information that we want to use in the future? We transfer it to some storage medium, like paper (disk). This way, we know that when this information is needed in the future, we can transfer it back into memory by reading it.

like hard drives and floppy disks operate magnetically, or by optical technology, and only lose information if it's intentionally erased or if it becomes corrupted during the writing process.

More importantly, the Macintosh can only work with data stored in RAM; it cannot directly manipulate data on any storage device. In order to open an application or file, it must be read from storage and written into memory. Once in memory, the application can be executed or the file can be modified, but to make these changes permanent, the information in RAM must be written back out to the storage device—this is what happens when you choose the Save command.

The Memory Control Panel

One of the realities Macintosh must face is the finite amount of memory available in their computers. Today's software seems to have an insatiable appetite for RAM, and new technologies—like multitasking, 24-bit color and sound, and particularly the Web and Web browsers—intensify the problem. The crusade for additional memory has traditionally encountered certain roadblocks: the operating system's limited ability to address the need for large amounts of memory, the computer's physical limitations, and the high price of memory chips.

System 7 began the process of breaking down these barriers, or at least temporarily pushed them back. The Memory Control Panel was one of System 7's new memory-related features. This Control Panel offers virtual memory, 32-bit addressing, and RAM disk options as well as the disk cache option, which is System 7's version of the RAM cache found in the General Control Panel of earlier systems. Each of these elements undergoes continual improvement as system software develops. Even when the outward appearance of the Memory Control Panel remains unchanged, you can detect speed enhancements due to underlying changes—particularly in Mac OS 8.6.

Mac OS 8.6

Applications And Memory Management 237

Because of certain limitations at the hardware or software level, the Memory Control Panel in older versions of the Mac OS doesn't provide the same options on all Macintosh models. If a certain Mac model doesn't support an option, then that option doesn't appear in the Control Panel. Figure 9.1 illustrates this point with the various Memory Control Panels found in System 7.5.

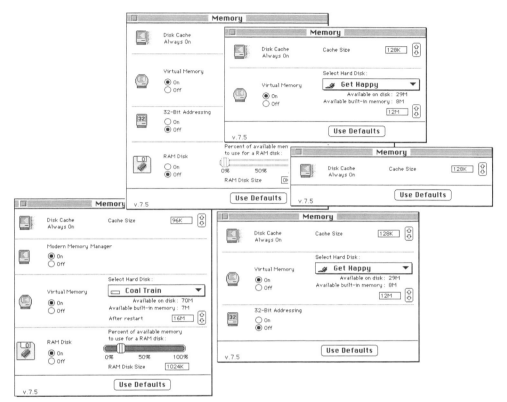

Figure 9.1 The five versions of the Memory Control Panel for System 7.5 that appear on various Macintosh models.

In Mac OS 8.6, however, the differences between models of the Macintosh (and Macintosh clones) are virtually nonexistent where the Memory Control Panel is concerned. Each has the following three sections:

➤ Disk Cache

➤ Virtual Memory

➤ RAM Disk

Figure 9.2 shows the Memory Control Panel in Mac OS 8.6; the sections that follow describe the different elements of this Control Panel.

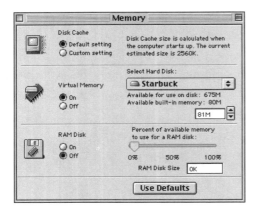

Figure 9.2 The Memory Control Panel for Mac OS 8.6.

Disk Cache

A disk cache is a small section of Macintosh RAM set aside to store a copy of the most recent data read from disk (or volume) into memory. Storing this copy makes the data readily available when it's needed again. Reaccessing data via the RAM-based cache rather than having to reread it from disk saves considerable time. A file subsystem cache scheme extends the current file system cache into temporary memory (RAM) when possible. This is of particular benefit to users with a large amount of physical RAM installed (i.e., actual RAM chips installed into the appropriate slots on the motherboard). Also, menus are cached so that the next time a menu is pulled down, it is displayed immediately. Because menu performance varies with CPU speed, this difference will be most apparent to users with slower machines.

The disk cache portion of the Memory Control Panel was reworked in Mac OS 8.5 to provide two types of cache settings:

➤ Default setting

➤ Custom setting

The Mac OS uses 32K of cache for every 1MB of RAM installed in your Mac. If you have 64MB of RAM, for example, 2048K would be the default cache setting. Clicking the Default button will allow the OS to select the setting that is best for most users according to this formula. Don't reduce the cache below its default setting unless you have specific memory limitations—the small amount of memory the cache consumes delivers a big return by significantly improving your Macintosh's performance.

In most cases, it's also a bad idea to increase the size of your cache too much. Settings over 32K per megabyte of installed RAM should be used only in very specific situations in which large cache allocations aid performance; your software's documentation should advise you on how to handle this. For example, Adobe's Type Manager can use large cache allocations when it's rendering several fonts for a document. Fonts can be stored in memory, and in that circumstance, the larger cache is helpful. Most applications use their own internal memory caching scheme and don't rely on the system software's cache for performance enhancement.

To use a custom cache setting (i.e., smaller or larger than the default), click the Custom button to reveal an information/warning dialog window, shown in Figure 9.3, and then select the Custom button within this dialog window.

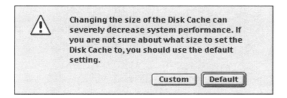

Figure 9.3 The Mac OS will present you with this dialog window when you first select the Custom setting button.

Next, increase or decrease the cache size. The minimum size is 128K and the maximum size allowed by the Mac OS is 8160K. The perfect disk cache size is a matter of great debate even among the most technically knowledgeable Macintosh users. Your Macintosh hardware and software configuration and the way you use your Mac significantly influence your optimal setting, so trial and error is really the only way to find what works best for you.

TIP
The Disk Cache option is always on; you may adjust its size downward or upward, but you may not turn it off.

Virtual Memory

Virtual memory is a hardware trick. It uses space on your hard drive to "fool" the Mac OS into thinking that the available amount of physical memory is greater than it really is. Using virtual memory, a Mac with only 32MB or 64MB of physical RAM can perform like a Mac that has 128MB or more. In fact, virtual memory can provide your Mac with over 1GB (1000MB) of memory. This number is one half of the disk space in System 7.1. System 7.5 has 4GB of addressable disk space, half of which is addressable as virtual memory (double the amount of potential virtual memory from earlier versions). Mac OS 8.6, however, can address up to 1 terabyte (1000GB) of hard drive space, so you could have up to several gigabytes of virtual memory.

Because virtual memory substitutes hard disk space for RAM, and hard drive space is generally much less expensive than actual RAM, virtual memory offers an obvious financial benefit. Furthermore, virtual memory can provide access to more memory than is possible with RAM chips alone.

However, using virtual memory has two main drawbacks. First, performance is slower than with real RAM since the mechanical actions required of your hard drive are no match for the electronic speed of RAM chips, which have no moving parts. Second, virtual memory appropriates hard disk space normally available for other activities. If you upgrade to a new drive, you'll notice a striking difference in hard drive speed while using virtual memory. An onboard hard drive disk cache (RAM installed on the hard drive itself) can greatly improve virtual memory performance.

Enabling Virtual Memory

To enable virtual memory, go to the Virtual Memory section of the Memory Control Panel, as shown in Figure 9.4. After you click the On button, the Select Hard Disk option becomes available. From the pop-up menu, choose the hard disk volume on which the virtual memory storage file will be created and stored. (If you only have one hard drive, the menu will offer only one option.)

Figure 9.4 The Virtual Memory option in the Memory Control Panel determines the size and location of the virtual memory file.

The amount of available space on the selected hard disk is displayed below the hard disk pop-up menu where it says "Available for use on hard disk". The amount of free space available determines the amount of virtual memory that can be configured. A virtual memory storage file equal to the total amount of memory available while using virtual memory will be placed on the selected disk. In other words, if your Macintosh has 64MB of actual RAM, and you wish to reach 128MB by using an additional 64MB of virtual memory, a 128MB virtual memory storage file must be created on the selected volume. This file, called VM Storage, is invisible, although you can use Sherlock to locate it by holding down the Option key while selecting the search criteria (see Figure 9.5).

Applications And Memory Management   241

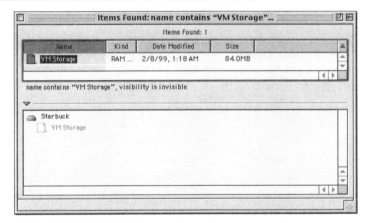

Figure 9.5 The virtual memory in use on your Mac is stored as an invisible file at the root level of your hard drive.

Appearing below the Available on Disk option is the *Available built-in memory* field, which tells you how much physical RAM is installed and recognized by the Mac OS. If you increase the amount of virtual memory to be used, a field labeled *After restart* will appear. The After restart option indicates the amount of memory specified, including actual RAM and virtual memory. Click on the arrows to modify this specification. If the After Restart option is not visible, click one of the arrows until it appears.

TIP

It's possible to have more RAM installed than is recognized by your computer. The RAM that is not recognized is either installed improperly or is not the right type of chip for your particular model of Macintosh. Consult your computer's documentation for the correct specifications.

Any changes made to the Virtual Memory option will not take effect until your computer is restarted. To verify that virtual memory is on, choose the About This Computer command to display the current memory status. (You'll find more

Mac OS 8.6

information on the About This Computer dialog box in the "About This Computer" section, later in this chapter.)

Virtual Memory Performance

Virtual memory works by moving information between a disk-based swap file and the RAM inside the computer; even when virtual memory is being used, the Mac OS communicates only with the real RAM. This movement of data between hard disk and RAM, technically known as paging, causes the Macintosh to perform slower than it does when using actual RAM alone.

The amount of paging slowdown depends on how much actual RAM is available and how virtual memory is being used. The more available RAM, the less paging interference. The activity called for also affects paging; working on multi-megabyte data files and frequent switching between open applications are the sort of activities that usually require more paging and therefore decrease performance. Problems with virtual memory show up as poor performance in animation, video, and sound. Games and multimedia content that require manipulation of large amounts of data are the first to suffer. Virtual memory is a prime energy drain for PowerBook computers.

A good rule of thumb in determining your own RAM/virtual memory mix is that you should have enough actual RAM to cover your normal memory needs and enough supplemental virtual memory to handle occasional, abnormally large requirements. If you find that approximately 64MB of RAM lets you work comfortably in the three or four open applications you use regularly, but you occasionally need another 32MB to open additional applications or work with large data files, then 64MB of real RAM and a combined total of 96MB of RAM and virtual memory would probably be adequate. However, if you don't need an additional 32MB of virtual memory on top of your 64MB of physical memory, use just one additional megabyte of virtual memory instead. This will help speed up things a bit and, as with using any amount of virtual memory, your applications won't ask for as much RAM.

Why is this, you ask? The presence of virtual memory allows only the code necessary for an application to launch to be read into memory upon launch. The remaining code used by an application is loaded only when needed. This allows for a quicker launch, but when you actually use the program, it may be slower to operate than if you weren't using virtual memory because all the code was loaded in the beginning. This is a trade-off inherent in using virtual memory: Applications launch faster, but any speed gained in the beginning might very well be lost as you continue to use the application.

Like the disk cache debate, exactly what ratios of real to virtual memory Macintosh users should set has long been the subject of speculation. Ultimately, the answer is for you to use as much virtual memory as is practical and useful. But remember, physical RAM is fairly cheap these days, and you should have at least 64MB on any model of Mac. And bear in mind that most entry level Macs ship with 32 or 64MB now—and some ship with 128MB of RAM.

Disabling Virtual Memory

Virtual memory can be turned off by clicking the Off button in the Virtual Memory area of the Memory Control Panel and restarting your computer. After disabling virtual memory, the invisible virtual memory storage file (VM Storage) is deleted from your hard drive automatically, and the space it occupied is returned to the Mac OS for use by other programs.

What Happened To 32-Bit Addressing?

Older versions of the Memory Control Panel had an option to enable or disable something called 32-bit addressing. This option is not present in OS 8.6 because it is obsolete. In the past, 8MB was the maximum amount of RAM that could be installed (or used) on the Macintosh. This limitation was imposed by the way the Macintosh system software addressed available memory chips, by including those parts that reside on the ROM chips on the computer's logic board. Newer Macintosh computers, of course, use newer versions of the ROM chips, allowing much more physical RAM to be installed.

This extended ability to use memory is called 32-bit addressing, referring to the number of digits used in the current memory-addressing scheme. The Mac's older memory scheme is 24-bit addressing, in which only 24 digits were used. Power Macintosh computers have 32-bit built-in addressing that cannot be turned off; therefore, you don't see a 32-bit addressing section in a Power Macintosh Memory Control Panel.

The ROM chips required for 32-bit addressing are 32-bit ROMs and are currently included in all Macs that contain ROMs. Certain "older" models, specifically the Plus, Classic, SE, SE/30, Portable, II, IIx, IIcx, and LC, did not have 32-bit clean ROMs and therefore couldn't normally use 32-bit addressing. The SE/30 and Macintosh II, IIx, and IIcx can be upgraded to 32-bit clean capacity using an extension called MODE32 or the 32-bit addressing system enabler, both of which were available without charge from user groups and online services. Apple no longer distributes or supports MODE32. Support for this function is built into later versions of the system software.

In some cases, launching a really old application that's not compatible with 32-bit addressing will cause your computer to crash.

Mac OS 8.6

What Happened To The Modern Memory Manager?

Older versions of the Memory Control Panel on PowerMacs have an option called the Modern Memory Manager. When you turned on the Modern Memory Manager option (first introduced in System 7.1.2), you enabled a memory processing scheme specially written for the PowerPC chip and native applications. Reduced instruction set computing (RISC)-based microprocessors such as the PowerPC (used in all PowerMacs) load so much more of the instruction set into RAM than complex instruction set (CISC)-based microprocessors (used in all other Macs) that virtual memory, paging, and other memory operations were among the first that were ported into native PowerPC (PPC) code.

The Modern Memory Manager contains algorithms that improve memory performance, not only when you're using native PPC programs, but also even when you're using older programs operating in 680x0 emulation mode. Just as the introduction of 32-bit addressing caused compatibility problems early on, so did the Modern Memory Manager—it was the single biggest cause of compatibility problems with the PowerMacs.

In Mac OS 8.6, the Modern Memory Manager is rolled into the system software and is on by default. It cannot be turned off.

Memory Control Panel Tips

Here are a few tips to keep in mind when configuring the Mac OS to use both physical and virtual memory:

➤ Use at least the minimum recommended disk cache as defined by the Default setting. The disk cache speeds up operation, so you should leave it set to at least 32K for every megabyte of RAM installed in your Mac. (That means a 1024K disk cache for 32MB of RAM, 2048K for 64MB, 4096K for 128MB, and so on.)

➤ Install enough physical RAM in your Macintosh. Real RAM chips should provide enough memory to cover your normal daily memory needs—at least 32MB, and in most cases, up to 128MB. Although virtual memory can provide inexpensive additional memory, 80 percent of your memory needs should be covered by real RAM. The performance drawbacks of relying too heavily on virtual memory don't justify the relatively small amount of money saved.

➤ Extend your available memory with virtual memory. Once you've installed enough RAM to satisfy your everyday needs, use the virtual memory to give yourself extra memory to cover special occasional situations, such as working with large color images, animation, or more than the usual number of simultaneously open programs.

Mac OS 8.6

➤ Some applications, especially multimedia games, movies, and audio programs, just don't like virtual memory. If these types of programs don't behave properly, check with their instructions for information about possible virtual memory incompatibilities.

TIP
Turn off virtual memory when you experience performance problems. Some programs, such as games and graphics programs, do considerable data input/output. Virtual memory can degrade performance, and rapid paging can also lead to system crashes.

Controlling Memory

Once you've determined how much memory you need and made it available to the Mac OS (by installing RAM and by using virtual memory), you'll want to manage that memory wisely and use it economically. Managing your Mac's memory ensures that each application has enough RAM to operate properly and that enough total memory is available to open as many different applications as necessary.

Mac OS 8.6 provides two excellent tools for memory management—the About This Computer dialog box and the Get Info dialog box. We'll look at both of these tools in this section.

About This Computer

Starting with Mac OS 8, the familiar About This Macintosh command was changed to About This Computer, and the dialog box associated with it was improved. The About This Computer dialog box provides information about the Macintosh you're using, including the system software version, installed and available memory, and the amount of memory used by each open application. Figure 9.6 shows the About This Computer dialog box.

Figure 9.6   The About This Computer dialog box.

The upper section of the dialog box shown in Figure 9.6 gives the version of operating system currently in use as well as the following data regarding the available memory:

- *Built-In Memory*—80MB. Displays the amount of physical RAM installed in your Macintosh, exclusive of virtual memory.

- *Virtual Memory*—81MB used on Starbuck. Documents the total memory available in your Macintosh, including installed RAM plus available virtual memory. The name of the hard disk storing the virtual memory file (in this case, Starbuck) and the amount of hard drive space being used are listed to the right of the Virtual Memory listing. Virtual memory and hard drive designations are set via the Memory Control Panel, described earlier in this chapter.

- *Largest Unused Block*—63.9MB. Calculates the largest contiguous section of memory currently not being used by open software applications. This number is important because it determines both the number and size of additional software applications you can open. In some cases, the largest unused block will not equal the amount of total memory available less the size of all open applications. That's because as applications are launched and quit, memory becomes fragmented—gaps are created between sections of memory that are used and those that are available. To defragment your memory and create larger unused blocks, quit all open applications and then relaunch them. As they're relaunched, applications will use available memory sequentially, leaving the largest possible unused block.

> **TIP**
> If you get an out-of-memory alert box when plenty of memory should be available, you could have a fragmented memory situation. This occurs when you launch and quit programs repeatedly. Try to "unlearn" techniques of the past by leaving programs you'll use later open. If you have a fragmented memory problem, try first quitting programs in the reverse order they were opened. If that doesn't do the trick, you'll have to restart to flush your Macintosh's memory.

Each software application requires a particular amount of memory in order to be opened successfully. The amount of memory is documented and can be controlled in the Memory section of the Get Info dialog box, as described later in this chapter. When a program is launched, it cannot be opened if its memory requirement is larger than the largest unused block. Therefore it's important to know approximately how much memory an application needs.

The lower portion of the About This Macintosh dialog box displays information about the memory used by the Mac OS, plus information about each open

Applications And Memory Management   247

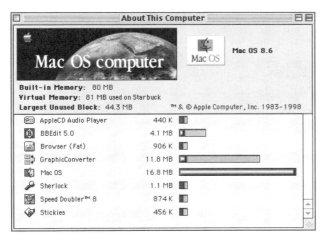

Figure 9.7 The About This Computer window showing multiple applications loaded into memory.

application, including its name, icon, and amount of memory allocated and used. Figure 9.7 shows the About This Computer window with multiple applications loaded into memory:

➤ *Application name and icon*—Each open application, along with a small version of its icon, is listed in alphabetical order.

➤ *Amount of memory allocated*—Just to the right of the application name, the total amount of memory that was allocated to that program when it was opened is displayed with a bar graph showing this amount in relation to amounts used by other open applications. The total bar represents total allocated memory; the filled portion of the bar represents the portion of allocated memory currently in use.

➤ *Amount of memory used*—In most cases, only a portion of an application's total allocated memory is used immediately upon opening it. Usually, some of the memory is used by the application itself, some is used to hold open document files, and some is left over for use by the software's commands and features. Only the memory currently being used appears as the filled-in percentage of the memory allocation bar.

Holding down the option key when choosing the About This Computer command changes the command into About The Finder, the result of which is shown in Figure 9.8. Choosing About The Finder brings up a copyright screen that first appeared in Finder 1.0 in 1984 (waiting a bit will get you a history of the Finder's programmers scrolling across the screen).

Mac OS 8.6

Figure 9.8   The secret About The Finder dialog box.

Memory-Related Utilities

Several great utilities that are either freeware (meaning they don't cost you anything), shareware (they may cost a few bucks), or commercial software (lots of bucks) are out there to help you analyze or test your Mac's memory. Of course, the About This Computer command is free, but it only gives you rudimentary information about your memory situation. Here are some of the best tools for a more thorough job.

Memory Mapper

If you want to know more details on your computer's memory usage, check out Bob Fronabarger's great utility called Memory Mapper (which is on this book's companion CD-ROM). Memory Mapper provides you with a detailed list of applications, extensions, and background processes that are currently loaded into memory on your Mac. Equally as important, Memory Mapper also tells you about virtual memory usage and in what order items have been loaded into memory. This is important because you should always try to quit applications in reverse order in which they were launched to prevent memory fragmentation.

Figure 9.9 shows an example of Memory Mapper with 26 entries for the Mac OS, applications, and free memory blocks. When the Mac OS is loaded into memory, it's loaded into the top portion of the memory area (called the High Memory area) as well as the bottom portion, which is occupied by portions of the Mac OS called the System Heap and the Lo-Mem Globals. The remaining elements of the Mac OS, such as the Finder, and all applications are loaded between the top and bottom portions of the memory area, in a zone referred to as the *application pool*.

Items are loaded from top to bottom in the application pool, and once all the memory has been used, you'll get an error message that says something like, "This cannot be completed because not enough memory is available." Not all errors are the result of an actual memory shortage. The System Heap (at the bottom of the memory pool) grows and shrinks dynamically as applications are launched and quit.

Applications And Memory Management   249

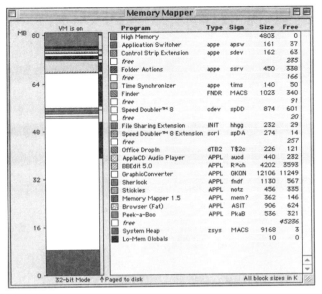

Figure 9.9 Memory Mapper provides detailed information on how much memory is used by the Mac OS and all running applications.

Some applications, like Microsoft Internet Explorer, grab all the available memory in the System Heap. If the System Heap is full and there is no memory available to an application that requests it, the Mac OS may return an error stating there is no memory available to launch the application even though plenty of memory is available in the application pool.

Figure 9.10 illustrates how one application can hog the System Heap. The image on the left is a detailed view of Memory Mapper while Internet Explorer is running with no open windows. The image on the right shows the same detail after the application was quit, which freed up over 1MB in the System Heap.

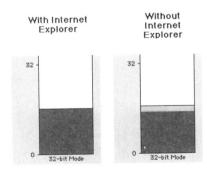

Figure 9.10 A detailed view of Memory Mapper, showing how the System Heap can be consumed by a single application.

Mac OS 8.6

Mac OS Purge

Mac OS Purge by Kenji Takeuchi is a simple, faceless utility that does two things. First, it purges the areas of memory occupied by stale data that was not automatically purged by an application, extension, or the Mac OS itself. This predicament occurs after you have launched and then quit applications that rely on large extensions or that, having written data to the System Heap, have not properly returned the memory to it or the application pool. Second, after the program has run (and because it's faceless, you won't actually interact with it) and quit, it will automatically open the About This Computer window.

To try this out, launch several applications and use them for a few minutes each, then quit them all. Then open the About This Computer window and take note of how much memory is used by the Mac OS. Finally, launch Mac OS Purge and compare how much memory is used by the Mac OS once the About This Computer window is displayed. For example, Figure 9.11 shows a before (top) and after (bottom) comparison of the results of this exercise. Notice that the Mac OS uses about 800K less memory after Mac OS Purge has been launched.

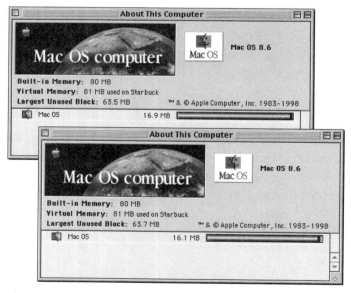

Figure 9.11 Use Mac OS Purge to free up memory that is no longer in use by the Mac OS or your applications.

The Get Info Dialog Box

As we've seen in earlier chapters, the Memory section of the Get Info dialog box allows you to take charge of your Macintosh's memory consumption using the information provided in the About This Computer dialog box. To minimize problems related to memory shortages, or to better allocate your available RAM to the different applications you want to open simultaneously, you can adjust the amount of memory each program uses.

The memory-related options of the Get Info dialog box differ among older versions of the operating system (such as System 7) and Mac OS 8.6, so we'll examine each of them separately.

Get Info In Earlier Versions Of The Mac OS

Earlier versions of the Mac OS provided fewer options for memory management than does Mac OS 8.6. For example, the Get Info dialog box's Memory option for System 7 is shown in Figure 9.12. The Memory option has two parts: Suggested Size and Current Size.

▶ *Suggested Size*—Displays the amount of RAM, as recommended by the developer, necessary to properly run the application. You can't change this option, but it's very valuable as a reminder of the original Current Size setting.

▶ *Current Size*—Specifies the actual amount of RAM that the application will request when it's launched. (By default, the Current Size is equal to the Suggested Size.) You can change the amount of memory that will be allocated by entering a new value in this option and then closing the Get Info dialog box.

Figure 9.12 An application's Get Info dialog box in System 7.0.

When an application is launched, the program requests the amount of memory specified in the Current Size option. If this amount is available in an unused block, the memory is allocated and the program is opened. You can check the size of the largest available block in the About This Computer dialog box, as described earlier.

If the amount of memory requested is larger than the largest available unused block, a dialog box will appear stating that not enough memory is available, asking if you want to try to run the application using less memory, or suggesting that you quit an open application to create enough free memory. See Figure 9.13 for examples of these messages.

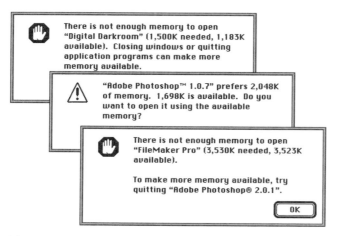

Figure 9.13 Examples of memory error messages that you may be familiar with from previous versions of the Mac OS.

Mac OS 8.6 uses a third option in the Memory section of the Get Info dialog box to provide greater control over how your applications use memory.

Memory Section Of Get Info In Mac OS 8.6

The Get Info dialog box's options in Mac OS 8.6 (as in System 7.6 and later) eliminate the need to change settings for different memory situations; they allow you to set options that determine how much memory will be used depending on the amount of memory available at launch time. Now, however, these memory requirements are set in the Memory section of the Get Info dialog box, as shown in Figure 9.14.

The Memory option here has four main parts: Suggested Size, Minimum Size, Preferred Size, and Note, described below.

➤ *Suggested Size*—Lists the amount of RAM the developer recommends to properly run the application. You can't change this option—it's a reminder of the memory requirements as defined by the application developer.

➤ *Minimum Size*—Designates the smallest amount of RAM in which the application will run properly. You can change this option by entering a new value, but your application may become unstable.

Applications And Memory Management 253

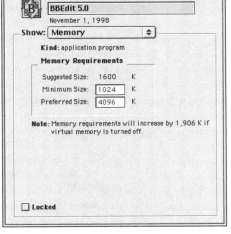

Figure 9.14 BBEdit's memory settings in the Get Info dialog box under Mac OS 8.6.

> *Preferred Size*—Specifies the actual amount of RAM that the application will request when it's launched. You can change the amount of memory that will be allocated by entering a new value in this option and then closing the Get Info dialog box.

> *Note*—Informs you how much additional memory will or will not be required if virtual memory is turned off or on.

When an application is launched, the program requests the amount of memory specified in the Preferred Size option. If this amount is available in a contiguous, unused memory block, the memory is allocated and the program is opened. You can check the size of the largest available block in the About This Computer dialog box, as described earlier.

If the amount of memory requested by the Preferred Size option is not available, but more memory is available than the Minimum Size option, the application will launch using all available memory. If the amount of RAM specified in the Minimum Size option is unavailable, a dialog box will appear offering advice on quitting other applications to free enough memory to complete the launch (see Figure 9.15). In previous versions of the Mac OS, one of two or three different boxes would appear; Mac OS 8.6 uses just one such dialog box.

Setting Memory Options

Optimally, 15 to 25 percent of the space in the memory allocation bar (displayed next to an application name in the About This Computer dialog box) should remain open, or unused, while the application is running. (As explained earlier, the

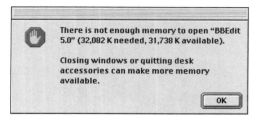

Figure 9.15 The unified "Not Enough Memory" dialog box in Mac OS 8.6.

bar illustrates total allocated RAM in gray and the portion of memory actually being used in blue.)

Some applications will not use all their allocated memory at all times—usage will vary as commands and features are used. Other applications, however, will automatically grab all the memory allocated to it from the Memory section of the Get Info dialog box. So to determine the actual, average, and maximum amount of memory used, keep the About This Computer window open while you work and monitor the changes in memory used by your applications in the lower half of the screen, as illustrated in Figure 9.16.

AppleCD Audio Player	440 K
BBEdit 5.0	5.9 MB
Browser (Fat)	1 MB
GraphicConverter	9.8 MB
Mac OS	28.6 MB
Memory Mapper 1.5	403 K
Peek-a-Boo	536 K
Sherlock	1.9 MB
Speed Doubler™ 8	1 MB
Stickies	456 K

Figure 9.16 Application memory use is documented in the About This Computer dialog box.

Given that having 15 to 25 percent unused space is the goal, watching the amount of actual memory used will tell you if the current memory allocation is too low, too high, or about right. As a result, you may need to increase a program's memory allocation, or you may be able to decrease it. Either of these modifications is done via the Size options.

Increasing memory allocation provides additional memory that can in many cases improve application performance, allow larger and more complete document files to be opened, and reduce or eliminate the possibility of memory-related crashes. These benefits are hardly surprising when you consider how an application uses its allocated memory: it must control and manage its own code, as well as data from

Mac OS 8.6

any open document files and all data manipulations performed by its commands and features. And it must do all this with an allocated memory that's less than the total size of the application program and its data files, let alone what it needs to manipulate its data. As a result, software must constantly shift parts of its own code and data from open documents back and forth between disk-storage memory and real memory. Providing additional memory minimizes this activity and allows the program to concentrate on operating efficiently.

For most programs, increasing the Current Size or Preferred Size option by 20 to 25 percent is optimal. If you experience frequent "out of memory" errors in any software application, however, continue increasing until these errors are eliminated. Increasing the amount of memory will sometimes fix problems associated with launching applications even though a specific error is not presented by the Mac OS.

Decreasing memory allocation allows you to successfully launch applications with less memory, thereby running more programs simultaneously. This is generally not a recommended practice, but in many cases software will operate successfully using less RAM than suggested by the developer.

The true minimum, although it will rarely be more than 20 percent smaller than the suggested size, cannot easily be determined. Don't be afraid to try, however—just be sure to test the application in this configuration before working on important data and save frequently once you begin working. Start by reducing the Current or Minimum Size option by just 5 to 10 percent; if you find that the About This Computer dialog box shows large amounts of unused space, you may be able to reduce the allocation even more.

With the low price of RAM and the availability of virtual memory, the need for most Macintosh users to reduce these sizes should become less common. Even if you have only 16MB of RAM installed, using virtual memory is preferable to reducing the Current or Minimum Size options. You're less likely to experience crashes or loss of data using virtual memory than with a reduced Current Size. (See the discussion of virtual memory earlier in this chapter.) Of course, the best long-range solution is to add enough RAM to your Macintosh so you won't have to depend on either virtual memory or Memory Requirements reductions.

Virtual Memory And Virtual Memory Requirements

We've discussed how PowerPC-native applications may be partially loaded into memory at startup if virtual memory is turned on. But what about the effect virtual memory has on the memory requirements of an application? Figure 9.17 gives you

Mac OS 8.6

an idea of how this works. On the left side of the figure is the memory section of the Get Info dialog box for BBEdit with virtual memory turned on, which is the default setting for Mac OS 8.6. Notice the Note section points out the application will require 1906K additional memory to run if virtual memory is turned off.

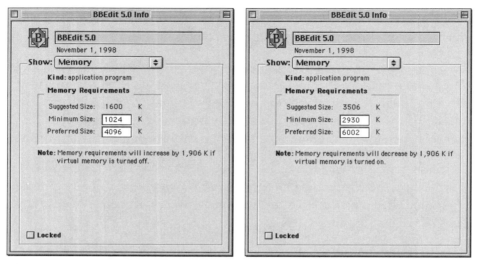

Figure 9.17 A comparison of memory requirements with virtual memory turned on (left) and off (right) for the same application.

The right side of the figure shows the same dialog box once the computer has been restarted with virtual memory turned off. The reverse is now true: The Note section says the application will require 1906K less memory of virtual memory is turned on.

A second benefit to using virtual memory, besides a quicker launch time for applications, is that you'll have more room to launch additional applications simply by turning on virtual memory. It doesn't matter how much virtual memory your computer is using, however; the changes in memory requirements for an application will never change in proportion to how much virtual memory is in use. It will only change if it is in use at all.

Wrapping Up

The amount of memory available on your Macintosh determines, in large measure, what you can do with your computer. As we've seen in this chapter, fine-tuned changes have been made to the OS since System 7. These improvements were designed to give you much more control over memory availability and how that memory is utilized:

➤ Virtual memory lets you "create" memory by using space on your hard drive as if it were RAM.

➤ Built-in 32-bit addressing makes it possible to access a vast amount of memory.

➤ The About This Computer dialog box provides constant feedback about what's happening with your Mac's memory.

➤ Utilities like Memory Mapper and Mac OS Purge can help you manage your memory usage.

➤ The Memory section of the Get Info dialog box helps you control the amount of memory an application uses.

In the next chapter, we'll look at one of the Mac OS's greatest strengths—the ability to launch and operate multiple applications at the same time. This chapter will focus on the multitasking abilities of the Mac OS, the commands and features it supports, and the ways in which you can use multitasking to work more productively.

Working With Multiple Applications

One of the exciting features of Mac OS 8.6 is actually an old feature that Macintosh users have been using for more than 10 years. Known as MultiFinder in previous system software versions and simply as the Finder in Mac OS 8.6, this feature lets you do the following:

➤ Run multiple applications at once

➤ Switch between open applications as necessary

➤ Leave one program working while you switch to another

➤ Copy multiple items at the same time and return to the Finder or another application while the items are copied in the background

MultiFinder was a separate utility file kept in the System folder of previous system software versions. Because the MultiFinder utility file is no longer used, the name MultiFinder is not appropriate. In this book, the set of abilities that allows you to open multiple applications simultaneously will be called *multitasking*. Other people and publications may continue to refer to them as MultiFinder features; you may also hear them described as the Process Manager. Some may avoid using any specific name, simply referring to the features as part of the system software or the Finder.

Technically speaking, multitasking comes in two varieties: cooperative and preemptive. Mac OS 8.6 provides cooperative multitasking, which means that all open applications have equal access to the Macintosh's computing power. In cooperative multitasking, applications are responsible for "letting go" of the microprocessor, whereas in preemptive multitasking, system software assigns a *time slice* to each application and shuttles processing between each running application. Time slices occur so frequently that each application appears to be running in real time.

Some purists consider preemptive multitasking, which ascribes priority to specific applications or tasks, to be the only "real" multitasking. You find preemptive multitasking in more "robust" operating systems such as Unix, where each computer supports multiple users. Apple is slowly migrating the system software toward full multitasking and memory protection.

The distinctions between cooperative and preemptive multitasking are unimportant—and probably uninteresting—to most Macintosh users. Faster hardware and more memory make running multiple applications much more practical, however. For convenience, we'll use the term multitasking to describe the Mac's ability to open and operate multiple applications simultaneously.

What Is Multitasking?

Multitasking allows several programs to be opened and used simultaneously. You can have your word processor, Web browser, and graphics package all running at the same time, and you can switch between them freely. It's even possible for an application to continue processing information while you're using another application. Figure 10.1 shows 13 applications running simultaneously, but with only three (Internet Explorer, GraphicConverter, and BBEdit) running as visible applications. The others have all been hidden using the Hide command in the applications menu.

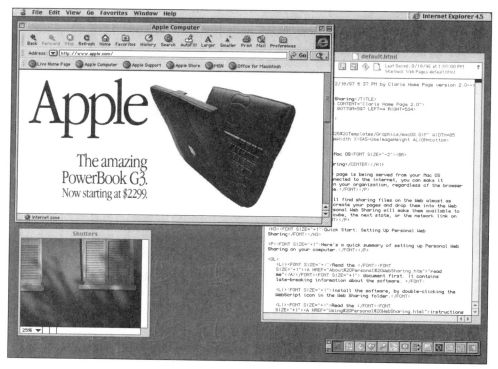

Figure 10.1 A Mac with several open applications.

Multitasking is a fantastic productivity booster, allowing you to use both time and resources with maximum efficiency. For example, you're working in your word processor when you receive a telephone call from your mother. She wants to know whether she'd be better off investing the $10,000 she just won playing bingo in a 10-year CD paying 8.25 percent, or if she should sink it into T-bills paying 6.15 percent tax-free. To help dear old Mom out of her dilemma, you need access to a spreadsheet. So you quit your word processor, launch your spreadsheet, perform the necessary calculations, offer your advice, quit the spreadsheet, launch the word processor, reload your file, and say good-bye to Mom.

Following this approach is fine—of course you want to help your mother—but much of the time it took to quit your word processor, launch the spreadsheet, quit the spreadsheet, relaunch the word processor, and reload your file could have been saved. Multitasking would have allowed you to run your spreadsheet without quitting your word processor.

This example points to one of the most obvious benefits of multitasking—the ability to use two or more applications together to complete a single project. To prepare a mail merge, for example, you can export data from your database manager, prepare the merge lists, and then execute the merge. In most cases, the raw data exported from your database will require some cleaning up before it's ready to be merged, and often you'll encounter a minor data formatting problem that requires you to repeat the whole export and data cleanup process. But by using multitasking, you avoid the delay and frustration of quitting the word processor to return to the database and then quitting the database to return to the word processor.

Suppose you need to read reports and view database or spreadsheet data while preparing presentation graphics, update graphic illustrations in a drawing package before importing them into a page layout, or use an optical character recognition package to read in articles for storage in a database. In these and many other cases, quickly switching from one application to another and using the Mac's Cut, Copy, and Paste commands allows transfer of information between applications that can't otherwise share data.

The third benefit of multitasking is the most exciting—and certainly the one yielding the greatest productivity gains: multitasking supports background processing. The result is that an open application can continue to process data even when you switch away from that application to work in another. Any task that ties up your computer, forcing you to wait for it to finish, can probably benefit from background processing. Common examples are printing, downloading files from the Internet, making large spreadsheet calculations, and generating database

Mac OS 8.6

reports. Examples of background processing and ways you can take advantage of this tremendous capability are discussed later in this chapter in the section entitled "Background Processing."

The Old MultiFinder

If you're familiar with MultiFinder from earlier versions of the system software, you'll find only a few differences between MultiFinder and the multitasking features of System 7 and Mac OS 8.6. The most notable differences are that multitasking is always available and, unlike MultiFinder, cannot be turned off. The other major difference is that the Finder is also multithreaded, which allows you to perform multiple copy operations and return to another application.

If you didn't use MultiFinder in previous versions of the system software, it was probably for one of the following reasons:

➤ *Insufficient memory*—MultiFinder required 2MB of RAM (at a minimum) and 4MB or more of RAM to be useful. The same is true of the multitasking capabilities of Mac OS 8, although the recent lowering of RAM prices and the addition of virtual memory in Mac OS 8.6 make having insufficient memory less of an issue than in the past. (Mac OS 8.6 memory requirements are discussed later in this chapter and in Chapter 9.) As the system software has continued to grow, so too has the Mac OS's memory appetite. In Mac OS 8.6, the current recommended minimum RAM for basic system software is 32MB. This increase is attributable more to additions of numerous features (Extensions, Control Panels, and the like) than to the memory management requirements of multitasking.

➤ *Reputation*—MultiFinder had a reputation for instability. Many people believed that using MultiFinder made the Macintosh prone to frequent crashes. As is often the case with software and hardware, this reputation was undeserved—the rumors of crashes were not based on the real facts. When MultiFinder was first released, many applications crashed when they were launched under MultiFinder. Crashing was not the fault of MultiFinder; it was usually because the application had not been written according to Apple's programming rules. Once these incompatible applications were made MultiFinder-compatible, almost all problems vanished. Another problem—again not attributable to MultiFinder—was the increasing use of start-up programs, which caused a memory conflict in the System Heap (an area of RAM used by the operating system), often resulting in crashes when using MultiFinder. This problem was easily cured with utilities such as HeapFix or HeapTool, which are freely available from user groups and bulletin boards. In any case, this type of problem is not apparent in Mac OS 8.6.

► *Complexity*—MultiFinder was considered too complex by many novice Macintosh users. This perception was understandable: after all, MultiFinder was offered as a virtually undocumented utility program. A Macintosh user had to be somewhat adventurous just to turn it on and learn how to use it. For the majority of users who didn't spend their free time attending user groups, browsing on CompuServe, or reading about the Macintosh, MultiFinder seemed intimidating and too risky.

In Mac OS 8 and later, multitasking was seamlessly integrated into the system software, making the simultaneous use of multiple applications a fundamental part of the working routine. The MultiFinder was replaced by just the Finder. Everyone who uses the Macintosh should take the time to learn, understand, and benefit from this powerful tool.

Multitasking In Mac OS 8.6

The ability to keep multiple programs in memory and recall them from the background to the foreground has been part of Macintosh system software since before MultiFinder. This kind of behavior is called context switching. An application in the background is suspended at its last point of execution. Context switching is not multitasking because only one process is running at a time. In technical parlance, your Macintosh stores the different threads of execution—but only a single thread in one application can execute.

Background processing started in System 6 and continues into Mac OS 8.6. Many lower-level I/O (input/output) functions have been enabled, allowing you to print, communicate, and display data in the background while a single application runs in the foreground. This was the beginning of multitasking: your Macintosh could run multiple processes, but it limited which types of processes could be concurrent. In this manner, the Macintosh was single-threaded because only one thread operates for the foreground and for any processes running in the background. That is, only one process is running at a time and your Macintosh CPU cycles between foreground and background tasks. This is commonly referred to as time slicing.

System 7.5 introduced the Thread Manager (compatible with all versions of System 7). The Thread Manager is an Extension that allowed for multithreading within a single application (see Figure 10.2). This was still lightweight, concurrent processing, but it was another step along the way toward a fully multitasked system.

Figure 10.2 The Thread Manager extension.

With the Thread Manager, you could work in your database, word processor, or spreadsheet while performing other functions in the same application. It was up to application developers to implement the programming necessary to take advantage of the Thread Manager, but the capability was ignored by applications that didn't implement it. Therefore, no compatibility problems were expected.

In Mac OS 8.6, however, the functionality provided through the Thread Manager has been integrated into the operating system itself, so the Thread Manager is no longer present. Some older applications written to take advantage of the Thread Manager may insist upon the Thread Manager being installed; Mac OS 8.6 will simply ignore it if it is installed.

One example of multitasking can be found in the OpenDoc compound document architecture. In OpenDoc, the architecture creates a document frame and manages parts within the document. When you add a part, the Part Handler checks to see whether the applet (text, sound, video, and so on) is open, and if not, opens it. As you work in a text part, clocks, animation parts, movie parts, or a live video feed can be running concurrently. It looks like multitasking, but it's really more a form of multithreading within a single application.

Currently, full multitasking is present in Mac OS X Server, and is being written into Mac OS X, which is slated to be unveiled to consumers in late 1999. In Mac OS X, Apple is building the heart of its operating system into a very small, fast, and portable core of code called a kernel. More importantly, the kernel comes with true memory protection. Memory protection isolates programs' threads in their own "containers" so that one thread cannot call for memory used by any other thread. A thread can crash and burn, but it will not bring your system to a halt. Along with preemptive multitasking, memory protection is the most important difference between the Mac OS and Unix-style operating systems such as Solaris and Linux. It will allow real-time multiuser transaction processing to run on a Macintosh.

Working With Multiple Applications

Mac OS 8.6 allows you to open multiple applications automatically, without any special configuration or initiation. In fact, when you launch your first application from the Finder, you'll immediately notice the effect: the Desktop (the volume icons, Trash, and so on) does not disappear as the new application is launched, as was the case in older versions of the system software. The Desktop remains visible in Mac OS 8.6 because both your new application and the Finder now run simultaneously (see Figure 10.3).

Working With Multiple Applications 265

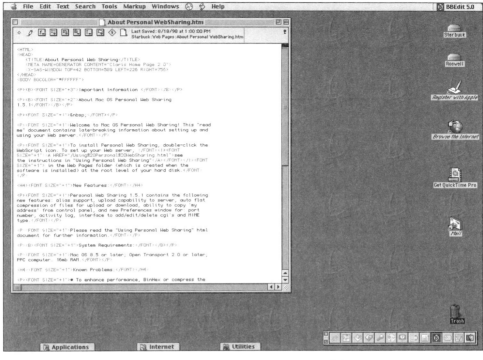

Figure 10.3 BBEdit running with Finder elements visible.

Note that beginning with System 7.0.1P, it became possible to "hide the Finder." In that instance, the Finder icons will disappear when you switched to another application. See the "Hiding The Desktop" section later in this chapter for more details.

When you launch additional applications, you continue to see the capabilities of multitasking. As each additional program opens, its menu bar and windows are displayed, and other open applications are unaffected.

When you first start using multiple applications simultaneously, the sight of several windows open at the same time may be a little disconcerting. As you learn to arrange and manipulate these windows and enjoy the benefits of multiple open applications, you'll soon find yourself wondering how you ever got along using just one program at a time.

The number of applications you can launch simultaneously is limited only by the amount of memory you have available. If your launch will exceed available memory, a dialog box will alert you to the problem, and the additional application will not be launched. (You'll learn more about memory and running multiple applications in "The Memory Implications Of Multitasking" section later in this chapter.)

Mac OS 8.6

Foreground And Background Applications

Although more than one program can be open at once, only one program can be active at any one time. The active program is known as the foreground application; other open but inactive applications are called background applications, even if you can see portions of their windows or if they're simultaneously processing tasks (see Figure 10.4).

Figure 10.4 The top-most window indicates which application is the current foreground application.

You can tell which program is currently active in several ways, three of which are shown in Figure 10.5:

➤ The menu bar displays the menu commands of the active program only.

➤ The active program's icon appears at the top of the Application menu.

➤ The active program name is checked in the Application menu.

➤ The Apple menu's About This Computer says About... (the active program's name appears here, in place of the word "Computer").

➤ Active program windows overlap other visible windows or elements.

➤ Active program windows display a highlighted title bar, which includes horizontal lines, the close box, and the zoom box.

➤ The Application Switcher will highlight the most active application.

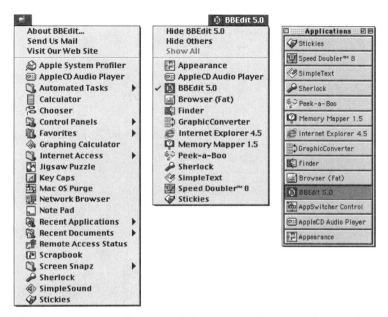

Figure 10.5 A collection of clues as to which application is the active application.

In contrast, a background application's menu bar does not appear, its icon is not checked in the Application menu, none of its windows are highlighted, and some or all of its windows may be hidden or obscured.

Because only one program can be in the foreground, it's important to be able to switch quickly and easily from one foreground program to another. Switching between applications is commonly referred to as "sending to the back" and "bringing to the front."

You can switch between open applications in at least four ways:

➤ *Use the Application menu*—Located in the upper right corner of the menu bar, the Application menu lists the names of all applications currently running. Choose the name of the application you want to switch to, and that program will bring its menu bar and windows to the front. For example, to switch from an application such as Internet Explorer to the Finder, choose the word *Finder* from the Application menu. The Finder's menu bar will appear, and any icons and windows on the desktop will become visible. (See Figure 10.6.)

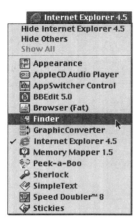

Figure 10.6 Switching between applications using the Application menu.

➤ *Use the Application Switcher palette*—If it is visible, click on an application's icon in the Application Switcher.

➤ *Use the Application Switcher's keyboard shortcut*—Press Command+Tab to cycle through the open applications one at a time.

➤ *Click any visible window*—Clicking any visible element on the screen brings the application owning that element to the front. For example, while working in your word processor, if you can still see the icons on the Desktop, clicking one of them will bring the Finder to the front, making it the current application. You can then return to the word processor by clicking its window.

Background Processing

You can bring any application to the foreground, which sends any other to the background, at any time except when non-Navigation Services-savvy dialog boxes are open. Applications that have the new Open and Save dialog boxes open can be moved safely into the background even if an Open or Save dialog box is active. You can even send most applications to the background while they're processing data—they'll continue to calculate or process in the background. Background processing brings to light an entirely new dimension of using multiple open applications simultaneously.

If you could use multiple open applications only sequentially, one after the other, the increase in productivity would be limited to the time you saved by avoiding repeated opening and quitting of applications. Background processing, however, lets you print a newsletter, calculate a spreadsheet, and dial up a remote bulletin board at the same time. This capacity is the ultimate in computer productivity.

Background processing is easy. Start by doing a lengthy process, such as loading a huge Web page using a slow modem; then bring another open application to the foreground. The background task continues processing while you use the computer for another task in another application. Because foreground and background applications are sharing the hardware resources, you may notice a slowdown or jerky motion in the foreground application. The severity of this effect will depend on your Macintosh's power and the number and requirements of the background tasks being performed, but your foreground application should suffer no detrimental effects.

TIP
Using virtual memory can emphasize any slowness when switching between applications.

Periodically, you may need to attend to a task left running in the background, or you may be given notice when the task is completed. If so, an Alert dialog box will be displayed, a diamond will appear before the application's name in the Application menu, or the Application menu icon will flash alternately with the alerting application's icon.

Background Printing

The first background processing most people use is printing. Background printing is not quite the same as using two applications at once, but it's close.

Without multitasking, you have to wait for the entire file to be printed because of the time it takes for the printer to mechanically do the job. In background printing, files are printed to disk as fast as the application and printer driver can handle them. Then a utility called a print spooler sends the print file from the disk to the printer. The advantage is that the print spooler takes over the task of feeding the pages to the printer while you continue working in your main application or even use another software application.

Since background PostScript printing support is built into Mac OS 8.6, the Background Printing option has been removed from the Chooser, as shown in Figure 10.7.

With background printing, files printed using the LaserWriter and other drivers are spooled to your hard drive automatically under Mac OS 8.6. At the same time, the Desktop PrintMonitor utility, automatically running in the background, begins

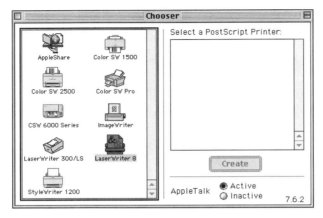

Figure 10.7 The Chooser.

printing the spooled file to the selected PostScript printer. While Desktop PrintMonitor is printing, you can bring it to the foreground by selecting its icon from the Desktop. The Desktop PrintMonitor dialog box is shown in Figure 10.8.

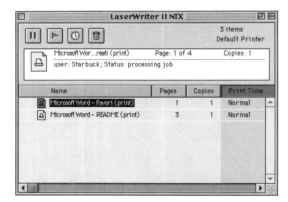

Figure 10.8 The Desktop PrintMonitor dialog box.

However, since background printing is now a part of the Mac OS, some applications will allow you to disable this feature and force a document that has been selected for printing to do so in the foreground. This is useful if you want a document to print immediately, not to mention faster. Foreground printing is faster because most Macs do not use a print server to handle Mac-to-printer communication, so printing is done on a peer-to-peer basis between the Mac and the printer, which requires processing power. In fact, many printers do not even contain a processor of their own and must rely on the Mac's processor to help things along. Foreground printing can assist in both these situations, but only for applications such as Microsoft Word 98 that allow this ability. Figure 10.9 shows the Background Printing section of the Print command in Microsoft Word 98.

Working With Multiple Applications 271

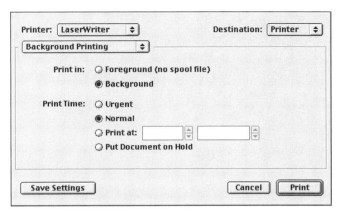

Figure 10.9 Some applications such as Microsoft Word 98 allow you to print in the foreground as well as the background.

Copying Files In The Background

Copying files from one location to another is a basic function the Finder has always provided, but through successive Finder versions, the capability has continued to evolve.

Early versions of the Finder provided only a simple dialog box during file copying. Later, a counter of files being copied was added. Then names of copied files were added, and finally the progress bar became a part of this dialog box. Despite these improvements, which seemed to make time pass more quickly, you were still forced to wait while files were copied.

In Mac OS 8.6, the process of copying files takes a huge step forward: you can now work in any open application while the Finder runs multiple copy operations in the background. To use this feature, follow these steps:

1. Open the application you want to use while the Finder is copying.

2. Switch to the Finder by using the Application menu, Application Switcher, or by clicking the Desktop.

3. Start the copy process in the normal way by dragging the desired files from their source location to the icon of the destination folder or volume (or by selecting Command+D). The copying process will begin, and the copying dialog box will appear. You can also select another item to copy while the first item is copying. For example, Figure 10.10 shows an item being copied three times simultaneously.

4. Then use the stopwatch cursor to select the Application menu and choose the name of the open application you want to use while the file copy is in progress.

Mac OS 8.6

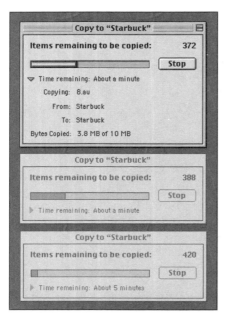

Figure 10.10 Initiating multiple copying tasks while programs continue to function.

This application will come to the foreground ready for you to use while the Finder continues its copy operation in the background.

5. Switch back to the Finder any time you like using the Application menu or clicking the Desktop.

Hiding Applications

Running several applications concurrently can result in an onscreen clutter of windows. To alleviate this problem, Mac OS 8.6 lets you "hide" open application windows and the Desktop, thus removing them from the screen without changing their status or the background work they're doing. You can hide an application at the time you leave it to switch to another application, or while it's running in the background. Figure 10.11 shows how your Desktop can become cluttered when running multiple applications simultaneously.

Hiding some programs while continuing to operate other programs can help clear things up a bit, as shown in Figure 10.12.

The Application menu provides three Hide commands: Hide <Current Application> (Current Application being the name of the current foreground application), Hide Others, and Show All:

Working With Multiple Applications   273

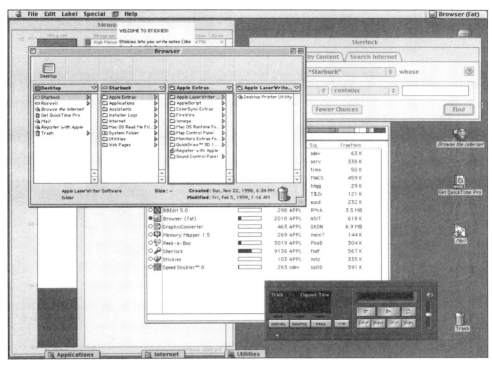

Figure 10.11   Running multiple applications without hiding can result in a crowded display.

▶ *Hide (current application)*—Removes all windows of the current application from the screen and brings another window of an open application to the foreground. The next-most recently used application is brought to the front when this command is selected. The icon of a hidden application is dimmed in the Application menu to signify that it has been hidden. To unhide the application, either select its name from the Application menu, which will bring it to the foreground, or choose the Show All command.

▶ *Hide Others*—Removes all windows from the screen except those of the currently active application. This is useful when onscreen clutter is bothersome, or if you're accidentally clicking the windows of background applications and bringing them forward. After the Hide Others command has been used, the icons of all open applications, except those of the foreground application, are dimmed in the Application menu as a visual reminder that these applications are hidden.

▶ *Show All*—Makes all current applications visible. You can tell which applications are currently hidden by their dimmed icons in the Application menu. When you choose the Show All command, the current foreground application remains in the foreground, and the windows of hidden background applications become visible; the applications remain in the background, however.

Mac OS 8.6

274 Chapter 10

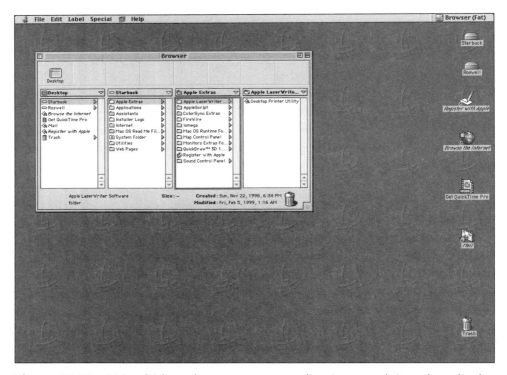

Figure 10.12 Using hiding, the same open applications result in a clear display.

While an application is hidden, it continues to operate exactly the same as it would if it were running as a background application and not hidden. If an application can normally perform tasks in the background, it will still perform these tasks in the background while it's hidden. In fact, because of the effort saved by not having to upgrade the screen display, the background operation of some tasks is faster when their parent application is hidden.

To hide the current foreground application when you send it to the background, hold down the Option key while bringing another application forward (either by choosing its name from the Application menu or by clicking the mouse on its window). You can retrieve applications hidden in this manner by using the Show All command or by selecting their dimmed icons from the Application menu.

Hiding The Desktop

A potential problem lies in wait for novices who are working with multiple applications at the same time. If you inadvertently click the Desktop, you switch into the Finder and out of your current program. Suddenly you've lost your place, and the menus have changed. Because the old Performa series was built for the home market (and for novices), Apple included in System 7.0.1P and 7.1P a feature

Mac OS 8.6

called Finder hiding that prevented users from switching to the Finder by inadvertently clicking on the desktop.

TIP

Some users simply close all of an application's windows and mistakenly believe that the application has therefore been quit. Some applications will automatically quit after the last window has been closed, but most will continue to run until "Quit" has been selected from the File menu.

Voluntary Desktop hiding appeared first in System 7.5 and continues to be a useful option in Mac OS 8.6. With Desktop hiding, when you switch into an application other than the Finder, the Desktop disappears (not unlike the way things worked before System 7—the difference is that this hiding is by choice). You can't click the background and switch out of your application. You turn on Finder hiding by disabling the Show Desktop When in Background check box in the General Controls Control Panel. So if you're working in an application and you can't see your hard disk, Trash, or file and folder icons where they should appear, Finder hiding is the cause. Figure 10.13 shows an example of Internet Explorer running with the Desktop hidden.

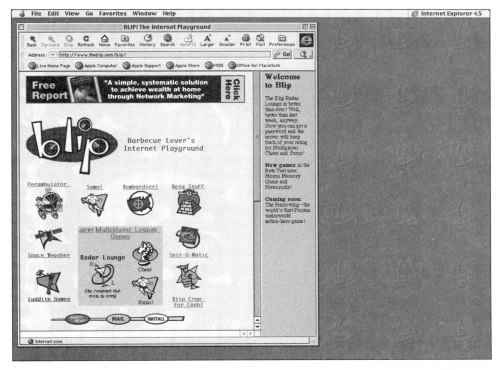

Figure 10.13 Internet Explorer running with the Desktop elements hidden.

Mac OS 8.6

Multitasking Tips

Once you start using the Hide commands to reduce screen clutter, you should be comfortable working with multiple open applications. The following tips can help:

➤ *Saving before switching*—Before bringing another application to the foreground, save your work in the application you're leaving so that if your Mac crashes or is turned off accidentally, you won't lose your work.

➤ *Resuming after crashing*—If an application crashes in Mac OS 8.6, you can usually force the Mac to close that application (referred to as a *force quit*) and regain access to your other applications by pressing Command+Option+Escape, the result of which is shown in Figure 10.14.

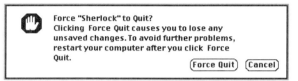

Figure 10.14   The Force Quit dialog box.

Note that after resuming after this kind of crash, your system may be unstable and prone to additional crashes. Using this option is a bit like driving a nail with a sledgehammer—it works but is likely to do some damage. You should save any unsaved work in other open applications, and immediately restart your Macintosh just to be safe.

➤ *Shutting down or restarting*—Selecting the Shut Down or Restart commands from the Finder's Special menu while multiple applications are open will cause all open applications to quit (if those applications have been properly programmed to accept the "quit" command using Apple Events). If any open documents contain changes that haven't been saved, the parent application will be brought to the foreground, and you'll be asked whether you want to save those changes (see Figure 10.15 for a few examples of this type of dialog box). Click Save to save the changes, Don't Save to discard the changes, or Cancel to abort the Shut Down or Restart operation and therefore the automatic quitting of that particular application.

➤ *Maintaining efficiency for background applications*—Applications in the background often run more efficiently if hidden with one of the Hide commands from the Application menu. This is true because often the onscreen display can't keep up with the application's processing rate; as a result, the application has to wait for the screen to be drawn. The extent of this delay depends on your computer system and video display. Using the Hide command eliminates all video-related delay.

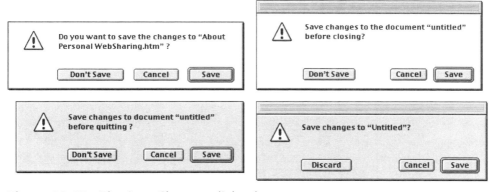

Figure 10.15 The Save Changes dialog box.

▶ *Switching and hiding*—To hide the active-most application while switching to another open application, hold down the Option key while clicking the new application's window or while selecting that application's name from the Application menu.

The Memory Implications Of Multitasking

Everything has its price. Macintosh users know this well (especially experienced Macintosh users). Multitasking is no exception—its price is memory.

Put simply, you can run only as many applications at once as your available Macintosh memory can handle. A predefined amount of memory must be dedicated to the application while it's open. Running multiple applications simultaneously requires enough memory to satisfy the cumulative amounts defined by those applications. Your total amount of available memory includes what's supplied by the RAM chips installed on your computer's logic board or on an expansion card (for PowerBooks), plus any virtual memory created with the Memory Control Panel. (See Chapter 9 for more information about virtual memory.)

When you first turn on a Macintosh running Mac OS 8.6, some of your memory is taken up immediately by the system software and the Finder. This amount varies depending on how many fonts and sounds you've installed, your disk cache setting, the Extensions you're using, and whether you're using File Sharing. In some circumstances, as much as 25 to 33 percent of your Mac's available memory can be consumed by the system software itself. Your Macintosh's memory usage is documented in the About This Computer dialog box, shown in Figure 10.16. If you would like to reduce the amount of memory your system software consumes, remove unused fonts or sounds, reduce the size of your RAM disk, and turn off File Sharing.

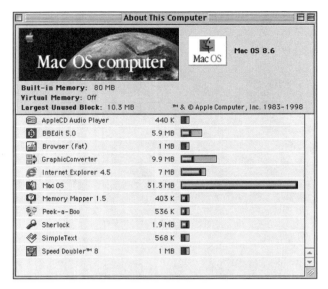

Figure 10.16 The About This Computer dialog box.

Each time you launch an application, it requests the amount of memory that it needs in order to run. If enough memory is available, the application is launched. If enough memory isn't available, one of several dialog boxes will appear warning you of the situation or offering a solution on how to make more memory available. The first, shown in Figure 10.17, informs you there's not enough memory available to launch the selected application.

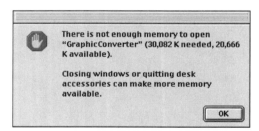

Figure 10.17 This dialog box appears when you're launching an application with limited memory available.

The second, shown in Figure 10.18, tells you the same thing but it also gives you the option of launching the application once another application has been quit to make room for the new application to be launched. Normally, launching the application under these circumstances will allow you to use the application without incident.

If available memory is insufficient to launch an application, quit one or more of the currently open applications to free up additional memory. Then try again to launch

Figure 10.18 This dialog box appears when you're launching an application with almost—but not quite—enough memory available.

the application you want. If this doesn't do the trick, quit additional open applications and retry the launch until you're successful. If all else fails, restart the computer.

For more information on your Mac's memory (including ways you can expand available memory), tips on reducing the amount of memory each application consumes, and more about using the About This Computer dialog box, go back to Chapter 9.

Wrapping Up

Working with several applications at once takes some getting used to, but it's the best way to make the most of your time and computing resources. As we've seen in this chapter, Mac OS 8.6's multitasking support is impressive:

➤ You can launch as many different applications as your available memory permits.

➤ Many applications can continue to process data while they're running in the background.

➤ Because the Finder is multithreaded, you can copy items in the background while continuing to use the Finder or other applications.

➤ Hiding open applications reduces onscreen clutter without affecting the operation of the applications.

Like many other Mac OS 8.6 features, multitasking is available to every program that's compatible with Mac OS 8.0 an higher. Next, Chapter 11 helps you unlock the world of desktop publishing by introducing you to the built-in font and printing capabilities of Mac OS 8.6.

Mac OS 8.6

Fonts And Printing

Mac OS 8.6 uses the best font and printing technologies that can be found in a personal computer, drawing on years of experience and technological advances. It's safe to say that a great measure of the Macintosh's success has been due to its capabilities in the graphics and publishing arena. Desktop publishing is the Macintosh's heritage. System 7 made major changes in this area, introducing sophisticated graphics, outline fonts, advanced typography, color matching, a new print architecture, a portable document format, and improved localization for international software. Many of these new changes were due to the release of QuickDraw GX in System 7.5.

Fonts are both the blessing and curse of the Macintosh, however. No other computer offers such a variety of fonts or typographic capabilities; but because of technical problems and corporate politics, no other aspect of the Mac has caused so many headaches for so many people.

System 7 extended Macintosh font technology, simplified font installation, improved the appearance of fonts onscreen, and introduced two new font formats called TrueType and TrueType GX. Mac OS 8.6 offers some relief from "font hell" from previous versions of the Mac OS. In this chapter, we'll look at the ways in which the Mac OS displays fonts and images to your screen and to your local and networked printers, paying special attention to fonts and type issues. Here you'll find out what's practical and what's possible.

Imaging Models

Fonts and images are generated for use on computer screens and printers by different ways, or models. Most monitors display information on screen at 72 dots per inch (dpi), but printers can create output at resolutions up to 1,440 dpi. Because of the disparity in quality between screen and printer output, different imaging models are required for displaying on screen and on paper. Apple has invented several imaging models over the last 20 years, including QuickDraw, QuickDraw

GX, and QuickDraw 3D. Apple is also considering using a new imaging model called OpenGL as a replacement for some of its own technologies, such as QuickDraw 3D, because of its cross-platform appeal. The components of the Mac OS that generate images and fonts on screen are not as important to most users as the fonts themselves, however.

Suffice it to say, the Mac OS is a powerful desktop publishing platform that is supported by many third-party imaging utilities such as Font Reserve, shown in Figure 11.1, to help users manage its imaging capabilities.

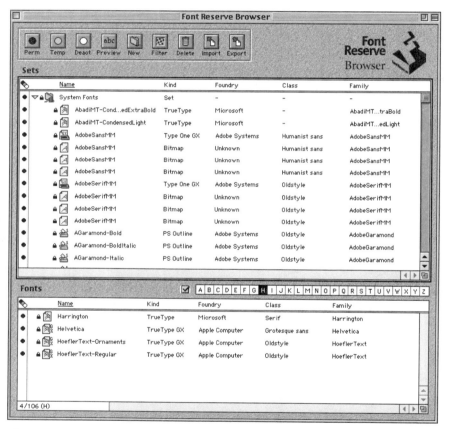

Figure 11.1 Use a tool like Font Reserve to help manage your fonts.

Several font technologies have been used to meet the needs of the various types of imaging models used by the Mac OS. Font technologies continue to improve and provide users with faster printing and better screen display using the following types of fonts:

➤ Bitmapped (fixed-size) fonts

➤ PostScript (variable-size) fonts

➤ TrueType (variable-size) fonts

➤ TrueType GX (variable-size) fonts

You can use all three of these types of fonts simultaneously under Mac OS 8.6, but as we'll see a bit later, each has its own advantages, as well as a few disadvantages. The Mac OS doesn't really allow you to change imaging models like you can change fonts, however. QuickDraw is the only real choice we have, but it is this model that allows for the Mac OS to use different types of fonts and printers.

QuickDraw

Of all the sets of components found in the Macintosh toolbox, few are as recognized as QuickDraw. QuickDraw shipped with the first Macintosh in 1984. MacPaint, MacDraw, and a generation of Macintosh programs that followed use QuickDraw for most of their capabilities. Anything you see drawn within a window on your Macintosh screen is due to QuickDraw.

QuickDraw is an imaging model—your Mac uses it to create and display fonts and images. These images are then sent to your monitor, printer, and any other output device that supports QuickDraw. As such, QuickDraw is really a page description language (or PDL) in the same way that PostScript is also a PDL.

> **TIP**
> PostScript is a page description language developed by Adobe and licensed to many operating system and printer manufacturers, including Apple Computer. The TrueType font technology was developed by Apple as a replacement technology to PostScript.

QuickDraw is responsible for the lines and shapes you draw; their patterns and fills; properties such as transparency or opacity; colors, color models, and color selection; fonts; and even what you see in a print dialog box.

Printers are deemed QuickDraw printers when they take QuickDraw output and rasterize (render) it to print its image. Similarly, PostScript printers rasterize PostScript output. PostScript printers are capable of printing QuickDraw because your Macintosh translates QuickDraw to PostScript when it is output to a PostScript device.

QuickDraw was never designed to meet the demands of high-quality output. Apple created QuickDraw to simplify and codify screen display at 72 dpi in black and

Mac OS 8.6

white (which were the screen characteristics of the classic Macintosh series), and to draw to simple printers such as the ImageWriter. For higher quality printing needs, Apple cut a co-marketing deal in 1985 with a small graphics programming company called Adobe to license the sophisticated PostScript language. Apple would sell Cannon's laser printing xerographic engine run by a PostScript controller, and QuickDraw would be converted to PostScript in the operating system of the Macintosh. The rest is, as they say, history.

One of the first QuickDraw upgrades came in 1988 when the Macintosh II was introduced. In its original release, only eight QuickDraw colors were supported. Color QuickDraw was incorporated into the system software in System 5, adding a 32-bit color modeling capability. Soon thereafter, with the introduction of the Mac IIx, Color QuickDraw was written into the new ROMs.

By 1989, high-quality type and graphics had become big business. Although the rest of the language was published, PostScript fonts were encrypted and proprietary, thus giving Adobe a lock on the type business for the Macintosh.

In response to their customers' needs, Adobe created an advanced version of PostScript called PostScript Level 2. PostScript had problems with complexity, file size, and with performance in particular. These problems were solved by adding a new memory model, new compression technology, and new methods for drawing (rasterizing) a page. Other needed improvements included better color support for printed (CYMK) color, color matching, advanced printing support, and several other technologies. QuickDraw had always suffered in comparison to PostScript, and PostScript Level 2 threatened to make QuickDraw an anachronism.

With System 7, Apple decided to make the break. An open outline font type standard called TrueType and a page description language called TrueImage were introduced. Apple set about addressing the other deficiencies in QuickDraw by revising it and adding new technologies through an Extension.

Because the TrueType font technology was ready to go in 1991, it was released with System 7.0. Some other components in the original System 7 list—the LineLayout Manager and the New Print Architecture—were not. Those two new features became part of a larger package, QuickDraw GX, meant to support the needs of color publishing. QuickDraw GX was designed to fix problems relating to color handling, text layout, typography, printing, and so on. Because these are industry-wide problems, it's not surprising that both QuickDraw GX and PostScript Level 2 address similar issues.

After nearly four years in development and testing, QuickDraw GX finally shipped in 1994. It received limited support in Mac OS 8, however, due to Apple's purchase of NeXT and the decision to move to Display Postscript. Applications that utilize both QuickDraw and QuickDraw 3D will work just fine under Mac OS 8.6, however, so it's unlikely that you'll experience any problems.

About QuickDraw GX

QuickDraw GX was a system extension that supplemented the capabilities of QuickDraw, and most of whose features have been incorporated into QuickDraw and other aspects of the Mac OS's printing capabilities. Mac OS 8.0 was the first release to exclude QuickDraw GX as a distinct component of the Mac OS. This change resulted from a decision on the part of Apple to move away from QuickDraw GX as development continued on the next major version of the Mac OS, called Mac OS X (Ten).

The capabilities formerly provided by QuickDraw GX that are now included in Mac OS 8.6 include:

➤ *Higher level graphics routines*—More complex shapes and transformations are supported. Applications that are QuickDraw-savvy can use these system routines; they require less memory to operate and less storage space.

➤ *Improved print architecture*—You will first notice QuickDraw GX's effect in printing because current applications and hardware can take advantage of it. A new, more powerful, and simplified print dialog box now appears in Mac OS 8.6. You can create virtual printers on your desktop as icons, drag and drop files to them, and have better control over your printers and spooled documents anywhere on a network.

➤ *Advanced typography*—QuickDraw GX used special TrueType GX fonts to create advanced type effects such as automatic kerning, justification, and special-character support based on context. These abilities are still available in Mac OS 8.6 and you can continue to use your current font collection, bitmaps or outline fonts, and converted PostScript Type 1 fonts.

➤ *Advanced layout*—Mac OS 8.6 provides support for international text such as Kanji, Hindi, Hebrew, Arabic, or any character set. You can mix right-to-left, left-to-right, or vertical arrangements of letterforms within a document, a paragraph, or a line.

➤ *Improved localization*—WorldScript provides a system for Macintosh developers to transform applications from one language and character set to another. The Mac OS performs the display and handling of fonts and supports character sets based on the Unicode standard. See "Unicode, WorldScript And Localization" later in this chapter for a description of these new capabilities.

► *Portable digital documents*—QuickDraw supports a new "universal" file format known as a portable digital document (PDD). A PDD created by an application can be opened, viewed, and printed by any other user who has QuickDraw on his or her computer whether or not the user has the creator application and typefaces.

► *Custom print functions*—Because fonts, printing, and other objects can be controlled by QuickDraw, developers can more easily create custom printer drivers, printer extensions, and solutions for specific markets.

► *Color matching*—QuickDraw incorporates ColorSync, Apple's color management technology. Because QuickDraw can profile device characteristics, colors can be reproduced as closely and as accurately as the device allows.

QuickDraw GX greatly extended the range of graphics primitives, or shapes, in QuickDraw. Beyond simple line movements that produce the basic shapes—lines, curves, rectangles, polygons, paths, and so on—QuickDraw GX added more advanced attributes. In this regard, outline type is just another shape, with both the same attributes and range of possibilities. Drawn or vector shapes are resolution independent and scale to any size correctly.

QuickDraw GX recognized three different attributes:

► *Style*—Style describes the pen thickness (line or stroke), line end cap (pointed, rounded, or flat), whether the line is drawn inside or outside a shape, line dashes and patterns, and line joins and corners. Text style includes font, size, and other attributes such as bold, italic, and so on.

► *Transform*—A range of shape transformations are supported, including scaling, rotation, perspective, skew, and clipping.

► *Ink*—The ink attributes are the descriptions of the color properties of a shape: data on the selection in a color space, transfer information (opacity, transparency, or mixing), and the description of how to view and display a selected color on a device.

These three words—*style*, *transform*, and *ink*—will enter the vocabulary of any application that uses QuickDraw GX to draw, manipulate type, work with color, and so on. Seasoned Macintosh users have worked with these concepts in their applications for years, but these capabilities were part of an application, not the system software. These capabilities are also part of the PostScript vocabulary. Adding them to QuickDraw makes them available to all QuickDraw applications, resulting in a wider range of possibilities in Macintosh applications with less development time.

Mac OS 8.6

What does the decision to stop supporting QuickDraw GX mean for the average user? Not much, unless you have applications that rely solely on QuickDraw GX and not on QuickDraw. In fact, such applications are so few and far between that none come to mind.

QuickDraw And Printing

Over the years, QuickDraw has introduced many changes to its print architecture that have made printing easier, more intuitive, and more convenient. Among the most important features are the following:

➤ *Desktop printers*—Printers can appear on your desktop—virtual printers that output files to real printing devices. You can drag and drop files to a printer, manage its print queue, and print to several printers without visiting the Chooser.

➤ *New Print dialog boxes*—Within the Print dialog box of any application, the new print architecture provides a redesigned Print dialog box in which you can select a printer.

➤ *Better print spooling*—Each printer manages its own print queue. You can reorder and delete print jobs and drag and drop print jobs from one printer to another.

➤ *Improved background printing*—You'll notice less drag on your foreground application when you print in the background; this is due to the redesigned print architecture.

➤ *Expanded print options*—You can mix page formats in a document. You could, for example, print a document with both landscape and portrait pages, or print a letter, envelope, and post card in a single print job. Multiple tray, double-sided, and other options are supported. You can also print a document to just about any printer; QuickDraw makes the needed conversions so that the page prints correctly—even if the page size or printable area changes.

➤ *Printer extensions*—Developers can create specialized printer drivers, called printer extensions, that provide your printer with special capabilities. Writing printer drivers is easier than ever, now that QuickDraw provides a ready-to-use toolbox for developers.

➤ *Portable digital documents (PPD)*—You can print PDD files on any Macintosh with QuickDraw installed; your having the creator application and fonts is irrelevant. A PDD file can be created by any Macintosh application, whether it's QuickDraw-savvy or not.

These changes are major—and far more numerous than in any other system software version. Nonetheless, most of it will seem intuitive and much easier than what came before.

Mac OS 8.6

Fonts And The Mac OS

The introduction of the Macintosh in 1984 brought with it many innovations, and one of the most important was the way the Mac OS enhanced the appearance of text. Whereas earlier personal computers reduced all communication to the drab, mechanical, and impersonal look of pica-12 (the original dot-matrix font), the Mac OS produced text in a wide range of typefaces, both onscreen and on the printed page. Typography—long an important part of printed communication—became a part of personal computing. As mentioned above, the Mac OS utilizes three basic types of fonts: bitmapped, PostScript, and TrueType, all of which are stored in the Fonts folder under Mac OS 8.6 (see Figure 11.2).

Let's look at the first two types now; TrueType fonts are discussed in another section because they're the preferred fonts for Mac OS 8.6.

Bitmapped Fonts

The original Macintosh fonts (New York, Monaco, Geneva, and Chicago) were fixed-width bitmapped fonts, which means that each character in each font was predefined by the series of dots necessary to create that character at a specific point size. Most bitmapped fonts were produced in 10-, 11-, 12-, and 14-point sizes, and were not scalable (meaning each font was incapable of having a variable width). Later versions used another kind of font altogether, called TrueType fonts.

The original bitmapped fonts, and the many bitmapped fonts that soon joined them, were optimized for display on the Macintosh screen and for printing on the Apple ImageWriter (which was the only printer available at the time). Limitations to working with these bitmapped fonts included:

➤ Dot-matrix bitmapped quality was unacceptable for most business uses. Although typeface variety was certainly a welcome improvement, most people still considered ImageWriter output quality unacceptable for business use regardless of the fonts.

➤ Font variety was limited. Although bitmapped fonts proliferated, almost all were "novelty" faces with little value beyond advertisements, invitations, and entertainment.

➤ The 400K system disks could hold only a limited selection of fonts. Because hard drives were not generally available at that time, it was necessary to boot the Macintosh from a 400K floppy disk. After you squeezed the System folder plus an application or two onto a floppy, only a small amount of room was left for font styles and sizes.

Mac OS 8.6

Fonts And Printing 289

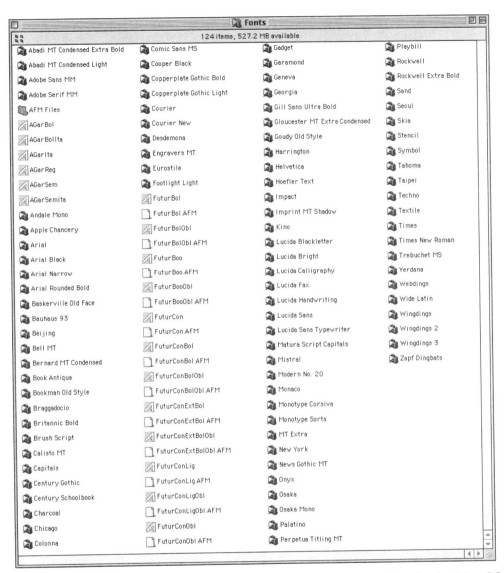

Figure 11.2 Many third-party fonts, in addition to those installed by the Mac OS, are installed in this Fonts folder.

> Macintosh applications could support only a limited number of fonts at one time. When too many fonts were installed in the System file, applications acted strangely, often providing only a random subset of the installed fonts.

These problems were solved, after some time, with new releases of system software, application software, and third-party utility programs. The next big change in the Mac font world was not based on software but on the introduction of the Apple Laser-Writer printer with its built-in support for the PostScript page description language.

Mac OS 8.6

PostScript Fonts

The introduction of the Apple LaserWriter printer brought a new type of font to the Macintosh: the PostScript font. Fonts of this kind were required in documents created for output to the LaserWriter (and to all later PostScript printers) so that the type could be printed at high resolution. Bitmapped fonts were inadequate for these new printers. Eventually, PostScript fonts came to be known by a variety of names, including laser fonts, outline fonts, and Type 1 fonts.

Each PostScript font consists of two files: a screen font file and a printer font file. The screen font file for a PostScript font is nearly identical to the font file of bitmapped fonts, providing bitmapped versions of the font at specific sizes optimized for onscreen use. Other similarities between the two include:

➤ Both are provided in different styles and sizes.

➤ Both appear in the font menu or dialog box in all applications.

Fonts usually have one of three or so icons, so it's easy to identify PostScript fonts when viewing the contents of the Fonts folder. Figure 11.3 shows some of the PostScript fonts in the Fonts folder.

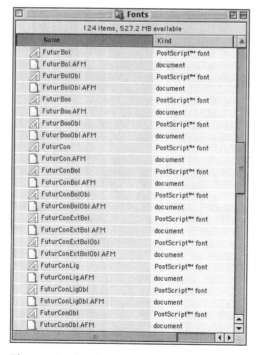

Figure 11.3 PostScript fonts in the Fonts folder.

Unlike bitmapped screen fonts, each PostScript screen font has a corresponding PostScript printer font. This printer font provides the PostScript printer with a mathematical description of each character in the font, as well as other information necessary to create and produce high-resolution output. When you're printing PostScript fonts, the screen font is only a general representation of the printer font. Your Macintosh works with the printer font descriptions to create text output.

Regardless of whether all screen fonts and printer fonts are matched, it isn't imperative that you use all the available screen fonts. You must, however, always use all printer fonts. In other words, you can *create* Helvetica Bold without installing the Helvetica Bold screen font (by using the Helvetica font and the Bold type style), but you cannot *print* Helvetica Bold without the Helvetica Bold printer font.

For a PostScript font to be printed correctly, the printer font file must be "available" to the PostScript printer. A font is available when it has been built into the printer's ROM chips, stored on a printer's hard disk, or kept on the Macintosh hard disk and manually or automatically downloaded to the printer.

PostScript Font Challenges

For a variety of reasons, using PostScript fonts in the real-world Macintosh environment has never been easy. The difficulties are generally related to the fact that the software and hardware environment in which PostScript fonts are utilized, as well as the PostScript fonts themselves, has been perpetually evolving. Most of these problems have been overcome through system software upgrades, new font management utilities, or "workaround" methods that have become well known and commonly accepted as necessary for font survival.

The following list describes many of the challenges PostScript font users have faced, along with the corresponding solutions, resolutions, or workarounds:

➤ *PostScript fonts versus non-PostScript fonts*—Because PostScript screen fonts are not noticeably different from non-PostScript screen fonts, it is difficult for inexperienced users to distinguish between them when creating documents that will be output on high-resolution PostScript printers.

This problem has been solved, at least partially, by PostScript's dominance in the Macintosh world; most Macintosh users now have access to PostScript printers. And PostScript fonts are now the rule rather than the exception.

➤ *Screen font availability*—It isn't always easy to determine which fonts a document contains in order to ensure the availability of all necessary screen and printer fonts at print time—especially if the person printing the file is not the one who created it. Over time, individual software vendors have developed schemes to help identify the screen fonts in a document. PageMaker displays the dimmed names of used but not currently available fonts in its font menu; both PageMaker and QuarkXPress produce a list of fonts used. Adobe has addressed the problem of screen font availability, making it possible for Illustrator to print files correctly even if the screen fonts used to create the file aren't available at the time of printing. Unfortunately, this solution hasn't caught on with some software vendors.

> *Printer font availability*—The most fundamental requirement of PostScript fonts is that for each screen font used in a document, a corresponding printer font must be available at print time. This requirement has caused tremendous difficulty for Mac users because of the lack of an automated way to track the screen font/printer font correspondence.

The advent of large font-storage printer hard drives, the Font Reserve and MasterJuggler font management utilities, the ability to download screen fonts, and the NFNT font resource have made the "Font Not Found: Substituting Courier" messages less common. But unfortunately, the only real solution to this problem lies with users and service bureau operators.

> *Too many font names in the font menus*—For non-PostScript screen fonts, a single font is provided in several different sizes, but you must create bold and italic versions using the Style command. PostScript fonts, on the other hand, provide a separate screen font for each size and style. As a result, font menus are very long. For example, Helvetica includes four entries (B Helvetica Bold, I Helvetica Italic, Helvetica, and BI Helvetica Bold Italic). Times has four as well, and so do many other fonts.

> *Font ID conflicts*—The original Macintosh system was designed to handle only a small number of fonts. With the font explosion that followed PostScript's introduction, there were soon more fonts than available Font ID numbers. The old Apple Font/DA Mover resolved Font ID conflicts as new fonts were added to the System file, but unfortunately, the Font/DA Mover did so by randomly renumbering the fonts. Renumbering fonts caused problems because some applications tracked fonts by Font ID number, and as a result, the same font would have different ID numbers on different Macintoshes.

Because many applications used the Font ID numbers to keep track of font assignments within documents, Font ID instability caused documents to "forget" which fonts were used to create them when they were transferred from one Macintosh to another. Working with a wide range of fonts on the Macintosh became like playing a low-stakes game of Russian roulette.

The release of system software 6.0 partially solved this problem by adding more complete support for a Macintosh resource called NFNT (pronounced N-Font).

Mac OS 8.6

NFNT offered a font-numbering scheme capable of handling over 32,000 different fonts. Of course, implementing the new system meant that millions of non-NFNT fonts already in use had to be replaced with new NFNT versions. A master set of new NFNT fonts had to be distributed for use in this replacement.

To make matters worse, Apple and Adobe used the same uneven, unplanned, and unprofessional distribution methods for the new font ID system that they used for Apple system software and shareware updates—user groups, bulletin boards, and friendly file sharing. Therefore, the problem was only partially solved.

To further complicate the introduction of NFNT fonts, Apple and Adobe chose not to "harmonize" the NFNT fonts by allowing only a single font menu entry to appear for each font (as discussed previously). It was left to users to perform this harmonization with their own utilities, which resulted in a non-universal set of fonts.

➤ *Different fonts with the same names*—As more vendors produced more PostScript fonts, another problem appeared: different versions of the same fonts released by different vendors.

This proliferation of fonts not only caused Macintoshes to become "confused" about which screen fonts and printer fonts were used in documents, but it also made it hard for service bureaus to know, for instance, if the Garamond specified in a document was the Adobe, Bitstream, or other font vendor version of Garamond. This point was crucial because font substitutions wouldn't work—and even if they did, character width differences would play havoc with the output.

➤ *The Type 1 font secret*—Because Adobe Systems had developed PostScript, they kept the specifics of the optimized format known as Type 1 for themselves. The Type 1 font format embedded "hints" in font outlines that made them look better when output in small type sizes on 300 dpi laser printers.

The Type 1 format was the only format compatible with Adobe's Adobe Type Manager (ATM) utility. This restriction excluded all other vendors' PostScript fonts from using these utilities because all non-Adobe PostScript fonts were in the Type 3 format.

Because Adobe fonts were compressed and encrypted, other vendors had to reverse-engineer the Type 1 font-hinting scheme to optimize their type. Bitstream and others were successful in "cloning" PostScript. Finally, after all the political turmoil surrounding the announcement of TrueType and the successful cloning of PostScript Type 1 fonts, Adobe released the specifications for the Type 1 font format. Today, most other font vendors have upgraded their fonts to the Type 1 format.

Mac OS 8.6

Printing PostScript Fonts

When a document containing PostScript fonts is printed to a PostScript printer, the printer driver queries the PostScript printer to determine whether the printer fonts required by the document are resident in the printer. These fonts may be built into a printer's ROM chips, or they may have been previously downloaded into the printer's RAM or onto the printer's hard disk. If the fonts are indeed resident, the document is sent to the printer for output. If the fonts are not resident, the printer driver checks to see whether the printer font files are available on the Macintosh hard disk. If they are, they're temporarily downloaded into the printer's RAM. If they are not available, an error message in the Print Status dialog box alerts you to that fact. This message usually states that Courier is being substituted for the missing font, and your document is then printed.

When the document is printed, the PostScript printer uses the printer font information to create each character. The information from the PostScript screen font is translated into printer font characters (screen fonts are only placeholders onscreen). The process of creating the printed characters—rasterization—is the most complex part of the PostScript printing process. During rasterization, PostScript uses the PostScript printer font file's mathematical character descriptions to select the output device pixels necessary to produce the requested character at the highest possible resolution.

When a document containing PostScript fonts is printed to a non-PostScript printer, such as a QuickDraw or dot-matrix printer, screen font information is transferred directly to the printer and is the only source used to produce the printed characters. None of the advantages of PostScript are employed. On a QuickDraw or dot-matrix printer, there is no difference between the use of a PostScript font and a non-PostScript font (except when ATM is being used, in which case PostScript fonts are superior).

Adobe Type Manager

Not long after Apple's announcement of System 7 and TrueType, Adobe Systems released Adobe Type Manager (ATM), a utility (rasterizer) that allows PostScript fonts to be drawn more smoothly at any resolution onscreen or on any non-PostScript output device. ATM incorporates the elements of display PostScript that Apple chose not to license. This development eliminated the biggest advantages that TrueType fonts initially had over PostScript fonts. It also proved that competition is often good for the consumer.

Adobe Type Manager 4.0.2 is a Control Panel, installed by applications like Adobe Acrobat Reader, that allows you to view PostScript printer font data onscreen.

Mac OS 8.6

When ATM is installed, PostScript fonts display at the best possible resolution onscreen at any point size for any font whose screen and printer fonts are installed. ATM also improves the output quality of PostScript fonts on non-PostScript printers. With ATM, almost any PostScript font can be printed successfully at any size on any dot-matrix, ink-jet, or QuickDraw laser printer. The effect of ATM on PostScript Type 1 type is shown in Figure 11.4.

Jagged Smooth

Figure 11.4 Without ATM (left), fonts appear jagged on screen at most point sizes. With ATM (right), the same fonts are smooth at any size.

ATM quickly became a huge success, and most people who worked with more than a few PostScript fonts either purchased the utility or received it in a bundle with some other software application or application upgrade. It was estimated that by the time System 7 shipped, over 80 percent of the installed base of Macintosh users were using ATM.

Some time after the initial shipment of System 7, Apple began offering ATM to anyone who purchased System 7 or a System 7 upgrade package. But Apple did not add ATM to the System 7 install disks, making it necessary to order the "free" copy of ATM from a toll-free number for a shipping and handling charge. This practice stopped with Mac OS 8, where ATM version 4.0.2 was installed into the Internet: Internet Utilities|Adobe|Fonts folder. Although a Control Panel, the ATM Control Panel may reside practically anywhere on your hard drive.

TIP
The ATM Control Panel needs to load after all other Control Panels have loaded, which explains why it is named ~ATM instead of ATM. The addition of the tilde (~) forces it to the end of the list of Control Panels to be loaded.

The primary drawback of ATM is that you must keep a printer font that corresponds to each installed screen font on your hard drive. Doing so requires more space and increases the cost of working with lots of fonts. You can obtain screen fonts without charge from service bureaus or online sources, but you must purchase most printer fonts at costs ranging from a few dollars to a few hundred dollars per type family.

Mac OS 8.6

To use ATM, you need the printer font files for any PostScript files you want ATM to work with. You must obtain or purchase these printer fonts separately. Open the ATM Control Panel, shown in Figure 11.5, to configure ATM for your Mac.

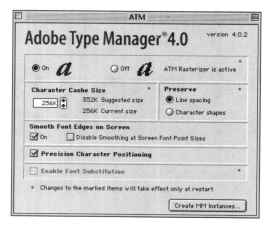

Figure 11.5   The ATM Control Panel.

ATM has few features to configure. As a rule of thumb, however, remember that your system's memory requirements will increase with each option that is enabled. For example, if you choose to have ATM smooth onscreen images and text in addition to printed images and text, the Character Cache Size will require more memory.

TrueType Fonts

In addition to supporting the same bitmapped and PostScript fonts that Macintosh users have worked with for years, Mac OS 8.6 utilizes a preferred font format that was introduced in System 7. TrueType fonts were designed to appear on the Macintosh screen at high resolution at any point size and to print at high resolution on virtually any output device.

TrueType was a fundamental shift from bitmapped fonts and PostScript fonts. Each TrueType font exists as a single file that does the work of both the screen font and the printer font. And when used along with Mac OS 8.6, TrueType fonts appear onscreen without "jaggies" at any point size and without the use of utilities such as ATM. TrueType fonts can be printed at full resolution on any dot-matrix, QuickDraw, TrueType, or PostScript printer.

TrueType is an open type format whose font specifications have been published for use by a wide variety of type vendors. It is supported by AGFA Compugraphic, Bitstream, International Typeface Corporation, Monotype, and others. Microsoft Windows and IBM's OS/2 support the TrueType standard, providing for strong cross-platform compatibility. You can buy TrueType font packages from most vendors, with the notable exception of Adobe—at least to this point. Both Apple and Microsoft now sell or freely distribute TrueType fonts.

TrueType GX

TrueType GX, an extension of the TrueType specification, takes advantage of the capabilities found in QuickDraw (and formerly QuickDraw GX). You buy QuickDraw GX fonts—as you would any other font format—as software bundles. QuickDraw GX and TrueType are notable for their handling of complex character sets and pictographic languages, which should make the Macintosh more attractive to users of non-Roman languages. TrueType GX introduces advanced typographical capabilities for fine control over letterforms and intelligent handling of characters in a layout. Apple describes GX fonts as "smart fonts" for their added intelligence.

TrueType GX and PostScript Type 1 fonts that follow the QuickDraw GX data structure can store information about justification, optical alignment, optical scaling, hanging punctuation, tracking, and kerning. Just like Adobe's Multiple Master technology, TrueType GX can create precise styling: bold, italic, and expanded or condensed along two, three, or four variation axes. Apple defines these axes as weight, width, slant, and optical size (optimal shape of a size).

Because it's possible to adjust letter size and spacing, you can use one TrueType GX font in place of another without changing line and page breaks. QuickDraw GX supplies the conversion that facilitates this substitution. TrueType GX fonts are the "ink" of Apple's new portable document format.

TrueType And PostScript

In Mac OS 8.6, TrueType is an alternative to PostScript, not a replacement for it. PostScript is fully supported in Mac OS 8.6. Neither is necessarily better than the other is; they're just different. Later in this chapter, we'll examine the realities of working in a world of mixed PostScript and TrueType fonts and offer some suggestions on the best ways to organize and utilize these font technologies on your system.

Although TrueType is in many ways a competitor for PostScript fonts, it's not a competitor for the complete PostScript language. TrueType printers use TrueType for fonts while employing QuickDraw descriptions for all other page elements. QuickDraw has proven itself on the Macintosh screen, and it's unlikely that the PostScript standard will be replaced in the near future; it has firm support from developers of high-end software, hardware developers, service bureaus, and end users. The PostScript language will likely continue to dominate personal computer printing.

Mac OS 8.6

TrueType Technology

TrueType fonts, like PostScript printer fonts, are outline fonts, which means that each character is described mathematically as opposed to the bit-by-bit description used by existing screen fonts. TrueType mathematical descriptions are based on quadratic Bézier curve equations rather than PostScript's standard Bézier curve equations. The difference between these equations is in the number of points used to determine the position of the lines and curves that make up each character. Apple claims TrueType's method creates better-looking characters at a wider range of output and display resolutions.

Because TrueType uses mathematical descriptions for onscreen and printer font versions, a single file can serve both the display and any output devices. As mentioned previously in this chapter, PostScript requires two files, a screen font file and a printer font file, to print or display at full resolution. Although it's easier to manage one font file than two, Adobe claims that putting its screen fonts and printer fonts in separate files is an asset because either can be updated or enhanced independently at any time without affecting existing documents or printer configurations.

When a document containing TrueType fonts is printed, the sequence of events depends on the type of printer used:

▶ *Dot-matrix printers*—When a document containing TrueType fonts is printed to a dot-matrix printer, the characters are reproduced in their natural contours, just as they appear on the screen. The output images are the results of the onscreen rasterization process, not the TrueType outlines. Therefore, dot-matrix output can only provide a more exact representation of the Mac's onscreen display.

▶ *QuickDraw printers*—When a document containing TrueType fonts is printed to a QuickDraw printer such as the LaserWriter II SC, the same process described for dot-matrix printers occurs—information from the onscreen rasterization process is sent to the printer.

▶ *68000-based PostScript printers with 2MB of RAM*—When a document containing TrueType fonts is sent to a PostScript printer using a Motorola 68000 CPU and at least 2MB of RAM, the printer driver queries the device to see whether the TrueType font scaler is available. The TrueType font scaler may be built into the printer's ROM, or it may have been previously downloaded onto the printer's hard disk or into printer RAM (using the LaserWriter Font Utility). If the TrueType font scaler is not available, it is automatically downloaded into the printer's RAM where it will reside until the printer is reset. This font scaler will consume approximately 80K of printer memory.

With the font scaler in place, the page is sent normally. Mathematical descriptions of any included TrueType fonts are sent to the printer and processed by the

TrueType font scaler. The page is then output at full resolution using any TrueType fonts rasterized by the font scaler software.

➤ *68000-based PostScript printers with less than 2MB of RAM, or RISC-based Adobe PostScript printers*—When a document containing TrueType fonts is printed to a PostScript printer or output device using a Motorola 68000 CPU and less than 2MB of RAM, or to a RISC-based Adobe PostScript printer, TrueType fonts are encoded into PostScript Type 1 font format and sent to the printer where they're processed just like all other PostScript fonts. The encoded Type 1 fonts do not contain PostScript "hints."

➤ *Printers with built-in TrueType scaling*—When a document containing TrueType fonts is sent to a printer with a built-in TrueType (TrueImage) font scaler, such as the LaserMaster 400XL or MicroTek TrueLaser, the TrueType outline information is sent directly to the printer, where the font is rasterized and imaged.

A Mixed World

In a laboratory environment, where some Macintoshes used only PostScript fonts and some used only TrueType fonts, where all documents using PostScript fonts were created only on the PostScript machines and those using TrueType fonts were created only on the TrueType machines, the daily use of these systems from a font-technology perspective would be very straightforward.

Unfortunately, none of us live or work in such a laboratory. Most Macintosh computers are more likely to be configured with PostScript fonts, TrueType fonts, and non-PostScript, non-TrueType bitmapped fonts. And most people will have some documents created with only PostScript fonts, some with only bitmapped fonts, some with only TrueType fonts, and many with mixes of TrueType, PostScript, and bitmapped fonts. So how can all this jumble work in the real world?

Picking Your Font Standard

When you install Mac OS 8.6, the Installer adds both the PostScript and TrueType versions of many default fonts, including Courier, Times, and Geneva. Over time, you will add additional fonts to your system—some PostScript, some TrueType—and sometimes you will add both PostScript and TrueType versions of the same fonts.

Once you've installed these fonts, their names will appear in the font menus or dialog boxes of all applications, but you will have no easy way to distinguish the TrueType fonts from the PostScript fonts, or to distinguish those for which both versions have been installed. Unfortunately, you cannot tell which formats are installed by looking at a name in a font menu. (Again, it's a shame Apple didn't make these distinctions visible.)

When you choose a font that is installed in both PostScript and TrueType formats, the Macintosh will decide whether to use the PostScript screen font or a scaled TrueType font for each occurrence, depending on the designated point size of the font. Assume, for example, that you have the PostScript screen fonts for Helvetica, Helvetica Bold, Helvetica Italic, and Helvetica Bold Italic installed in your Fonts folder, each in 10-, 12-, and 14-point sizes. Also assume that the TrueType Helvetica, Helvetica Bold, Helvetica Italic, and Helvetica Bold Italic files are installed. In this case, most applications would use the PostScript versions of Helvetica for instances of 10-, 12-, or 14-point type and the TrueType version in all other cases. In other words, PostScript screen fonts are used when they're available at the size specified, and TrueType fonts are used for all other sizes.

Of course, when no TrueType font has been installed, PostScript versions are used for all sizes. If ATM is installed, ATM will scale the onscreen font display to provide smooth character representations. PostScript outlines will be used at print time to produce smooth type at the resolution of the output device (assuming the output device is equipped with a PostScript interpreter).

> ***TIP***
> This process of alternating PostScript screen fonts and TrueType fonts is controlled by each application. Some software developers choose to use TrueType fonts even when PostScript screen fonts of the exact size requested are available. Until the document is printed, it's impossible to tell whether TrueType or PostScript fonts are being used, so consult your application manuals for more information.

This situation is clearly confusing. It gets worse if you consider the possibility that some older documents on your hard drive were created using only PostScript fonts. When you open them, you may be instead using TrueType versions of those same fonts. These old documents will then be forced to use TrueType fonts and extensive text repositioning may occur as a result. You'll experience the same outcome if you're using an application that ignores PostScript screen fonts and uses the True-Type fonts in all situations.

Text repositioning occurs because character widths for TrueType fonts will not always exactly match PostScript font character widths, even in the same font and family. The width of a 14-point Helvetica Bold **H** may be slightly different in TrueType than it was in PostScript. The cumulative result of the character width accommodations in your document will be text repositioning.

Because using both PostScript and TrueType versions of the same font makes it impossible to determine which version is being used at any one time, it is best not to install both PostScript and TrueType versions of the same fonts. This is especially true for fonts used in documents being prepared for high-resolution output that will be printed at a remote site (such as a service bureau).

If you use the default Mac OS 8.6 fonts (Times, Helvetica, and so on) for high-resolution output, you may want to remove either the PostScript or the TrueType versions of them from your Fonts folder. If you just use these fonts onscreen and print them from your local laser printer, however, it's probably not worth the trouble to remove one of them.

Font Reserve

With so many types of fonts and considerations about their use, you might need to seek the help of a utility such as Font Reserve from DiamondSoft (www.diamondsoft.com) to help manage your fonts. Font Reserve works by cataloging all your fonts and allowing you to create sets of fonts. It's AppleScriptable, and you can even share your sets of fonts with other users, which is especially important if you collaborate with graphic designers, printers, or service bureaus.

Font Reserve is comprised of several components. The Font Reserve Settings application is the primary configuration interface for the application itself, but not for the fonts (see Figure 11.6). The Font Reserve Settings application sets the location of the database that controls the fonts, which can be on a local hard drive or an AppleShare server. It also sets memory requirements for the database application.

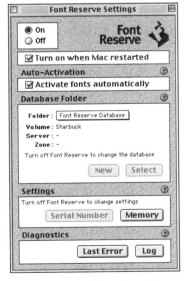

Figure 11.6 The Font Reserve Settings application.

Mac OS 8.6

The Font Reserve Browser application is the main pathway for interfacing with your sets of fonts. Shown in Figure 11.7, this application has a highly configurable interface that allows you to view all your fonts according to the following categories:

➤ Name

➤ Kind (TrueType, bitmap, TrueType GX, and so on)

➤ Foundry (manufacturer or vendor)

➤ Class (Serif, Sans Serif, and so on)

➤ Family (AdobeSansMM, Future, and so on)

The upper portion of the browser window lists the sets of fonts, while the bottom half lists the individual fonts in the selected set. You can view all the fonts in the

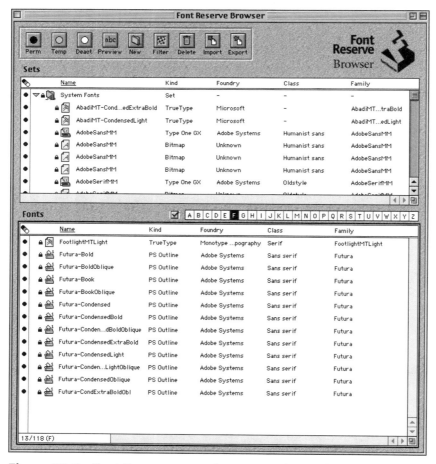

Figure 11.7 Font Reserve uses a browser-style window to view the various fonts and font sets installed on your computer.

set, or only those fonts whose names begin with a particular character in the alphabet. The example in Figure 11.7 shows all the fonts in the set in the upper half, while displaying only those fonts whose names begin with the letter F in the lower half of the window.

Getting detailed information on a particular font is a snap when using the font browser. Just double-click on a font to open that font in a preview window, as in Figure 11.8. You'll have easy access to detailed information about the font, including general information, a map of all the characters in the font, information about kerning, as well as three previews of the font (sentence, paragraph, and a cascading preview of the font in various sizes).

Figure 11.8 Previewing a font in Font Reserve.

Access to this type of information about a font is a dramatic improvement over the information provided by the Mac OS. The information it provides, either through a list view like the one in Figure 11.3, or by double-clicking on a font suitcase, as in Figure 11.9, is limited to the type of font and a preview of the font.

Finally, to create a new set of fonts that you can use on your Mac, archive, or share with other users, choose File|New Set and drag fonts from one set to the new set. It's that easy!

Figure 11.9 Double-clicking on a font while in the Finder reveals very limited information, making applications such as Font Reserve a wise investment for avid font collectors.

Advanced Typography

The development of computer-aided design tools has led to both an explosion in type design and a typographical revival. More high-quality typefaces are available now than ever, in almost any format you choose to buy. However, several technical challenges remain in typography: contextual use of letterforms, international character sets, and more flexible type handling. TrueType GX fonts may provide some solutions to these problems.

The contextual use of characters is a style issue. Characters are language elements that include letters, numbers, punctuation marks, and other linguistic symbols that have a value or meaning in a certain language. QuickDraw GX introduced the concept of a glyph. A *glyph* is a representation of a character. Glyphs are what the characters looks like in that particular instance, but they don't contain any meaning beyond the characters they represent. An application specifies a character, and QuickDraw in Mac OS 8.6 automatically draws the appropriate glyph of the right size, style, and so on.

A TrueType GX font follows the Unicode specification for an international character set. It can contain up to 65,000 glyphs (called characters in other systems). This expansion of the character set and of the LineLayout Manager's line layout capabilities makes it easier to support digital type in non-Roman languages. Roman language users will benefit from augmenting character sets with small caps, fractions, superior/inferior characters, ligatures, swashes, fleurons, and borders are included in a single font. The LineLayout Manager creates these special characters in context based upon the intelligence built into the font.

In Roman languages, glyph substitution places ligatures where two or three characters make the text more readable and attractive. For example, _ is substituted for the letters *f* and *l*, and _ for *f* and *i*. Because these glyphs retain the original two character definitions, they spell check, search and replace, and substitute correctly. Ligatures can be made to appear inside or at the end of words.

Whereas glyph substitution is a nice type style feature in Roman languages, it assumes added importance in text systems such as Arabic or Hindi in which characters change their shape based upon their positions in a word. QuickDraw makes the appropriate placement of glyphs, cutting down on data entry and character selection.

Glyph substitution also lets developers create animated fonts. The animation occurs between different glyphs of the same characters in the same manner that cursors can be animated in Macintosh system software.

As applications become savvier, use glyphs, and apply glyph substitution, you'll find that much of the work you once did to style a document is now done for you automatically. You may also discover that applications come with menus or dialog boxes that allow you to select which of these typographical features you wish to apply in a document. Figure 11.10 shows an example of some of the font preferences for Microsoft Word 98.

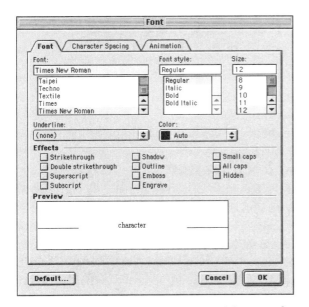

Figure 11.10 Selecting advanced font preferences in a popular word processing application.

Mac OS 8.6

Text Effects

Because QuickDraw treats text as a shape, it offers designers the same latitude in applying special effects that illustrators have in creating artwork. Certain of the more tedious tasks that designers require have already been automated inside TrueType GX fonts, including optical scaling and alignment, glyphs, automatic kerning, and tracking.

You can expect to see a proliferation of text effects, including applying transformations such as skew, rotation, mirroring, and perspective to a line of text. The results of such transformations rival programs such as Adobe's PageMaker and Quark's QuarkXPress. However, since these effects are now part of system software, they will appear in many other (often smaller) programs. Other effects, such as ductile type, may be new to you. In ductile type, a character can expand or contract to provide script continuity.

Because written languages can be like English (read left to right), Hebrew (read right to left), and Japanese (read top to bottom), QuickDraw can mix a variety of scripts together—even on the same line.

Anyone who has traveled abroad—say to Japan, where Japanese and English are mixed on the same page—will understand why this capability is a boon. With ideographic languages (those using pictures for characters, such as Japanese, Chinese, or Korean), QuickDraw can apply proportional vertical writing and automatic alignment to centered baselines. That line can be rotated to any angle or transformed like any shape. You also can mix different lines of text, such as Kanji and Roman type, and apply the baseline of your choice.

Typography is not the subject of this book, however; Mac OS 8.6 is. The typographical capabilities that QuickDraw gives Macintosh users are unique for any computer system—probably a landmark in the type and computer industries.

Unicode, WorldScript, And Localization

Computer vendors have long struggled with the task of translating software between languages and cultures. A version of software for another language or culture is called a *localized version*, and the process is called *localization*. The problem is compounded by several issues. Different languages use different character sets. Even when the languages are the same, as is the case for American and British English, the character sets may differ. Character sets can even be based on different alphabets, with different numbers and characters. Ideographic languages—Japanese Kanji, Chinese Han, and Korean—have thousands of characters. These differences make translation difficult, affect sort orders, and slow down the spread of innovative software worldwide.

Many standard character sets have been used locally throughout the years. The ASCII standard for American text is one such standard. A consortium of industry vendors has created and codified a system of 65,000 characters incorporating all the modern languages in the world and some of the ancient languages as well. That system is called Unicode, and was adopted by Apple in Mac OS 8.

Apple has developed a technology called WorldScript that manages a variety of localization issues such as date and time formats, sort orders, and input methods. To change the text features for the script system on your Macintosh, open the Text Control Panel and choose the feature you want from the pop-up menu. You can also select dates, times, and numbers from the Date & Time and Numbers Control Panels.

Input methods are important in non-Roman languages such as Japanese or Chinese. For these languages, users enter phonetic values used in speech and the input method translates to a character. This way, with an ideographic language, you can use a standard keyboard for data entry. For example, Japanese users type Roman characters until the Kanji characters are recognized and substituted. WorldScript works by using a user-installed script or onscreen instructions that make the appropriate character translations.

QuickDraw expands WorldScript's capabilities by providing the advanced typographical capabilities for text and characters that have been described previously. Now WorldScript can provide sophisticated scripting of text handling in any language. With these new tools, developers have a method for localizing software quickly.

Installing Fonts

Before the release of System 7, you installed screen fonts using the Font/DA Mover, which transferred them between their font suitcases and the System file. Over the years, however, the Font/DA Mover became a scapegoat for many of the Mac's larger font management problems. Because of this, and due to the fact that the Font/DA Mover's interface was seen as inconsistent with the drag-and-drop method by which other files were moved from one location to another, a new method of installing screen fonts was introduced in System 7.

This method requires no utility program—you simply drag fonts onto the System Folder icon or the icon of the System file. They are then placed into the System file automatically. This method works with all kinds of fonts (TrueType fonts, bitmapped fonts, and PostScript screen fonts), and the only limitation is that fonts cannot be installed while any application other than the Finder is open. If you tried to drag fonts into the System file or the System Folder while applications were open, a dialog box would appear telling you that you couldn't do so until all applications had been quit.

Another change in System 7 was that you could open screen font suitcases directly from the Finder by double-clicking them as if they were folders. This action opened a suitcase window, displaying individual icons for each screen font in the folder. You could distinguish PostScript screen fonts or bitmapped fonts from ones in the new TrueType format by the icon they displayed. TrueType fonts use an icon with three *A*s, and PostScript screen fonts or bitmapped fonts use an icon with a single *A*, as shown in Figure 11.11. This is still true with Mac OS 8.6.

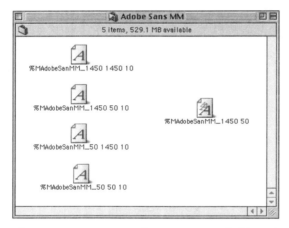

Figure 11.11   Icons for PostScript (left) and TrueType (right) fonts.

Double-clicking an individual screen font icon opens a window showing a brief sample of the font, as we've already seen.

In System 7, individual font icons were always stored in a font suitcase or in the System file; they could not be stored as files in any other folder. System 7 provided no easy way to create new empty font suitcases, so if you needed a new suitcase to store your fonts, you would've created one by duplicating an existing suitcase file and then discarding the fonts contained in that duplicate. You could then copy any fonts you wanted into that suitcase and rename it as necessary. In Mac OS 8.6, all fonts and font suitcases are stored in the Fonts folder in the System Folder. This makes keeping track of fonts much easier than in older versions of the Mac OS.

Changes In Fonts

In Mac OS 8.6, all fonts are stored in the Fonts folder and are easily installed and deinstalled. This wasn't always the case, however. Although System 7 eliminated the Font/DA Mover, it did little to correct the more fundamental problems of Macintosh font management. One such problem was that installing fonts into the System file—when done by the system software or by some utility—resulted in large System files that tended to cause crashes. Sometimes these crashes were so severe that they required a complete system software reinstallation.

The release of System 7.1 corrected this problem by adding a Fonts subfolder to the System folder. All screen fonts and printer fonts now reside in this folder; they are no longer stored in the System file. Up to 128 screen font files or font suitcases (each containing any number of fonts) stored in the Fonts folder could be loaded at startup and become available in the font menu or dialog box of your applications.

Mac OS 8.6 continues to employ a Fonts folder within the System folder, but the practical limit on the number of fonts has been removed. You can add font suitcases or individual font files to the Fonts folder by:

➤ Dragging the fonts to the Fonts folder.

➤ Dragging fonts onto the System Folder icon, where they will be placed into the Fonts folder automatically (see Figure 11.12).

➤ Merging the fonts from one font suitcase with another by dragging one suitcase onto another.

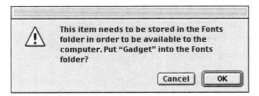

Figure 11.12 The Mac OS knows to store fonts that have been dropped onto the closed System Folder into the Fonts folder.

You may not be able to add fonts to the Fonts folder when most other applications are running. Some utilities may be open at the time the fonts are copied, moved, or otherwise installed by another program. When you add fonts to the Fonts folder, they will not become available to any applications that are already open until you quit and relaunch those programs. Fonts or suitcases with the same names as existing fonts or suitcases cannot be added to the Fonts folder; you must first move the previously installed font to another folder or into the Trash.

Mac OS 8.6

Removing Fonts

Removing fonts is essentially the same as installing them. You must first quit all open applications, then move or delete the selected fonts from the Fonts folder. Moving fonts in use by the Mac OS will not be allowed. To get rid of these, you'll need to boot from an alternative startup disk such as an emergency boot floppy or the Mac OS 8.6 installation CD-ROM.

Desktop Printing

As you learned in Chapter 2, you select printers using the Chooser, specifying a serial port or network connection for the printer. When you want to add a new Desktop printer, you must go back to the Chooser to make another selection. Printers that are connected via AppleTalk will be listed in the right-hand side of the Chooser window, as in Figure 11.13. Printers that are available to you via serial or TCP/IP will require additional steps.

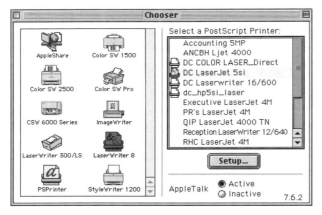

Figure 11.13 The Chooser is still the main place you'll go to select a printer.

You can check the status of print jobs, delete print jobs from the queue, and suspend or resume printing by double-clicking the Desktop printer's icon or clicking it once and choosing from the options in the Printing menu (see Figure 11.14).

You can select several printers of different types and in different locations and then place them on your desktop or in a folder on your hard drive. Any output device, either a network printer or personal printer, can be mounted on your desktop. Connections to shared devices are controlled through the standard File Sharing Users and Groups Setup dialog box and passwords schemes, which are described in Chapter 17. Not only can you mount printers, but you can also mount film recorders, fax modems, or any device that can currently be selected in the Chooser. With

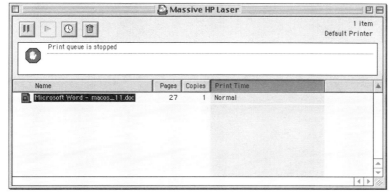

Figure 11.14 Elements of a Desktop printer.

appropriate controls, selected individuals can utilize only the devices you want them to, saving on wasted materials or inappropriate usage.

The Print Dialog Box

In Mac OS 8.6, printing from within an application has been enhanced with a new Print dialog box, shown in Figure 11.15 for the application Microsoft Word 98. Although many of the options in the Print dialog box will be familiar, over time you will see new print options for different applications and printers. Some of these features are application-specific, while others are printer-specific. Therefore the print dialog box you see will depend on the application and the printer.

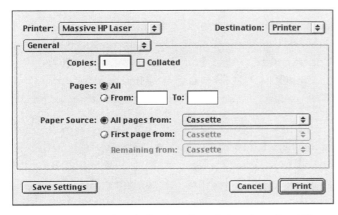

Figure 11.15 The default print dialog box for Microsoft Word 98.

312   Chapter 11

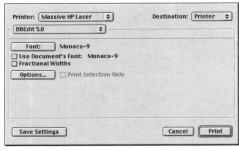

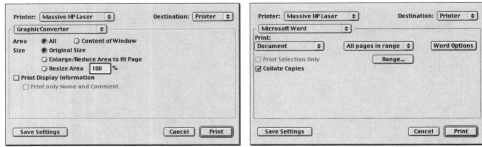

Figure 11.16   The application-specific portions of the print dialog box for three applications.

Most applications, such as BBEdit, GraphicConverter, and Microsoft Word 98, have application-specific settings, as shown in Figure 11.16.

When you click the Print button in the Print dialog box, the document is spooled and sent to the printer of your choice. It's placed in a print queue, as discussed in the next section. If the printer is connected, the document is printed. If not, it prints when you connect to that printer again.

The Mac OS enables device-independent printing, which means that you can format a document to print on a specific printer. Page formatting is preserved even when the size of the page or printable area changes. For extreme changes in size, in which the text would be unreadable or the quality of the page compromised, the Mac OS will apply user-selected defaults to tile, scale, or clip the printed image. You can also select to format a print job for any printer. This is done when sending a document to an unknown printer. In that case, the document's line and page breaks are preserved.

As it stands now, applications provide their own page definitions. QuickDraw provides standard definitions for page formatting that allow one application to copy and paste pages to another without having to reformat the document. Because pages have uniform definitions, you can also break documents into separate pages, each with its own format and page setup. These options will appear as standard Print and Page Setup dialog box options across all Macintosh applications.

Mac OS 8.6

Fonts And Printing 313

> **TIP**
> To print the contents of your Mac's Desktop or any Finder window, click on any item on the Desktop and select Print Desktop, or Print Window, from the File menu.

Letters, mailing labels, envelopes, or anything can be mixed within a document that you print appropriately. Because you'll have control over tray selection and other features, these capabilities are most practical with multi-tray printers. As you print to a standard printer with just one tray, you will be signaled to feed odd-sized paper or envelopes manually into the printer. When you have multiple trays, the new print architecture automatically routes pages to the correct tray. It's not necessary to select a bin number; just feed your printer print stock.

The Print Spooler

When you print a document, the data goes to the print spooler portion of the Desktop printer, where it is sent on to the printer itself or a print server. Some printers have their own processor, memory (RAM), and storage space (hard drives), while others rely on your Mac's resources for printing. Some networked environments employ a print server. Print servers are usually computers or networked devices that take the print request off the hands of your computer and feed the items to the printer for you. Macs tend to serve as their own print queues, while Microsoft Windows-based computers often have print servers do the job.

> **TIP**
> In addition to issuing the Print command to print a document, you can also drag and drop a document onto a Desktop printer icon to print that document.

In any of these cases, the document you want to print must go through the Mac OS's print spooler first. When a printer has a queued document, the Desktop printer's icon will change to indicate that it's processing the contents of the spool, as in Figure 11.17.

Figure 11.17 A Desktop printer icon with documents in the print queue.

Mac OS 8.6

Each Desktop printer manages its own print queue, an example of which is shown in Figure 11.18. To manipulate the print queue, do the following:

➤ To open a print queue, double-click the printer icon.

➤ To reorder the queue, drag the document icon to a new position.

➤ To move a print job to another printer, drag the document icon to that printer icon.

➤ To delete a job, select a document icon and click the Trash icon.

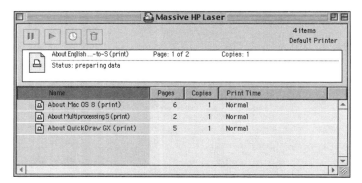

Figure 11.18 A print queue with several documents waiting to be printed.

Several other changes become apparent when you print using a print queue. The background printing architecture ensures that you take less of a performance hit when working in the foreground. You'll notice this benefit more on slower, older Macintosh computers, but it's a welcome change anywhere. The Mac OS monitors the needs of the foreground application and allocates more resources to printing when that application is idle. Resources are returned to the foreground when activity increases.

The print queue is smarter, too. If your Macintosh crashes, you'll find after rebooting that your print job resumes from the point where it stopped, even if that point was in the middle of a job. Therefore, for a multipage print job, the most recently printed page prints again, followed by the next one. You no longer have to reprint the entire job or respecify the print job when you crash.

Chooser Extensions And PostScript Printer Descriptions

For the most part, printers require specific Chooser extensions in order to communicate with a particular printer. Mac OS 8.6 provides several Chooser extensions in the Extensions folder, and each one shows up in the Chooser. The LaserWriter 8 extension is used to access the majority of laser printers. In addition to Chooser extensions, PostScript printers also rely upon PostScript Printer Description (PPD) files to print. These files contain printer-specific information on such things as the number of trays, printer resolution, and color matching. PPDs are stored in the Printer Descriptions folder inside the Extensions folder. If you don't see a PPD for your specific printer when you go to create a Desktop printer icon, just choose the closest match or choose the Generic button. Figure 11.19 shows both the Chooser Extensions and a few of the PPDs installed by Mac OS 8.6.

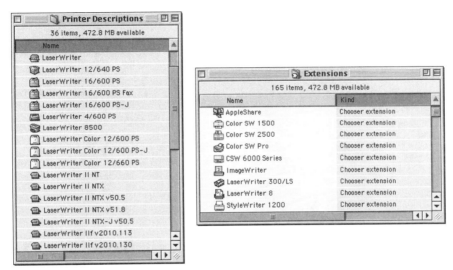

Figure 11.19 The default printer extensions for Mac OS 8.6.

For each printer, you'll find a corresponding Chooser extension in the Extensions folder in the System Folder. Using the Extensions Manager, you can disable the extensions that you don't need such as the StyleWriter extensions. This will free up a little memory used by the Mac OS.

Desktop Printer Utility

For those printers you cannot access using the Chooser, there's always the Desktop Printer Utility, located in the Apple LaserWriter Software folder in the Apple Extras folder (see Figure 11.20). This utility connects to four types of printers:

➤ AppleTalk

➤ LPR (using TCP/IP)

➤ No printer

➤ PostScript

Figure 11.20 The Desktop Printer Utility.

To connect to an LPR printer using the Desktop Printer Utility, follow these steps once you know the printer's IP address:

1. Launch the Desktop Printer Utility.
2. Select Printer (LPR) from the window shown in Figure 11.21.

Figure 11.21 Use the Desktop Printer Utility to create a Desktop printer via TCP/IP.

3. Select a Printer Description File. If one cannot be found, choose the Generic button.
4. Enter the printer's IP address after clicking the Change button in the LPR Printer Selection portion of the window shown in Figure 11.22.
5. Save the Desktop printer, which will appear like any other printer on the Desktop.

ColorSync And Color Matching

The Mac's proficiency and popularity as a publishing computer is well known. And in the past few years, advances in processing power, storage capacities, scanning, and output technology have earned the Mac OS the leading role in even the most

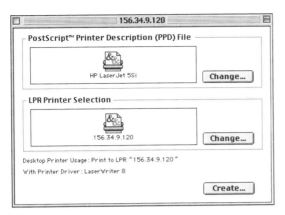

Figure 11.22 The main configuration window for the Desktop printer.

demanding high-quality color publishing situations. Publications from *The New Yorker* to *People* are now produced fully or partially on the Macintosh. In fact, many reports indicate that some 70 percent of all desktop publishing is done on the Mac.

Despite this acceptance, and the overall improvements in color publishing technology, one aspect of color publishing has remained a challenge: matching colors that appear onscreen to those that are printed on color proofing devices and, finally, to the colors of the finished product, which are usually based on film output. Maintaining the consistency of colors as they move from an onscreen display to different output devices has been difficult for two basic reasons.

First, computer monitors produce colors by adding together differing percentages of red, green, and blue light. This method of mixing light from original sources is called *additive color*. Output devices, on the other hand, work by applying color to a page that will selectively absorb light waves when the document is illuminated via an external white light (such as that from light bulbs or the sun). This method of creating colors is called *subtractive color*. Additive and subtractive color produce fundamentally different ranges of colors. For this reason, onscreen color (additive) offers bright, highly saturated colors that invariably appear darker when printed (subtractive) on paper or other materials.

Second, variations between different printers, monitors, and presses make it impossible for each of them to produce the exact same range and quality of colors. An inexpensive ink-jet printer has one set of printable colors, a color laser printer another, a dye sublimation printer yet another, a web press another, and a high-quality sheet-fed press another still.

Differences in the color models and technical characteristics of color devices result in each having its own specific gamut, or range, of colors. To achieve consistent color across different devices, the trick is to map colors from one device to another so that when a file is displayed or produced on each device, the differences between the devices' gamuts are accounted and compensated for and the color remains as consistent as possible.

Apple's ColorSync System Profile performs this task exactly. When ColorSync is installed, colors are converted from their original definitions into a device-independent definition based on the international CIE XYZ color standard or color space. (A color space is a three-dimensional mapping of a range of possible colors.) This conversion is done using a device profile, a small file that tells ColorSync about the color characteristics and capabilities of the input device or monitor. Once a color is defined in CIE XYZ, it can then be translated using a set of color matching method (CMM) algorithms for output using the device profile of the output device. Figure 11.23 shows the ColorSync Control Panel and the selection dialog window that you'll use to select the display for your computer.

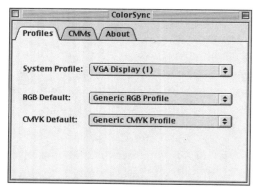

Figure 11.23 The ColorSync System Profile.

Apple will provide device profiles for its own monitors, scanners, and color printers, but the success of ColorSync will be dependent upon third-party developers producing and distributing their own device profiles for their scanners, monitors, and printers. In order for you to use ColorSync effectively, you must have device profiles for the specific scanners, monitors, and printers you're using for any given project.

When ColorSync translates colors into or out of the CIE XYZ color model, it does so with the goal of providing the best possible match between the original color and the final color. Differences in devices do not always make an exact match possible, as explained earlier. The algorithm ColorSync uses to perform this translation was designed for optimum results, but it was also designed to use a small amount of memory and provide good performance. Other companies, such as EFI and Kodak, have developed other conversion methods—based on lookup tables

Mac OS 8.6

rather than algorithms—which will produce superior results but require much more memory, information, and expertise about each input and output device. These methods are compatible with ColorSync, however, and can be put to good use by anyone working in high-quality color who desires improved results.

By providing an automated color-matching system, Apple has taken the uncertainty out of using color. What was once tedious work is now handled for you by hardware vendors and solutions providers. The quality of this translation will no doubt improve over time.

For a detailed description of how to configure your Mac to use ColorSync, refer to Chapter 15 and the discussion of multimedia applications and the Mac OS. ColorSync is as much an issue of color matching as it relates to multimedia as it is an issue of printing.

Wrapping Up

Fonts continue to be an exciting part of the Macintosh, and as shown in this chapter, font technology remains a source of innovation and controversy. Mac OS 8.6 supports four different font formats: bitmapped, PostScript, TrueType, and TrueType GX. It supports five if you count Adobe's Multiple Masters font technology.

In this chapter, you learned about the following:

➤ *Imaging models using QuickDraw and QuickDraw GX*—Apple's system-level graphics and type page description language allow for easy development of sophisticated applications.

➤ *Fonts*—How to select, install, and work with fonts on the Macintosh. You also learned about TrueType GX fonts and their effect on foreign language applications.

➤ *Desktop printing*—How to select a printer and how the Mac OS processes print jobs.

➤ *Color matching*—ColorSync can help your images look their best on your Mac, someone else's Mac, or even in print.

In Chapter 12, you'll learn about how applications and the Mac OS communicate with each other and about Apple's compound document standard that allows pieces of applications to be easily reused among different applications.

Interapplication Communication And OpenDoc

As you saw in Chapter 10, launching several applications simultaneously can dramatically improve your productivity on the Macintosh. Mac OS 8.6 makes it possible to integrate your applications more closely: messages and commands can be passed from one application to another, and text and graphic elements can be shared between documents. These capabilities are made possible by the Interapplication Communication (IAC) feature of the Mac OS and the Edition Manager, respectively.

Although the power of IAC and the Edition Manager is provided by Mac OS 8.6, neither feature is automatically available to an application. Each capability must be specifically added by software developers; and in the years since IAC and Edition Manager were first offered in System 7, only a handful of developers have done so. Fortunately, Microsoft Office 98 provides support for these features, arguably the most important suite of applications available for the Mac OS. Other popular applications also support the Editions Manager, including Adobe PageMaker, ClarisDraw, and QuarkXPress.

Taken to the extreme, the best way to mix different data types and application capabilities is to use a compound document architecture. With this model, a document—rather than an application—is the central construct. When you add data to a compound document or try to modify it, a small application capable of handling that part is called up.

This architecture is what OpenDoc is about. Using AppleEvents and the Open Scripting Architecture, OpenDoc provides a document framework to enable a new class of application and a new style of computing. Best yet, when you use OpenDoc, you are using concepts you already know (such as cut and paste) in a familiar way. Your Macintosh still feels like a Macintosh.

OpenDoc's future is uncertain, however. It is no longer under active development at Apple; instead, it's in "maintenance mode," meaning that only bug fixes will continue to be made. But OpenDoc support is built into the Mac OS, and as long as developers create applications for it, it will continue to be the more natural way to work. Chances are that, over time, OpenDoc—or something very much like OpenDoc that is built on the Mac OS X framework, such as Java—will bring about profound changes in the way Macintosh users buy applications and do their work. Because it's still supported by the Mac OS, we'll look at how OpenDoc works, its components, and what it can do for you.

Interapplication Communication (IAC)

The Copy and Paste commands are simple examples of how the Mac OS allows applications to share data and communicate indirectly with each other. The Mac OS also provides broad application-to-application communication, known as Interapplication Communication (commonly abbreviated as IAC among programmers and serious Mac geeks). IAC provides a structural framework within which software applications can send messages and data to other software applications. These sharing capabilities make the Mac OS more powerful in many ways. They reduce the pressure on any one application to "do it all," allowing each application to specialize in what it does best, such as word processing, database connectivity, or spreadsheets.

Spellchecking is a good example of IAC. Many applications allow text to be created, edited, copied, and pasted, and over the last few years many have added built-in spelling checkers, each with its own dictionary files. Initially this sounds like a good deal—until you realize that you have to learn and remember how each spellchecker works and make room for each data file on your hard drive. And the developers of each program have to spend time and money developing and testing utilities.

Suppose, instead, that one independent spelling checker was the best of them all, offering the biggest dictionaries, the most features, and the best user interface. Using IAC, each of your software applications could access this one spelling checker, saving you the hassle of learning multiple commands, customizing multiple dictionaries, and wasting hard drive space on duplicate files. And your software developers could spend their time and money on other things, such as improving their applications' unique features. BBEdit is a good example of this type of setup; it can use an external spellchecker in place of its built-in spellchecker. Figure 12.1 shows the BBEdit Spelling Preferences window, in which the application Spellswell has been chosen as the default spellchecker. Spellswell can check the spelling of any application that uses the Word Services Apple Event Suite, including Eudora Pro (email client), Word Perfect (word processor), or Writeswell Jr.

Mac OS 8.6

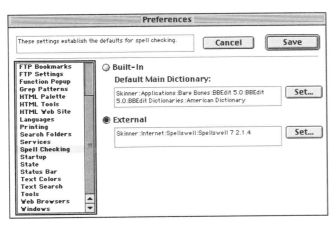

Figure 12.1 Spellchecking is a good example of Interapplication Communication.

Understanding AppleEvents

The mechanics of IAC are quite technical, but fortunately you don't need to know anything about them unless you intend to write your own Macintosh programs. You'll be aware of IAC when your software takes advantage of its features, but the entire IAC operation will be translated into friendly Macintosh commands and dialog boxes you're already familiar with (so you can skip the rest of this section, if you'd like). However, if you have an interest in AppleScript, Apple's system-wide object-oriented programming language (the subject of Chapter 13), this topic will interest you because AppleEvents is the fundamental messaging system upon which AppleScript is based.

IAC is a protocol that defines a type of communication between applications and provides a mechanism for the delivery and implementation of that communication. You can think of IAC as a set of grammatical rules that make up an acceptable format for messages sent between applications. A message in this format is known as an AppleEvent.

For example, an application issues an AppleEvent to another application. The AppleEvent is usually a command like "Open filename and Copy Data record #, fieldname," followed by the sending application's pasting the data somewhere. Using this kind of mechanism, you can link a directory, a to-do list, and a calendar. In fact, some of the first and best implementations of AppleEvents have been in the Personal Information Manager (PIMs) category.

In addition to the AppleEvents format, IAC provides a messenger service to transmit the properly formatted message from one application to another. Although IAC defines the communication format, it doesn't specify the message content. The "language" of AppleEvents is defined by Apple and by the Macintosh software developer community in cooperation with Apple. This cooperation is very important—a computer language designed to communicate between a variety of software applications developed by different companies must be carefully constructed in order to accomplish its goal of facilitating precise communication.

For an application to send an AppleEvent or to understand an AppleEvent it receives, the application must be specifically programmed to handle it properly. This interoperability makes it impossible for applications built to run under old versions of the Mac OS to use IAC. Only when the AppleEvents language is clearly defined can software developers update their programs to properly engage in an AppleEvents dialog.

AppleEvents are described by commands and actions that act on objects. You can think of these constructs as being roughly equivalent to verbs and nouns in the programming language, which we'll discuss in the next chapter. AppleEvents include nouns and verbs in their definition descriptors, as you can see when you open an application's AppleEvent dictionary. To help software developers implement program support, Apple classified AppleEvents into categories called suites. The suites are as follow:

➤ *Required suite*—Open Application, Open Document, Print Document, Run Application, and Quit Application are the four basic AppleEvents and the only ones required for applications. Think of them as the Hello, Please, Thank You, Start, and Good-bye of AppleEvents. This is the smallest of the standard suites.

➤ *Core suite*—Though not as universal or fundamental as those in the Required suite, these AppleEvents are general enough that almost every Macintosh application should support them. The list of Core AppleEvents, quite large already, is growing as Apple and its software developers work to make sure every type of communication that may be needed is provided for. You can perform a wide range of tasks using the Core suite, including opening and closing windows, counting words or lines, and saving documents.

➤ *Text suite*—The Text suite supports AppleEvents used by word processors, page layout applications, and other applications that utilize text editing functions. The Core suite contains minimal text functions, so the Text suite is for a level of support higher than simple text functions used in dialog boxes.

➤ *QuickDraw Graphics suite*—QuickDraw events define actions required to draw simple graphics to your monitor, printers, or other devices. Most graphics programs adopt this suite. The QuickDraw Graphics Supplemental suite contains additions and extensions to the original suite, such as the ability to rotate objects, and it is yet another level of graphics messaging support.

➤ *Table suite*—Tables are a fundamental property of spreadsheets, databases, and other systems that use two-dimensional data arrays. This suite provides data addressing, retrieval, and modification capabilities. Other suites, like the Database and Spreadsheet suites, provide complementary functions.

➤ *Finder suite*—Beginning with System 7.5, a set of 13 Finder commands and actions was added to the Finder. Actions such as copying, trashing, and other Finder events are supported. See "The Scriptable Finder" in the next chapter for more information. The Finder suite contains the following items: open about box, copy to, duplicate, empty trash, make aliases for, move to, sleep, shut down, open, print, put away, restart, and select.

➤ *Miscellaneous suite*—Events that don't quite fit into other suites are grouped into this grab bag of miscellaneous events. Utilizing this suite allows Apple to extend Interapplication Communication without having to define large numbers of small suites. The AppleEvent Registry now contains many specialized suites. Some examples are the Mail, Personal Information, and Telephony suites.

➤ *Custom suites*—A Macintosh software developer may need AppleEvents designed for proprietary or cooperative use by the developer's own applications. If a developer's word processor included a unique feature not controllable with any existing Core- or Functional-area AppleEvents, the developer's company could define its own Custom AppleEvent. This AppleEvent could be kept secret and used only by the software developer's applications, or it could be shared with other software developers. Some examples of custom suites are Aladdin System's StuffIt suite, Apple's HyperCard suite, and CE Software's QuicKeys suite. FileMaker Pro contains a custom suite that is a subset of Core, Table, and Database suites. This custom suite also contains some FileMaker-specific commands. FileMaker Pro also contains a FileMaker suite with several classes: go to, find, request, menu item, and menu. You can view supported suites using the Open Dictionary command in the File menu of the Script Editor, a standard part of the AppleScript package. Figure 12.2 shows the FileMaker-specific suite in the FileMaker scripting dictionary. For more information, refer to the discussion in Chapter 13 on application dictionaries.

The entire current list of AppleEvents, along with detailed descriptions of each, is regularly sent to all Macintosh software developers so they can incorporate these AppleEvents into their software updates. Apple compiles a standard AppleEvent Registry to which developers can refer when creating their own applications.

Mac OS 8.6

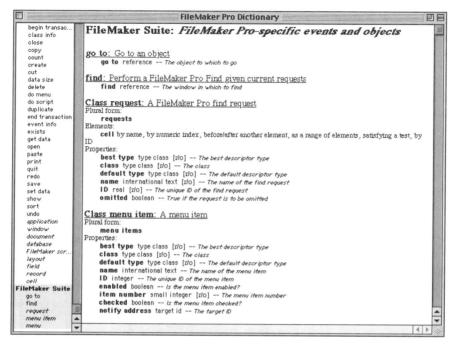

Figure 12.2 The FileMaker suite viewed in the FileMaker Pro dictionary.

AppleEvents And Program Linking

When an application sends an AppleEvent to another program, the receiving program is usually launched and then asked to perform a task. Of course, this process assumes that the receiving program is available. In addition to being able to communicate with programs that exist on the same hard drive, AppleEvents, through IAC, can communicate with programs that reside on other parts of a network as well.

AppleEvents have found their first important use linking small, related programs together into a larger, more capable system. Several Personal Information Managers use AppleEvents to exchange data between modules, such as calendars, contact managers, and notepads, and to make the various modules more powerful and seamless. Other candidates for AppleEvents projects are flat-file databases that require relational capabilities and application or system macros. In the next chapter, you will learn how to use the Script Editor to record AppleScripts.

Chapter 17 introduces the capability that allows any user on the network to share data with any other user on the network. In Chapter 18, you'll learn about the Program Linking option that allows you to access software from other Macintoshes on the network via IAC commands. If you use this option, applications on one Macintosh can use AppleEvents to communicate with applications on other Macs across the network. As with other aspects of IAC, it remains to be seen how this capability will be translated into new Macintosh software features.

The Edition Manager

Creating text and graphic elements within one application and using them in other applications has always been a hallmark of the Mac OS. Its legendary Cut and Paste commands are now offered in most all operating systems, but when these OSs were just getting around to adding such features, the Mac OS had already introduced even more powerful features through the Edition Manager's Publish and Subscribe commands.

By using Publish and Subscribe in your applications, you can move elements between applications, and those elements can be manually or automatically updated as you modify them. In other words, when text, graphic, sound, or video elements are moved from one document to another, original and duplicate elements remain linked. When the originals are changed, so are the duplicates. The Publish and Subscribe commands use IAC to take cutting and pasting to a much higher level.

The benefits of using the Publish and Subscribe commands are obvious:

➤ Charts created in spreadsheets or databases and used in word processors or page layout applications can be automatically updated any time the data changes.

➤ Legal disclaimers and other boilerplate text commonly used in documents (such as dates on a copyright notice, for example) can be automatically updated.

➤ Illustrated publications can be created using preliminary versions of graphic images that will be automatically updated as these graphics are completed.

You can use Publish and Subscribe commands for more than simple "live copy and paste" between two applications on your Macintosh. These commands support Macintosh networks (using File Sharing), so your documents can include components that were created, manipulated, and stored by many people on many network file servers.

Although the term Edition Manager is the technical programming term for this set of capabilities, we'll use the term Publish/Subscribe for the remainder of this chapter to refer to the entire set of Edition Manager capabilities.

How Publish/Subscribe Works

Although Publish/Subscribe is a powerful feature, its basic premise is simple: any elements—text, graphics, sound, or video—or combinations of elements can be transferred from one document to another using Publish/Subscribe. It happens like this:

Mac OS 8.6

1. The transfer begins when elements to be shared are selected and then published to a new edition file, such as the selected spreadsheet cells in Figure 12.3. This process is similar to the Cut or Copy process except that instead of being transferred into memory, the selected elements are saved to the edition file on disk. When you publish these elements, you name the edition file and specify where on your hard drive it will be stored.

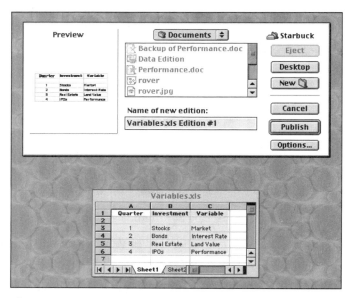

Figure 12.3 An edition file consists of selected elements, such as text, images, or other data.

2. The section of your document used to create an edition is called the Publisher. A link is automatically maintained between an edition file and the document that created it. When changes are made in the Publisher, the edition file is updated to reflect these changes. Figure 12.4 shows an edition file selected for publishing in a word processing document. Updates can be made any time the original document is changed or at any other time you initiate them.

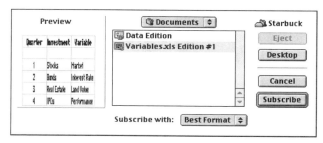

Figure 12.4 An edition file selected for publishing.

3. To complete the transfer of elements between documents, the receiving document subscribes to the edition file by importing the edition file elements and establishing a link between the edition and the subscribing document. The document section imported from an edition becomes a Subscriber (to the edition). Figure 12.5 shows a sample word processing document that has subscribed to a portion of a spreadsheet.

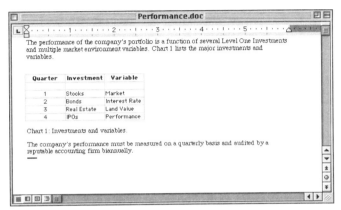

Figure 12.5 Edition files can be subscribed to by any number of other documents, and are automatically updated after they have been subscribed to (inserted) in these documents.

At this point, the edition file is an independent disk file, linked to the document that published it and any documents subscribing to it. As elements in the publisher document change, the edition file is updated according to options set in that original document. As the edition file is updated, the edition data used by subscribers is also updated according to options set in the subscribing document. The entire process is shown in Figure 12.6.

Publish/Subscribe Commands

In applications that support Publish/Subscribe, a small handful of commands, including the following, usually appear in the Edit menu or in a submenu:

➤ Create Publisher

➤ Subscribe To

➤ Publisher Options/Subscriber Options

Some applications use other command names for these functions, but they should work in essentially the same way. For example, take a look at Figure 12.7, which shows the Publishing submenus for Microsoft Word (left) and Microsoft Excel (right), both components of Microsoft Office 98. Note that Excel has an additional

Mac OS 8.6

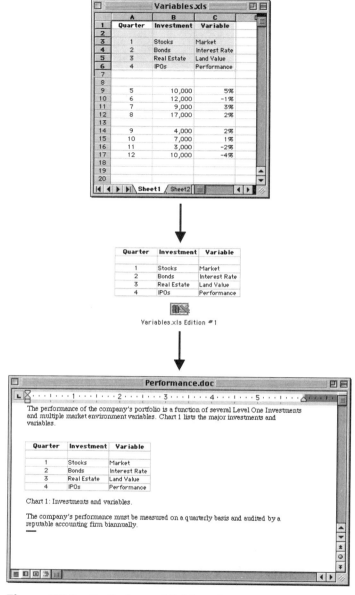

Figure 12.6 Both the publishing document and the subscribing document are linked to the edition file.

submenu called Links, which contains many of the options found in Microsoft Word's Subscriber Options submenu.

The following sections describe the main features found in most applications that support Publish/Subscribe.

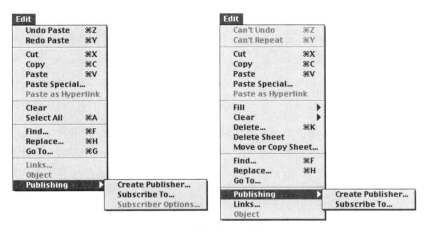

Figure 12.7 Two example Publisher submenus.

The Create Publisher Command

Create Publisher creates a new edition file, which you name and store in any desired location on any available volume. The edition file contains the text and graphic elements selected when you choose the command. To publish any elements, select the areas of the current document that you wish to share and choose the Create Publisher command from the appropriate menu. The Create Publisher dialog box, shown in Figure 12.8, then appears.

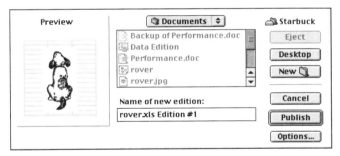

Figure 12.8 The Create Publisher dialog box.

The left side of this dialog box previews the elements that will be included in the edition, but be aware that not all selections provide a preview. To complete the creation of the edition, enter a name in the Name of New Edition option box and select a location where the file will be saved. Then click the Publish button, which saves your new edition to disk.

A new file (separate from the document you're currently working in) that contains a copy of the elements you selected to publish is created on the selected disk or network volume. This file—the edition—will be placed in other documents and

Mac OS 8.6

applications using the Subscribe To command. According to the options set in the Publisher Options dialog box, the edition will be updated to include any changes made to the elements it contains.

The Subscribe To Command

The Subscribe To command (the Publish/Subscribe equivalent of the Paste command), imports a copy of an edition file into the current document. When you choose this command, the Subscribe To dialog box appears (see Figure 12.9). The names of edition files appear in the scrolling list, and a preview of an edition appears when you select its filename. Select the edition you want, click the Subscribe button, and the chosen edition appears in your document.

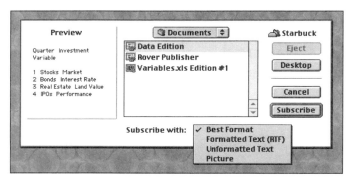

Figure 12.9 The Subscribe To dialog box.

When you're working in text-based applications, as opposed to graphic applications, the edition appears at the point where the cursor is positioned when you chose the Subscribe To command. In graphics applications, the edition file usually appears in the current screen display area, but not at the exact X and Y pixel coordinates. Details on how to use these included editions follow.

Publisher Options

The next Edition Manager command is either Publisher Options or Subscriber Options, depending on what you select. The Publisher Options command presents a dialog box like the one shown in Figure 12.10.

Additional Publisher options may be found in the Edit|Links menu in Excel 98.

This dialog box presents four important options:

➤ *Publisher To*—This menu is not really an option because it offers no alternatives; it simply shows you where the edition is stored and the path to that location. To see the storage location, click on the Publisher To pop-up menu.

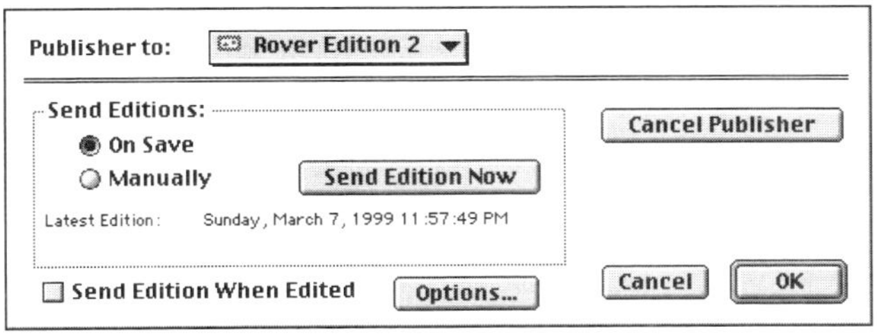

Figure 12.10 The Publisher Options dialog box for Word 98.

➤ *Send Editions*—This option lets you choose when the file associated with the selected edition will be updated. If you choose On Save, the edition file is updated each time the current document is saved; if you choose Manually, you must click the Send Edition Now button to update the edition file.

This option also displays the date and time the edition file was last updated. If On Save is selected, this information probably indicates the date and time the created file was last saved. If Manually is selected, the time at which the elements included in the edition were last changed is also listed, letting you know how up-to-date the edition is in relation to the file's current status.

➤ *Send Edition Now*—Clicking this button updates the edition file to reflect the current status of the published elements. This button is normally used only when Send Editions Manually is selected.

➤ *Cancel Publisher*—The Cancel Publisher button removes the link between the published elements in the current application and the edition file. Canceling the publisher does not delete the edition file, so it doesn't directly affect any documents that subscribe to that edition.

You can't reestablish the link to an edition once it's been canceled (although you can use the Create Publisher command to create a new edition with the same name, saved in the same location), so you should use the Cancel Publisher button only in certain situations. It's better to use the Send Editions Manually option to temporarily prevent editions from being updated.

If you accidentally use the Cancel Publisher button, you may be able to undo it by exiting your document with the Close command, clicking the Don't Save button to avoid saving your changes, and then reopening the document with the Open command (of course, doing so means you lose any changes you've made). The Revert command offered by some applications may also return your document to the state it was in before you canceled the Publisher.

In many cases you'll be able to select a few additional options like the ones shown in Figure 12.11 for Microsoft Word (top) and Excel (bottom) by selecting an

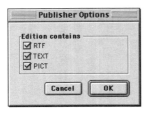

Figure 12.11 Examples of the options for saving a Publisher in Microsoft Word (top) and Excel (bottom).

Options command. Such options usually relate to features that determine how an edition appears within a document, such as the file format in which an edition is to be saved. Deselecting the file formats that are not desired will decrease the file size.

For example, publishing a small image and selecting RTF, TEXT, and PICT in the Publisher Options window results in an edition that's 83K in size. The same edition published using only PICT format (the native image format for the Mac OS) results in a file size of only 28K.

Some applications, such as Excel 98, allow users to configure publishing options through additional menu options. For example, the menus shown in Figure 12.12 are accessed by choosing Edit|Links|Options, which is essentially the same as the Edit|Publishing|Publisher Options in Word 98.

The Subscriber Options Command

The Subscriber Options command can be selected from the Edit|Publisher submenu only when a subscribed edition is selected, as indicated by the border around the edition. When you select an edition, the Subscriber Options dialog box (shown in Figure 12.13) appears.

The Subscriber dialog box usually presents the following options:

➤ *Subscriber To*—This menu offers no alternatives; it simply lets you see where the edition is stored and the path to that location. To see the storage location, click the Subscriber To pop-up menu.

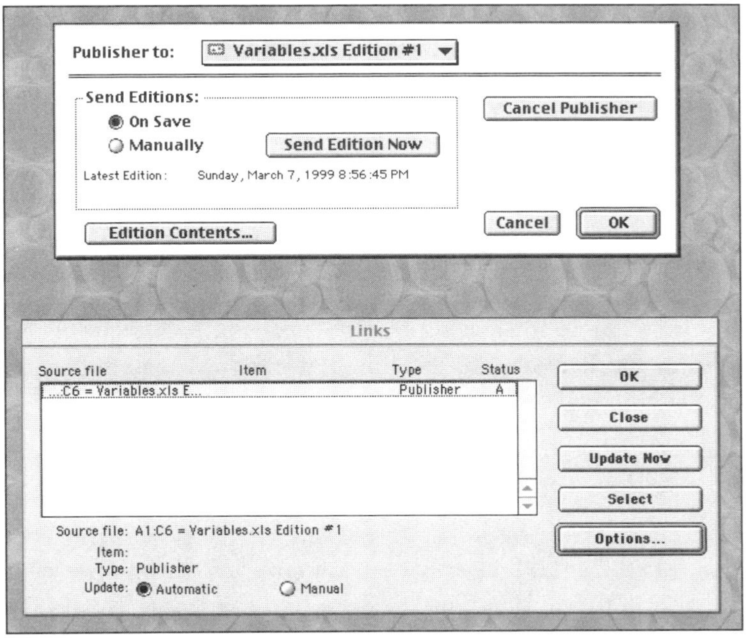

Figure 12.12 Publisher options in Excel 98 are also found through the Publisher|Links menu.

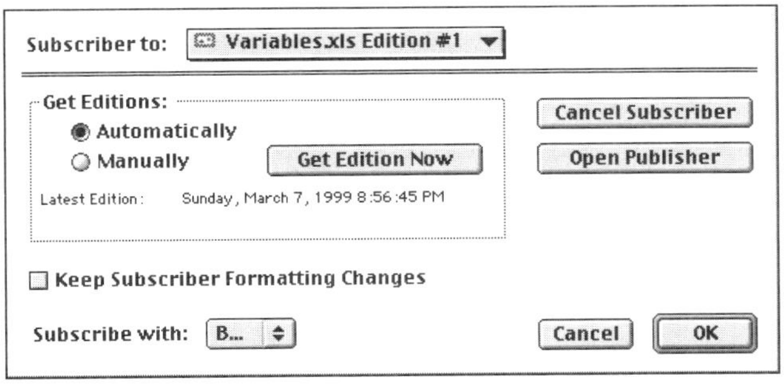

Figure 12.13 The Subscriber Options dialog box.

▶ *Get Editions*—This option lets you choose when the edition elements will be updated to reflect any changes made to the edition file. The Automatically option causes any changes to the edition file to be imported each time you open the document or whenever the edition file changes; the Manually option requires you to click the Get Edition Now button in order for changes to the edition to be reflected in your document.

If you choose Automatically, your document will always have the latest version of the text or graphic elements contained in the edition file. If you choose

Manually, your document may not always reflect updates to the edition file, but you can choose when those updates are made.

The date and time when the current edition was last changed by the application that created it are displayed below the Get Editions option. If you selected Manually, the date and time when the edition was imported into the current document are also listed. If these dates and times are not the same, the edition data contained in the current document is not up-to-date with the current edition file.

If the dates and times are dimmed, the edition file can't be located; it's been deleted or moved to another volume. The link between the current document and the edition file has been broken.

➤ *Get Edition Now*—Clicking this button imports the contents of the current edition file into your document. It's normally used only when the Manually option is selected.

➤ *Cancel Subscriber*—The Cancel Subscriber button removes the link between the imported elements and the edition file. The imported elements remain in the current application, but future changes to the edition will not be reflected in the current publication.

You cannot reestablish the link to an edition once it's been canceled (although you can use the Subscribe To command to create a new link to that same edition), so you should limit using the Cancel Subscriber button to particular circumstances. A better strategy would be to use the Get Editions Manually option to temporarily prevent editions from being updated in the subscribing document.

If you accidentally use the Cancel Subscriber button, you may be able to undo it by exiting your document with the Close command, clicking the Don't Save button to avoid saving your changes, and then reopening the document with the Open command (of course, following these steps means you lose any changes you've made). The Revert command offered by some applications may also return your document to the state it was in before you canceled the subscriber.

➤ *Open Publisher*—The Open Publisher button performs a neat trick—launching the application that created the selected edition and opening the document from which the edition was published. This lets you edit the contents of the edition using all the tools and capabilities of the application that originally created it.

You can use the Open Publisher button to both launch an application and open a document that created an edition, or you can perform the same tasks using the Finder—it makes no difference to the outcome. The Open Publisher button just makes the process convenient. Changes you make to the open document will be

Mac OS 8.6

reflected in the disk file and related edition files, depending on the settings you use in the Publisher Options dialog box and whether you use the Save command.

You also can modify the edition file without changing the original document, using the following steps after launching the application with the Open Publisher button:

1. Set the Publisher options for the edition to Send Editions Manually.
2. Make the necessary changes to the text or graphic elements.
3. Click the Send Edition Now button in the Publisher Options dialog box.
4. Close the document or quit the application without saving your changes.

The edition file will now be updated, but the original document and any other editions will remain unchanged.

Editing Subscribers

Because the contents of a subscriber are provided by an edition file and are usually updated periodically (according to the setting in the Subscriber Options dialog box), there are limits to manipulating a subscriber within any document. In general, you can't make any changes that would be lost when a new version of the edition becomes available.

The following are some of the limitations in editing subscribers:

- *Text subscribers*—With subscribers that include only text, you can't edit the text when subscribing to the edition. The only exception is that you can set the font, type size, or type style of the text as long as the change applies to the entire subscriber text. You can't make one word in the edition bold or set one sentence in a different font.

- *Graphic subscribers*—When using subscribers that include graphics, you can reposition the editions you've subscribed to, but in most cases you can't resize them. (Graphic handles appear on the corners of the subscriber border in the event that you are permitted to resize the subscriber.)

- *Text in graphic subscribers*—The text in a graphic subscriber cannot be modified in any way. In the subscriber, the text is considered a part of the graphic element.

The correct way to edit a subscriber is to reopen the document that published the edition, make changes in that document, and then save those changes or use the Send Edition Now button to update the edition. You can quickly access the original document for any edition by clicking the Open Publisher button in the Subscriber Options dialog box.

Mac OS 8.6

Edition Files In The Finder

The edition files created with the Create Publisher command look just like any other files on your disks. They use a small shaded rectangle icon like the one surrounding editions in publishing or subscribing applications; you can add comments to them using the Get Info command.

Double-clicking an edition file in the Finder opens a window (shown in Figure 12.14) that contains the edition contents, the edition type (PICT and so on), and the Open Publisher button. The Open Publisher button launches the application that created the document from which the edition file was created and then opens that document.

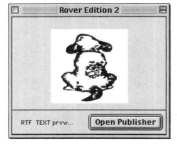

Figure 12.14 These windows are opened by clicking edition files from within the Finder.

You work only on the document that created the edition, not on the edition file. Any changes made to the edition elements are then updated to the edition file (based on the options in the Publisher Options dialog box). Therefore, deleting a file that has published editions makes it impossible to modify or update those editions again—the data in the editions cannot be accessed from either the edition file or the subscriber document.

Edition File Links

The link between edition files and their publishers and subscribers is automatically maintained even if you rename or move these documents to new locations on the current volume. If you move an edition file, publishing document, or subscribing document to a new volume and delete the copy on the original volume, the links to and from the file will be broken.

When links to or from an edition file are broken, it's impossible to automatically or manually update the edition file or the version of that edition file used in any subscribing documents. You can tell that a link is broken by the notification "Edition cannot be found" in the Subscriber To dialog box, or the error dialog box shown in Figure 12.15, which appears when the Get Edition Now button is selected.

Figure 12.15 Error messages like this can occur if you change the link between edition files.

Although you can't directly "reconnect" a broken Publisher or Subscriber link, you can recreate a link between an application and an edition published from it:

1. Open the application and select the border surrounding the previously created edition. Even though the link has been broken, the border will still be visible.

2. Select the Create Publisher command and save the edition with the same name as the previous edition to the same location as the previous edition, overwriting the unlinked copy that remains.

3. Any Subscribers using this edition will now update according to their option settings, using the information in this new version of the edition.

To re-create a link between an edition and a subscribing application:

1. Open the subscribing application and select the element that was imported as a subscribed edition.

2. Select the Subscribe To command and locate the edition file to which you want to recreate a link. Then click the Subscribe button.

3. The data from the edition file as it now exists will appear in your document, replacing the older version that was selected. This edition is now linked to the edition file on disk and will update according to the settings of the Publisher and Subscriber options.

Unavailable Edition Files

When you open a document containing subscribers, the Mac OS attempts to locate edition files linked to each subscriber. If any of these edition files reside on unmounted floppy disks or removable volumes, you'll be prompted to insert the disks or volumes. Then the document will open normally, and the links between the subscribers and their edition files will be maintained.

Edition Files And Your Network

Edition files can be published to or subscribed from any available network or File Sharing volume. They operate in pretty much the same way on network/File Sharing volumes, except that documents containing publishers and subscribers must access the editions over the network in order to keep all files updated properly.

To expedite sharing editions via a network, you can create aliases of editions stored on network volumes that you access frequently. You can then browse these aliases on your local hard drive (from the Subscribe To dialog box), and when the editions are used, the aliases will automatically connect to the appropriate network volumes and access the edition files.

To subscribe directly to editions on network volumes, aliases will also mount automatically when you open documents subscribing to the editions.

Edition Manager Tips

The following are several tips you can use when working with the Edition Manager:

- *Republishing an edition*—If you overwrite an edition (by creating a new edition with the same name in the same location as an existing edition), the new edition will be linked to all documents that subscribed to the old edition. For example, if you wanted to replace an existing edition file named Corporate Logo with a new graphic, you could use the Create Publisher command to create a new edition named Corporate Logo and save it in the same volume and folder as the old Corporate Logo edition. (When you're asked to confirm that you want to overwrite the old file, click the Yes button.) At this point, all documents that subscribed to the old Corporate Logo edition file will begin using the new Corporate Logo edition file the next time they're updated.

- *Using nested editions*—You can create editions that contain text or graphics subscribed from other editions (see Figure 12.16), so-called nested editions. After you set appropriate updating options in all associated Publish To and Subscribe To dialog boxes, changes you make to elements of the original documents will be correctly updated everywhere they occur.

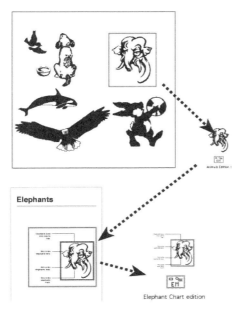

Figure 12.16 Edition files can contain other editions.

For example, if your page layout program subscribed to your Corporate Logo document for the purpose of using it, along with some text and ornamental graphics, to create a corporate insignia, you could use the Create Publisher command to save an edition file named Corporate Insignia. This edition could then be subscribed to for use on the first page of all corporate reports created in your word processing programs. If the Corporate Logo edition were updated, this update would appear in the page layout file (where the insignia was created) and extend to the Corporate Insignia edition when the page layout document was opened (assuming the Publisher options and Subscriber options were set correctly). The updated Corporate Insignia edition would then be updated in all documents in which it was used (if you set the appropriate Subscriber option).

➤ *Saving Publisher documents*—When an edition is created, the edition file appears on disk and can be subscribed to immediately. If the document that published the edition is closed without being saved, however, the edition file will be deleted, and all subscriber links will be broken.

For example, you open a drawing application and quickly create an illustration of a cow jumping over the moon. Using the Create Publisher command, you create an edition named Cow Over Moon and then switch to your word processor where you subscribe to the Cow Over Moon edition and continue to work on your text document. Later, when you're ready to quit for the day, you choose the Shut Down command from the Finder's Special menu, and your drawing

Mac OS 8.6

application asks whether you want to save the untitled file you used to create Cow Over Moon. At this point, if you don't name and save this file, the Cow Over Moon edition will be deleted from your disk. The image will remain in the word processing document that subscribed to it, but the link between the word processing document and the deleted edition file will be broken. It will be impossible to edit the graphic in the future without re-creating it.

➤ *Using edition aliases*—You can subscribe to edition file aliases just like you subscribe to standard edition files. As always, the alias file will maintain a link to the original file even if you move or rename the alias or the original. If the alias's original document is on a network server or File Sharing volume, the volume will be mounted automatically.

The ability to Publish and Subscribe has been available now for many years, but it gets very little press in Macintosh literature. Apparently, few users make good use of this powerful feature. Perhaps having the data and publisher application available remotely is difficult for people to conceptualize. That's too bad, because Publish and Subscribe is powerful—and easy to use.

A similar concept in Microsoft Windows is the linking in Object Linking & Embedding, or OLE. You can link data automatically (hot link) or manually (warm link). When you open a linked document, Windows posts a dialog box asking whether you want the data updated. OLE uses Dynamic Data Exchange, or DDE (introduced in Windows 3.0), as its messaging system. DDE is similar to AppleEvents, described in the previous section. DDE allows one application to pass data to and from another through the Windows clipboard with a reference to the source of the data. DDE is just one layer of OLE's functioning. OLE is similar to OpenDoc; both are discussed in more detail later in the chapter.

OpenDoc

As computers become more powerful and the industry matures, you would expect that the technology would be easier to use. That hasn't been the case. The trend in the industry has been to release ever more feature-filled software packages, as if the quality of a program is measured by the number of check-offs it can warrant on a feature list. Word processors now contain spell checkers, grammar checkers, thesauruses, page layout modules, graphics, charting, outlining, idea processing, table of contents and index generation, databases and mail merges, envelope label printers, telephone and fax machines, and email message centers.

What's a user to do? You can hardly find these features, let alone learn about them. Only "get-a-lifers" can love the current state of the software industry. In an ideal world, you could safely ignore the stuff you weren't interested in. However, extra features burn up processing power and disk space. Checked your hard drive lately? Don't be surprised if you find half a dozen spellcheckers lurking about in there. This trend has probably reached its peak with the release of huge, everything-including-the-kitchen-sink packages such as Microsoft Office and the WordPerfect office package.

Vendors have long been aware of the problem; it's both a resource management opportunity and an industry barrier. Large programs from large software houses crowd out innovative small products from small companies. One solution is to link small programs into a compound document architecture with an object-oriented framework and Interapplication Communication. Then you can buy and learn just the functions you need—one text editor, one spellchecker, one paint module, and so on.

With this goal, Apple and a consortium of partners, including IBM, pursued an industry-wide standard called OpenDoc. OpenDoc is an architecture under which documents are built. OpenDoc is the result of the "Amber" project at Apple, with other technologies added to the mix by the other vendors in the program.

TIP

For the latest version of OpenDoc, see www.info.apple.com/swupdates/.

What Is OpenDoc?

Users viewing demonstrations of OpenDoc described it as a "bug fix" because it fits into a natural way of working with data objects as parts of a compound document. A compound document is much more natural than an application-centered document: you don't have to do context switching between applications to get the capabilities you need. Just click a part and the menu changes. You don't even notice it. But when you go to the menu, the command you expect to use for that part is there. Need a part? Just add it. OpenDoc supplies the reference to the appropriate part handler.

OpenDoc offers the following user benefits:

▶ *Easy creation of compound documents*—You use the same Cut and Paste, Drag and Drop, Publish and Subscribe, and other metaphorical commands that you're used to. OpenDoc looks and feels like a Macintosh. It uses the Open Scripting Architecture (OSA), of which AppleEvents and AppleScript are a part, as its messaging medium.

Mac OS 8.6

> *In-place editing*—Point at and click what you want to change. Cut and Paste, Drag and Drop, and most other aspects of data handling that you've come to know are also supported.

> *Improved multitasking*—You can have several parts "playing" at the same time in the same document. For example, you could have a clock and a video running while you work in a text file. OpenDoc provides multithreaded, multitasked system time-slicing among all three parts.

> *Central data storage and unified document management*—All your data pieces are in your document; only the services needed to use them are referenced. Therefore, data can't be lost or inaccessible as it can be in the Publish and Subscribe model. You also can track the revision history of your document.

> *Cross-platform support*—OpenDoc is a vendor-neutral, platform-neutral specification supported by major industry players. As yet, Microsoft doesn't directly support OpenDoc. They sell a competing compound document architecture called Object Linking & Embedding.

In order to promote OpenDoc and make it an open standard, a nonprofit association called the Component Integration Laboratories (or CI Labs) was formed. CI Labs published the OpenDoc standard. It was not only responsible for making OpenDoc available to everybody, it also provided rigorous testing and evaluation procedures to approve software under the program. Apple pulled out of CI Labs in early 1997, and the organization was dissolved soon thereafter.

> *Consistency of operation and uniformity of interface*—Use one part editor for each data type. When your needs grow, you can upgrade to a more powerful editor. OpenDoc defines a consistent user interface for documents, parts, and part handlers.

OpenDoc has the potential to profoundly impact the way you use your Macintosh. It will make it much easier for you to customize your environment or for vendors to provide quality vertical market packages (software written for a niche audience) suitable for your line of work.

Documents And Parts

OpenDoc adds a few additional words to the vocabulary of the Macintosh user. These words are based on common ones you use in your everyday speech, so they shouldn't be much of a burden. We all work with *documents*, and we all know that most documents are comprised of *parts*. Let's look at how the concepts of documents and parts are used in conjunction with OpenDoc.

Documents are the central framework in OpenDoc. A document is no longer tied to a single application but is composed of small pieces of content called parts. Parts are the fundamental building blocks in OpenDoc. They have the same relationship to documents that atoms have to molecules. Parts come in flavors, which are content containers. Text parts contain characters; graphics parts contain lines and shapes; spreadsheet parts contain cells, formulas, and a spreadsheet engine; video parts contain digitized video sequences and a player; and so on. OpenDoc makes its best effort to compartmentalize capabilities within part types, although some mixing occurs. The type of data in each part is known as the part's intrinsic content.

Parts can contain other parts (embedding), so a document has a part hierarchy. That is, at its root level, a document has a single part in which other parts are embedded. Developers must decide whether their parts can embed other parts; if the parts can be embedded, they can accept any type of part.

Parts are created and modified by part editors. These editors are small programs that are called upon by an OpenDoc document—they're actually system routines. Some part editors will ship with the OpenDoc package so that in system software you'll have basic capability right out of the box. This capability is similar to current functions of system software such as TextEdit, QuickDraw, the Communications Toolbox, and other routines that let you work with parts of the Macintosh interface in standard ways.

Part handlers are more complex editors created for OpenDoc by third parties. You buy them shrink-wrapped in stores. Part handlers are the equivalent of applications; they are responsible for the following functions under the OpenDoc architecture:

➤ *Displaying*—Drawing the part onscreen and rendering it to a printer.

➤ *Editing*—Editing the part.

➤ *Storage and management*—The part handler reads and writes the part to and from memory and disk. For this reason, part handlers can be of two types: editors and viewers. Many will be both.

➤ *Acting as an interface modifier*—The editor part handler is responsible for switching menu commands, adjusting dialog boxes, and changing the interface to make available whatever tools a part requires. A viewer part handler is a subset of an editor; it allows users to display and print a part but not edit it. You use viewers to provide security lockout features for parts in documents.

Another important concept in OpenDoc is that of frames. Whereas parts are areas of one kind of content, frames are the boundaries separating the collection of objects and operations supported by one part from those supported by another. You can embed a button in a part, and that compound construct is a frame that can be manipulated. Frames have properties such as layering (front to back), transparency, and so on that will be familiar to users of draw graphics programs.

Mac OS 8.6

In Figure 12.17, you see a frame with a clock. Other parts in the document—the button, the text, and the molecule graphic—are not part of the clock frame. It may be helpful to think of frames as grouped collections of objects; each grouped collection has its own identity.

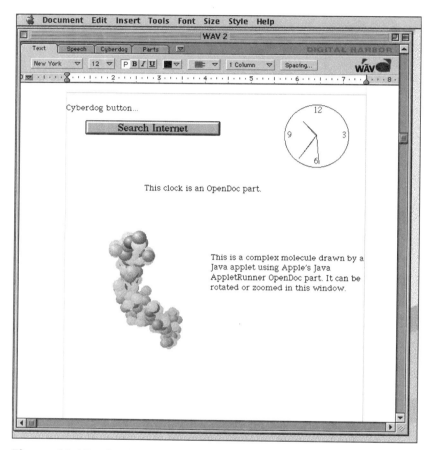

Figure 12.17 An OpenDoc document with a frame and several parts.

Thankfully, it's much harder to explain what a frame is than it is to use one. The notion is almost entirely transparent to the user. Frames are not simply windows that appear or disappear from view; they are persistent. When you open a frame in a window, you see the frame. When you close that window, the part returns to the condition it was in before you opened the window. A frame can show, however, much of its contents is displayed. That is, if a frame contains a graphic larger than the frame, you see the cropped part of that graphic within the frame.

Storage of compound documents requires a system of saving the document to disk with each part referenced to its part handler. OpenDoc uses an object-oriented storage model based on Apple's Bento standard. Storing a document to disk compartmentalizes each part as a data object and provides references to appropriate part handlers. Opening that document begins a process of calling appropriate part handlers one after another to "build" the document in memory. When you move an OpenDoc document to another computer or type of computer, these part handler references allow the OpenDoc document to be opened by other appropriate handlers when the creator part handler isn't available. This system ensures cross-platform capabilities and also provides a mechanism for collaborative access. You can write part handlers that are both multiuser and version-history sensitive.

OpenDoc Menus

OpenDoc applications have a slightly different menu bar than the usual Mac program. The File menu is replaced with a new menu, the Document menu. Since the basic idea behind OpenDoc is that users will work on "documents" instead of individual files, this makes more sense. However, it is a bit disconcerting to see the familiar File menu replaced. Other menus work, act, and look the same as with non-OpenDoc applications.

Take a look at Figure 12.18, the Document menu from Digital Harbor's WAV word processor. All of the things you'd expect from the File menu are there. Here are the items you can expect from any OpenDoc Document menu:

Figure 12.18 The OpenDoc Document menu isn't very different from the old-fashioned File menu.

- ▶ *New*—Opens a new, blank document.
- ▶ *Open document*—Opens a previously created document from the disk drive.
- ▶ *Insert*—Inserts the contents of the file you select into the current document.
- ▶ *Close*—Closes the current document.
- ▶ *Save*—Saves the current document.
- ▶ *Page Setup and Print*—These items work just as you'd expect.

OpenDoc Control Panels

Since OpenDoc is completely modular, you might have more than one editor that can work on a particular piece of data. For instance, you might have a text frame in a document. If you want to edit that text, any text editing part will do. But what if you have more than one? Luckily, you can choose which editor you want to use on a particular kind of data.

The Editor Setup Control Panel (in Figure 12.19) is where you make your selections. To choose an editor, simply open the Control Panel, find the part type, select it, and click the Choose Editor button. It will display all editors you have installed that can work with that kind of data. In Figure 12.20, a Cyberdog editor has been chosen.

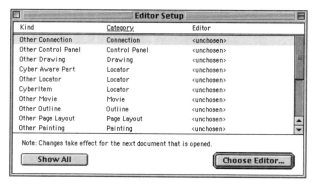

Figure 12.19 The Editor Setup Control Panel lets you match parts to editors.

Figure 12.20 The Choose Editor dialog box shows you all parts that can edit the data type you've selected.

One more Control Panel you should know about is OpenDoc Setup (Figure 12.21). This Control Panel lets you set two things: the amount of RAM allocated to new OpenDoc documents and whether and when OpenDoc is on (loaded into RAM) or off (unloaded).

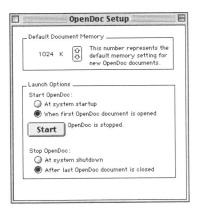

Figure 12.21 The OpenDoc Setup controls RAM settings for OpenDoc.

If you use OpenDoc all the time, you might decide to leave it on from system start-up to system shutdown. To do this, simply click the radio buttons for Start OpenDoc at System Startup and Stop OpenDoc at System Shutdown. However, the default settings start and stop OpenDoc so that it's not loaded when it's not being used—this is probably the best setting for most people.

Wrapping Up

Using just a few simple commands, Edition Manager allows you to transfer text and graphics between applications while maintaining a "live link" to the original data:

➤ *Create Publisher*—This command saves the selected data to a new edition file on disk.

➤ *Subscribe To*—This command imports an edition file from disk into the current document.

➤ *Publish/Subscribe options*—These commands control the way changes to original documents are updated to the edition file and documents subscribing to the edition file.

The OpenDoc architecture provides a framework for creating compound documents using small applications. Although OpenDoc provides a glimpse of the possible future of software, it isn't included in Mac OS 8.6. Apple has put the project into maintenance mode and no further updates other than bug fixes are expected.

AppleEvents provides a rich object-oriented messaging language that IAC uses to let applications talk to one another. As you will see in Chapter 13, this system software programming tool uses AppleEvents and a natural programming language to let you automate many actions into easy-to-use programs.

AppleScript

When the first version of MS-DOS shipped with the IBM PC in 1983, it came bundled with a version of the Basic programming language, which made it possible for PC users to control their computers and operating systems. With programs called batch files, users could start applications automatically, repeat actions, perform timed backups, set the operating environment, and more. Over the years, Macintosh owners longed for the PC's capacity for do-it-yourself programming—one of the few areas in which the PC was more gifted, out of the box, than the Macintosh.

Although several third-party developers offered system-wide macro programming tools—most notably UserLand's Frontier, Binary Software's KeyQuencer, Affinity Microsystems' Tempo II Plus, WestCode Software's One Click, and CE Software's QuicKeys—none of them were officially blessed by Apple, nor have they achieved enough support in the Macintosh community to become standard. They also didn't provide a wide enough scope; the ability to control applications, repeat actions, and automate system tasks is something that has to come from the operating system if it is to be successful. Apple finally released its own programming language, AppleScript, to provide these much needed capabilities as part of an overall strategy meant to supply automation tools across Macintosh applications and beyond. AppleScript is now an integrated part of the operating system. It is automatically installed when you install the Mac OS.

AppleScript can be used in an impressive variety of ways:

➤ AppleScript lets you tailor applications and desktops to meet your needs.

➤ AppleScript simplifies the work of developers, systems integrators, and Value Added Resellers (VARs) by providing custom solutions based on standard Macintosh applications.

➤ AppleScript allows you to write an *applet*, an *intelligent agent*, or *a smart document* that can seamlessly integrate small components into larger solutions. This capability is part of Apple's strategy for downsizing applications, which also includes Inter-Application Communication, AppleEvents, and OpenDoc (described in Chapter 12).

➤ You can create new product opportunities with AppleScript. You'll see some of these possibilities in Apple Guide and PlainTalk, which incorporate, can be controlled by, and in turn can use AppleScript to control other applications.

AppleScript is a pervasive part of the Mac OS—even if you don't use it for programming, many elements of the OS itself require it, and it is now a mandatory part of Mac OS 8.6.

What Is AppleScript?

AppleScript is a high-level, object-oriented, natural-language programming language. And as far as programming languages go, AppleScript is the real thing: it can store variables and lists (records or arrays); repeat through looping; make decisions based on cases; do IF branching; compare; do Boolean logic; and manipulate text, numbers, dates, times, and other values. AppleScript can also declare variables, create user-defined commands or subroutines, and store and manipulate data to return values.

AppleScript is an object-oriented programming language because it imposes actions on objects that are defined as part of its programming model. Objects can be applications (Finder, Scriptable Text Editor, FileMaker, and so on), files, resources, interface elements (buttons, windows, and so on), or data. In the Finder, objects can be a variety of Macintoshes, printers, and even AppleTalk zones on a network. Objects you can see on your Desktop can be manipulated with AppleScript, a capability made even easier with the Scriptable Finder (introduced in System 7.5).

Objects have two additional characteristics that are programmatic: *inheritance* and *encapsulation*. Objects, like applications, can contain other objects (encapsulation); objects derived from other objects share common characteristics (inheritance). Third-party applications behave as if they are object-oriented databases to AppleScript because they encapsulate a group of scriptable objects. These features impose regularity to objects by making them behave in ways you expect and have come to learn intuitively.

AppleScript uses *words* and *statements* to form scripts. As in non-programming languages, words are nouns (objects), verbs, and modifiers. Verbs are common action commands such as open, close, print, or delete. Often verbs are derived from standard menu commands. Statements are commands that can be communicated in the form of messages to objects in other applications. Applications themselves are objects because they can be commanded to do actions.

As an example of an AppleScript statement, consider the following:

```
tell application "Scriptable Text Editor"
to activate the window name "Untitled."
```

This one-line statement (it appears as two lines because of page constraints in the book) is a complete script that instructs the Scriptable Text Editor to search its list of opened windows, and if an "Untitled" window is open, make it the frontmost active window. The formatting of this statement with bolded verbs, plain nouns, and italicized variables is traditional but not required. Often you'll see AppleScripts written in clegic logic (or display) format, with indentations for each command structure. You can see an example of this formatting in the Add Alias to Apple Menu AppleScript, which is shipped with the collection of Automated Tasks (discussed later in this chapter). It is shown in the Script Editor window in Figure 13.1.

As much as possible, AppleScript is written in a manner similar to the way you normally write and speak, although the syntax is much more precise and demanding. The intent is to lower the learning curve for AppleScript by employing words, expressions, and modifiers that you use in your everyday life.

Programs written in AppleScript, called *scripts*, are like those written for all other high-level programming languages. Scripts must be interpreted and compiled to run on your Macintosh. You can store scripts for interpretation at run time, or you can transform your script into interpreted read-only programs that you can distribute freely to other users. When you compile an AppleScript, it is transformed into a dialect-independent format called *Universal AppleScript*. Upon opening an AppleScript, you'll see the script displayed in the default language of the Macintosh you're working on—not necessarily the language in which the script was originally written. This means that a translation from Universal AppleScript has been done.

If you've ever used the HyperTalk programming language in HyperCard, AppleScript will seem familiar. Unlike HyperCard, however, AppleScript is extensible by other applications within the language. AppleScript uses a dictionary of commands (verbs), objects (nouns), and modifiers that are defined within each program that has chosen to implement AppleScript. Applications codify their data and functions by establishing dictionaries of objects and commands. You can view an application's dictionary by selecting the File|Open Dictionary command of the Script Editor. Figure 13.2 shows you the Appearance Control Panel's dictionary.

Each scriptable application will have different elements in its own scripting dictionary, although many of the same elements will appear in each dictionary. Also, you can use several applications to write AppleScripts and open dictionaries in addition

Mac OS 8.6

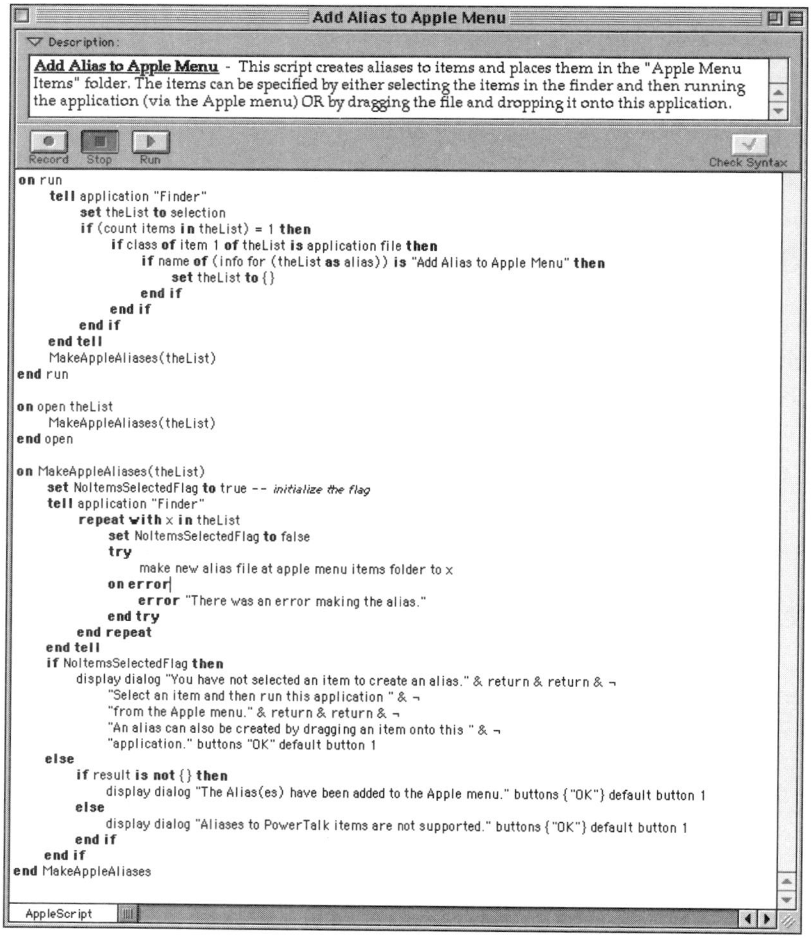

354   Chapter 13

Figure 13.1   The Add Alias to Apple Menu AppleScript shown in the Script Editor window.

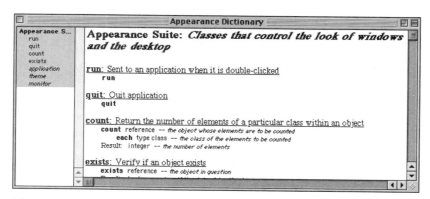

Figure 13.2   The Appearance Control Panel's AppleScript dictionary.

Mac OS 8.6

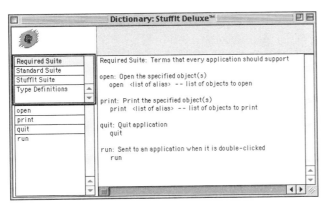

Figure 13.3 The AppleScript dictionary for StuffIt Deluxe, viewed with Scripter instead of Apple's Script Editor.

to the Script Editor, including Scripter from Main Event (www.mainevent.com). Figure 13.3 shows the dictionary for StuffIt Deluxe, a very popular application for compressing and decompressing files.

When AppleScript loads an application's dictionary, external data becomes objects and external functions become commands, and the language of that application becomes part of AppleScript's syntax.

The AppleScript Architecture

Most programming languages require that you learn a new language. To minimize this inconvenience, Apple introduced the Open Scripting Architecture (OSA) as a language standard that other software venders could adopt, so that their applications could communicate with each other. A software vendor merely has to follow the OSA specifications to make a scriptable application.

The standards definition phase of OSA began in 1989 and is ongoing. OSA and Apple Event Registry were released concurrently with System 7.0 in 1991. This marked the beginning of Inter-Application Communication, which is the foundation of the AppleScript architecture. Some key applications that supported AppleScript with the original architecture (such as Excel 4.0, FileMaker Pro 2.0, PageMaker 4.2, and others) were released in 1992. Bundled with System 7 Pro, AppleScript 1.0 premiered as a separate product in 1993. Version 1.1 and the Scriptable Finder appeared in System 7.5. The Scriptable Finder was a very important addition to the AppleScript architecture; it removed the final advantage of text-based operating systems by allowing users to script the operating system. Mac OS 8.6 includes the latest version, AppleScript 1.3.5. This update is completely written in PowerPC-native code, making it the fastest yet. The many added abilities of AppleScript 1.3.5 are covered later in this chapter.

AppleScript is just one expression of OSA. OSA includes AppleEvents (which you learned about Chapter 12), the object model, and a reference library of objects and events that are codified by third parties through Apple. These components form the basis for an open standard that Apple hopes others will build upon in the years to come.

As you may remember from the preceding chapter, AppleEvents is a messaging language that has made Inter-Application Communication (IAC) possible since System 7. With AppleEvents, programs communicate with one another, performing interapplication operations. One expression of the power of IAC is Publish and Subscribe, which allows applications to "publish" any AppleEvent that other applications might be interested in, and other applications to "subscribe" to that event. This means that an application can use the capabilities of another application, saving a lot of programming effort. AppleEvents works between applications that are either on the same computer or connected through a network.

AppleScript uses AppleEvents as the messaging medium through which commands are passed and results returned. A script is sent to the AppleScript Extension, which then interprets the statements in the script and sends AppleEvents to the appropriate application. The Apple Event Manager Extension serves as the traffic cop that deciphers these messages and routes them appropriately. You see the Event Manager in System 7.1; in later systems its function is incorporated into the System file.

To prevent AppleScript from growing in nonstandard ways, Apple imposes a standard language. Objects in AppleScript are identified by compound names, called *references*. The overall naming scheme is called the *Object Model*. With this lexicon of references, the language allows you to refer to individual objects in one of several alternate ways without worrying about how each application prefers to describe an object. Some commands have alternate expressions, as do some objects—fortunately, AppleScript validates both kinds in any application.

A standard syntax is imposed on developers only for common language tasks. Apple has organized events and objects into *event suites*. These suites are common ways to do tasks based on application categories: text processing, databases and spreadsheets, communications, page layout, and so on. They extend across the programming language the concept of common menu-command language elements such as *copy* and *paste* to scripting commands such as *delete, contain, get,* and *set.*

Event suites are evolving as developers register their commands, objects, and suites in the AppleEvent Registry (available from the Apple Professional Developers Association, or APDA). The event suites in this registry are the standard language for Inter-Application Communication implemented at the machine level and a

Mac OS 8.6

standard reference for developers on implementing AppleScript support within their own applications.

The commands that compose the language of AppleScript are contained in files called OSAX, which stands for Open Scripting Architecture Extension. These files are also called Scripting Additions. In previous versions of the operating system, Scripting Additions were contained in a single file called Standard Additions. This file, and other OSAX files, are now located in a folder called Scripting Additions in the System Folder (See Figure 13.4). In addition to this unification, new features that extend the developer's abilities have been added:

- *Clipboard Access*—Scripts can now access the data that is contained in the clipboard. A script can access data in the clipboard, set new data, or get information on the data.
- *Delay*—Scripts can incorporate a delay of a certain amount of time, specified in seconds. Scriptwriters use this to give scripts a more natural feel.
- *Choice Menus*—A list of items can be presented to users, allowing them to make selections.
- *Mounting Remote Volumes*—This powerful new feature enables scripts to mount a volume with either AppleTalk or AppleShare IP.
- *Say*—The Apple Text-to-Speech technology is now easily accessible via scripting. The rate of speech and inflections within the text are optionally controllable with special tags that can be inserted into the text. The rest of the process is automatic.
- *Summarization*—The summarize command takes a file and returns a brief summary. The number of lines in the result can be controlled.
- *Timed Dialog Boxes*—A dialog box now has the ability to assume a default value if a user does not respond to it within a specified amount of time.

Scripting Basics

AppleScript has been implemented using different components over the years. In earlier versions, AppleScript wasn't a mandatory part of the Mac OS, but once installed it added three items in the Extensions folder: AppleScript, the Record Button, and the Apple Event Manager. Things have changed a bit in Mac OS 8.6, including the following elements:

- *AppleScript (extension)*—This extension contains the AppleScript language and the code necessary to interpret it for your Macintosh. It also passes messages between applications. The AppleScript extension loads at boot-up as a 2-K handler in system memory when no scripts are running. When scripts are running, the full 330K of the extension is loaded.

Mac OS 8.6

▶ *AppleScriptLib (extension)*—This extension implements the AppleScript Open Scripting Architecture (OSA) component.

▶ *Scripting Additions (folder)*—These language extensions can be written in another programming language and added to AppleScript. They are often referred to as user-definable programs. In AppleScript, these scripts are called up using simple syntax with the named command or filename. Figure 13.4 shows the components of the Scripting Additions folder that are installed by Mac OS 8.6.

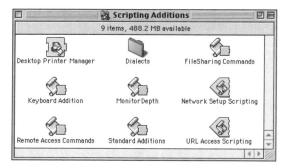

Figure 13.4 The Scripting Additions folder in the System Folder.

As AppleScript continues to develop, you'll discover scripting additions in third-party books and as shareware or freeware on online services. You'll also find scripting additions located in the Scripting Additions folder located in your System Folder. This folder also contains the Dialects folder (only English for now). You can open a Scripting Addition with the AppleScript Script Editor (this process is explained a little later in this chapter). Figure 13.5 shows the commands that are associated with the URL Access Scripting Addition.

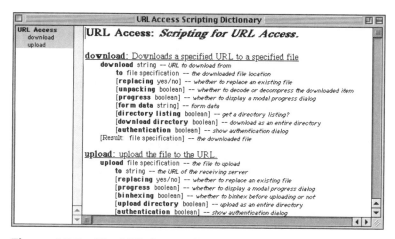

Figure 13.5 The URL Access Scripting Addition dictionary.

➤ *Scripts (folder)*—The Scripts folder provides a central location for storing AppleScripts. The Folder Actions folder, shown in Figure 13.6, is new in Mac OS 8.6. This folder, which is installed automatically, makes it possible to attach scripts to folder actions. This feature will be described in detail later.

Figure 13.6 The Scripts folder stores AppleScripts, including the new Folder Actions scripts.

The Apple Extras folder (part of all installations since System 7.5) contains an AppleScript folder. Additional non-system components of AppleScript are housed there: the Script Editor, AppleScript Guide, and a folder of Useful Scripts. The following list describes what these components do:

➤ *Script Editor (application)*—This application allows you to write or record, edit, check the syntax of, compile, and run scripts. Shown in Figure 13.7, the Script Editor is a basic but effective means of manipulating AppleScripts.

➤ *AppleScript Guide (AppleGuide file)*—The AppleScript Guide helps you learn the basics of writing AppleScripts and using the Script Editor. Choose Help|Help Center|AppleScript Help to activate the Help Viewer application, shown in Figure 13.8.

➤ *Automated Tasks and More Automated Tasks (folders)*—Automated Tasks and More Automated Tasks are a series of example AppleScripts that you can use in your daily work. The Automated Tasks folder includes these scripts:

  ➤ Add Alias to Apple Menu

  ➤ Share a Folder

  ➤ Share a Folder (no Guest)

  ➤ Start File Sharing

  ➤ Stop File Sharing

Mac OS 8.6

Chapter 13

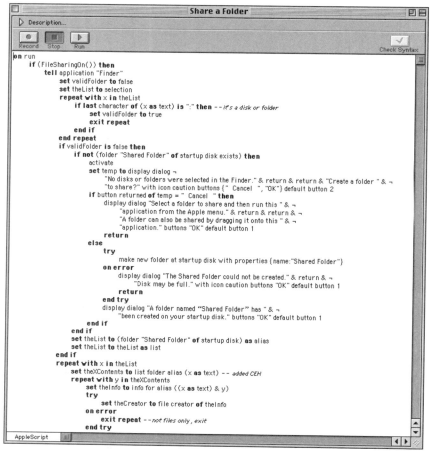

Figure 13.7 The Script Editor.

The More Automated Tasks folder includes the following scripts:

- Alert When Folder Changes
- Hide/Show Folder Sizes
- Synchronize Folders

An alias of the Automated Tasks folder is included in the Apple Menu Items folder. You can initiate the script by choosing it from the Automated Tasks submenu. We'll take a look at some of these scripts later in the chapter.

Although AppleScripts can be placed anywhere, it makes sense to keep them in one place. Mac OS 8.6 provides such a place. Within the System Folder is a folder named the Scripts folder in which you can store all of your scripts. If you want to use a script in another place (such as the Startup Items folder), you can create an

Figure 13.8 AppleScript Help provides a great deal of information about using AppleScript and the Script Editor.

alias to the original, which you should keep in the Scripts folder. As with any alias, alterations or updates made to a script in one location will take effect in all other locations. If you drop a script on the System Folder, the Finder will automatically put it in the Scripts folder, or create a Scripts folder if one does not already exist.

Because AppleScript support is added to an application by its developer, it is not universally available. Moreover, an application may or may not support three different levels of AppleScript:

➤ *Scriptable*—A scriptable application represents the highest level of AppleScript support. These applications can understand and respond to AppleEvents generated by scripts. A scriptable application can be controlled by an AppleScript script.

➤ *Recordable*—A recordable application is capable of sending itself AppleEvents and reporting user actions to the Apple Event Manager so that a script summarizing these actions can be recorded. When you use the Record button of the Script Editor, recordable applications allow you to create and compile scripts as applications. This is probably the easiest way to create a script, as it requires no knowledge of scripting. For example, pressing the Record button and then opening an application is easier than typing the corresponding "tell" command.

➤ *Attachable*—This type of application can trigger a script as a response to a user action (such as clicking a button or entering a text string). Apple describes an attachable application as "tinkerable." Attachable applications are useful as a "front end" to other applications.

Any combination of support is possible; you can have an application that is scriptable and recordable, recordable and attachable, scriptable and attachable, or all three. Apple publishes a booklet entitled *AppleScript Guide to Scriptable Applications* with a listing of each application's capabilities. To get this brochure or to add an application to the list, you can visit the Apple Web site at www.apple.com/applescript/.

The Script Editor

The Script Editor, which Apple provides with AppleScript, is the application that opens and runs scripts, records or writes scripts, and saves scripts in various forms. It illustrates many of the basic principles used in creating and working with AppleScripts.

Recording A Script

The Script Editor comes with a recorder feature that lets you create scripts based on your actions. Other macro programs call this a "watch me" kind of programming. As described previously, applications can only be scripted in this way if they are recordable. TeachText is neither scriptable nor recordable, but SimpleText is. The Finder, for example, is only scriptable and recordable in System 7.5 and later.

Start the Script Editor, and in the script window, enter the script name. Click the Record button to turn on the recorder. Go about switching to the program of your choice and performing other actions as desired. The Apple menu icon flashes as a script is being recorded. To complete your recorded script, switch back to the Script Editor window and click the Stop button; now you run your new script by name whenever the Script Editor is open (see Figure 13.9). You can also use the commands in the Control menu of the Script Editor in place of the buttons you see in the window.

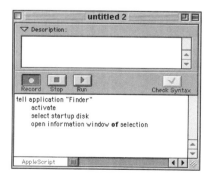

Figure 13.9 The Script Editor window with a sample recorded script.

You will notice that the Script Editor has entered all the commands that correspond to your actions. It also formats the script commands in stylized clegic logic (hierarchical indentions), which makes it much easier to read if you are going to modify the script later. As with other keystroke macro recorders, only certain actions can be captured by the Script Editor: using menu commands, pressing keys, saving files, opening and closing windows and files, and clicking the mouse. Drags and clicks are not normally captured because they don't result in any actions or changes. When a click or drag does result in an action, such as activating a button, or moving a file to a new folder, that action is recorded.

Because the actions were recorded to a script, the syntax does not require checking. Therefore, the Check Syntax option (described later) is not available in the Script Editor window.

Saving A Script

When you stop the recording of a script in the Script Editor, you save it within the Script Editor. It's more advantageous, however, to save the script as a document that you can call up from the Finder. Via the Save command in the Script Editor, you can bring up the standard Save dialog box shown in Figure 13.10. Scripts are normally compiled when saved. To save a script without compiling it first, choose the Save As command from the File menu and save the script as Text. The following list describes the three formats to which you can save scripts in the Script Editor:

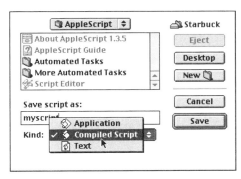

Figure 13.10 The Script Editor Save dialog box.

➤ *Application*—When you double-click on an AppleScript that was saved as an application, the application runs by itself without the assistance of the Script Editor. By choosing check boxes when you save a script as an application, you can specify that applications be kept open after the script is run (Stay Open) or that the Script Editor be closed (Never Show Startup Screen) when the script starts up (see Figure 13.11).

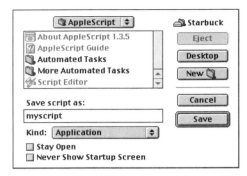

Figure 13.11 Saving an AppleScript as an application.

➤ *Compiled Script*—You can use compiled scripts independently or as commands within other scripts. Because run-time and compile engines are separate, scripts execute quickly and with few memory requirements. The icon for a compiled script differs from that of a script saved as an application. Figure 13.12 shows the various icons associated with AppleScript, including those of scripts saved as applications, compiled scripts, and as text.

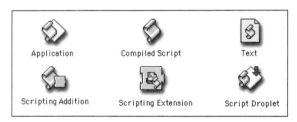

Figure 13.12 AppleScript icons.

Compiling a script changes the script from the "dialect," or (generally speaking) normal English, that you can read into Universal AppleScript, a pseudocode that your Macintosh can read. A compiled script requires additional translation, but is much more easily executed by the OS than a script written in a dialect.

➤ *Text*—You can open scripts saved as text files from within other programs and reuse the code. It's best to save a script as a text file if you intend to use it in programs such as BBEdit, a program that's popular with application and script authors. Notice that the icon in the title bar is that of a script saved as text, rather than a BBEdit document icon (see Figure 13.13).

You can save an application or compiled script as a *run-time*—or as AppleScript calls it, *run-only*—version of your script, but you cannot save text files as run-only. To save a run-only version of a script, choose the Save As Run-Only command from the File menu. The dialog box that appears will ask you to specify its location, name, and format.

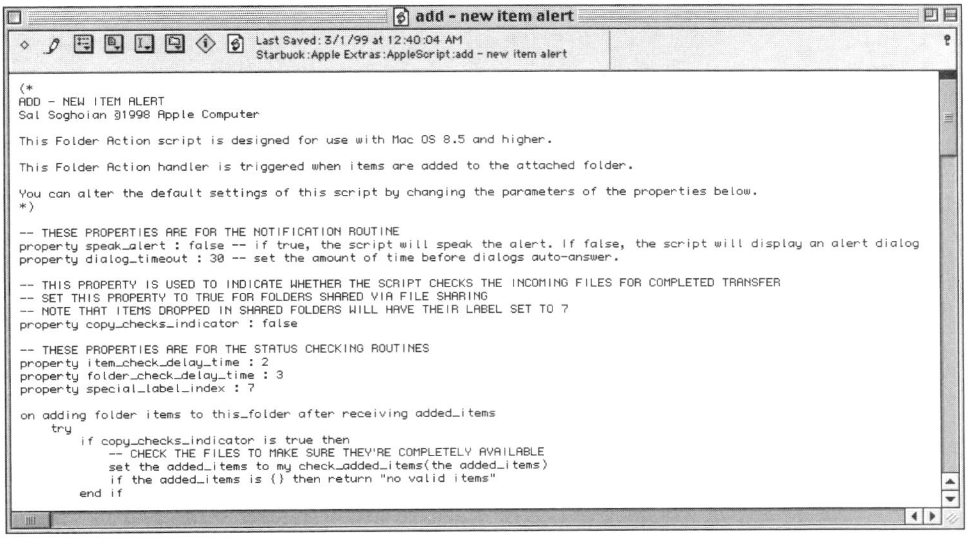

Figure 13.13 An AppleScript saved as a text file, viewed in BBEdit.

Running A Script

Depending on how a script was saved, you can run it several ways. You can select scripts recorded in the Script Editor by double-clicking them, or by choosing File| Open and then clicking the Run button. You can also double-click the name of a script to run it. You can stop scripts from within the Script Editor by using the Stop button.

TIP
To save a script as a non-editable, choose Save As|Run-Only from the File menu.

You can run a script that was saved as an application by opening the file just like any other application. Double-click an application or select that application and give the File|Open command to start the script. When you launch an AppleScript application, a start-up screen (see Figure 13.14) may appear if you chose that option from within the Save dialog box. Click the Run button or press the Return key to run the script; click the Quit button or press the Command+Period keystroke to abort the script.

Running a script results in an action. Some scripts return a value or expression based on their results. If you expect an outcome that you wish to see displayed in a window, choose the Show Result command from the Script Editor Control menu. If there is an error in your script, you may see an error message in the Result window.

Figure 13.14 An AppleScript application start-up dialog box.

Scripts also can be saved in the form of a *droplet*, that is, a drag-and-drop-enabled application. Droplets are indicated with a down-pointing arrow on their icons, as shown in Figure 13.15. To initiate the action supported by an AppleScript droplet, simply drag the icon of the object you wish the action to take place with over the icon or alias of the droplet. This process is similar to dragging a file icon over a Desktop Printer icon to print the file. If the droplet supports the object, the action takes place immediately; otherwise, an error message is posted. To make a script a droplet, the object acted upon has to be scripted into the AppleScript program.

Figure 13.15 An AppleScript droplet icon.

Scripts can, of course, be embedded inside other applications or files. Scripts in this form can be called up in many ways. Some embedded (or attached) scripts will be under your control; others will not. You'll often see scripts attached to buttons; when you click the button, the script runs. Other scripts will look for a text string in a field, check a condition, or do other tasks that may not be obvious to you, such as when an action automatically triggers the script. These scripts can often run in the background and escape your detection.

Modifying A Script

Scripts recorded in the Script Editor are fully editable in the script window, as is any text document. To begin modifying a script, you must launch the Script Editor and use the Open Script command from the File menu to open the script by name.

Most of the text editing actions in the Script Editor should be familiar to you from your word processor. Just type in your changes and save the results. In addition to simple clicks and drags, you can use the following shortcuts in the Script Editor window:

➤ Double-click to select a word; triple-click to select a line.

- Use the arrow keys to move the insertion point.
- Use the Command+Left arrow or Command+Right arrow keystrokes to move to the beginning or end of a line, respectively.
- Use the Command+Up arrow or Command+Down arrow keystroke to move to the beginning or end of the script, respectively.
- Use the Tab key at the beginning of a line to indent it. Tabs typed in the middle of a line are converted to space characters when you apply syntax formatting.
- Use the Return key at the end of an indented line to apply indenting automatically to the next line.
- Use the Option+Return keystroke to insert a continuation character (¬) and move to the beginning of the next line. This shortcut lets you work with a line that is too long to fit in the view of the active window. AppleScript ignores the continuation character and treats the lines on either side of it as one line.
- Use the Shift+Return keystroke to move the insertion point from the end of an indented line to the beginning of a new, unindented line.

Notice that the Script Editor has a Check Syntax button for written or modified scripts. This feature will run through a script to check that the syntax of programming steps is correct. Syntax is the collection of grammar rules for a programming language. That is, if you have a command that requires a certain command step (an end to an IF command, for example), that step is in the syntax—if you forgot to put it in, you'll get an error when you click on the Check Syntax button. The Check Syntax button will correct errors in construction only, not errors in programming logic.

When applied, the Check Syntax feature returns the first error as selected text. If there is an error in the text, no formatting is applied to the text in the Script Editor window. When the error is corrected, the Script Editor compiles the script, showing it with clegic (indented) formatting and other formatting options.

Some Script Editor features let you set the formatting of the script to make it easier to read. Some programs call this *beautifying* the program. You can change fonts, styles, sizes, and colors that are used in your scripts. These formatting styles make it easier to read the script and understand it, but they have no effect on the operation of the script. To set formatting options, choose the AppleScript Formatting command from the Edit menu. The dialog box shown in Figure 13.16 will appear. Changes you make in this dialog box will affect any script you open from the Script Editor. Other programs that work with scripts, such as the Scriptable Text Editor, have similar features.

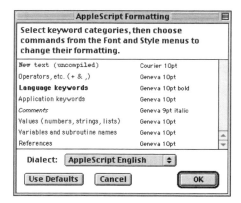

Figure 13.16 The AppleScript Formatting dialog box.

The elements of formatting that you can apply, based on the AppleScript formatting dialog box, are as follows:

➤ *New text*—Any modifications you make to a script before you check its syntax, run it, or save the results. Formatting these modifications allows you to easily discern your changes from a "wall of text."

➤ *Operators*—Actions (verbs) applied to objects in AppleScript.

➤ *Language keywords*—Commands available as part of the AppleScript language. They are often also actions and verbs.

➤ *Application keywords*—Language Extensions added to AppleScript by an application called within a script.

➤ *Comments*—Explanatory text that you add to a script to make its purpose understandable. Some people add comments to the beginning of a script as a header, to the beginning of a procedure, or even after important lines.

Comments in AppleScript are preceded by a double hyphen. Anything on a line to the right of the double hyphen is set in Italics when compiled and then ignored at execution time or during a syntax check. For multiline comments, use an asterisk to mark the beginning and end of the comments. Supplying cogent commenting without overdoing it is an art and the sure sign of a good programmer. For beginners, it's better to over-comment script than under-comment it.

➤ *Values*—Data or information, such as names, words, and numbers, used by AppleScript.

➤ *Variables*—Containers you name that can contain values. Values can change based on conditions.

➤ *References*—A pointer to an object is a reference. When you describe "window 1 of application Scriptable Text Editor," AppleScript knows you're referring to the topmost window open in the application. You see reference formatting in the Result window, not in the script window.

Scripting Applications

Every application has its own set of terms that it can add to the AppleScript vocabulary. Those terms are described in the dictionary within the application. At a script's run time, a called application's vocabulary is added to AppleScript for its use. To view an application's dictionary, choose the Open Dictionary command from the File menu of the Script Editor. Then select the application in the standard Open dialog box. Items, commands, and other verbs are described in the left scroll panel. These items are organized in event suites supported by the program.

Mac OS 8.6 has added a list of system software components that are now scriptable. Several Control Panels can now be controlled by scripts:

- Appearance
- Apple Menu Options
- File Exchange
- File Sharing
- Location Manager
- Users & Groups
- Web Sharing

Several Extensions are also now scriptable:

- Apple Guide
- Application Switcher
- ColorSync Extension
- Folder Actions

Finally, several of the applications that are part of the Mac OS package are now scriptable:

- Apple Help Viewer
- Apple System Profiler
- Desktop Printer Manager
- Sherlock
- Network Setup Scripting

Mac OS 8.6

When you click on an item, you will see the definition of the command in the right panel. Figure 13.17 shows part of the dictionary for BBEdit. You will see information about the item such as the kinds of objects that it acts on, the information or values that it requires, and the results that are returned. Nearly every AppleScript-aware application supports the required suite and the standard suite of AppleEvents. Refer to Chapter 12 for more information on this topic.

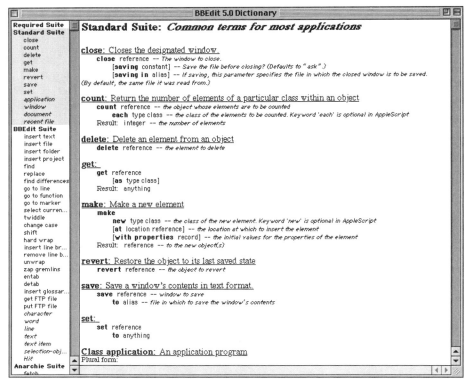

Figure 13.17 The scripting dictionary for BBEdit.

For applications that support AppleScript, you may find that you can select an object in the application and paste that object's reference into an AppleScript that you are building in the Script Editor. This system is still in its infancy, so this important feature is likely to be extended in the future. For now, you'll have to try out objects based on what you see in an application's dictionary to see what works. An object can be scriptable and recordable without allowing the pasting of object references.

When you can paste an object, the procedure is simple. Select the object in your application, and use the Copy command from the Edit menu. Then switch to the

Script Editor and place the insertion point where you desire. Issue the Paste Reference command from the Edit menu. That reference then appears. For example:

```
"word 2 of document 'Untitled'"
```

One complaint scriptwriters have had with former incarnations of AppleScript is that the dictionaries of various applications are very hard to understand. The greatest difficulty has been the tendency of the commands that are specific to an application to be presented in one solid chunk. While this presentation format is concise, it's difficult for a scriptwriter to find the name of a script command without having some idea of where the command is located alphabetically. With Mac OS 8.6, the Finder, Scripting Additions, and many other system software components have revised the internal structure of their dictionaries. The dictionaries are subdivided into sections that represent different types of functionality. This allows a scriptwriter to narrow a search without previous knowledge of the component.

The Scriptable Finder

To use AppleScript to automate tasks of the 7.0 and 7.1 Finder, you needed to use an external library of functions called the FinderLib, which was distributed by Apple. These 13 Finder routines, 5 input-checking and utility routines, and 2 properties-checking routines form the basis for the suite that was incorporated into System 7.5's Finder. Now when you open the Finder's dictionary under Mac OS 8.6, you'll see the Finder suite shown in Figure 13.18, which has a greatly expanded dictionary.

Scripting the Finder means that these commands can be employed directly in scripts that use the Finder without having to call scripts from an external library. As a matter of convenience, you can record scripts using the recorder function of the Script Editor and using the Finder as one of your applications.

A Few New Tricks In Mac OS 8.6

Some of the new features of AppleScript 1.3.5 have already been mentioned—the performance has been drastically increased; a host of new abilities with Scripting Additions (OSAX) is available; and development and administration of scripting is much easier thanks to the Scripts folder and the new organization of dictionaries. Here are a few of the other changes:

➤ *Unit Types*—For a script to be useful internationally, it must be capable of manipulating data in many different formats. The latest version of AppleScript enables a script to present a measurement with many different unit types, and automatically does the conversion.

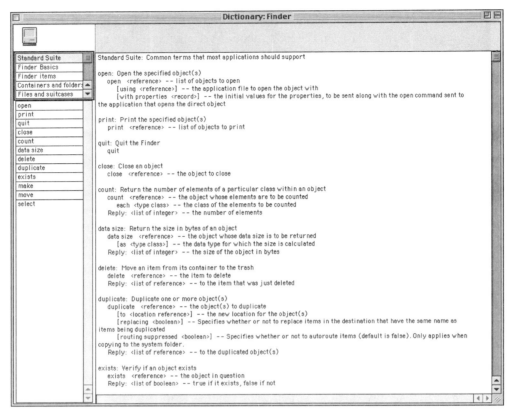

Figure 13.18 The Finder's scripting dictionary as viewed in Scripter.

> *Internet Suite*—The Common Gateway Interface (CGI) is the HTTP interface for executing programs on a server from an HTML form. The Internet Suite is an addition to AppleScript that allows easy access to the information in the HTTP header, so that CGI can be created using AppleScript instead of a programming language such as C, C++, or Pascal.

> *Folder Actions*—This allows a script to be associated with a folder interaction. For example, a script can be designed to run every time a certain folder is opened. The other interactions are closing a folder, adding items to a folder, removing items from a folder, and moving or resizing a folder window. Scripts associated with adding and removing are only executed when the folder's window is actually open. You associate a script with a folder by holding down the Control key while clicking the folder's icon, and selecting "Attach a Folder Action" from the menu. This presents a file selection dialog box in which you select the desired script. A folder with an attached script gains a special icon, as shown in Figure 13.19.

Figure 13.19 The Folder Actions icon indicates that an AppleScript has been attached to a particular folder.

These changes should be very exciting to all users and developers of the Mac OS. The Folder Actions, for example, lead to very interesting possibilities. If you would like to experiment with Folder Actions a little further, take a look at 10 samples in a folder called Folder Action Scripts in the new Scripts folder in the System Folder. The samples include:

- add - duplicate to folders
- add - new item alert
- add - reject added items
- add - set view prefs to match
- close - close sub-folders
- mount/unmount server aliases
- move - align open sub-folders
- open - open items labeled 1
- open - show comments in dialog
- remove - retrieve items

It's not difficult to create your own Folder Action Scripts script. Many more samples and tutorials can be found in the Mac OS help system and also on the Web. Here's a sample that uses Folder Actions, as well as a new capability of AppleScript: timed dialogs. This new feature gives AppleScript the ability to dismiss (close) a dialog box after a predetermined amount of time measured in seconds. This example (taken from the AppleScript Help guide) beeps, displays a welcome message, and closes the message after 30 seconds if the OK or Cancel buttons are not first selected.

```
on opening folder this_folder
    tell application "Finder"
        activate
        set the folder_name to the name of this_folder
        beep
        display dialog "Welcome to folder: " & ¬
            the folder_name giving up after 30
```

Mac OS 8.6

```
        end tell
end opening folder
```

To attach a folder action to a folder:

1. Compose a script and save it as a Compiled Script in the Folder Actions section of the Scripts folder in the System Folder.
2. Control+Click a folder in the Finder and select Attach a Folder Action, as in Figure 13.20.

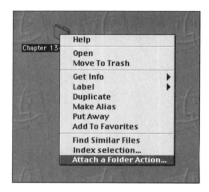

Figure 13.20 Attaching a folder action.

3. Select the folder action script, and the special icon (described above) will then be present to indicate that the folder action is active.

When you open a folder that this script is attached to, it will verbally welcome you and a dialog will repeat the welcome, displaying any comments that are associated with the folder you've opened (see Figure 13.21).

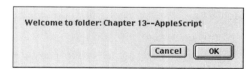

Figure 13.21 The result of a sample folder action script.

Once attached, a folder action script can easily be detached or modified by Control+ Clicking the folder and making the appropriate selection (see Figure 13.22).

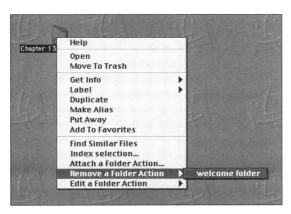

Figure 13.22 Modifying a folder action.

Sample Scripts

Mac OS 8.6 includes a set of preprogrammed AppleScripts that users can access from a hierarchical submenu of the Apple menu. An alias in the Apple Menu Items folder points to the Automated Tasks folder found in the AppleScript folder.

These scripts are, in fact, very useful because they add additional compound functionality to the Finder. A short SimpleText file, "About Automated Tasks," is included in the Automated Tasks folder describing its contents.

A folder called More Automated Tasks includes additional AppleScripts. You may wish to add these to the Automated Tasks folder so that you can access them from the Apple menu. Over time you may find many other AppleScripts that you can add to the Automated Tasks folder.

When Mac OS 8.6 was released, the initial set of Useful Scripts included the following:

➤ *Add Alias to Apple Menu*—To create an alias to an item in the Apple menu, select this script. Because the Add Alias to Apple Menu is a droplet script, you can also drag the item over the AppleScript icon.

➤ *Start File Sharing/Stop File Sharing*—These two scripts turn File Sharing on and off without your having to open the Sharing Setup Control Panel. You can also use the Control Strip of a PowerBook for this function.

➤ *Share a Folder/Share a Folder (No Guest)*—A shared folder is one that is available to other users on the network (as described in Chapter 17). Another File Sharing user can copy files that have been put in a shared folder; others can copy files into it. If you drop a folder onto this script, this script makes the folder a shared folder and turns on File Sharing. Use the No Guest script if you don't want guest users to access the folder. When you restart your Macintosh, reapply this command to reactivate the shared folder.

The scripts in the More Automated Tasks folder are:

- *Hide/Show Folder Sizes*—This script turns on and off the Calculate Folder Sizes option in the Views Control Panel.

- *Alert When Folder Changes*—When you select a folder and apply this script, AppleScript will watch the folder to see what new items are added to it while the script is running. When a new item is added, you're switched to the Finder, the folder is opened, and the new item is highlighted. This script is useful for monitoring a download or communications folder.

- *Synchronize Folders*—With this script, two folders are compared and the contents of both are synchronized. That is, both folders are made identical by having missing files added to and files with recent modifications replace older versions. To use this script, select two folders and apply the command.

> **TIP**
> Older versions of AppleScript included the Scriptable Text Editor. Even though many text editors and word processors, such as BBEdit and Microsoft Word, are scriptable, a lightweight scriptable text editor is still necessary. If you have this need, check out Style, a comprehensive scriptable text editor from Merzwaren. It is shareware (about $10) and can be downloaded at www.merzwaren.com.

Learning More About AppleScript

The AppleScript Web site (www.apple.com\applescript\) has links to several valuable resources for learning more about AppleScript, including these online resources:

- AppleScript User Guide
- AppleScript Language Guide
- The AppleScript Source Book
- ScriptWeb

The AppleScript site also links to several companion software developers who make products that complement AppleScript, including:

- FaceSpan
- Real Basic

➤ PreFab Player

➤ Script Debugger

➤ Scripter

➤ ScriptDEMON

Finally, check out Amazon.com and Barnesandnoble.com for the latest books about AppleScript.

Wrapping Up

AppleScript fulfills a long-standing promise to provide automation capabilities within the Macintosh operating system. Although still developing, AppleScript is thorough and rigorous in its implementation, laying the groundwork for more important and convenient expressions to come.

In this chapter, you've learned how to use AppleScript to:

➤ Record actions with the Script Editor

➤ Save scripts that you can run as applications, or as compiled scripts that you can call from within other scripts

➤ Work with applications that are AppleScript aware; that is, recordable, scriptable, and attachable

➤ Attach compiled scripts to folders (folder actions)

In the next chapter, you'll look at one of the most important features of Mac OS 8.6: Mac Runtime for Java. Java is a powerful cross-platform language that is used to enhance Web pages or create double-clickable applications.

Java

It seems that anyone who knows anything about computers these days has heard about Java. Hailed as the greatest advance in computer programming since the one and the zero, to some extent Java has yet to live up to the hype.

Java was developed by Sun Microsystems as a platform-independent language for the Internet. It was originally designed as a language for embedded systems (the tiny computers in your car or VCR, for example). Before long, Sun realized how Java could be used to create software that would perfectly suit the needs of the Internet. Because most users access the Internet over modems and phone lines, Internet-based software must be relatively small so that it can be quickly downloaded. It's also essential that Internet-based software understand TCP/IP as well as the higher level applications that use it, such as Web servers and FTP servers. Java meets these needs, having both small executable files and vast networking capabilities.

Java, in fact, isn't all that new, claims to its breakthrough status notwithstanding. Many of the concepts it uses come from other languages; its syntax is very close to C++, and its object orientation is very much like Smalltalk. But Java's networking ability is fairly unique, and that's important in today's interconnected world. As a matter of fact, you have almost certainly used Java already! Many Web sites use Java applets (small applications) to make a page dynamic.

Java has a great future, and Apple has embraced the technology in a big way. Mac OS 8.6 ships with Java, as will all future versions of the operating system, including OS X. Mac OS 8.6 adds the ability to use AppleScript with Java programs, brings more complete support for the Java language, and has several performance enhancements. A variety of exciting features, such as complete support for QuickTime, are on the horizon. In fact, Apple expects programmers to move to Java, and is ensuring that their new system software can be accessed by Java programs. That's a pretty big endorsement! So you can see why you, as an Apple user, should spend some time getting to know Java. This chapter will tell you what Java is and how you can run Java on your Macintosh.

Java On The Macintosh

Apple began supporting Java with the Macintosh Runtime for Java in late 1996. Now, support is bundled into Mac OS 8.6 so that all Macs can run Java programs without needing any new software.

A Java program is often called an *applet*, which refers to the fact that most Java programs are tiny in size and focused on providing a small set of features. However, there's no reason why a full-featured application couldn't be written in Java—in fact, most software vendors would love to have their applications written in Java. Why? Because a program created in Java could be written and debugged once, and then work on everybody's computer without the necessity of porting between all the different platforms. Software developers could make more money for less effort, and updates would be released more quickly for all platforms. In fact, Corel has released a beta of a Java-only version of its well-known Corel Office suite of applications. The only drawback, to cross platform compatibility is the resulting sacrifice in performance. The Corel Suite worked fine, but because it took a lot longer to get anything done, Corel abandoned the project. Over time, however, more developers may use Java to create the programs we use every day because Java offers many unique features:

➤ *Cross-platform compatible*—Java applets use what's called *byte code*, which any computer can read using a Java Virtual Machine (commonly abbreviated VM). All an operating system needs to run Java applets is a Virtual Machine. In this way, a single Java applet can be run on a Mac, a Windows computer, or a Sun workstation.

➤ *Apple-supported*—Apple has, in its infinite wisdom, provided the Mac Runtime for Java (often abbreviated MRJ) since Mac OS 8. Owners of earlier Macs with earlier operating systems need to install MRJ separately.

➤ *Small*—Since Java is an object-oriented language, applets "inherit" features of the language that reside on the users' computer and therefore these features don't need to be downloaded. Java also features built-in compression features so that bitmaps and sounds, for example, can be as small as possible.

➤ *Secure*—Java applets are restricted in many ways so that your computer can't be harmed by applets written by malicious (or inept) programmers.

➤ *Network-ready*—Java includes a rich feature set for connection over the Internet. Java applets can connect to Web servers, FTP servers, chat servers, or just about anything else that uses TCP/IP.

> *Performance*—Although the execution speed of many Java programs is slower than programs written for one operating system, special technologies such as JIT and HotSpot compilers are closing this gap. Java also offers other performance benefits, particularly in networked applications. The Java Virtual Machine monitors the memory use of Java programs with a technique called Garbage Collection, which ensures that the programs don't suffer from memory leaks, one of the biggest causes of crashes with most software.

These features make Java a great language for any computer, but especially for the Mac. Over the years, Mac users were often left out in the cold waiting for developers to make Mac versions of new software developed for Windows-running PCs. Java eliminates this discrepancy because any Java applet that runs under Windows will run under the Mac OS. As more and more software is created for Java, the Mac will benefit greatly.

Art Safari, shown in Figure 14.1, is an applet that is served from the Web site of the Museum of Modern Art (MoMA). This Java program, which works on all Java-enabled browsers, offers a palette for young artists to experiment with. Take a look at this article on the Web about Art Safari at http://java.sun.com/features/1999/02/moma.html. Like all Java programs, Art Safari became available to Mac users as soon as it was available to Windows users.

Mac Runtime For Java

When you install Mac OS 8.6, Java is installed automatically. Apple's Java is called the Macintosh Runtime for Java, or MRJ, for short. There isn't a whole lot to the installation. The Java installation consists of an Extension, the class libraries necessary for Java to run (shown in Figure 14.2), and a few configuration files—all located in your Extensions folder. Configuration preferences are also added to your Appearance Control Panel and the Text Encodings folder that resides in your System Folder.

The MRJ Libraries folder is installed inside your Extensions folder, but it's not an Extension—it's actually a shared code library. Unlike most of the files in your Extensions folder, the Java libraries aren't loaded unless you're actually running a Java applet. The Java libraries can't conflict with other Extensions at boot time, so you don't have to worry about Extension conflicts.

A folder entitled "Mac OS Runtime for Java," located in the Apple Extras folder, contains a file called "About MRJ 2.1" and a folder full of License Agreements. In previous versions of the OS, Java samples were in this folder. Apple removed the samples from the current installation because many users felt they were unnecessary. The next section explains how to obtain and use these examples.

382 Chapter 14

Figure 14.1 The Art Safari applet.

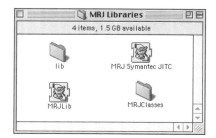

Figure 14.2 The MRJ installation places these files in your Extensions folder.

Mac OS 8.6

Running Java Applets

Previous versions of the Mac OS included Java samples. If you want Java samples with Mac OS 8.6, however, be prepared to download them yourself. The latest version of the MRJ SDK (the Mac Runtime for Java Software Development Kit) can be downloaded from www.apple.com/developer/java/. (Don't be intimidated by the words "software development.") To run one of the many example Java applets installed by the kit, just drag and drop an applet's HTML file onto the Applet Runner. The program will launch and the Java applet will start. That's all it takes! Running Java on the Macintosh is incredibly simple.

The Applet Runner application has a menu of Java applets you can try out. To try an applet, navigate through the hierarchical menu to the applet HTML file you want to try. Figure 14.3 shows some of the applets that come with the MRJ SDK.

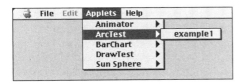

Figure 14.3 The Applet Runner has a menu of sample applets for you to try.

The Applet Runner has a File menu with the usual items:

- *Open URL*—Opens an HTML file from the Internet using the Uniform Resource Locator (URL) you specify.

- *Open Local HTML File*—Opens an HTML file from your local hard disk.

- *Properties*—Shows a dialog box that displays the attributes for that applet.

You can also use the File menu to run an applet, or you can just drag an HTML file onto the Applet Runner (although this won't work for a network-based HTML file). An applet's Properties, also found under the File menu, specify its security settings. For security purposes, applets are usually restricted in what they can do. For instance, applets usually can't write files to the user's hard disk, and therefore are prevented from overwriting important files (such as the Finder and System, or your precious data). However, this restriction can be a pain—especially if you're using a Java-based productivity application and really *want* to save files to the hard drive.

Fortunately, the Applet Runner lets you change the Properties of an applet. When you open the Properties dialog box, you have seven options (as you'll see in Figure 14.4):

- *Network Access*—This controls how your applet connects to the Internet, with three options to choose from:

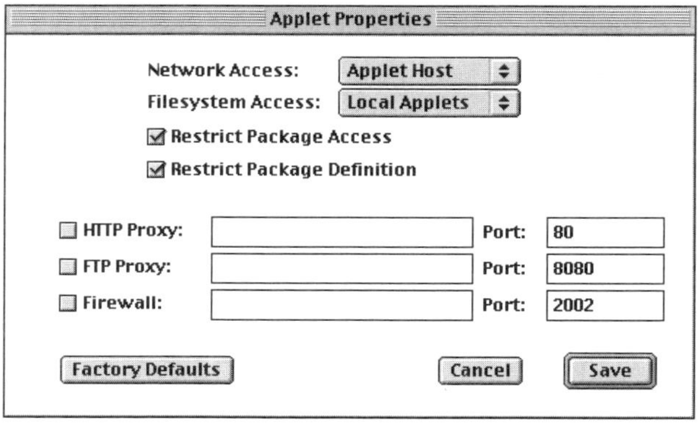

Figure 14.4 The Applet Properties dialog box lets you restrict an applet's abilities.

- *No Access*—The applet can't use the network at all.
- *Applet Host*—The applet can use the restricted network access provided for applets.
- *Unrestricted*—The applet can use the network in any way it wishes.
- *File system Access*—This controls how your applet uses your hard drive. There are three options here as well:
- *No File System*—The applet can't use the hard drive at all.
- *Local Applet Access*—The applet can read and write files to the local directory in which it's stored, but nowhere else.
- *Unrestricted*—The applet can access and modify any file anywhere on the drive.
- *Package Access and Package Definition*—These control how the applet interacts with the Java VM system and whether or not the applet can change your Java's built-in classes. These settings are either restricted or unrestricted.

If you're working with a company that uses a firewall, the next three controls are for you. They control how the applet connects to the Internet through a proxy server:

- *HTTP Proxy*—Enter the address and TCP/IP port of the Web proxy server.
- *FTP Proxy*—Enter the address and TCP/IP port of the FTP proxy server.
- *Firewall Proxy*—Enter the address and TCP/IP port of the firewall proxy server.

In the above case, where you wanted to save files to your hard drive, you can set your applet to have permission to use the file system and hence write files. If you do this, however, you should be very sure that the applet comes from a reputable source and isn't a "Trojan horse," a program that looks angelic but is actually a destructive virus.

Mac OS 8.6

> **TIP**
> Unless you make changes, the default settings ensure that a Java applet cannot cause harm on your system. You don't need to take any other safety measures.

In addition to the File menu, the Applet Runner has an Applet menu that affects the currently running Java applet:

- *Reload Applet*—Dumps the applet from RAM and loads it freshly from the disk.
- *Restart Applet*—Forces the applet to start again from the beginning.
- *Suspend*—Pauses the applet.
- *Resume*—Continues a paused applet.
- *Show Applet Tag*—Shows the HTML tag used to specify the applet (applets are run from HTML files). Usually, this tag includes some special initialization commands for the applet.

These options only affect the frontmost applet. To affect another applet, click on its window to bring it to the front.

Other Java VMs

Apple isn't the only maker of a Java VM for the Mac OS. Because Java is an open standard, any company is welcome—in fact, encouraged—to try its hand at producing Java software. At least three other companies make Java Virtual Machines that you can easily get for your Mac:

- *Metrowerks*—The makers of CodeWarrior, the premiere programming environment for the Mac, have created a fast VM that Microsoft includes with its Internet Explorer.
- *Symantec*—Another maker of compilers and developments tools, Symantec, makes a VM for the Mac for use with its Cafe Java visual programming environment. It's not widely used on the Mac, however.
- *Roaster*—The first Java for the Mac just might be the best. Roaster, Inc. produced the first VM for the Mac, and Apple licensed it for the first release of the MRJ. The Roaster VM was the first to provide a Just-In-Time (JIT) compiler for the Mac. Its speeds make the Mac equal to any other platform for running Java.
- *Apple*—Apple now uses its own Java VM for the MRJ. The Apple VM gains more critical acclaim with each new version.

These "outside" Java VMs aren't integrated into the OS like the MRJ is. Each Java applet uses its own applet-running program. Apple's MRJ, however, is available to all programs (such as Web browsers) as an application-level service, so it's easy for programmers to add applet-running ability to their own programs. At some point, Apple may offer the ability to add plug-in Java Virtual Machines, thereby enabling you to switch to the VM of your choice. Internet Explorer already lets you do this to some extent by giving you a choice between the MRJ and Microsoft VM. To do this, select Preferences from Internet Explorer's Edit menu, and then select Java. You will see a pull-down selection box where you can choose from any installed Virtual Machines. Figure 14.5 shows a Java applet called ArcTest. Although this applet isn't

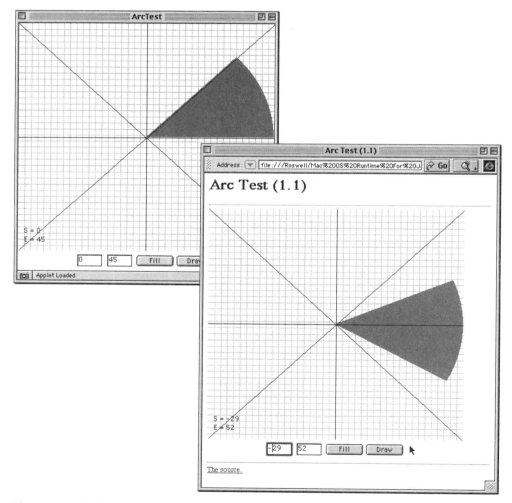

Figure 14.5 The ArcTest Applet in Applet Runner (left) and in Internet Explorer (right).

particularly helpful in real-life situations it could be a useful example of how to draw angles if you're trying to learn how to program with Java. Here you see the applet in both the Applet Runner and in Internet Explorer.

Some of the example applets, such as the Bar Chart Applet, are actually useful. This applet takes configuration data from an HTML file and makes a Bar Chart. Figure 14.6 shows the Bar Chart Applet.

Figure 14.6 The Bar Chart Applet.

One of the advantages of using applets on Web pages over plain HTML is that Java is so dynamic. HTML is limited to loaded images and components such as buttons. Java allows interactive pictures to be drawn, such as with the DrawTest Applet shown in Figure 14.7. The DrawTest Applet presents a canvas that can be drawn upon by dragging across it with the mouse pointer.

Applets have varying degrees of utility on Web pages. They can be used for navigation or for messages. The LED Sign Applet in Figure 14.8 is just such an applet. A separate text file is used to configure this applet so that any message can be displayed and different fonts can be used.

The LED sign is eye-catching, but sometimes it's desirable to include actual custom images or photographs. The Neon Sign Applet shown in Figure 14.9 does exactly that. The applet flickers between two different images, creating the look and feel of a neon sign.

Applets contribute to the content of a page by adding interactivity, a feature that's being utilized by several institutions for training. With Java applets, it doesn't matter what type of computer the student is using, and no plug-in has to be

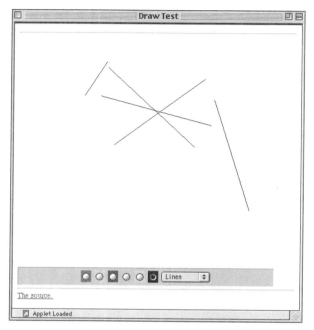

Figure 14.7 The DrawTest Applet.

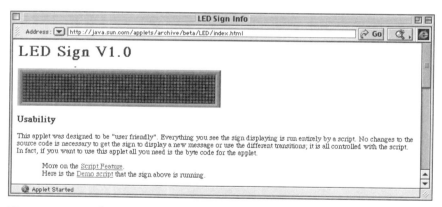

Figure 14.8 The LED Applet.

downloaded. Figure 14.10 shows an applet called Voltage that illustrates the use of resistors in a circuit. This kind of visual tool is especially good when the student has no opportunity for hands-on experience.

Mathematics departments have also begun to put applets to work as teaching tools. Many schools use applets to demonstrate concepts in analytical geometry. Even in the case of high school geometry, applets can be used to demonstrate concepts effec-

Mac OS 8.6

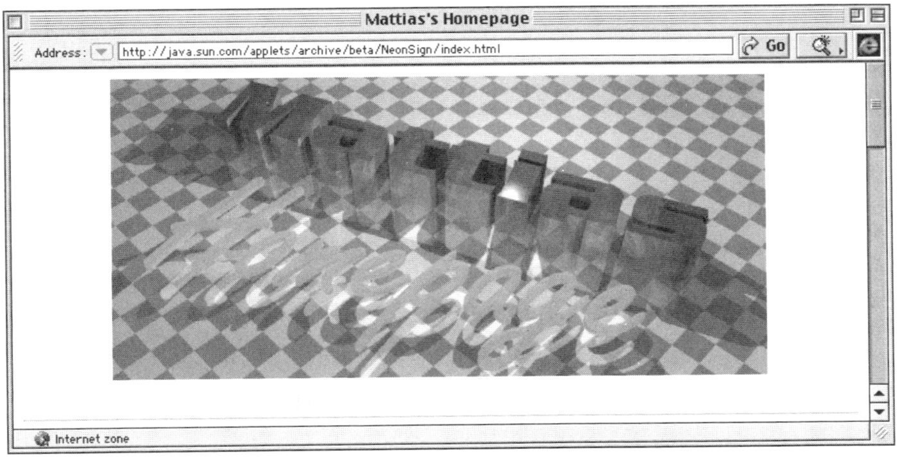

Java **389**

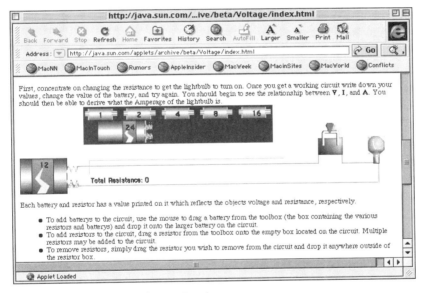

Figure 14.9 The Neon Sign Applet.

Figure 14.10 The Voltage Applet.

tively. Figure 14.11 shows a demonstration of a proof of the Pythagorean Theorem; this applet was designed to help the student understand the proof graphically.

The "Look" Of Cross Platform Programs

From the beginning, Java programs were designed to blend in with other programs on each operating system. When a Java program contains a button and the program is run on a Macintosh, the button appears to be a Mac button. When the same Java program is run on a Windows computer, the button looks like a Windows button.

Mac OS 8.6

390 Chapter 14

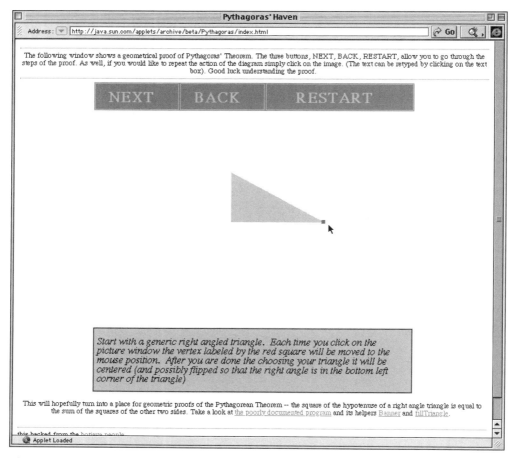

Figure 14.11 The Pythagorean Theorum Applet.

The person who writes the program has no control over this—it's an element of Java itself.

Figure 14.12 shows an applet called Card Test Applet running on a Mac.

Now, take a look at Figure 14.13, which shows the same applet running on a Windows 98 machine.

Swing: The Java Foundation Classes

Although in some ways it's desirable to have your applets automatically assume the look of an operating system, there are definite disadvantages:

▶ *Excessive need for testing*—A program that will use different components on different platforms must be tested on each platform to make sure that it really works.

Mac OS 8.6

Java **391**

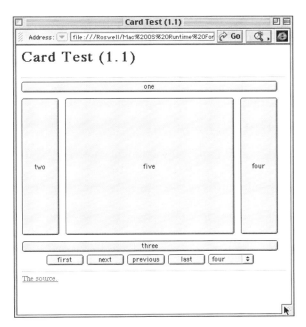

Figure 14.12 The Card Test Applet on a Mac.

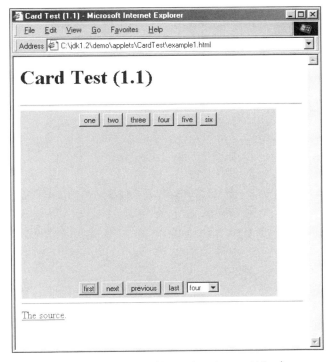

Figure 14.13 The Card Test Applet on Windows.

► *Limited number of components*—This mechanism imposes a limit on the number of components that could exist in Java. The only components that can be used are components that are available on all platforms.

► *Loss of control*—In the software business, it's never good to completely remove options. A developer should have ultimate control over how a component will look.

When Sun and other companies realized these limitations, writing the components completely in the Java language became the solution. In Java Foundation Classes (JFCs), developers were taught to use the Java language to overcome the problems described above. ("Swing" was the original code name for the Java Foundation Classes. One of the Sun creators of JFC was a big fan of Duke Ellington, who popularized a song containing the lyric "it don't mean a thing, if it ain't got that swing". He assigned the Ellington reference as a temporary name for the evolving JFCs, which were so eagerly anticipated even before their release that the code name became a common term.)

The Java Foundation Classes not only give developers the option to use more components, but also the ability to determine exactly how each component will look. For example, instead of having to use the buttons that are available from all operating systems, Java buttons can contain pictures, or even animations. Figure 14.14 shows an example of buttons that contain images. Although you can't tell from this illustration, the active button is actually an animation.

Figure 14.14 JFC buttons containing images and animation.

The Grass Is Always Greener—Pluggable Look And Feel

With Swing, Java developers can make components look any way that they want. They can also create completely new types of components. This is not enough for some developers, however, who yearn to make their application blend in with the operating system. The latest solution from Java is called Pluggable Look and Feel. This feature makes it possible for an application to automatically assume the look of a Windows application, and then with one small change be made to look like a Motif application (Motif is the windowing toolkit used on some Unix platforms). A native Java look is also possible. The Macintosh look and feel was added with the latest version of the MRJ, but legal problems ensued regarding use of the Macintosh

Mac OS 8.6

look and feel with non-Macintosh computers; this feature has therefore been temporarily disabled. For an example, Figure 14.15 shows how an example component would look with the Macintosh look and feel (*if* it was legal), compared with the same component with the Windows look and feel, the Motif look and feel, and finally the pure Java look and feel.

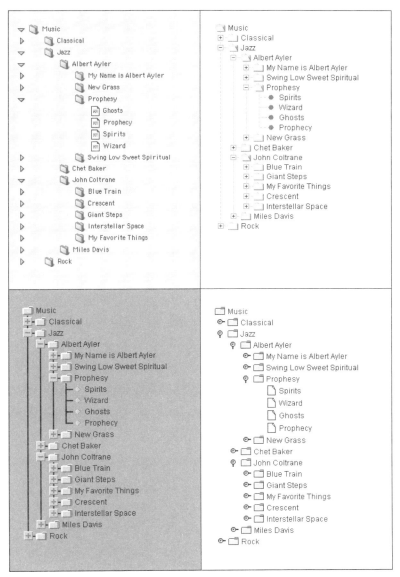

Figure 14.15 The Java Tree View component with each look and feel.

Wrapping Up

Java is the newest element to the Mac OS, as well as the one with the most promise. The most significant characteristic of Java is that it allows computer programmers to write one version of a program, such as a word processor, which can then be run on many different types of computers without modification. Programmers refer to this as the "write once, run anywhere" capability. Developers no longer have to choose a target platform when writing software. The popularity of Java means that software debuts for the Mac at the same time that it comes out for Windows. With Java-written software available for every platform at once, users will be free to choose the operating system that is most comfortable, and businesses will choose the OS that is easiest to support. In the next chapter, we'll look at one of the oldest elements of the Mac OS—support for multimedia applications.

15

Multimedia

The way the word *multimedia* is bandied about in the computer press, it seems to refer to the progress we've made toward making computers like we see on *Star Trek*—you know, a computer that does flashy things with sound and animation, charts space in 3D, and talks back to you. That's multimedia, as far as the average user is concerned. However, in our universe, computers aren't quite powerful enough to make a convincing holodeck.

At a minimum, multimedia refers to the combination of sounds and images on a computer. In the past few years, however, the definition of multimedia has grown to encompass QuickTime movies, MIDI, virtual reality, and 3D rendering.

Ironically, as its definition grows, the term seems to specify less: what exactly is a "multimedia-ready computer" ready for? If the computer in question is a Macintosh powered by Mac OS 8.6, we know exactly what this means. In the standard installation of Mac OS 8.6, you'll get these components:

➤ QuickTime and QuickTime VR

➤ QuickDraw 3D

➤ Text-to-Speech

And depending on what model of PowerMac you have or what accessories your particular computer has, you might have these multimedia capabilities as well:

➤ CD player

➤ AM/FM radio tuner

➤ Cable/TV tuner

➤ DVD player

Together, these components give you a high-performance multimedia computer that can play movies, sounds, and MIDI files, and even speak back to you using a variety of voices. Captain Picard would be proud of our progress, don't you think?

QuickTime

For years, Macintosh has led the way for personal computers in typography, graphics, sound, and high-resolution color. With the advent of QuickTime, the Macintosh continues this tradition by blazing the trail in video and multimedia capabilities.

QuickTime is a set of extensions and applications that gives your Macintosh the ability to play and record moving video images, animation, and sound in completely new ways. It makes moving images and sounds a basic type of Macintosh data. All kinds of applications—word processors, databases, presentation graphics packages, page-layout programs—can now incorporate these moving images as easily as standard graphics.

QuickTime is now an essential component of the Mac OS, and is also an option for Windows 95, 98, and NT users. QuickTime for Java, discussed below, is now in beta and will allow any computer that can run Java to also benefit from many QuickTime features found on the Mac and Windows platforms.

QuickTime is available at no charge, although—in typical Apple fashion—that doesn't necessarily mean you'll be able to get it easily or without cost. QuickTime is being distributed in a number of different formats and channels:

➤ QuickTime 3 is included as part of Mac OS 8.6.

➤ The QuickTime Starter Kit features QuickTime, a player utility, a few sample movies, and more, and can be purchased from any Apple reseller or most mail-order software dealers.

➤ QuickTime can be downloaded from Apple's QuickTime Web site (www.apple.com/quicktime). It can also be downloaded from online services or obtained from most Macintosh user groups.

➤ Many QuickTime-dependent applications include QuickTime on their distribution disks.

Actually, QuickTime comes in two versions: QuickTime and QuickTime Pro. QuickTime is free and comes with Mac OS 8.6; QuickTime Pro, on the other hand, will cost you about $30 and enable you to perform significantly more tasks. The Pro version provides many additional features, including:

➤ Creating new QuickTime movies from existing movies

➤ Editing QuickTime movies, including individual tracks within a movie

➤ Playing or exporting more than 30 types of multimedia file formats

- Using the QuickTime Plug-in to view almost all the multimedia types on the Web
- Creating slide shows

The standard version is fine if all you need to do is view movies over the Web, but the Pro version opens up several new doors to the world of multimedia.

What's New With QuickTime 3?

QuickTime 3.0 has many new features, most of which are performance related. You'll notice improved performance in part because more of the code is PowerPC-native. Movies can now vary from 240×180 pixels at 1fps up to 320×240 pixels at 30fps, depending on the type of Mac. The MoviePlayer 3.0 application replaces the SimplePlayer application that shipped with earlier versions of QuickTime. The following aspects of QuickTime have undergone improvement since versions 2.0 and 2.5:

- *QuickTime DataPipe*—The DataPipe improves performance on all types of CD-ROM drives. Tracks can be preloaded into memory prior to playback.
- *Music*—Movies can now contain music tracks. Data is stored as a series of note commands like music is stored in MIDI files.
- *MPEG*—MPEG is an international standard for digital video. QuickTime 2.5 can play MPEG if you have an MPEG board installed in your computer or if you have a PowerMac and the MPEG playback extension.
- *Timecode*—QuickTime 2.0 can store a timecode (SMPTE or otherwise) in a movie. Timecodes point to the source tape.
- *Burnt text*—QuickTime 1.6 introduced anti-aliasing text. Version 2.0 adds the capability to store pre-rendered text in a compressed image for faster redraw.
- *Drag and Drop*—With version 2.0, you can drag one movie to another to perform a paste operation. When you're in MoviePlayer, you can also pull a movie from the Finder to drag it into a sequence. When you drag a text movie into a SimpleText document, the text is extracted into the document.
- *Power Macintosh*—All compressors and decompressors are now native on the PowerPC. Cinepak compression is two and a half to three times faster on a model 8100 than on a Quadra 950.
- *Copyright dialog*—You can now add copyright information directly to a movie by using the Set Movie Information command in the MoviePlayer 2.0 application to add the information in the authoring mode. View the information with the Show Copyright command.

- *Sprites*—A sprite is a graphic that can be animated using commands that tell how the sprite moves (as opposed to storing a full frame for each step of the animation). Sprites are like MIDI for image files: you don't need to store the digital video for an animation.
- *Improved Web support*—When you download QuickTime movies over the World Wide Web, the movie will begin to play as soon as enough data has arrived.
- *Miscellaneous*—A number of other small changes have been added. They include the ability to play AIFF, MU-LAW, and WAV sound files directly, a standard export dialog box, and an improved grayscale slider bar.

QuickTime 4.0, which should be released shortly after Mac OS 8.6 in mid-1999, promises further performance improvements as well as eye-catching features like live digital effects and vector graphics. You can follow its progress at www.apple.com/quicktime.

QuickTime Basics

QuickTime adds support to your Macintosh to play several types of file formats, including movie, sound, and image formats, that enable the following capabilities:

- Play multiple types of movies
- View pictures
- Navigate QuickTime VR panoramas
- Play many different types of audio formats

The basic movie file format is called Movie (the file type is MooV). Like other file formats, such as PICT, EPS, or TIFF, the Movie file format saves a certain kind of data—in this case, moving video, animation, or sound (or all of these)—in a way that can be viewed at a specified rate and quality. By defining this file format at the system-software level, Apple makes it easy for application developers to support this kind of data, which encourages them to develop sophisticated ways to create and use data that changes or reacts over time (such as moving images or sounds) on the Macintosh. Other file formats supported by QuickTime 3 are shown in Table 15.1.

A QuickTime movie acts much like any other text or graphic element—you can select, cut, copy, or paste it either within or between QuickTime-savvy applications and store it in the latest version of the Scrapbook. In some cases, you can't even tell that an object is a movie until you select it; before that, it looks just like any other graphic element. When you select a movie, however, it displays an identifying set of controls that allow you to adjust the volume (if it has sound) and play the movie, as well as fast forward, reverse, or randomly adjust it, as shown in Figure 15.1.

Mac OS 8.6

Table 15.1 QuickTime import/export file types for the Mac OS.

Format	Import	Export
Video		
AVI	Yes	No
DV	Yes	Yes
MPEG	Yes	No
OpenDML	Yes	No
Audio		
AIFF/AIFC	Yes	Yes
Audio CD	Yes	No
DV	Yes	No
MPEG Layer 1 & 2	Yes	No
Sound Designer II	Yes	No
System 7 Sound	Yes	Yes
µLaw (AU)	Yes	Yes
WAV	Yes	Yes
Still Image		
3DMF	Yes	No
BMP	Yes	Yes
GIF	Yes	No
JPEG/JFIF	Yes	No
MacPaint	Yes	No
PhotoShop	Yes	No
PICT	Yes	Yes
PNG	Yes	No
QuickDraw GX	Yes	No
QuickTime	Yes	No
SGI	Yes	No
Targa	Yes	No
TIFF	Yes	No
Animation		
Animated GIF	Yes	No
FLC/FLI	Yes	No
PICS	Yes	No

(continued)

Mac OS 8.6

Table 15.1 QuickTime import/export file types for the Mac OS *(continued)*.

Format	Import	Export
MIDI		
Karaoke MIDI	Yes	No
Standard MIDI	Yes	Yes
Text		
Text	Yes	Yes

Figure 15.1 A QuickTime movie with its controls.

The image you see in a movie element when the movie isn't playing is called its *poster*. The poster is a selected image from the movie. Because it's often not the first frame of the movie, you'll see the image of the poster jump to another image when the movie begins.

A *preview* is a moving representative of the movie. Not all movies have previews, but most longer ones do. A preview gives you a quick look at the movie highlights. A series of standard file dialog boxes lets you choose whether to see the poster or a preview before you open a movie.

As in previous versions of Mac OS 8, all these features are available whether you are viewing QuickTime files in a Web browser using the QuickTime plug-in (Figure 15.1) or QuickTime's MoviePlayer application (Figure 15.2).

Mac OS 8.6

Figure 15.2 You can use the MoviePlayer application to view any QuickTime file.

Configuring QuickTime

QuickTime uses a standard Control Panel to configure several aspects of QuickTime, as well as register your name and serial number for QuickTime Pro. The configuration options include:

- *AutoPlay*—Enables audio CDs to begin playing or multimedia CDs to launch automatically upon insertion. Because of a particular type of computer virus known as the AutoStart virus, it is recommended that you disable both options to prevent the virus from infecting your computer and being spread to others.

- *Connection Speed*—Allows you to tell QuickTime the speed of your network connection. QuickTime uses this information to help download the best file size for movies that have been optimized for various connection speeds. As a general rule, faster connections can handle larger files, and larger files are capable of better image and sound quality.

- *Media Keys*—Provided by content creators to allow you to access private files.

- *QuickTime Exchange*—Allows you to view files associated with other platforms, such as Microsoft Windows and the AVI movie file format.

- *Registration*—The Registration section is where you go to register the Pro version.

In addition to these configuration options, you can also configure the most popular Web browsers (Netscape Navigator 3.x and 4.x, and Internet Explorer 3.x and 4.x) to use the QuickTime plug-in. To configure the QuickTime plug-in, follow these steps:

1. Make sure the QuickTime plug-in is in your Web browser's plug-ins folder, which is usually located in the browser's application folder. Both Netscape Navigator and Microsoft Internet Explorer use Netscape plug-ins, so don't be alarmed if the plug-ins in your Internet Explorer folder have Navigator icons.

Mac OS 8.6

2. Review your browser's file helper configuration options to make sure QuickTime is properly defined as a file type. If not, open the Internet Control Panel, shown in Figure 15.3, while in Advanced user mode and configure Preferences| Helper Apps with the settings shown below.

Figure 15.3   The Internet Control Panel may need a bit of assistance in recognizing QuickTime files, although the presence of the QuickTime Plug-in should be sufficient for most Web browsers to auto-detect and be properly configured.

3. Next, visit the QuickTime home page at www.apple.com/quicktime and load one of the movies listed in the QuickTime Showcase section. If it won't load, check your browser's preferences and make sure it's configured to view QuickTime files via the QuickTime Plug-in.

4. If the QuickTime Plug-in is properly recognized by the browser, the movie will begin streaming and the same QuickTime controls found in MoviePlayer will be present, with one additional control, as in Figure 15.4.

5. To configure the QuickTime Plug-in, click on the triangle in the lower right-hand corner of the controls to reveal a menu, as in Figure 15.5.

6. The settings dialog box is very straightforward; just confirm a few general settings, your connection speed, and the MIME settings, and you're set (see Figure 15.6).

7. When you're ready to save a movie or sound file, just click on the triangle again and choose to save the files as a source (to preserve the original file format) or as a QuickTime file.

Multimedia   403

Figure 15.4   A streaming QuickTime movie view with the QuickTime Plug-in and Internet Explorer.

QuickTime And Data Compression

One of QuickTime's most important technological breakthroughs is the real-time compression and decompression it provides to video, animation, photographs, and other graphics. QuickTime supports several built-in compression schemes and can easily support others as necessary. The built-in compression is a software-only solution, capable of achieving ratios as great as 25:1 without any visible loss in image quality. With specialized hardware, compression ratios as high as 160:1 are possible.

Compression is particularly important because of all the data needed to generate moving images and accompanying sounds. A good rule of thumb for estimating movie size is that every minute of motion consumes 10MB of disk space. As another example, a seven-minute, full-size, full-resolution movie could consume 200MB in its uncompressed form. Compressed, that same movie might need only 45MB. Of course, most movies are significantly shorter (lasting between 5 and 30 seconds), so files in the 200K to 1MB range are common.

Mac OS 8.6

404 Chapter 15

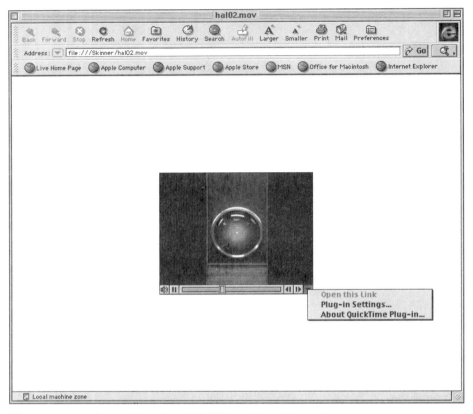

Figure 15.5 Accessing the QuickTime Plug-in's settings.

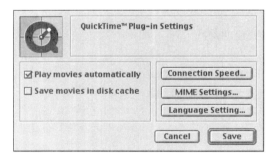

Figure 15.6 The QuickTime Plug-in's settings are easy to follow.

The actual size of a QuickTime movie depends on the following:

➤ *Image size*—Measured in horizontal and vertical pixels, the image size determines how large the movie will appear onscreen. The larger the image, the larger the movie file. Movies default to 160×120 pixels in QuickTime 1.0, but version 1.5 expands this default to 240×180 pixels. Version 2.5 takes it all the way to 640×480 pixels.

Mac OS 8.6

- *Resolution*—QuickTime supports all the Mac's resolutions—depths of color—including 1-, 2-, 4-, 8-, 16-, 24-, and 32-bit. The higher the resolution, the larger the movie file.

- *Frames per second*—Most QuickTime movies are recorded using 10, 12, 15, or 30 frames per second (fps). Without additional hardware, 15fps is the QuickTime standard; 30fps, which is the standard for commercial-quality video, is supported by QuickTime 1.5. Version 2.5 supports 29.97fps (which matches the frame rate of professional video equipment). The higher the frame rate, the larger the resulting movie file.

- *Audio sampling rate*—This rate can be thought of as the "resolution" of the sound. The Macintosh supports 8, 11, 22, or 44kHz audio sampling, although anything higher than 22kHz requires additional hardware. The higher the sampling rate, the larger the sound portion of a movie file.

- *Compression*—As mentioned earlier, QuickTime supports a number of compression schemes. You can select the degree of compression for each scheme. Increasing compression reduces movie size, but sometimes compromises playback quality. New compression schemes introduced with QuickTime 2.5 should reduce or eliminate these kinds of problems.

- *Content*—Beyond the previously mentioned technical factors, the actual set of sounds and images contained in a movie is what will ultimately determine its size. This factor makes it difficult to estimate the size of a QuickTime movie based solely on its length or technical characteristics.

Using QuickTime

You can use QuickTime to watch movies (which may be included on CD-ROM disks, obtained from user groups or online services, or come embedded in documents you get from other Mac users), or you can create your own QuickTime movies. It's easy for almost anyone with a Mac to view a QuickTime movie, but creating one requires a fairly substantial investment in hardware, software, and the development of what may be brand-new skills.

Most QuickTime movies that are available now are part of CD-ROM-based information discs that provide education or information on music, history, sports, news, entertainment, or computer-related topics. CD-ROM is the perfect media for QuickTime because it has huge storage capabilities (650MB), can be inexpensively reproduced, and has access times sufficient to deliver good-quality playback. CD-ROM support for QuickTime has recently been enhanced by faster CD drives (such as the 32x drives that are standard on most new Macs and Mac clones) and performance improvements included in QuickTime 2.5.

To view movies and sounds, you can use the MoviePlayer application, included in the QuickTime folder within the Applications folder. To view images, you can use the PictureViewer application.

QuickTime MoviePlayer

The venerable MoviePlayer application has been revised to support the customized presentation and export of movies as well as the playing of them. When playing a movie, as in Figure 15.7, MoviePlayer looks pretty much the same as in previous versions.

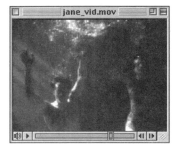

Figure 15.7 The MoviePlayer application, part of QuickTime 3.0.

The Pro version allows you to selectively play the audio or video track of a movie, as well as export it as a Digital Video (DV) stream, among other formats (see Figure 15.8).

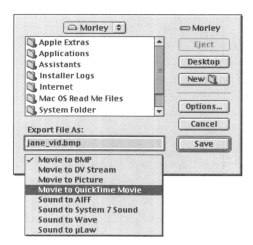

Figure 15.8 The Export options enabled as part of QuickTime Pro.

QuickTime PictureViewer

The PictureViewer application is also a new component of QuickTime 3. PictureViewer uses the QuickTime component of Mac OS 8.6 to view, manipulate, and convert images into several popular file formats, including BMP (for Microsoft Windows) and PhotoShop. It's a no-frills application, but an essential one for anyone who uses the Web and downloads images. Figure 15.9 shows a sample GIF image as viewed through the PictureViewer application.

Figure 15.9   The PictureViewer application is a handy utility to view images downloaded from the Web.

QuickTime VR

QuickTime VR (QTVR) is a powerful extension to QuickTime. It allows you to actually walk through a movie, spin around, look up and down, and manipulate objects within a movie. QTVR takes digital images, stitches them together, and makes them look as if they were taken with a movie camera. Pretty neat stuff. If you have Internet Explorer or Netscape Navigator, you can download a QTVR plug-in that lets you view QTVR movies within a browser window. For more information on this, see the QTVR home page at www.apple.com/quicktime/qtvr.

QTVR movies come in two basic types: one in which you move through or around inside a movie, and another in which an object, such as a book, car, or planet, is manipulated. The difference lies in whether it's you or the object that is moving. A really complex QTVR movie can contain both. For example, Figure 15.10 shows a sample QTVR movie of the interior of a U.S. Navy ship.

Like regular QuickTime movies, QuickTimeVR movies can be viewed from within a Web browser window, as in Figure 15.11, or using the MoviePlayer application, as in Figure 15.12. You can find links to many examples of QuickTimeVR on Apple's QTVR Web site at www.apple.com/quicktime/qtvr.

408   Chapter 15

Figure 15.10   Take a virtual tour using QuickTime VR.

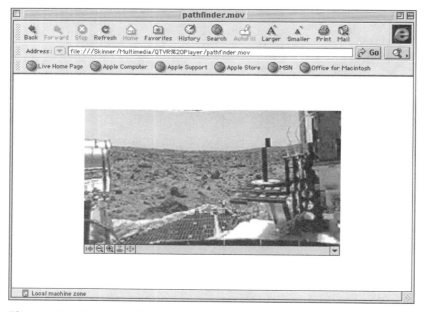

Figure 15.11   Use a Web browser to view QuickTimeVR movies.

Figure 15.12   Movie Player will also let you view QuickTimeVR movies.

Mac OS 8.6

QuickDraw 3D

The final frontier in multimedia must be 3D. Ever since *Jurassic Park* and the stunningly popular game *Doom*, creating 3D worlds on a desktop computer has seen an explosion of interest. Over the years, a variety of companies created many different Mac applications to allow a user to create objects in 3D and render (draw) them realistically. However, these programs could not interoperate in any significant way. Each had their own data file format and each had the ability to use plug-ins—but only their own special kind of plug-in.

Why is this? Well, it's difficult to write a 3D program. A programmer must learn a vast array of skills just to get a basic image on the screen. Although it would be neat, it wouldn't be very cost-effective to have the creators of ClarisWorks add true 3D support to their program.

Apple created QuickDraw 3D in a bold attempt to cut this Gordian knot. QuickDraw 3D makes it possible for different programs to share files, 3D models, textures, and camera positions. QuickDraw 3D adds standard renderers as well as a method for adding new renderers. Best of all, QuickDraw 3D makes it simple for programmers without any 3D experience to support it.

Installation

The Mac OS 8.6 installer has a check box for QuickDraw 3D. Just check this box and the program will be installed. Once the installation is done, you'll find that QuickDraw 3D adds a few more extensions to your System Folder:

- *QuickDraw 3D*—The main QuickDraw 3D Extension that enables creation and manipulation of 3D objects.

- *QuickDraw 3D IR*—A QuickDraw 3D plug-in that accelerates the rendering (drawing on screen) of objects.

- *QuickDraw 3D RAVE*—This file allows programmers to gain rendering speed by accessing the low-level portions of QuickDraw 3D. It's mostly utilized by 3D games that don't require the user-interface features of QuickDraw 3D but do need to be able to render models. Ambrosia Software's Avara is an example of a program that uses RAVE.

- *QuickDraw 3D Viewer*—This group of extensions provides basic 3D support for all applications. An application can use QuickDraw 3D to load a model, position it in space, light it, and render it.

If you're low on hard disk space, you can remove extensions that you're not using. For example, if you don't have a hardware accelerator, you don't need the HW Driver and HW Plug-in files.

Mac OS 8.6

The standard installation also includes new versions of the Scrapbook and SimpleText, which enable these programs to open and manipulate model files. Also, a set of sample models is included so you can play around with them in SimpleText.

3D MetaFile Format

Apple created a special file format, the 3D MetaFile format, for use with QuickDraw 3D. Although a plethora of formats for 3D files (including DXF and 3DS) already exists, none includes all of the features found in the 3DMF format. A 3DMF file stores: The geometrics that make up an object; saved camera views; and textures, shading, and coloring information for all objects.

Unlike the DXF file format, 3DMF files can store complex geometrics like splines and NURBS (Non Uniform Rational B-Splines). These allow the designer to specify things like smooth curves and cut-out surfaces. In the DXF file format, you'd have to specify a curve as a series of short straight-line segments; if you enlarge the model, these straight lines become obvious and the model seems less realistic.

3DMF files can be saved in one of two ways: Text, which you can open with a text editor like BBEdit, or binary, which is smaller but not readable by humans. Not every application gives you a choice, but when one does, binary is usually the best choice. Text is useful mainly when trying to figure out why a model doesn't work in a particular program or when sending files over the Internet in text (as opposed to binary) mode.

Apple gives away information on the internal structure of the 3DMF file format. Sample code for reading and writing these files is available for developers who want to support these kinds of files from their software. No other file format offers so much. Now you see why 3DMF has become so popular!

In fact, the 3DMF file format has rapidly become a cross-platform standard for 3D model files. All major 3D programs on Macs, Windows, and even Unix machines provide the ability to read and write 3DMF files. Portions of 3DMF have even been incorporated into the specifications for VRML, the Internet-based 3D "virtual worlds" specification. So it's safe to say that 3DMF will be around for a while.

In your Apple Extras folder you'll find a sampling of models available from different companies, all of which you can buy and use in your own 3D designs. You can also find a rich treasure trove of models to download on the Internet.

User Interface

QuickDraw 3D, like its big brother QuickTime, is more than just a file format. QuickDraw 3D includes a set of tools that allows you to manipulate 3D models.

Mac OS 8.6

Multimedia   411

You can move, rotate, and zoom a 3D model. You can reposition the camera (the point in 3D space from which you are seeing the model) and save camera positions. Applications can use these built-in user interface tools or implement their own, just like they can with the standard QuickTime window.

Take a look at Figure 15.13. You can see a 3DMF model in the Scrapbook. A bank of controls along the bottom edge of the window includes the following features:

➤ *Camera*—Lets you look at the model from the front, back, top, bottom, left, or right.

➤ *Scale*—Lets you scale the object up or down, making it bigger or smaller in the window.

➤ *Rotate*—Allows you to rotate the object in the view. When clicked, the cursor changes to a hand; you can "grab" the model and rotate it around a central point.

➤ *Move*—Lets you move the model in the window. When clicked, the cursor changes to a hand; you can "grab" the model and move it left or right.

➤ *Home*—Returns you to the "home view," or the original view of the object as was specified in the 3DMF file.

Figure 15.13   A QuickDraw 3D model in the Scrapbook can be rotated, moved, or scaled.

Making Models

One thing QuickDraw 3D doesn't include is a program with which you can create models. If you're serious about 3D, you'll want to purchase a top-notch program like Infini-D, Strata Pro, Macromedia Extreme3D, or ElectricImage Studio. These programs support QuickDraw 3D's support for hardware acceleration, user interface standards, and the 3DMF file for import and export. In addition, they offer professional features and control, but at a cost: the cheapest is priced at $395 and the most expensive costs $7,995.

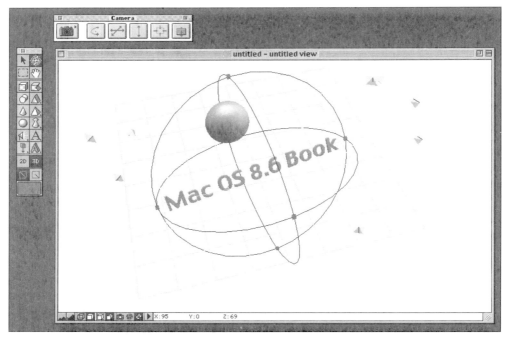

Figure 15.14 It's easy to create 3D text in 3D World!

If you just want to play around with QuickDraw 3D, like in the example shown in Figure 15.14, I recommend a cheaper solution: Microspot's 3D World. This low-cost program ($139) offers a good basic set of tools and features. You can create simple shapes, shade them, group them, and apply textures to them. You can also create 2D or 3D text using whatever TrueType fonts you have installed. You can even create simple animations that you can export as QuickTime movies.

A demo of 3D World is available from Microspot's Web page at www.microspot.com. This demo won't let you save, export models, or print. However, it's a great way to play around with QuickDraw 3D and learn the basics of 3D modeling.

Drag And Drop

QuickDraw 3D makes great use of Mac OS 8.6's drag-and-drop features. You can drag a model from one program to another or drop it on the Scrapbook (for use later) or Desktop. Both SimpleText and the Scrapbook implement the standard QuickDraw 3D user interface tools, making it possible for you to manipulate images inside them.

You can also drag a QuickDraw 3D model into a program that only accepts pictures. QuickDraw 3D will render the view you're currently looking at and drop it into the application as a PICT clipping. This way you can use all your existing applications with QuickDraw 3D—no upgrades necessary!

Speech

Computer-generated speech has had an interesting history on the Macintosh. The very first program anyone saw running on a Mac in public was Macintalk, a text-to-speech generator that could create fairly realistic-sounding speech. At the introduction of the Macintosh, Steve Jobs pulled a Mac out of a carrying case and the Mac joked, "Thanks, it was hot in there." Ah, progress.

Apple eventually released Macintalk for developers to use, but few took the opportunity since Macintalk wasn't part of the standard system installation. Mac OS 8.6 comes with the Speech Control Panel, which provides far more power than the old Macintalk.

Text-To-Speech

The Speech Control Panel implements a form of Text-to-Speech whereby any text on the screen can be read aloud by the computer. Programs must be designed to support this feature, and many already do. For instance, SimpleText can speak any portion of a document.

Take a look at the Speech Control Panel in Figure 15.15. You can choose the voice your computer will use and also set the speed at which the computer speaks. Some of the voices are slow and could use a little speeding up.

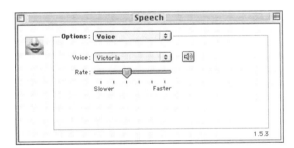

Figure 15.15 The Speech Control Panel lets you pick your computer's voice.

A number of different voices are available. They run the gamut from pleasant and understandable to difficult and unintelligible. Some are quite amusing—the Deranged voice speaks through a lunatic laugh, and the Good News voice sings your text to the tune of "Pomp and Circumstance."

In the Speech Control Panel (see Figure 15.6), you can tell your computer to read any alert dialog boxes that pop up. The Speak the Alert Text setting means that the computer will speak whatever text is in the alert dialog box; the Speak the Phrase option will add a prefix of your choice beforehand. I find that any delay before speaking is annoying, so I set that option to zero.

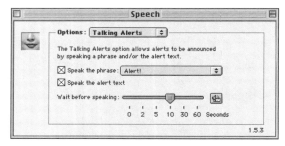

Figure 15.16   The Speech Control Panel can be set so that any alert dialog box will be read to you.

Other Multimedia Applications

Depending on your computer's hardware and software configuration, you may have one or more of the following applications installed. Apple makes some of the following items, but you may also have multimedia capabilities by third-party vendors.

Apple FM Radio

The Apple FM Radio application is a FM tuner that has a familiar interface for most Mac OS users (see Figure 15.17). It is a simple application that allows you to listen to your favorite stations in either mono or stereo, change the channel and volume level, and record a broadcast to disk.

Figure 15.17   The Apple FM Radio application.

One neat feature of the Apple FM Radio application is that it allows you to preset your station preferences so you can organize the application like you would a car radio, for example (see Figure 15.18).

Apple Video Player

The Apple Video Player, shown in Figure 15.19, is often found on the Performa series and the 20th Anniversary Macintosh, or any other Mac with Apple's TV tuner card installed. However, it's also often found on Macs without such hardware, so don't be confused if it is present on your computer but doesn't work.

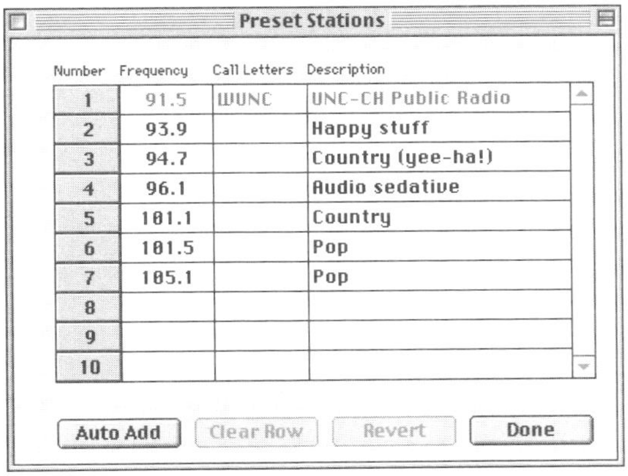

Figure 15.18 Configure stations for easy access to your favorites.

Figure 15.19 You can watch TV on your Mac if you have a TV tuner card installed.

The video controls for the Apple Video Player allow you to select various video and audio input options (see Figure 15.20). You can also configure your channel preferences and reminders so you don't miss your favorite shows (see Figure 15.21).

Figure 15.20 Configuring video input sources in the Apple Video Player is very easy.

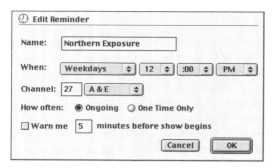

Figure 15.21 The Apple Video Player helps you remember your favorite shows!

AppleCD Audio Player

The AppleCD Audio Player, shown in Figure 15.22, has been around for a long time, and is no different in Mac OS 8.6 than in previous versions of Mac OS 8. You can mount and play an audio CD, as well as customize the playlist, just as before.

Figure 15.22 The AppleCD Audio Player.

To configure a playlist with the AppleCD Audio Player, follow these steps:

1. Insert an audio CD into your computer's internal or external CD-ROM player.
2. Click on the Track List show/hide triangle to reveal the track list.
3. Enter a title for the CD and a name for each track in the playlist area. You can use any name, as shown in Figure 15.23.

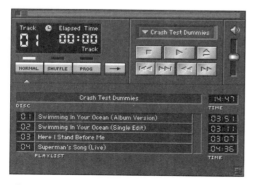

Figure 15.23 The AppleCD Audio Player's track list.

The user interface mimics many household CD players. The buttons in the upper-left quadrant of the AppleCD Audio Player window are (from left to right):

➤ *Normal*—Plays the tracks in their original order, then stops.

➤ *Shuffle*—Reorders the tracks randomly, then stops.

➤ *Prog*—Allows you to program the order in which the tracks are played, as shown in Figure 15.24.

➤ *Repeat*—Repeats the CD without stopping.

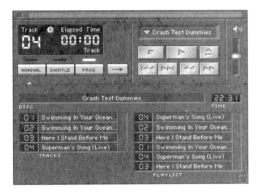

Figure 15.24 Use the Prog button to program your own playlist.

The buttons in the upper-right area of the Audio Player window use conventional icons to control volume as well as the commands to start, stop, pause, jump to the previous or next track, and scan forward and backward. Clicking on the Show/Hide Tracks pop-up menu (the small green triangle) allows you to skip to a specific track; double-clicking on a track number in the track list accomplishes the same thing.

Apple DVD Player

The newest member to the Mac OS multimedia application family is the Apple DVD Player, which allows those of us lucky enough to have a DVD player to play laser disc-quality video on a Macintosh. Of course, you must have a DVD drive installed, which is becoming more and more common every day. But DVD is more than just a new way to watch movies.

DVD stands for digital video disk or digital versatile disk, because it comes in several flavors. Too many, some say! Currently there are the following DVD formats in use that allow for the storage of audio, video, and data. Some are read-only, while others are writable as well:

➤ *DVD-Video*—Full-screen, full-motion video via hardware or software compression.

- *DVD-ROM*—Read-only multimedia discs, capable of reading and playing CD-ROMs as well.

- *DVD-RAM*—A 5.2G storage drive that is readable and writable.

- *DVD-ROM/RAM*—All the capabilities of DVD-ROM, and can write DVD-RAM storage drive.

- *DVD +RW*—An erasable DVD format similar to CD-RW technology.

- *DVD-R*—A DVD format that allows for one recording session for up to 3.95G.

- *Divx*—A special DVD format that allows a disc to be used for a limited amount of time.

Of all these formats, Apple makes drives that support the DVD-ROM, DVD-ROM/RAM, and DVD-Video formats. For now, however, most users will be using the Apple DVD Player to view movies on discs formatted for the DVD-Video format. This is a unique format that allows content creators to produce one disc with many levels of language support and other controls.

If you haven't already discovered your DVD player, look in the Apple Menu and select the Apple DVD Player and choose Edit|Preferences and select the Language tab (see Figure 15.25). Choose the appropriate language for the audio, subtitle, and menu languages. Next, review the Parental Controls tab (Figure 15.26) to explore the options that parents might find useful.

When you're ready, just pop in a DVD disc and use the stylish remote control to navigate through the disc (see Figure 15.27).

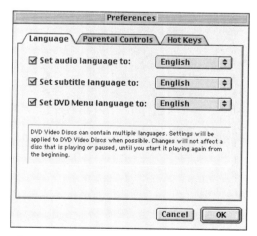

Figure 15.25   The Apple DVD Player's Language preferences.

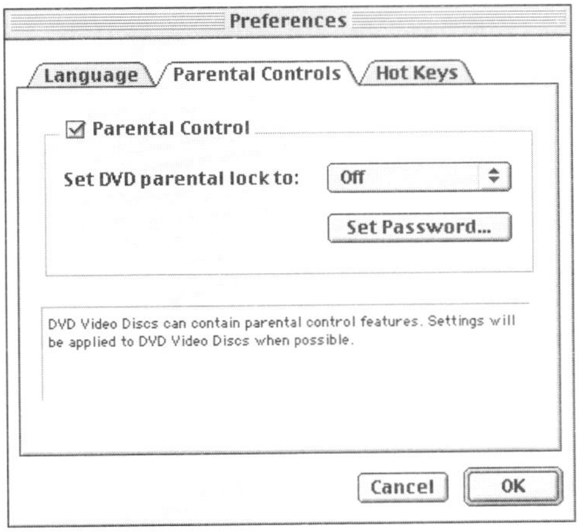

Multimedia 419

Figure 15.26 The Apple DVD Player's Parental Controls preferences.

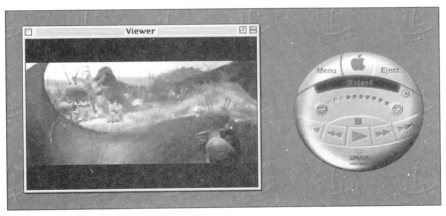

Figure 15.27 The Apple DVD Player's remote allows you to navigate through a DVD disc and activate its menu.

Note that each DVD disc will have its own menu, so options that are available in one disc, such as Closed Captioning or alternative language tracks, may not be available in other discs.

Extended CD-ROMs

Many new audio CD-ROMs come with a bonus multimedia track as well. It's no big surprise that the multimedia portion is based on QuickTime with a front-end created with Macromedia Director, one of the most popular CD-ROM gaming creation tools. Because these CDs are hybrid (audio and data) CDs, you can insert them into your Mac's CD-ROM drive and either play the audio portion using the AppleCD Audio Player as usual, or follow the directions on the data portion.

For example, Figure 15.28 shows a QuickTime movie placed in the center of the screen with Macromedia controls in the lower half of the screen that allow you to advance through the CD or return to the main menu.

Figure 15.28 An example of an audio CD with a bonus multimedia track.

Since Mac OS 8.6 installs the latest version of QuickTime, you usually don't need to install anything else; you can just double-click on the application icon and start watching, listening, or interacting with the CD, just like a Mac should.

MPEG 3 Players

The latest craze in the multimedia world is MPEG 3 (abbreviated MP3), an ultra-efficient file format that is about 10 times more efficient than standard audio formats, for example. The greatest thing about MP3 is that you can shrink an entire audio CD track, which is usually about 30MB, into a file about 2-3MB in size. This is a very manageable file size for use on the Web, and it opens up new possibilities for artists who want to break into new markets without the overhead of mastering and distributing CDs.

All you need to use MP3 is an MP3 player, such as MacAmp from @soft, and some sound files. MacAmp, shown in Figure 15.29, uses a standard Mac OS application interface and is very easy to use. It consists of a player (top), an equalizer (middle), and a playlist window (bottom).

Multimedia   421

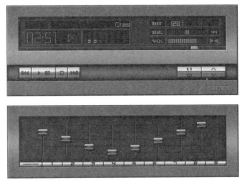

Figure 15.29   MacAmp's player, equalizer, and playlist.

You can create and edit your own playlists, and even export them for others to use. For the latest information about MP3 and links to FAQs and MP3 files, see the MacAmp Web site (www.macamp.com) and the MP3 site (www.mp3.com).

Wrapping Up

In this chapter, you've learned about the multimedia features of Mac OS 8.6. You've seen how to play digital video and audio with QuickTime and view 3D models with QuickDraw 3D; how to use the text-to-speech features of Mac OS 8.6; and the basics of the Mac OS's most common multimedia applications.

Next, in Part III of this book, you'll see how Mac OS 8.6 interacts with the world outside via networking. You'll learn how to work on a network, how to connect to the Internet, and even how to set up your own Web page!

Troubleshooting

Every type of computer and operating system has its own quirks and challenges, and the Mac OS is no exception. Compared to other operating systems, however, the Mac OS 8.6 has significantly fewer issues to overcome, and those that do present themselves are more easily fixed. In fact, each version of the Mac OS has improved on the previous version in terms of stability and quashing *undocumented features* (bugs). This type of evolutionary improvement has been possible because the core fundamentals of the Mac OS have not changed over the past decade. This constancy enables Apple software engineers to refine the stability of the Mac OS and third-party software authors to increase the interoperability of their applications and utilities with the Mac OS. The evolution of the Mac OS makes troubleshooting it a bit like learning to swim: once you've learned the basics skills of floating, the dog paddle, and the backstroke, you're capable of teaching yourself most everything else. This chapter will teach you all the basics of troubleshooting Mac OS 8.6 so you can swim in the kiddie pool, the deep end, or the Atlantic Ocean.

Common Problems And Their Solutions

The vast majority of problems you're likely to encounter with Mac OS 8.6 revolves around a handful of common scenarios that are easily resolved. You might encounter some of the following problems on more than one occasion, and never see others. Take a look at each of the following scenarios so you'll at least be familiar with each problem, its possible cause, and solutions. For more information, see Appendix A to learn where to go for additional help with these and other issues.

Computer Won't Start Up

Problem
On startup or restart, the computer won't start at all. There is no activity on screen and/or you don't hear anything coming from the central processing unit (CPU).

Cause
The computer and/or the monitor aren't getting any power, or the power isn't reaching the CPU or monitor. The first is easy to detect, but the second is a little more difficult.

Solution
Be sure that the computer is plugged into a surge-protected outlet that is itself receiving power. If your monitor is plugged in through the courtesy outlet on the back of the CPU, make sure the connection is secure. If it isn't secure, the CPU may be getting power but the monitor is not, even if it's turned on. To test the outlet for power, plug in a lamp or other device and turn it on; if it works, the outlet is receiving power.

If your computer is plugged into a surge protector (and it should be!), check to see if the surge protector is in the On position. Most surge protectors have an On/Off switch. If it has a Reset button, try selecting it; it may have been tripped by a power surge. Finally, if your surge protector has a fuse, shut down everything that's plugged into it, unplug the surge protector from the outlet, and check the fuse.

If your computer is receiving power but still doesn't start up, two possible explanations remain—but both require the services of an Apple-authorized repair center. First, the power supply in your CPU, which converts the current received from an outlet into a form that is usable by the computer, may be damaged. It's not uncommon for a power supply to go bad, especially of the computer is left on for extended periods of time. The minimal life span for a power supply left on 24 hours per day should be several years, however. Finally, the worst-case scenario requires replacing the logic board because it cannot transfer the power received from the outlet through the power supply to the necessary components of the computer. PowerBooks are especially susceptible to simultaneous power supply and logic board failure because of the way the power cord plugs into the back of many older models, such as the 5300 series.

Blinking Question Mark On Startup

Problem
On startup, the CPU and monitor receive power, but a blinking question mark appears on screen and no further startup activity occurs.

Cause
The Mac OS cannot detect a valid startup disk containing the Mac OS. Either the drive is bad, or the Mac OS is not available.

Mac OS 8.6

Solution

In about half the cases, the infamous blinking question mark is present because the computer cannot locate the designated startup disk. Most Macs only have one hard drive, and the solution in this case is fairly simple: zap the computer's parameter RAM, or PRAM, which is kind of like giving the computer a loud wakeup call to restart and behave!

To zap the PRAM, follow these steps after reading the remainder of this solution:

1. Restart the computer by pressing Control+Command+Power key (also know as a hard restart or a hard boot).

2. Hold down the Option+Command+P+R keys while the Caps Lock key is *not* depressed.

3. Keep holding down these keys until you hear the startup chime a second time, then release.

Zapping the PRAM has a peculiar side effect that you should be aware of before executing. Certain Control Panels and settings are cleared by this action, and you'll have to check them and reset some to return your computer to its normal settings:

➤ Apple Menu Options

➤ Energy Saver

➤ Keyboard

➤ Map

➤ Memory

➤ Monitors & Sound

➤ Mouse

➤ Trackpad

Other Control Panel settings (such as alternative Ethernet settings in the TCP/IP Control Panel if you have a third-party adapter installed) may also be affected so it won't hurt to check all the settings after zapping the PRAM.

In the other half of cases when the blinking question mark appears at startup, the computer can't find a valid System Folder. The solution is to start from another bootable source and help the computer locate the System Folder. You can boot from the Mac OS CD-ROM or a bootable floppy, such as the Emergency Startup Disk that comes with each Macintosh. When the Mac OS boots, it looks for a valid System Folder in the following order:

Mac OS 8.6

1. Floppy drive
2. Hard drive designated in the Startup Disk Control Panel
3. Additional hard drives
4. CD-ROM drive

The most common method is to start up using a bootable CD-ROM. You can do this in two easy steps:

1. Insert the CD-ROM.
2. Restart holding down the C key until it boots from the CD-ROM.

To boot from a bootable floppy:

1. Insert the floppy disk.
2. Restart.

Once the computer has restarted, open the designated boot drive and look for a System Folder with the special icon which indicates that it is *blessed*, or designated as bootable. Figure 16.1 shows two System Folders, only one of which is blessed (left).

Figure 16.1 The blessed System Folder (left) has a special icon to indicate that it is a valid System Folder.

To bless a system folder:

1. Open the startup Disks Control Panel and select the disk containing the System Folder.
2. Open the System Folder and double-click the Finder icon.
3. Ignore any messages about the Finder not being able to be opened; double-clicking it is just a trick to get it to be recognized by the Mac OS.
4. Restart.

If the computer doesn't start up properly, you'll need to reinstall the Mac OS from the installation CD-ROM (see Appendix C for detailed information about installing, reinstalling, and updating to Mac OS 8.6).

Hangs When Starting

Problem
The Mac OS hangs (freezes) when starting, leaving the computer in an unusable state.

Cause
There is an Extension conflict, corrupted preference file, or a missing component of the Mac OS.

Solution
The computer has power, starts to boot up, but stops before it completes the full startup process—these are the symptoms of one of the most common problems for Mac OS users. At startup, the Mac OS displays icons for many Extensions and Control Panels as they load, illustrating for users what is—or is not—loading at startup. Some of these items have the option of not showing their *startup icon* during startup, or a red X may be drawn through the icon to indicate that the item did not load properly. For the most part, however, you'll be able identify at what point the Mac OS stops loading properly by watching the startup icons load.

An Extension conflict at startup occurs when one Extension cannot load because it conflicts with an Extension that has already been loaded. Disabling and reenabling Extensions in a process of trial and error to see which are in conflict, based upon your analysis of the startup icons and eliminating the offending Extension, is the cheapest approach to solving this type of problem. The best way to do this is with the Extensions Manager Control Panel, after you have started the Mac with Extensions off using the following steps:

1. Restart the computer.
2. Hold down the Shift key *before* the Welcome to Mac OS screen appears.
3. Release the Shift key once the "Welcome to Mac OS Extensions Off" screen appears.

If this succeeds, try going to the Extensions Manager and selecting the Mac OS 8.6 Base set, and then the Mac OS 8.6 All set. This eliminates the possibility that something installed by another application or utility is the cause of the problem, and not Mac OS 8.6 itself.

A more costly way to deal with an Extension conflict is with a product like Cassidy & Green's Conflict Catcher (www.conflictcatcher.com), a very sophisticated program that can help you work through almost any Extension conflict. Another great tool is the wonderful shareware program Extension Overload by Teng Chou Ming, which is included on this book's companion CD-ROM. Both Conflict

Mac OS 8.6

Catcher and Extension Overload are discussed again in the section below entitled "Useful Tools."

Another possible solution for when your Mac freezes on startup is to *trash the prefs* (Mac-speak for throwing away the Preferences files) for the offending Extension, Control Panel, or the Finder. An item's configuration and resource settings are often stored in a Preferences file; if this file is corrupted and unreadable by the Mac OS, it may prevent the item from loading at startup.

Follow these steps to trash the prefs for a specific item:

1. Restart with Extensions off or from an alternative boot source.
2. Open the Preferences folder of the System Folder of the boot drive.
3. Move the Preferences file of the selected item to the Trash, but *do not empty the Trash*.
4. Restart the computer.

On restarting, a new Preferences file will be created. You'll have to reenter any customizations.

Finally, if a critical component of the Mac OS is missing at startup, it can cause symptoms similar to an Extension conflict or a corrupted Preference file. The only recourse at this point is to reinstall the Mac OS (see Appendix C).

Freezes During Use

Problem
The Mac OS or an application freezes during use and displays an error message or will not return control to the user.

Cause
The Mac OS or an application performs an illegal operation or attempts to write to the memory space occupied by another application, Extension, or the Mac OS itself.

Solution
Application programming is an extremely sophisticated business, and sometimes programmers make mistakes that result in an application, or the Mac OS, crashing during use. If the error is one of many types of known errors, the Mac OS may be able to identify the error and display a message like "The application XYZ has crashed because of a Type -36 error" and give you the opportunity to quit the application. Often, however, you'll just get a frozen screen or a blank dialog box, in which case you should try the following solutions to recover from the error:

Mac OS 8.6

1. Press Command+Period.
2. Press Command+Escape.
3. Force quit the application by pressing Option+Command+Escape and select Force Quit from the window shown in Figure 16.2.
4. Reboot (Control+Command+Power key).
5. For those computers that have a small hole near the access panel, such as the iMac, straighten a paperclip and insert it into the hole. This performs a manual restart and should be used as a last resort.

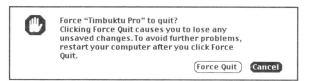

Figure 16.2 Choose Option+Command+Escape to force quit an application that is misbehaving.

If you succeed in regaining control of the computer, you should immediately save your open documents and restart the computer. By continuing to work without restarting after a crash, you are courting disaster because of the increased likelihood of a secondary crash.

Won't Shut Down

Problem
The Mac OS won't respond to the Shut Down command.

Cause
The Mac OS or an application is preventing the partial or full execution of the Shut Down command, or an item in the Shutdown Items folder is interfering with the computer's ability to shut down properly.

Solution
When you select Shut Down, the Mac OS issues an AppleEvent instructing all open applications to quit. If an application doesn't receive the AppleEvent or cannot interpret it properly, then the Mac OS will not comply with the final steps of the shutting down process. The best solution is to retry the Shut Down command. If that fails, then manually quit any applications that have not successfully quit in response to the AppleEvent. If all the applications do indeed quit, leaving only the Finder open, force quit the Finder or restart the computer using what experienced computer users refer to as the three-finger salute (Control+Command+Power key).

Mac OS 8.6

Once you have rebooted the computer, check to see if contents of the Shutdown Items folder (assuming you have anything in it) could be interfering with the Shutdown process. Programs in the Shutdown Items folder are launched after all other applications have quit in response to the Shut Down or Restart commands. If these other applications do not quit properly, the Mac OS may try to shut down the programs that are supposed to be launched on Shutdown.

Drive Not Recognized

Problem
One or more hard drives are not recognized during startup (they don't appear on the Desktop).

Cause
The Mac OS cannot find a boot partition or driver for a drive.

Solution
If the Mac OS cannot find a hard drive , try booting from the Mac OS CD-ROM or the Emergency Startup Disk. You can also try booting from a third-party CD-ROM or diskette, such as FWB Hard Drive ToolKit, Norton Utilities or TechTool Pro, and then run the appropriate utility (see the "Useful Tools" section below for a list of the best tools to use in this situation). Every hard drive contains a special section for driver information called the boot partition. The OS must be able to access the boot partition in order to mount the disk on startup. If the boot partition is corrupted or the driver information is unreadable, the drive will not be mounted until it has been repaired.

In the case of Apple-brand hard drives, the Drive Setup utility is the best solution to try first. If you can afford it, however, you can't go wrong with purchasing a commercial utility that specializes in disk storage. In the worst-case scenario—in which you cannot reinstall the proper driver for a drive or repair it—you may have to reformat the drive, which will cause all of your data to be lost.

Can't Connect To A Network/Internet

Problem
Cannot see AppleTalk devices over the network or access the Internet.

Cause
Your computer has been physically disconnected from the network or a software error has occurred. Also, the network may be "down," in which case there's nothing wrong with your Mac.

Solution

Network-related errors are familiar to most users, and the first possible solution is to make sure your Ethernet cable or modem is properly connected. Network cables and hardware devices such as Ethernet cards and modems rarely go bad, however. The most likely solution to this type of problem can be found by checking your AppleTalk and TCP/IP Control Panel settings. Third-party Ethernet adapters typically require additional drivers, which—if not present—will prevent your computer from seeing the network. For example, Figure 16.3 shows an alternative Ethernet source selected in the AppleTalk Control Panel. This source, like Apple's built-in Ethernet adapter, relies on an Extension, which if not present, will result in a network access error.

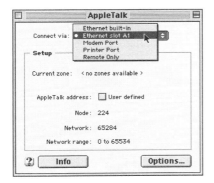

Figure 16.3 Network drivers must be present in order for the Mac OS to use certain types of networking hardware, such as this Fast Ethernet adapter.

Modems present different types of errors, which are usually related to configuration errors in the Modem and Remote Access Control Panels. Dial-up connections are often very difficult to troubleshoot because of the differences between dial-up servers and the many, many different types of clients that access these servers. In such cases, check your ISP's configuration requirements and your settings, such as those found in the Remote Access Control Panel, an example of which is shown in Figure 16.4.

Mouse And Keyboard Won't Work

Problem
The mouse and/or keyboard won't work.

Cause
The ADB (Apple Desktop Bus) or USB (Universal Serial Bus) cables connecting the mouse and keyboard to the CPU have become disconnected, or the mouse or keyboard is broken.

Mac OS 8.6

432 Chapter 16

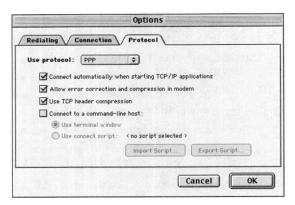

Figure 16.4 Dial-up networking problems are usually the result of a misconfigured Control Panel setting such as the PPP settings in the Remote Access Control Panel.

Solution

In about 70 percent of cases, the answer to this problem is simply that the cables connecting the mouse or keyboard have become disconnected. Pre-iMac computers all use the ADB-style cable to connect the mouse to the keyboard and the keyboard to the CPU. In some of these computers, the ADB cable passes through the monitor, connecting the mouse and keyboard independently to the monitor, which is then connected to the CPU. First check to see if any of these cables is loose, especially if you have your keyboard is one of the models that has ADB connectors on either side. These are notorious for becoming bent and broken. If all are connected properly and the problem persists, you could have a bad mouse or keyboard. Try using someone else's mouse or keyboard before buying new ones.

For iMac owners, the USB cable could have become disconnected. The connectors on USB cables are a great improvement over ADB connectors and are much less prone to failure.

TIP
Whenever possible, shut down the computer before connecting and disconnecting ADB cables. USB cables may be freely connected and disconnected at any time, however.

Application Crashes

Problem
An application crashes, either periodically or consistently.

Cause
The application may have a bug or may conflict with the Mac OS or another application.

Solution
Check the documentation on the offending application to see if it mentions any "known problems" with the application itself, or when interacting with other applications. Next, check the Web site of the vendor to see if any new information or updates to the application have been posted. Applications crash for hundreds of reasons, but the cause usually boils down to two main issues:

➤ Memory problems

➤ Memory problems

That's right. Memory problems are the biggest issue for the Mac OS because of the way the Mac OS allocates memory for use by itself and by applications. In a nutshell, the Mac OS doesn't use *protected memory space*, which is available with Mac OS X Server and will be available in Mac OS X sometime in 2000. Protected memory space allows an application to run in a block of memory that cannot be infringed upon by other applications. It also allows an application to access additional memory when needed. Mac OS 8.6 relies on programmers to write their applications with a "good faith" attitude, in the hope that applications won't invade the memory space of the Mac OS itself or other applications. Basically, there's nothing you can do about this type of problem.

A common type of application crash can be attributed to an application needing more memory than is currently available. Fortunately this is a solvable problem. Refer to Chapter 9 for the details on how to allocate more memory to an application using the Memory section of the Get Info dialog window, an example of which is shown in Figure 16.5.

A final possible solution to stop an application's repeated crashing is to not quit an application out of the order in which it was launched. Quitting out of order can lead to memory fragmentation and application instability. For example, if you launch Application A, Application B, and then Application C, you should quit Application C before you quit Application B. Fortunately, the tear-off portion of the Application Switcher can be configured with AppleScript or a utility such as AppSwitcher Control to show applications in the order in which they were launched, as in Figure 16.6. This provides a helpful visual clue as to the sequence in which applications must be quit *before* quitting the target application.

Mac OS 8.6

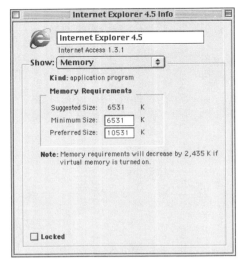

Figure 16.5 Increasing the amount of memory for an application can often prevent frequent crashing of that application.

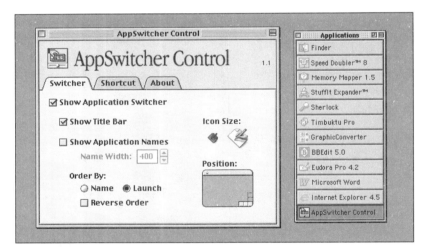

Figure 16.6 Use a utility such as AppSwitcher Control to show applications in the order in which they were launched.

If you want to learn more about application error codes, refer to a utility such as SysErrors by Caerwyn Pearce, which is included on the CD-ROM. When you see an error like the one shown in Figure 16.7, just fire up SysErrors and look for the error in question.

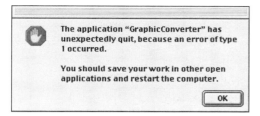

Figure 16.7 When you see errors such as this, heed the advice and restart after saving as much of your work as possible.

Colors Won't Display Properly

Problem
Colors on screen look odd, especially when browsing the Web.

Cause
A loose connection, corrupted preference file, or Monitors & Sound settings are not set properly.

Solution
Color problems are typically due to one of three causes. First, your monitor cable could be loose, preventing one or more of the pins in the cable from making a good connection. The result will be a display with an unusual color balance, such as a green or amber wash over the entire screen. Securing the cable will usually take care of this problem.

Next, the Monitors & Sound preferences file could be corrupt, which is easily fixed by trashing the preferences and restarting.

Finally, open the Monitors & Sound Control Panel and check the color depth and resolution settings. As a rule of thumb, configure your computer's display as follows:

➤ As many colors as possible

➤ The highest resolution you're comfortable with

➤ A refresh rate of 75Hz or higher

Figure 16.8 shows how these criteria are met in the Monitors & Sound Control Panel for a 19" ViewSonic PS790 monitor in Mac OS 8.6.

The color depth setting is especially important because it controls the quality with which Web images are displayed. To illustrate this point, look at Figure 16.9, which shows the color depth preview section of the Monitors & Sound Control Panel. Notice the difference between the smoothness of the transition between the colors?

Mac OS 8.6

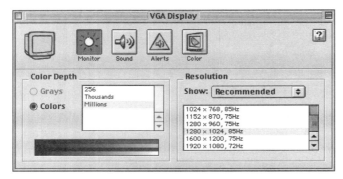

Figure 16.8 An optimally configured Monitors & Sound Control Panel.

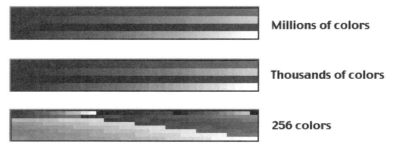

Figure 16.9 Configure your computer to display as many colors as possible to eliminate the possibility of poor image quality.

Won't Print

Problem
Computer won't print.

Cause
Printer is physically disconnected or print driver is improperly selected via the Chooser.

Solution
Check your serial cable to ensure connectivity, if connected locally. Or check the network connectivity for your computer and the printer, if it is a networked printer. Physical connectivity is usually pretty easy to troubleshoot:

1. Shut down the Mac and the printer.

2. Start up the printer, and then the Mac once the printer is online.

If you're sure the printer is connected properly, open the Chooser and look for the printer using the proper Chooser extension, such as LaserWriter 8, shown in Figure 16.10.

Troubleshooting   437

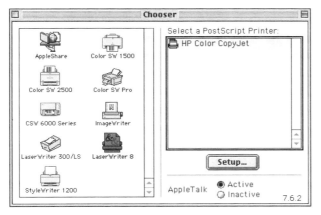

Figure 16.10   Using the Chooser, confirm that your printer is available.

If necessary, create a new Desktop Printer using the Chooser, or launch the Desktop Printer Utility from the Apple Extras folder and create a new Desktop Printer. Another option is to open an existing Desktop Printer to confirm connectivity to the printer and its configuration options. The Desktop Printer Utility will work with many non-Apple printers, but you may need to locate and use any third-party diagnostic utilities that came with your non-Apple printer.

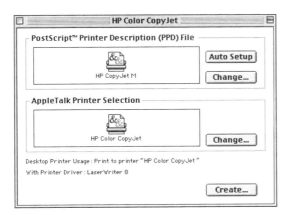

Figure 16.11   Use the Desktop Printer Utility to troubleshoot printing problems.

Documents Won't Open

Problem
A document won't open even though you have the application that created it and you can create new documents using the same application.

Cause
A corrupt Desktop database.

Mac OS 8.6

Solution

The Mac OS uses a database called the Desktop to keep track of information about files and the applications used to create them. Many computers contain tens of thousands of files, and it isn't too surprising that the Mac OS gets a bit confused about which documents were created with what application. The answer is to ask the Mac OS to repair the Desktop database as follows:

1. Restart the computer.
2. Hold down the Command+Option keys until a dialog box appears asking you if you want to rebuild the Desktop.

Rebuilding the Desktop will take several minutes, depending on how many files are on your hard drive. If you have more than one drive, you will be asked if you want to rebuild the Desktop on each available drive. If this doesn't succeed in fixing the problem, try trashing the Finder prefs (described earlier) and rebuilding the Desktop. For more information about the Desktop and how the Desktop database is structured, see Thomas Templemann's Web site about the Desktop at www.tempel.org/macdev/dtdb_secrets.html.

Useful Tools

Hundreds of tools are available to help you troubleshoot the Mac OS, your applications, and your computer's hardware. Some are expensive commercial applications, while others are shareware or freeware. Start with the tools that come with the Mac OS, then branch out as needed, keeping in mind that it never hurts to be familiar with a utility before it's needed in an emergency!

The following list describes some of the more frequently used tools that you should consider adding to your troubleshooting toolkit, and tells you where you can get the latest versions.

Disk First Aid

asu.info.apple.com

The Disk First Aid utility, shown in Figure 16.12, comes with the Mac OS and is an essential tool for diagnosing and repairing Apple hard drives. It can verify the physical integrity of a disk, as well as make some repairs and reformat disks.

Troubleshooting 439

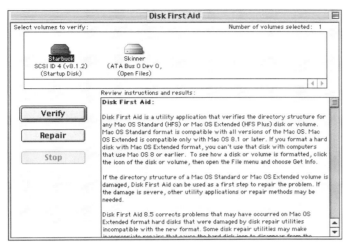

Figure 16.12 The Disk First Aid utility.

Drive Setup

asu.info.apple.com

The Drive Setup utility is the tool used to format and reformat drives, including partitioning, low-level formatting, and updating disk drivers (see Figure 16.13).

The Disk First Aid and Drive Setup utilities are included on the Mac OS CD-ROM and the Emergency Startup Disk.

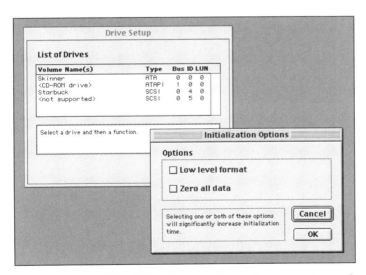

Figure 16.13 The Drive Setup utility allows you to perform essential formatting tasks such as low-level formatting of hard drives.

Mac OS 8.6

Apple System Profiler

asu.info.apple.com

The Apple System Profiler, located under the Apple Menu, is a tool that catalogs your computer's hardware and software attributes for reference and for use by trained support professionals. It catalogs just about every conceivable aspect of your Mac, including hardware specifications, Mac OS version and components, network connectivity, printer connections, and all Extensions, Control Panels, and applications (see Figure 16.14).

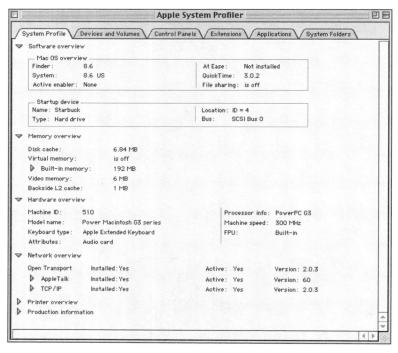

Figure 16.14 A small portion of the information gathered by the Apple System Profiler.

Extension Manager

asu.info.apple.com

As we've seen in Chapter 2, your Mac relies on Extensions to provide essential functionality for your computer, and the Extension Manager is the best way to manage these Extensions, as well as Control Panels, and Startup Items.

Mac OS Installation CD-ROM

store.apple.com

The Mac OS installation CD-ROM is bootable, contains tools for verifying and formatting discs, and, of course, the Mac OS itself.

Bootable Floppy

asu.info.apple.com

Because of the prevalence of CD-ROMs, and of the Mac OS installation CD-ROM in particular, a bootable floppy isn't as essential as it once was. However, not all Macs that are capable of running Mac OS 8.6 have CD-ROMs, especially PowerBooks. It's probably a good idea to make a bootable floppy like the one shown in Figure 16.15 and keep it with the Mac OS CD-ROM just in case a CD player is unavailable.

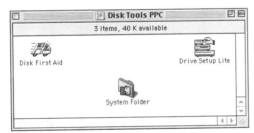

Figure 16.15 A bootable floppy with two essential troubleshooting tools.

MacsBug

asu.info.apple.com

MacsBug is an advanced programming utility that loads before the Mac OS at startup and is particularly useful in identifying what causes an application to crash. When an error occurs and is trapped by MacsBug, a really funky screen appears that provides detailed information about what crashed and why. The benefit for the beginner user is that at least you'll know what crashed and be able to recover control of the computer by typing one of several commands, such as *es* to exit the offending application, *ea* to restart the offending application, or *rb* to reboot the computer.

FWB Hard Disk ToolKit

www.fwb.com

FWB Hard Disk ToolKit is a powerful application that specializes in the formatting, performance optimization, and repair of hard drives. In addition to individual drives, it also supports RAID (Redundant Array of Inexpensive Disks) drives as well. If you aspire to be a power-user, then you should have this utility. Figure 16.16 shows the main view of the FWB Hard Disk ToolKit utility.

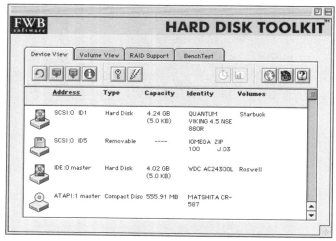

Figure 16.16 FWB's Hard Disk ToolKit.

Norton Utilities

www.norton.com

Norton Utilities is a suite of utilities that provides serious repair capabilities along with disk optimization (see Figure 16.17), added protection against crashes, and file and disk recovery. Norton Utilities is probably the best-known repair utility for the Mac OS, and for good reason. Be sure to add this to your toolkit.

TechTool Pro

www.micromat.com

Another tool that has become essential to the Mac OS troubleshooting toolkit is TechTool Pro from MicroMat, shown in Figure 16.18. TechTool Pro is a real geek's tool, but it provides a clever front end that allows you to select a Simple or Standard interface—in case you're intimidated by the Expert interface.

Troubleshooting 443

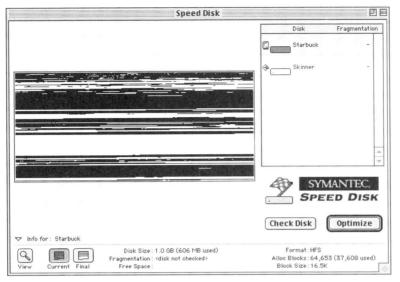

Figure 16.17 Use the Speed Disk utility from Norton Utilities to optimize and defragment your hard drive.

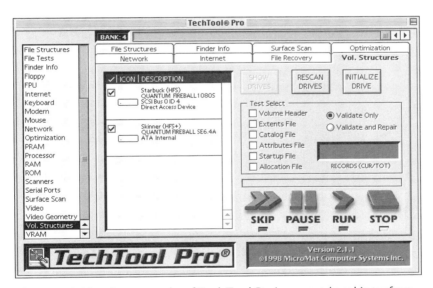

Figure 16.18 An example of TechTool Pro's expert-level interface.

File Buddy

www.skytag.com

File Buddy is a wonderful (and cheap!) utility that provides a number of functions such as finding duplicate or hidden files, checking the integrity of aliases, cleaning

Mac OS 8.6

out unnecessary files, inventorying drives, and rebuilding the Desktop. One of the most popular features of File Buddy, however, is its powerful Get Info command, an example of which is shown in Figure 16.19.

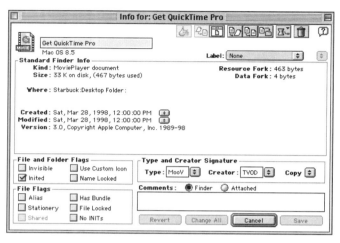

Figure 16.19 File Buddy's powerful Get Info command.

Extension Overload

www.mir.com.my/~cmteng

Extension Overload by Teng Chou Ming is an award-winning utility that helps users manage the dozens of extensions in the System Folder. In fact, this utility contains information on over 1,200 items! Shown in Figure 16.20, Extension Overload provides detailed information about each item and offers a searchable interface to help you locate a specific Extension or Control Panel.

Conflict Catcher

www.conflictcatcher.com

Conflict Catcher helps resolve Extension conflicts and startup problems by identifying offending items. It works by cataloging your System Folder and performing a series of restarts, identifying problems along the way.

SysErrors

perso.club-internet.fr/caerwyn

SysErrors by Caerwyn Pearce is a database of error codes with a handy interface that allows you to search for a particular error, as in Figure 16.21, or browse

Troubleshooting 445

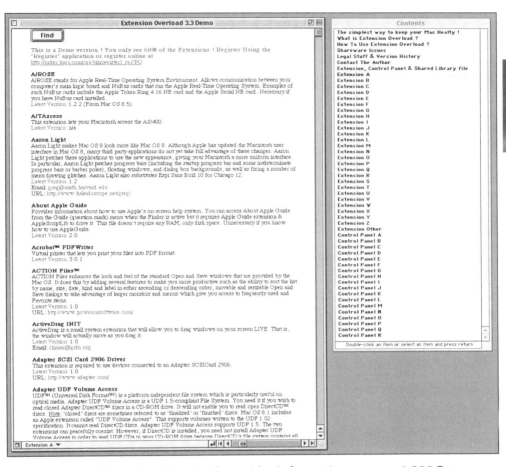

Figure 16.20 Extension Overload provides information on over 1,200 Extensions and Control Panels.

Figure 16.21 Search for a specific error using SysErrors.

Mac OS 8.6

categories of error codes for specific elements of the Mac OS, such as the Memory Manager.

Remember that Mac OS error codes come in two formats, positive errors and negative errors.

Disinfectant

hyperarchive.lcs.edu/HyperArchive/Abstracts/Recent-Summary.html

Disinfectant by John Norstad is an antivirus utility that, although no longer supported, is the best freeware antivirus utility available. It has a basic interface, an example of which is shown in Figure 16.22, and is a useful tool to have around.

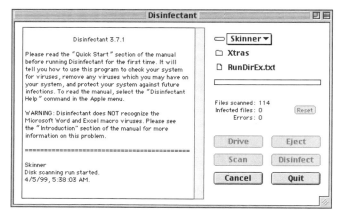

Figure 16.22 Disinfectant is an older, but free, antivirus utility.

Norton AntiVirus

www.norton.com

Norton AntiVirus is a powerful commercial application that detects and automatically repairs viruses, including Microsoft Word macro viruses, and updates its virus library over the Internet. It includes a bootable CD-ROM.

Virex

www.mcafee.com

Virex is another commercial application that provides substantial protection against viruses, as well as automatic updates and scheduled scans of your drives and network volumes.

Preventing Problems

Problems are a fact of computing life, but you can take several steps to prevent trouble down the road. These steps are no guarantee that you'll never have problems, however. Instead, they're more like vaccinations that help ward off problems. Consider these steps as a first line of defense against problems on your Mac.

➤ *Backup*—Performs full backups on a regular basis, and incremental backups in between. At a minimum, back up your documents and have the installation disks and CDs handy in case you have to reinstall the Mac OS and/or your applications.

➤ *Rebuild the Desktop*—Rebuilding the Desktop isn't as critical as in previous version so the Mac OS. However, if you have 20,000 files, the Desktop just might need a little help now and again.

➤ *Clean out unneeded files*—The fewer files on your drives, the easier (and faster) it will be for the Mac OS to manage your file systems. If you really need to keep files around for a while, look into a CD recorder to create archival copies of important collections of folders and files.

➤ *Write down or print out important settings*—If your disk crashes and you reinstall all your software, how will you be able to reconfigure your Internet settings? Periodically write down or print out any information that is critical to getting you up and running after a catastrophic failure.

➤ *Restart strategies*—Because of the way the Mac OS handles memory, it's a good idea to restart your Mac every day to help prevent memory fragmentation and increase system stability. Systems that are left on 24 hours a day should be restarted as well.

Wrapping Up

Troubleshooting the Mac OS is fairly easy when compared to other operating systems, but a lot of good this observation will do if you're the one trying to resolve a problem! If you do have a problem, keep in mind the most common problems and their solutions discussed in this chapter, including the software tools that are available from Apple and others. Also, don't underestimate the effectiveness of preventative maintenance, and above all else, *back up your data on a regular basis*. Your number *will* come up one of these days!

In the next section, we'll look at how to use your Mac on a variety of networks, starting with Apple's built-in File Sharing capability.

Mac OS 8.6

PART III

Networking

17

File Sharing

File Sharing is one of the many areas in which the Macintosh was ahead of its time when it was introduced in 1984. The first Macintosh supported the AppleTalk networking protocol, allowing any number of Macintosh computers to be strung together with inexpensive telephone cable to form what is known as a peer-to-peer network. Back then, however, sharing word processing documents was probably the most compelling reason to create a Macintosh network.

Today, AppleTalk networking is still provided on every Macintosh, and the number of good reasons for putting a Mac on a network has increased. AppleTalk is no longer the preferred networking protocol for the Mac, however; TCP/IP, Ethernet, and Fast Ethernet networks are available as well. You might want to put your Macintosh on a network for these three main reasons:

- *Computer-to-computer communications*—Networked Macs can use email and messaging systems, and can transfer files directly from one computer to another.

- *Shared peripherals*—Laser printers, color printers, slide recorders, high-speed modems, fax/modems, and scanners are all expensive peripheral devices that can be shared among networked Macintoshes.

- *Centralized or distributed file servers*—Storing large amounts of data on file servers provides an easy way to share information, allows a number of people to participate in workgroup projects, and reduces the data storage requirements of individual users. File Sharing, Apple's version of peer-to-peer networking over AppleTalk, is the way that most Macs communicate over a network, although Macs can network other ways as well using the AppleShare Filing Protocol (AFP).

It's in this last category that earlier versions of the Mac OS first provided the abilities that were greatly expanded in later generations of the operating systems. In Mac OS 8.6, users can share files from their hard drives and other storage devices, such as Zip or SyQuest drives, with other computers on the network, as well as access files being shared by these other computers. This capability is called File Sharing. In this chapter, you'll learn the basics of File Sharing and how to use it to allow others to access your files. The next chapter discusses additional File Sharing features, including accessing the data shared by other Macs and ways you can connect to your own Macintosh from another computer on your network using the Chooser and the Network Browser.

What Is File Sharing?

File Sharing is a feature of the Mac OS that lets you designate up to 10 folders and volumes on your computer to be shared with other computers on your network. For each shared folder or volume, you can assign access privileges limiting the use of your shared data to only the users you specify. Figure 17.1 shows the first of three File Sharing strategies: sharing the contents of your computer with other users.

Figure 17.1 File Sharing lets you share your data with others.

In the second File Sharing strategy, shown in Figure 17.2, you can access folders and volumes other Macintoshes are sharing—provided you've been granted access privileges. Once accessed, folders and volumes from other Macs appear on your desktop. Now you can use them as if they were your own.

Figure 17.2 File Sharing lets you access data from other computers.

In networking parlance, when your computer is sharing files, it's acting as a server; when it's accessing files from another computer, it's acting as a client. File Sharing allows every user on a Macintosh network to become a server, a client, or both, as in Figure 17.3.

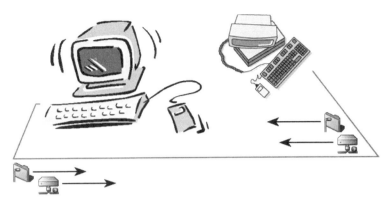

Figure 17.3 Using File Sharing, every Mac on the network can be both server and client.

Sharing data from your Macintosh and accessing data shared by others on your network can increase your capabilities and productivity in many ways. Here are some examples of resources that can be shared:

➤ *Central libraries*—Reference files such as clip art, templates (or stationery), and historical records can be kept in one location and shared with the entire network.

➤ *Drop-box folders that send and receive files*—Each network user can define an electronic "Out box" and "In box." By assigning access privileges, you can use an Out box to let everyone add files (but not look at the folder's contents), and an In box to let users "pick up" the files they need (but not add any files).

➤ *Shared edition files that create living "workgroup" documents*—The Edition Manager features (described in Chapter 12), together with File Sharing, give network users access to edition files created by many users and stored on several hard drives.

The Limits Of File Sharing

Although the capabilities of File Sharing are impressive, it's important to understand that File Sharing is only a "personal" version of AppleShare IP or Mac OS X Server, Apple's dedicated file server software that uses TCP/IP as well as AppleTalk. AppleShare IP accommodates hundreds of shared items and allows Windows-based computers to connect as well. Mac OS X Server provides the same level of access as well. For a small number of Macs, File Sharing is sufficient, whereas larger or more heavily used networks should utilize a combination of AppleShare IP and

File Sharing. In these situations, File Sharing will supplement AppleShare IP, not replace it.

Here are a few considerations about using File Sharing that you might consider:

- *Administration requirements*—As you'll see later, the administrative requirements of sharing files are not incidental. When many users need frequent access to numerous files and folders, centralized File Sharing administration (provided by central file servers such as AppleShare) is usually more efficient than distributed administration.

- *Security risks*—To avoid the burden of administrative requirements, users often neglect security issues, leaving confidential or sensitive data unprotected and available to anyone on the network. This is less likely to occur on centralized, professionally managed file servers.

- *Performance degradation*—Even with a very fast processor and a very fast hard drive, File Sharing takes a noticeable toll on computer performance. Macintoshes or peripherals that aren't particularly speedy to begin with make the problem even worse. The benefits outweigh the inconveniences for casual or infrequent users. For frequent uses, however, continually having to deal with long delays can be annoying and counterproductive. A centralized server with resources dedicated to the burdens of serving network users is the practical alternative in these circumstances.

- *Access limitations*—File Sharing can serve only 10 folders or volumes from one Macintosh at a time, and support only 50 logged-on users at one time (and that would be pushing it) with a maximum of 15 to 20 concurrent users. In many cases, these constraints are too restrictive. Furthermore, the sharing Macintoshes must be left on all the time to ensure that files are always available on the network.

A File Sharing Quick Tour

File Sharing's capabilities are powerful and therefore require more preparation and attention than most other Mac OS 8.6 features. Here are the steps necessary to use File Sharing:

1. *Prepare your Macintosh*—This includes physically connecting to a network, installing the File Sharing files, and activating AppleTalk.

2. *Start File Sharing*—The File Sharing Control Panel provides configuration information and the master switch. In Mac OS 8.6 you can start (and stop) File Sharing using one of the AppleScripts found in the Automated Tasks folder under your Apple menu. If you have the Control Strip active on your desktop (for PowerBook as well as desktop users), you'll find a File Sharing switch as one of the modules there.

3. *Configure Users & Groups*—Users must be defined and user preferences and access privileges must be set in the Users & Groups Control Panel. In most situations, user groups will also require definition. You'll need to specify what access privileges your Macintosh will enforce when network "guests" log on.

4. *Specify folders/volumes to share*—To share any folder or volume, the Sharing command must be applied and sharing options set.

5. *Connect with others using File Sharing*—In order to access folders and volumes being shared by others, the Chooser or Network Browser may be used to log on to other computers (Mac, Windows, or Unix).

6. *Use the File Sharing Activity Monitor to track access to your shared data*—The Activity Monitor within the File Sharing Control Panel constantly updates you on who's accessing what on your computer.

The remainder of this chapter looks in detail at the first four of these steps. The last two are covered in Chapter 18.

Preparing For File Sharing

File Sharing success depends on correctly connecting your Macintoshes and installing network drivers. The simplest and most common Macintosh networking scheme uses Ethernet connections, although LocalTalk or PhoneNet-style connectors and cabling are still in use as well. However, sophisticated networks require Ethernet or Fast Ethernet (or even TokenRing) adapters via NuBus or PCI slots. Almost all PowerMacs come equipped with built-in Ethernet or Fast Ethernet ports; a few PowerBooks do not have Ethernet, but it can always be added using a PCMCIA card or internal adapter. When the network is physically connected, network availability and the presence of network software drivers must be verified by opening the AppleTalk Control Panel, which displays the available network drivers (shown in Figure 17.4).

Figure 17.4 The AppleTalk Control Panel displays the available network drivers in the Connect via section.

Mac OS 8.6

After verifying that network drivers are recognized by the Mac OS, open the AppleTalk Control Panel and choose Options to confirm that AppleTalk is active, or open the Chooser. If your network is divided into zones, the Chooser also displays a list of available AppleTalk zones. Figure 17.5 shows the Chooser with and without zones.

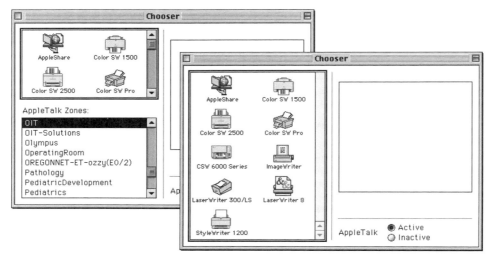

Figure 17.5 The Chooser turns on AppleTalk and selects network zones.

Starting File Sharing

Once your network is ready to be accessed, you can configure and turn on File Sharing with the File Sharing Control Panel located in your Control Panels folder. The File Sharing Control Panel (shown in Figure 17.6) lets you define your

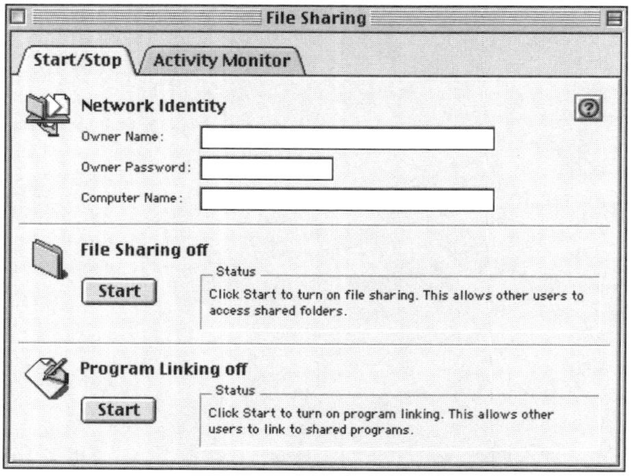

Figure 17.6 The File Sharing Control Panel.

"network identity," turn File Sharing on and off, start and stop Program Linking, and monitor File Sharing activity.

The File Sharing Control Panel hasn't changed much since Mac OS 8. One feature that's new with OS 8.6 is that once you enter an Owner Name or Computer Name, the other fields in the Control Panel cannot be left blank. The options in the Start/Stop portion of the File Sharing Control Panel include:

➤ *Owner Name*—The name of the primary user of a computer. Any name of up to 32 characters is acceptable, and you can change the Owner Name at any time.

➤ *Owner Password*—A security gate, allowing you as owner to access this Macintosh's entire hard drive from anywhere on the network when File Sharing is turned on. It also allows you to access any shared folders or volumes. (By default, you're assigned ownership of all folders and volumes shared by your Macintosh. You can then assign this ownership to others, if you wish, as described in "Configuring User Preferences" later in this chapter.) The password is not case-sensitive and is limited to eight characters in length.

Note that this password can be changed at any time, and it's not necessary to know the old password to define a new one. This means you don't have to worry about forgetting your password. This may seem like a breach of security—and it is. File Sharing controls only remote user access to your Macintosh; it doesn't apply to anyone who sits down at your Mac's keyboard. Unfortunately, the ability to change the password at any time is consistent with the Mac's total lack of local security.

➤ *The Computer Name*—The name that other network users see when looking at your Macintosh from the network. It appears in the Chooser when they click on the AppleShare icon, and when they print to network printers. This computer name is the equivalent of the Chooser name used in earlier system software versions.

➤ *File Sharing (Start/Stop)*—The master control switch. When the Start button is clicked, File Sharing is turned on and the folders and volumes on your Macintosh are available to the network, based on the access privileges assigned to them. As File Sharing starts, the message in the Status area documents the startup process (see Figure 17.7).

➤ *Program Linking (Start/Stop)*—This function allows remote users to control programs residing on your Macintosh with interapplication communication (IAC) commands.

Once File Sharing is running, the Start button becomes the Stop button. When you click on the Stop button, a new dialog box asks you how many minutes remain

458 Chapter 17

Figure 17.7 Click the Start button to start File Sharing; a status message will document the progress of File Sharing.

until file sharing is turned off. Enter a number between 0 (for immediate shutdown) and 999 (for delayed action). Figure 17.8 illustrates this action.

After you click OK in this dialog box, the Status message tells you how many minutes remain before File Sharing is turned off, as shown in Figure 17.9. As turn-off time approaches, other users accessing your Macintosh files are warned of impending shutdown to give them an opportunity to save their work and release any volumes or folders they're using. Regardless of whether users have released your

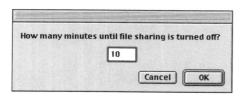

Figure 17.8 The Shut Down dialog box.

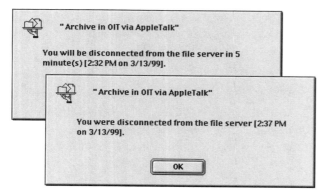

Figure 17.9 Clients are warned before a File Sharing server closes and after it has closed down.

Mac OS 8.6

files, contact with your Macintosh is terminated immediately. The Mac simply extends the courtesy of warning other users so they won't lose work or be abruptly interrupted. If you choose the 0 minutes option, cutoff will occur without warning. (To check the number of users connected to your Mac, refer to the Activity Monitor window in the File Sharing Control Panel, as described in "Monitoring File Sharing" later in this chapter.)

When File Sharing is on and users are connected to your Macintosh, the Shut Down or Restart command brings up the Alert dialog box shown in Figure 17.10. Again, be sure to give your network users enough time to save their work before shutting down. If possible, cancel the Shut Down or Restart and leave your Macintosh running so that network use can continue.

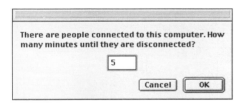

Figure 17.10 The alert that appears at Restart or Shut Down.

As a convenience, Mac OS 8.6 gives you two other places where you can turn File Sharing on and off. In the Automated Tasks submenu of the Apple menu, you'll find two commands (AppleScripts, really): one called Start File Sharing, the other called Stop File Sharing. These commands have the same results as clicking the Start and Stop button in the Sharing Setup dialog box. If you have the Control Strip installed, one of the panels is for controlling File Sharing, as shown in Figure 17.11. It works similarly.

Figure 17.11 The File Sharing section of the Control Strip.

Registering Users & Groups

Before making your Macintosh folders and/or volumes available to other network users via File Sharing, you must decide who may and may not share your files. You may want to share your files with every user on your network, but it's more likely that you'll want to restrict access to some or all of your shared files.

To designate access, open the Users & Groups Control Panel (shown in Figure 17.12). This Control Panel displays a window containing one icon for each user and one icon for each group registered to access your Macintosh, in addition to a guest icon and an icon for you, the Macintosh owner.

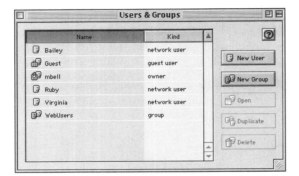

Figure 17.12 The Users & Groups Control Panel.

Of course, when you open the Users & Groups Control Panel for the first time, no users or groups are yet defined; therefore, only the guest and Macintosh owner icons will appear.

Via the Users & Groups Control Panel, you can grant access to four categories of users:

➤ *Registered Users*—These are specific users whom you want to have access to your shared folders or volumes. Registered users are given access to your data as individuals or as members of a defined group.

➤ *Groups*—A group is a collection of designated registered users. Individual registered users can be included in any number of groups.

➤ *Guests*—Any non-registered user on your network can attempt to log on to your shared folders or volumes as a guest. You determine whether you want a guest to have access to your data.

➤ *Macintosh Owner*—As the owner, you can give yourself special remote abilities and access privileges to your computer.

In addition to the definitions and privileges mentioned so far, the Sharing dialog box provides additional security safeguards. This dialog box specifies Registered Users and Groups who have access privileges to particular folders and volumes (see Figure 17.13). (More on the Sharing dialog box in "Sharing Folders Or Volumes" later in this chapter.)

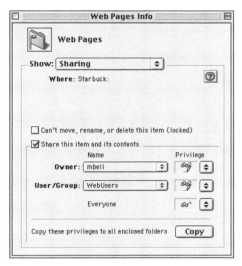

Figure 17.13 Registered Users and Groups are assigned access privileges via the Sharing portion of the Get Info window.

Creating New Users

To designate a new user, open the Users & Groups Control Panel and choose the New User button, or choose New User from the File menu (see Figure 17.14). This creates a new "New User" registered user in the Users & Groups window and opens the File Sharing options window (we'll discuss File Sharing options in the section entitled "Configuring User Preferences"). Enter the name of the user you want this icon to represent. You can use the person's real name, a user name such as "first initial+last name," or any other user name you care to dream up.

Figure 17.14 The File menu provides the New User and New Group commands.

Up to 100 registered users can be defined, but Apple recommends staying under 50. If more than 50 people need regular access to certain shared folders or volumes, consider moving your data to a dedicated AppleShare IP server or allowing all guests access to that data. (There is no limit to the number of guests who can access your Macintosh, only to the number of registered users.)

You don't need to register users individually unless you want to limit access privileges. If you plan to allow everyone on the network to see and change your data, they can all log on as guests. If not, you should define Users & Groups.

Configuring User Preferences

After registering a new user, or to alter a user's password or preferences, click on the user's name in the Users & Groups Control Panel to open the File Sharing options window, as shown in Figure 17.15. This dialog box sets the user's password and allows (or disallows) the user to connect via File Sharing or Program Linking. This dialog box also displays a list of all groups in which the user is included (you can change or modify group memberships from this dialog box by double-clicking the group name, which opens the group properties window).

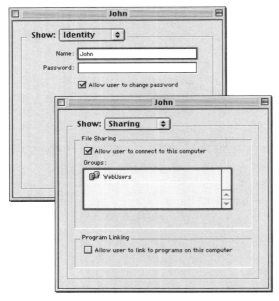

Figure 17.15 The User Preferences dialog box.

Let's look at the options under the pop-up menu "Identity" in this dialog box:

▶ *User Password*—In order to access your data from another Macintosh on the network, a username and, in most cases, a password must be entered. By default, the user has no password, and logs on by simply entering the username and leaving the password option blank. Unfortunately, this doesn't provide much assurance that the user who's logging on is supposed to have network access.

To add a password, type one into the User Password option box. For security, bullets will appear instead of characters once the cursor has left the Password field.

When you add or change a user password, you must notify the user, for obvious reasons. Another approach is to allow the user to define his or her own password when logging on for the first time. The user can change the password periodically after that. This process is enabled with the Allow User to Change Password option, described below. A variation would be to start with an obvious password like the user's first name or *changeme*, then encourage the user to change it at the first opportunity.

You can change any user password at any time. For example, if a user forgets his or her password, it's impossible for you to find it; you must "change" it to resolve this problem. Changing a password also lets you bar a particular user's access until you provide a new password.

Avoid using obvious passwords like names, zodiac signs, and birthstones. Change your passwords regularly.

➤ *Allow User to Change Password*—This option allows registered users to change their passwords using the Change Password button that appears in the Chooser as they log on to your Macintosh. In most cases, this option should be selected; changing user passwords frequently increases the security of your data. Of course, because you as the Owner can always change passwords directly in this dialog box, you lose no privileges by allowing users this option.

Select the pop-up menu "Identity" and select "Sharing" for these options:

➤ *Allow User to Connect*—This check box is the "personal" master switch that makes it possible for a specific user to connect as a registered user (they still may be able to connect as a guest). This option is on by default, but you may want to turn it off occasionally. Using this option to revoke access privileges is less drastic than deleting the user, which makes later reinstatement more difficult.

➤ *Program Linking*—Users can take advantage of this option if the feature is turned on in the File Sharing Control Panel.

Creating And Working With Groups

Because a network comprises many individual users, assigning access privileges to each user for each item would be a very tedious job. To avoid this, File Sharing lets you define groups, add registered users to these groups, and then assign access privileges that apply to all group members.

New Groups are created by selecting the New Group button while the Users & Groups Control Panel is open. This action places a new "New Group" group icon in the Users & Groups window and launches the Group Preferences dialog box. Enter the name of the group you want this icon to represent (descriptive names are

Mac OS 8.6

best). Registered users never see the group names you assign, nor do they need to know which groups they're assigned to.

You can't make a guest icon a member of any group, but you can add yourself as the Macintosh Owner to any group. Why would you want to do this? If you assign ownership of folders or volumes to another user or group, you won't have network access to that folder unless you're a member of a group that has access privileges—or if you use the Allow User to See Entire Volume option in your Owner Preferences (described later).

To add registered users to the group, drag their icons onto the group icon and release them. Or you can double-click on the group icon to open the group's window and then drag user icons directly into this window. You can also combine groups by dragging one group icon over another. Adding a user to a group does not remove the user icon from the main Users & Groups window. You can drag a single user icon into any number of groups. To determine which groups a user is part of, double-click the registered user's icon and refer to the list in the User Preferences dialog box. See Figure 17.16.

Figure 17.16 A defined group containing five registered users.

To remove a user from a group, open the group window, select the user's icon, and choose the File menu's Remove command or press the Delete key. This deletes the user from the group; it does not remove the user entirely or remove the user from any other groups he or she belongs to. Similarly, you can delete an entire group by selecting the group and choosing the File menu's Remove command, which removes the group but does not affect any group member individually.

Configuring Guest Preferences

Occasionally you may want to share files with someone on your network who isn't a registered user. This is made possible by File Sharing's support of guests. A single guest icon, which is automatically included in the Users & Groups Control Panel, is used to control access to your shared data for all non-registered users. The guest icon cannot be deleted. Double-clicking on the guest icon brings up the Guest Preferences dialog box, shown in Figure 17.17.

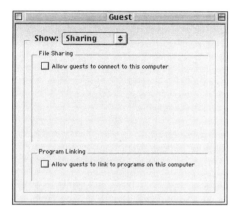

Figure 17.17 The Guest Preferences dialog box.

In this window, the Sharing pop-up menu lists only two options:

▶ *Allow Guests to Connect to This Computer*—This option is the master switch that allows guests to log on to your Macintosh. When this option is deselected, network users can't log on to your Macintosh as guests.

Allowing guests to log on does not automatically give them access to data. Guests can access folders and volumes based only on the "Everyone" access privileges in the Sharing dialog box, as described later in this chapter. If no folders or volumes are available to Everyone, guests who attempt to log on will find no data available.

▶ *Allow Guests to Link to Programs on This Computer*—Program Linking, the ability to use applications located on computers other than your own, is used by the Mac OS's IAC feature. Guests can link to your programs only if you've selected this option.

Configuring Owner Preferences

The preferences you set for yourself, the Macintosh Owner, affect the way you can access your Macintosh from elsewhere on the network. They have no effect on what you can do directly from your keyboard. The Macintosh Owner icon is created automatically and assigned the Macintosh Owner Name as designated in the Sharing Setup Control Panel. The Owner icon appears with the label "Owner" in the Users & Groups window. Double-clicking on this icon opens the Macintosh Owner Preferences dialog box shown in Figure 17.18.

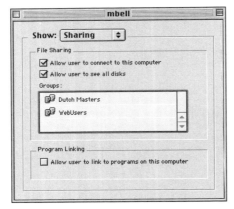

Figure 17.18 The Macintosh Owner Preferences dialog box.

The options in this dialog box are the same as those described previously for any registered user, with the exception of the Allow User to See All Disks option. This option lets you access entire volumes on your Macintosh from anywhere on the network at any time—even when the volumes have not been specifically shared via the Sharing command. When accessing volumes in this way, you have full access privileges to all files, folders, and applications.

> **TIP**
> This feature is very powerful—and potentially dangerous. It allows you to work on your Macintosh, or access any data stored on your Macintosh, from any Mac on the network just as if you were at your own keyboard. The danger is that anyone else who knows your Owner Name and password could gain the same access.

If you don't need the Allow User to See All Disks feature, leave it deselected. If you decide to use this option, be very discreet with your password and be sure to change it frequently. If you won't be using this feature over an extended period of time, temporarily deselect it. Of course, the possibility exists that someone might sit down at your Macintosh keyboard and access your data or change your password, then remotely access your Mac. File Sharing should not lull you into a false sense of security. If you have good reason to believe this could happen, other security measures should be taken.

File Sharing   467

Sharing Folders Or Volumes

For any folder or volume to be shared with others on your network, you must initiate sharing and specify access privileges with the Sharing command. Any mounted volume—including hard disks, hard disk partitions, removable cartridges, CD-ROMs, and any folder on any mounted volume—can be shared. Floppy disks and folders on floppy disks cannot.

To initiate sharing, select the folder or volume and:

➤ Choose the Sharing command from the Get Info submenu of the File menu

➤ Activate the contextual menu and select Get Info|Sharing

➤ Press Command+I and select the Sharing portion of the Get Info window that appears

Each of these actions brings up the Sharing dialog box (shown in Figure 17.19). This dialog box allows you to turn on Sharing and assign the access privileges for this item. Access privileges, as you learned earlier, determine who can see the folders and volumes, who can see the files inside those folders and volumes, and who can make changes to existing files or store new files. (We'll talk more about access privileges in the "Access Privileges" section, later in this chapter.)

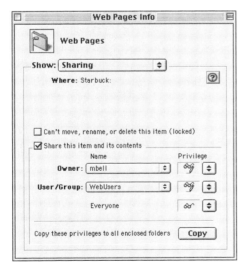

Figure 17.19   A Sharing dialog box.

The Sharing dialog box presents a number of important options:

➤ *Can't Move, Rename, or Delete This Item*—This option gives you a safety net to ensure that the folder or volume you share is not moved, renamed, or deleted

Mac OS 8.6

by any network user—including the owner. It's a good idea to select this option in all cases, unless you know that repositioning, renaming, or deleting the item will be necessary. Checking this box will prevent accidental changes with unpleasant results.

- *Share This Item and Its Contents*—This check box is the master switch that turns Sharing on or off for the selected folder or volume and the contents of that folder or volume. Until this option is selected, all other options in this dialog box are dimmed.

- *Owner*—This option specifies the owner of the selected folder or volume and the owner's access privileges. In most cases, you (as the Macintosh owner) will remain the owner of shared folders and volumes.

  By way of the pop-up menu, you can designate any other registered user as the owner of the selected folder or volume. The assignee can then reset access privileges for the item. Your access to the selected folder or volume from another Macintosh on the network is then dependent on your inclusion in the User/Group option (discussed in the following subsection). Of course, your access to the folder or volume from your own Macintosh will not be affected; the options in the Sharing dialog box affect only network access.

  Once an owner has been specified, use the check boxes to assign access privileges. (We'll discuss available access privileges and their use in the "Access Privileges" section later in this chapter.)

- *User/Group*—Via the pop-up menu, this option grants one user or one group access to the selected folder or volume and defines the access privileges available to this user or group. In many ways, this is the most important Sharing option. It usually designates the person or group of users who will most frequently access the shared data. (See the "Access Privileges" section of this chapter for the ways this feature can be utilized, including bulletin boards, drop boxes, read-only filing systems, and true workgroup File Sharing and storage systems.)

- *Everyone*—This option specifies access privileges granted to guest users on your Macintosh. As mentioned before, anyone on your network can log on to your Mac as a guest—providing you've specified that Guest logins are permitted. In that case, the "Everyone" option determines which volumes and folders they can access.

- *Copy These Privileges to All Enclosed Folders*—When you share a folder or volume, all enclosed folders are also automatically accessible to users with access privileges. You cannot "unshare" a folder that's enclosed in a shared folder or on a shared volume, but you can change the access privileges of an enclosed folder so that they don't match those of the enclosing folder. This option also can reset the access privileges of the enclosed folders so they match those of the currently selected folder or volume. Confused?

For example, a folder called Web Pages is shared, with full access privileges by everyone belonging to the group named Dutch Masters. Enclosed in the Web Pages folder is a folder called Sample Files & Templates. We want to limit access to this folder (Sample Files & Templates) so that only members of the group named WebUsers can access it. To do this, after configuring the Sharing command for the Web Pages folder, select the Sample Files & Templates folder and choose the Sharing command again. Now, access privileges must be changed to limit access to the WebUsers group members only. Figure 17.20 displays the Sharing dialog box for the Web Pages folder and the Sample Files & Templates folder.

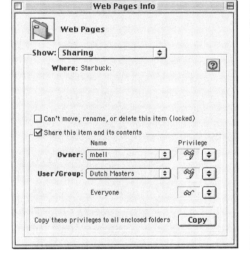

Figure 17.20 The Sharing dialog box for a parent and child folder.

Notice that the Share This Item and Its Contents option has been replaced in the Sample Files & Templates folder dialog box with a Use Enclosing Folder's Privileges option. This occurs because the Sample Files & Templates folder is inside a folder that is already shared. By default, this new option is selected and its access privileges match those specified for the enclosing Web Pages folder. Deselecting the Use Enclosing Folder's Privileges option makes it possible to change the access privileges to allow only the owner and members of the Web-Users group to access this particular subfolder in the Web Pages folder (see Figure 17.21).

After making any changes to these options, click the close box in the title bar to close the dialog box and apply these options to the selected item. If you've made

Mac OS 8.6

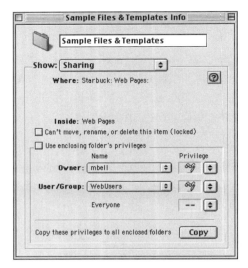

Figure 17.21   Configuring File Sharing privileges for a group of users.

changes to the item's ownership, dialog boxes will ask you to confirm or cancel the changes requested. A dialog box will also appear if you chose the Copy These Privileges to All Enclosed Folders option.

Icons Of Shared Items

The Mac OS uses custom folder icons to indicate whether a folder is shared, and if it is shared, whether any users are currently logged in. This feature helps owners determine whether or not users are accessing their computers. For example, Figure 17.22 shows a folder icon and its changes. After you have specified and implemented Sharing options, the shared folder's icon will modify itself, confirming the folder's Sharing status.

Figure 17.22   A folder as it appears before Sharing (left), after Sharing (center), and when users are connected (right).

Unsharing

Shared items can be made unavailable to network users by two methods: you can turn File Sharing off completely, or you can turn File Sharing off for individual folders and volumes. Of course, turning off your Mac or disconnecting its network cables will also do the trick!

To turn File Sharing off completely, open the File Sharing Control Panel and click the File Sharing Stop button, as described earlier. When File Sharing is turned off, the settings and access privileges that you set with the Sharing command are retained for all shared folders and volumes, and will go back into effect when File Sharing is turned on again.

To turn off the Sharing of a particular folder or volume only, select the appropriate folder or volume, choose the Sharing command, and deselect the Share This Item and Its Contents option. When you close the Sharing dialog box, the selected folder or volume will become unavailable for network access. (An Alert dialog box like the one shown in Figure 17.23 will appear if users are currently accessing the shared item.) Note that all of an item's access privilege settings are lost when Sharing is turned off for that particular folder or volume; you'll have to reset the settings the next time the item is shared.

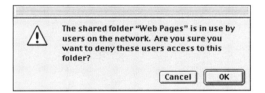

Figure 17.23 Unsharing with users.

An alternative to turning off File Sharing either completely or for particular folders or volumes does exist: you can change the Allow User to Connect and Allow Guest to Connect options in the user icons found in the Users & Groups Control Panel. Although this method is not generally recommended, it does allow access privilege settings to remain in force while temporarily making it impossible for some or all users to connect.

Access Privileges

Shared folders, volumes, and folders enclosed within shared folders and volumes are available to other network users according to access privilege settings you apply in the Sharing dialog box. These privileges, along with users and groups designated in the Users & Groups Control Panel, are the keys to controlling File Sharing.

As shown in Figure 17.24, the three access privilege options are assigned to three different users or groups. Your choice of option settings and combinations determines how network users can access and modify your shared data and storage space.

Figure 17.24 The access privilege options.

Let's look at these access privileges, the users and groups they can be assigned to, and the results of applying them in different combinations, starting with the fewest privileges offered to the most users:

➤ *None*—With no privileges specified, a shared folder is inaccessible to users. If that folder is enclosed within another folder to which a user has at least read access, the folder lacking any privileges will look like the one shown in the top portion of Figure 17.25. If the folder is a share point (tech-speak for a shared folder or volume) that is not contained within a shared folder or volume, it will appear in the Chooser as nonselectable, as in the lower portion of Figure 17.25.

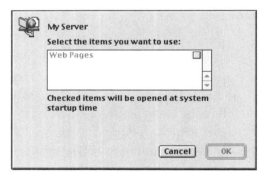

Figure 17.25 A shared folder with no privileges as seen in the Finder (top) from the Chooser (bottom).

➤ *Write Only (Drop Box)*—This privilege hides the contents of folders from a specified user or group—users don't even know what, if anything, is inside this type of folder (selecting Get Info will reveal 0K of contents). Users can place files in the shared folder but only the owner can see and manage its contents. When the Write Only option is selected, the folder icon changes to that shown in Figure 17.26.

Figure 17.26 A shared folder with Write Only privileges (drop box).

Mac OS 8.6

▶ *Read Only*—This option limits a user to viewing the contents of the folder. No changes can be made within the shared item. When the Read Only option is selected, an icon appears in the upper-left corner of the title bars of all windows accessed via File Sharing to let the user know that the folder or volume is write protected (see Figure 17.27). In addition to not being able to write to this folder, users are unable to edit files and folders, or delete them.

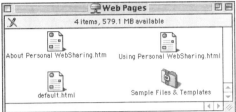

Figure 17.27 A shared folder with Read Only privileges.

▶ *Read & Write*—When the Read & Write privilege is set, the user can save new files, change existing files, and create new folders. He or she enjoys almost unlimited access to the folder and its contents. The folder will have no special icons, as in Figure 17.28.

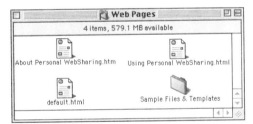

Figure 17.28 A shared folder with Read & Write privileges.

The last three privilege options described above can be assigned individually to users in three categories:

▶ *Owner*—The owner of a folder or volume is the individual or group who can change the access privileges of that folder or volume while accessing it over the network. The person who creates a folder is automatically the owner of it, so by default you're the owner of the folders and volumes on your Macintosh. When a user creates new folders in shared folders or volumes, however, that user becomes the owner of the new folders.

Using the pop-up menu, the owner can be designated as any user or group. Selecting the *<Any User>* option gives any guest who accesses the folder or volume full owner privileges (including the right to reassign access privileges).

When setting access privileges on remote volumes, the Owner pop-up menu does not appear and the Owner Name must be entered manually.

➤ *User/Group*—The User/Group category assigns access privileges to a specific user or group. When sharing folders or volumes, select the desired User/Group from the pop-up menu of all registered users and groups. When setting access privileges on remote volumes, the User/Group pop-up menu does not appear and the Owner Name must be entered manually.

➤ *Everyone*—The Everyone category grants access privileges to all guests who connect to the Macintosh that contains the selected folder or volume. Of course, in order for guests to log on, the Allow Guests to Connect option must be set in the Users & Groups Control Panel.

Access Privilege Strategies

This elaborate matrix of categories and access privilege levels allows precise control over the way shared files can be used. Several common ways of using access privileges are as follows:

➤ *Create an Inbox folder*—The key aspect of an Inbox is that people can drop items into the folder but can't see what's already there or delete items from the folder. This is accomplished by granting write only privileges to everyone, an individual, or a group of users, as shown in Figure 17.29.

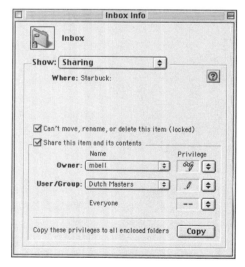

Figure 17.29 A set of access privileges that defines an Inbox.

➤ *Create an Outbox folder*—The opposite of an Inbox, an Outbox allows users to see files and folders, but not to add or delete items. This limited access is designated by granting read only access to an individual, a group, or to everyone, as in Figure 17.30.

▶ *Provide a workgroup area*—Creating a folder with several subfolders for access by groups working on related projects is a common way to utilize access privileges. For example, you can create a folder to which the members of the "Marketing" group have some privileges, whereas members of the "Sales" team have different privileges. An additional folder might contain documents that are readable, but not writable, by everyone, as in Figure 17.31.

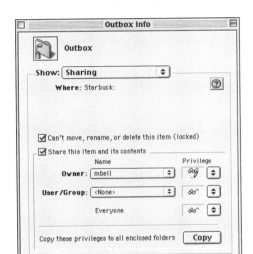

Figure 17.30 A set of access privileges that defines an Outbox.

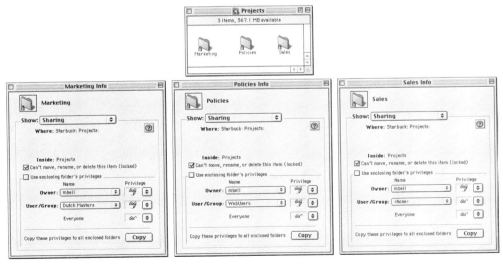

Figure 17.31 Privileges for several folders in a workgroup-style File Sharing arrangement.

The key, however, is to create a parent folder for all the workgroup's subfolders, with read-only access granted to all users of the parent folder. This prevents users from disturbing the parent folder (called Projects in this example) while providing different levels of access for members of various groups working on a project. Figure 17.32 shows how such a folder might be configured in conjunction with File Sharing.

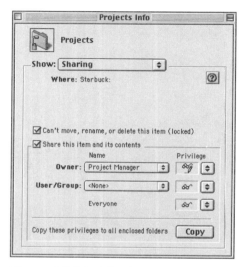

Figure 17.32 The key to creating a workgroup environment is configuring File Sharing access to a parent folder.

Monitoring File Sharing

The File Sharing Control Panel gives you information about the items shared, the users connected to your computer, and the activities of these users. Open the File Sharing Control Panel, select the Activity Monitor tab, and the dialog box in Figure 17.33 appears.

The first item in this Control Panel is the File Sharing Activity Monitor. This gauge fluctuates with the demands on your computer system as connected users access your Macintosh. When the demand is high, the local operation of your Macintosh slows. If slowdowns caused by remote users are a persistent problem, you may need to limit the access of registered users and guests by reducing the amount of shared data you make available. Alternatively, you can shift some shared data to dedicated AppleShare file servers.

The window labeled Connected Users lists network users currently connected to your Macintosh. You can disconnect any user by selecting the user's name from this

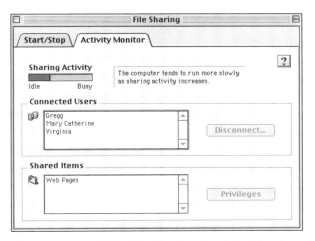

Figure 17.33 The File Sharing Activity Monitor dialog box.

list and clicking the Disconnect button. A dialog box lets you give the selected user warning by delaying disconnection for the number of minutes you select, or you can use 0 minutes and disconnect immediately.

The last window of this dialog box presents a list of the folders and volumes you've shared. To see the access privileges for an item, select one and click the Privileges button; the Sharing dialog box will appear.

Wrapping Up

The power and flexibility of File Sharing will undoubtedly change the way you work on a Macintosh network. File Sharing removes almost all the barriers—physical and psychological—that previously inhibited the flow of data between computers. With File Sharing, you can:

➤ Make any folder or volume on your computer available to anyone connected to your Macintosh network.

➤ Designate who can access the files and folders you share.

➤ Specify privileges extended to each regular user and network guest.

In Chapter 18, you'll see the other side of the File Sharing coin—accessing data shared by other Macs and by centralized file servers.

Mac OS 8.6

Working On A Network

Mac OS users have long known the benefits of computer networking. Shared printers, Mac-to-Mac communication, and remote access to network file servers are commonplace on almost every Mac network. This chapter focuses on using your Macintosh network to access AppleShare and File Sharing volumes, the effects of access privileges, and how you control files stored on remote volumes. We'll also look at using Program Linking to allow applications to talk to each other over a network.

Accessing Network Volumes

As described in Chapter 17, every Mac on your network is capable of sharing up to 10 folders or volumes with other network users. This ability is based on Users & Groups access privilege designations for each Mac that shares network data. In addition, dedicated AppleShare file servers can make an unlimited number of complete volumes available to all network users according to specified access privileges.

Connecting to other computers running the Mac OS for File Sharing and Apple-Share file server access is easy. This section describes how to do it and how to manage shared data.

Before connecting to your file server, make sure that you've selected the appropriate network services. Open the AppleTalk Control Panel and click on the Ethernet, Modem Port, Printer Port, or an alternate means of connectivity. Then proceed with the instructions that follow. If you don't understand the options as they're presented, talk to a network administrator if one is available.

Connecting With The Chooser

The first step in accessing network data is to open the Chooser (in the Apple menu) and click on the AppleShare icon, which is shown in the upper left corner of Figure 18.1.

The available network file servers appear on the right side of the window, and if your network is divided into zones, those zones are listed in the lower left corner of

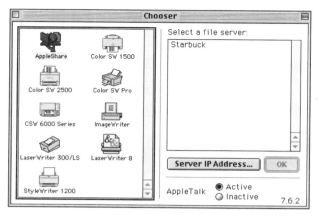

Figure 18.1 The Chooser with a file server listing.

the Chooser. If a zone list appears in your Chooser, select the zone in which your Macintosh is registered. That zone's available server volumes will then appear.

The list of file server names includes both dedicated AppleShare file servers and the Macs on your network that use File Sharing. From the listing, it's not easy to tell which names are AppleShare servers and which are File Sharing Macintoshes. In any case, as a client accessing data over the network, it makes no difference to you whether you're accessing data from a dedicated AppleShare file server or from a File Sharing Macintosh.

When you've located the name of the file server you wish to access, double-click on the filename or click the OK button below the file server list. The Connect dialog box appears (shown in Figure 18.2). This dialog box gives you the option of connecting to the selected file server as a guest or as a registered user.

In order to connect as a registered user, a user icon with your name and password must exist on the AppleShare server or File Sharing Macintosh. This shows that

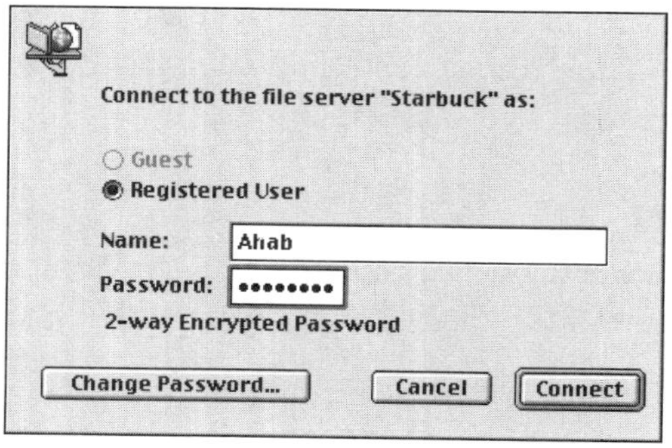

Figure 18.2 The Connect dialog box.

the systems administrator or Macintosh owner has defined your Macintosh as a registered user, as described in Chapter 17.

You can now click the Registered User option. The owner name specified in your Sharing Setup Control Panel will appear as the default in the Name option box. If this is not the name under which you're registered, make the required changes to the Name option. If a password has been assigned, enter it in the Password option. If none is needed, leave the option blank. Then click the OK button.

Connecting as a guest is simpler but may restrict your access privileges. Of course, this is your only option if you're not a registered user. To connect as a guest, click the Guest option and then click the OK button. If the selected file server does not allow guests to connect, the Guest option will be dimmed. In this case, the only way to connect is to contact the Macintosh owner or server administrator and ask to become a registered user.

The final option in the Connect dialog box is the Set Password button, which allows registered users with appropriate access privileges to reset their passwords for a particular file server. Changing your password affects only the currently selected file server, not all servers on which you're a registered user.

Selecting Specific Volumes

After you identify yourself as either Registered User or Guest (and then click the OK button), a list of available volumes on the selected server appears, as shown in Figure 18.3. If an incorrect name or password was entered, an Alert dialog box appears, and you'll be returned to the Connect dialog box.

This dialog box lists all volumes that the selected server is sharing with the network. When accessing File Sharing volumes, it's not possible to differentiate between shared folders and shared volumes, so the term volumes will be used generically. Refer to the Chapter 17 for more information.

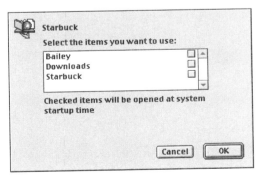

Figure 18.3 Available server listing.

Mac OS 8.6

The names of any volumes you're not allowed to access will be dimmed. You can mount any one non-dimmed volume by double-clicking on the volume name or selecting the volume name and clicking the OK button. You do not have to click in the box next to the volume that you want to select (the auto-mount feature is described below). To mount more than one volume, hold down the Shift key while selecting volume names and then click the OK button.

You can also configure the volume to mount automatically each time you start up your Macintosh by clicking on the check box next to a volume name. You'll have to enter your password manually each time you start your Macintosh because, by default, your password is not stored as part of the automatic-mount process. To simplify the automatic mount (but at the same time reduce security), click the Save My Name and Password option and then double-click the volume name or click the OK button.

After mounting a volume, you're returned to the Connect dialog box. To mount additional volumes from the selected file server, click the OK button again to return to the volume list and repeat the mounting process for another volume.

Remote Volumes And Access Privileges

Any remote volumes you've mounted appear on your Desktop as AppleShare Volume icons (see Figure 18.4) unless they have a custom icon associated with the folder or hard drive, in which case the custom icon will be displayed instead. The AppleShare Volume icon also accompanies these volumes in Open or Save As dialog boxes. These volumes are used in the same way as local volumes (those physically connected to your Mac) except that any restrictions imposed by your access privileges apply. When your Macintosh is communicating with remote volumes, arrows flash just to the left of your Apple menu.

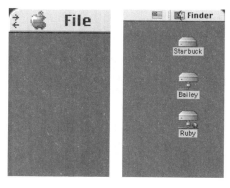

Figure 18.4 A volume icon on the Desktop (right), and the activity arrows that flash while remote volumes are accessed (left).

As described in Chapter 17, access privileges determine whether you can see folders, see files, or make changes to available volumes. The Finder windows for remotely accessed volumes indicate your access privileges by displaying small icons in the upper left corner just below the title bar (shown in Figure 18.5). To see your assigned access privileges, choose the Sharing command from the File menu while the folder is selected or open.

Figure 18.5 The Cannot Write, Cannot See Folders, and Cannot See Files icons.

When you don't have Make Changes privileges, you can't save or copy a file to a volume. In Save dialog boxes, the Save button is dimmed when the selected volume is write-protected in this way; and at the Finder, any attempt to copy or create files will bring up the dialog box shown in Figure 18.6.

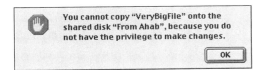

Figure 18.6 A sample Not Enough Access Privileges dialog box.

This same dialog box will appear if you attempt to create a new folder on a volume for which you don't have See Folders privileges.

Use the Sharing command to see the complete access privileges for any volume you're allowed to mount. Select the volume icon and choose the Sharing command from the File menu. If you own the volume, you can change these access privileges. When you create a folder on a shared volume, you're automatically designated as the folder's owner and allowed to use the File menu's Sharing command to reset the access privileges.

A Volume Access Shortcut

Want to avoid this lengthy process every time you mount a networked volume? You can create an alias of the volume icon that appears on your Desktop and store that alias in a convenient spot on your hard drive, perhaps in your Apple Menu Items folder. In fact, you can create a folder full of network volume aliases, as shown in Figure 18.7.

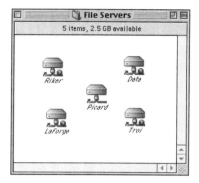

Figure 18.7   Folder of volume aliases.

Double-clicking on the network volume alias icon mounts the volume as soon as you supply any necessary passwords. After you have mounted a network volume, it will appear in the Recent Servers selection under the Apple Menu. This is another method that can save you a lot of time when you frequently use the same network volume.

Disconnecting From Remote Volumes

You can disconnect a mounted network volume by any of three ways:

➤ *Trash the volume*—Simply drag the volume icon into the Trash. Just as this action ejects removable disks, it releases mounted file server volumes.

➤ *Shut Down or Restart*—All mounted volumes are released when you implement the Shut Down or Restart commands.

➤ *Put Away*—The File menu's Put Away command, or its keyboard equivalent, Command+Y, dismounts any selected volumes.

Accessing Your Hard Drive Remotely

When File Sharing is on, you can access your entire hard drive and all volumes currently mounted from anywhere on your network. Just be sure you haven't deselected the Allow User to See Entire Volume option in the Owner Preferences window of the Users & Groups Control Panel. This option is accessed by double-clicking on the user icon that displays your Owner Name.

To reach your hard drive from another Mac on your network, select the Chooser just as you would to log on to any network volume. Locate the name of your Macintosh in the scrolling file server list and double-click on it. After you log in, a new dialog box appears, listing the name of each hard drive connected to your Macintosh. These are not volumes you've shared with the Sharing command; they're complete hard drives as they appear on your Macintosh's Desktop. To mount your drive, double-click on the drive name or select the drive name and click the OK button.

Your hard drive then appears with AppleShare volume icons on the Desktop of the Macintosh you're using. You now have complete access to your drive, including all files and folders, with no limitations based on access privileges. You can create files and folders, delete files, redefine Users & Groups, set File Sharing access privileges, or do anything else you could do if you were sitting at your own Mac keyboard.

When you're finished using a remotely mounted hard drive, you can release it just like you would any other volume—by dragging it to the Trash, using the Put Away command, shutting down, or restarting.

The Network Browser

Mac OS 8.6 uses the Network Browser, introduced in Mac OS 8.5, as a new way to look at remote volumes. The Network Browser is a program, located in your Apple Menu, that enables you to see all the servers and zones available on your network. It does not list network printers, however. Although it seems quite similar to the Chooser, the Network Browser adds many of the useful features of a Web browser. The Network Browser will probably take over the position of the Chooser as the technology becomes more mature. The Network Browser is shown in Figure 18.8.

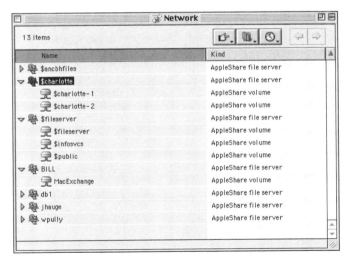

Figure 18.8 The Network Browser.

The Network Browser provides some extra functionality compared to the Chooser, but its most useful feature may actually be a side effect. The Shortcuts, Favorites, and Recent buttons that enable the Network Browser (described in the following text) are available to many applications in their Open and Save dialog boxes. This means that other actions can now be just as easy as connecting to servers. The Macintosh has become very network savvy.

The Network Browser, like the Chooser, allows the user to connect to a server by IP address. To do this, click on the Shortcuts button shown in Figure 18.9 and choose Connect to Server. This will present a dialog box (Figure 18.10) that allows you to specify the address of the server you want to locate. This functionality is very similar to the Open Location command on a Web browser.

Figure 18.9   The Shortcuts button.

Figure 18.10   The Connect to Server dialog box.

The Shortcuts button has another function, in addition to connecting to servers by IP address. Once the Network Browser is pointing to another location, whether it's displaying the contents of a zone or the contents of a server, the Network option of the Shortcuts button will return the browser to its initial state, pointing at the topmost level of the zones. This is somewhat similar to the Home button of various Web browsers.

> **TIP**
>
> A zone refers to a group of servers. It's much easier to navigate 100 servers if they are divided into 10 groups of 10 servers! The actual grouping process usually corresponds roughly to the physical layout of the network. For example, a company might put all of the computers on a single floor into one zone. If your AppleTalk network isn't divided into zones, all the servers will appear in an untitled *default* zone instead.

The Favorites button is another feature borrowed from Web browsers. It allows you to make a list of your favorite servers, the same type of list that the Microsoft browser calls Favorites and the Netscape browser calls Bookmarks. The Favorites button is shown in Figure 18.11. You can add a server to the listing by clicking the Favorites button and selecting Add to Favorites. You can remove a server from the listing by clicking the Favorites button and selecting Remove From Favorites.

Figure 18.11   The Favorites button.

The Recent button, which is shown in Figure 18.12, displays the most recent servers that you've visited. You can usually access this feature in Web browsers by clicking on the Location, or Address, field. This feature is very useful when you're dealing with network volumes that you want to use frequently over a short period of time. In this type of situation, you might not want to bother to put the server in the Favorites menu. The Recent button remembers the servers with no effort.

Figure 18.12   The Recent button.

No browser would be complete without Forward and Backward buttons. They're the same standard buttons that are used in Mac OS Help and in many other places in the operating system (Figure 18.13). They take you back and forth between network servers, following the order in which you visited those servers.

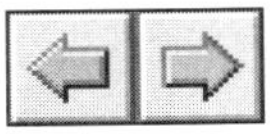

Figure 18.13   The Backward and Forward buttons.

Program Linking

As mentioned in Chapter 12, applications specifically programmed to support AppleEvents can communicate with application programs residing on any AppleShare server or File Sharing volume on the network. If you want programs that can take advantage of Program Linking to communicate with each other across your network, you must specifically enable Program Linking.

The master control for Program Linking is found in the File Sharing Control Panel, as shown in Figure 18.14. The message in the Status area documents the Program Linking start-up process. Once Program Linking is running, the Start button becomes the Stop button.

Mac OS 8.6

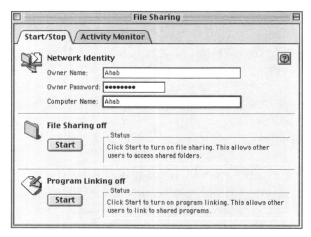

Figure 18.14 The Sharing Setup dialog box provides the master control for Program Linking.

Program Linking must also be enabled in the Macintosh Owner icon found in the Users & Groups Control Panel (the Macintosh Owner icon is different than the others and displays the name entered in the Sharing Setup dialog box; it also says "owner" under the file description). Double-clicking on this icon displays the dialog box shown in Figure 18.15. The Program Linking option, in the lower portion of the dialog box, enables Program Linking. The Owner refers to the person who is administrating the machine. Even when Program Linking has been turned on and enabled in the File Sharing dialog box, it's only available to applications that support it. To initiate Program Linking for an application that supports it, highlight the application you wish to use and then choose the Sharing command from the File menu.

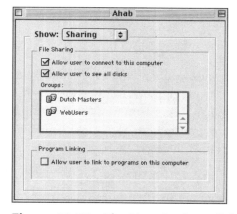

Figure 18.15 The User Options dialog box for the Macintosh owner.

Mac OS 8.6

The Allow Remote Program Linking check box is displayed if the application you selected supports Program Linking. Otherwise, this option will be dimmed. To make the application available for Program Linking, click the check box and then close the Sharing dialog box.

Program Linking is a nice feature, but few people use it today—even most "power users" haven't worked with it much, if at all. Program Linking has two main benefits that you should think about:

➤ If you have a computationally intensive task, such as 3D rendering or visualization studies, you can off-load the assignment to a more powerful computer on your network. The result can be returned to you over the network much more quickly than if you had to process the task on solely your own computer.

➤ Through AppleEvents, Program Linking provides you with additional capabilities that are not resident in your own computer. With Program Linking, you can access a remote copy of the application that has the capabilities you need without having to load the outside program on your own computer. This saves you both money and time—you avoid additional purchases, and you don't have to install the application.

Wrapping Up

Most Macintosh users are initially interested in connecting to a network in order to share peripheral devices such as laser printers or network modems. But networks also make it possible for computers to communicate with each other and for data to be shared between computers or by accessing centralized file servers.

In this chapter you've seen how to make the most of these abilities:

➤ Using the Chooser and Network Browser to select an available File Sharing or AppleShare server.

➤ Mounting volumes and setting up automatic mounting connections.

➤ Working with assigned access privileges.

➤ Setting up and using Program Linking.

Next, in Chapter 19, we will look at how Mac OS 8.6 prepares you to connect to the biggest network in the world—the Internet.

Internet Connectivity

If the big story of the eighties was the advent of affordable personal computers, then the big story of the nineties is the Internet and the World Wide Web. The Net is *the* hot news topic of today, and in just a few years the World Wide Web has grown from a handful of university pages to a massive conglomeration of commercial, personal, governmental, and educational sites. The interconnectivity the Internet provides is a powerful solution for many business, educational, and entertainment needs, and the Web provides an easy-to-use interface to the Internet much in the same way the Mac OS serves as an interface to powerful and complex computer hardware.

If you've ever worked on the Web with other computers, you know that a Mac is the best way to get online. Combining text, sound, images, and movies, the Net is actually a form of multimedia itself, and the Mac OS is a superior multimedia platform. The people at Apple realized this, and have integrated Internet connectivity into the operating system itself. In addition, they included everything you need to connect to the Net as part of the basic installation of Mac OS 8.6.

Each of the major applications and utilities you'll need to master the Internet and the Web is already installed on your machine. Your home or office Mac can even become a Web server. We'll discuss these new applications and server abilities in the next two chapters; for now, let's talk about how the Mac OS can help you get online in just a few minutes.

Getting Connected: ISP Vs. LAN

People connect to the Internet in two basic ways: through an account with an Internet Service Provider (ISP), or through a local area network (LAN). Most people connecting to an ISP at home use a modem, whereas most commercial users connect via a corporate or educational LAN. In fact, many large colleges and universities use their LANs to provide Internet access for their faculty, staff, and students.

> **TIP**
>
> Modem connections make use of two sets of rules, called *protocols*: Transmission Control Protocol and Internet Protocol, commonly referred to as TCP/IP. The first determines how information is split into smaller parts and then reassembled at the destination, while the latter determines the best path for the information to travel.

ISP/Modem Access

Most users who access the Internet from home connect to their ISP with a modem and special software. Once the account is set up correctly, the settings rarely need to be changed.

With old versions of the Mac OS, it was sometimes tricky to get all the settings tweaked, all the software working together, and the modem talking to the ISP. Previous versions of the Mac OS didn't ship with the proper software to connect your Mac to the Internet unless commercial software, such as America Online, was added by a value-added reseller (VAR). This oversight can be attributed, for the most part, to third-party developers of Internet connectivity software who were not interested in corralling a lot of disparate programs.

Fortunately, Mac OS 8.6 allows you to bypass much of this hassle by automating the process of registering with a new ISP or updating your old account.

LAN Access

Many businesses now have networks that connect the various computers throughout an office or group of offices. These networks are called local area networks (LANs). A group of LANs makes up a wide area network (WAN), and when several WANs are connected, they comprise what's referred to as an intranet. LANs, WANs, and intranets use communications software such as email clients, Web browsers, and collaboration software that utilize the same protocols as the Internet.

Connecting to the Internet through a LAN is generally less confusing for novice users than connecting through a modem. The steps that are necessary to connect to the Net by way of a LAN are extraordinarily easy, and most businesses with large networks have full-time computer and networking professionals on staff to take care of all the nasty configuration details. The Mac OS 8.6 has automated the process to such a degree that most people will be able to set themselves up on a LAN with little effort. The automation takes the form of three Internet Assistants.

Internet Assistants

Mac OS 8.6 comes with a suite of helper applications that enable you to get up and running on the Web without even breaking a sweat. Whether you're accessing the Web from home via a modem or from work via a LAN, these helpers will have you surfing in no time. Figure 19.1 shows the programs you're most likely to use to connect to the Internet. They are located in the Internet Setup folder, which is in the Internet Utilities Folder, inside the Internet Folder of your System Folder.

Figure 19.1 The Internet Setup folder contains everything you'll need to connect to the Internet.

The applications you'll use most frequently are:

➤ Internet Setup Assistant

➤ Internet Editor Assistant

➤ ISP Referral Assistant

These assistants were developed by Apple after years of observing the trials and tribulations of users who were trying to connect to the Internet using ISPs and all the major types of modems. Apple developers observed that the worst problems stemmed from a handful of difficult tasks related to configuring your modem hardware to communicate with the Mac OS. The assistants do this for you and make the entire process very easy.

Internet Setup Assistant

Mac OS 8.6 doesn't waste time on formalities. At the end of the setup process, the installer asks you if you want to launch the new Internet Setup Assistant (don't worry—if you want to spend a little time playing around with the new OS first, the assistant will wait for you in the Internet Setups folder). Figure 19.2 shows you what the Internet Setup Assistant looks like when it is launched.

The Internet Setup Assistant is used primarily to set up new accounts or modify old ones; it also provides links to the other two assistants. The assistant's interface

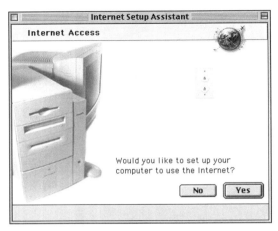

Figure 19.2 The Internet Setup Assistant guides you through the process of setting up Internet connections.

has greatly improved since OS 8—besides being more attractive, the Internet Setup Assistant also functions as a streamlined system, asking a series of questions instead of presenting a giant form for the user to complete. It shields you from information that's irrelevant to you.

Internet Editor Assistant

The Internet Editor Assistant, a component of the Internet Setup Assistant, helps organize the information needed to connect to an ISP. With this assistant, you can collect various telephone numbers and server addresses into set configurations, as shown in Figure 19.3. The top of the Internet Editor Assistant window says

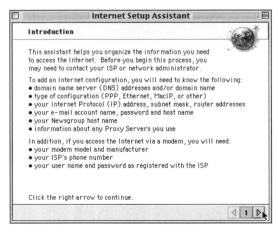

Figure 19.3 The introduction to the Internet Editor Assistant lists what information you will need to configure your setup.

Mac OS 8.6

Internet Setup Assistant, a reminder that the three assistants are all parts of the same configuration tool. Figure 19.4 shows how the Internet Editor Assistant lets you store multiple configurations.

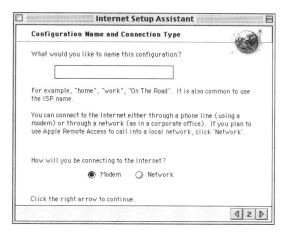

Figure 19.4 The Internet Editor Assistant lets you store different Internet configurations.

For users who have more than one ISP account or who access the Internet with both a modem and a LAN, the ability to store different configurations is a godsend. It allows you to designate a series of settings—one for accessing from home, one for calling in to the work LAN, for example—to choose from when connecting. Figure 19.5 shows some of the available options for adding a new Internet configuration that utilizes a modem. After you complete each window of the configuration

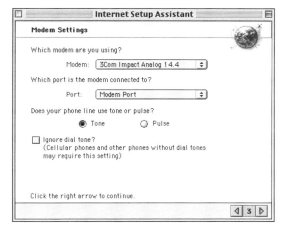

Figure 19.5 A list of some available modem options set up through the Internet Editor Assistant.

Mac OS 8.6

process, the system tries to perform viability tests on the settings you've entered. This gives you a chance to correct most errors right after you make them, and saves you the frustration of going through the entire setup process and then receiving an ambiguous error message at the end.

To create a new Internet configuration file with the Internet Editor Assistant, you'll need some basic information that your LAN administrator or someone at the ISP can provide. You'll need the following information:

➤ *User information*—Your username and password.

➤ *Modem dialing information*—The name and type of modem (for modem connections) and the phone number of your ISP.

➤ *Your IP address*—This is a series of four groups of numbers separated by periods (for example, 122.95.6.789). Most people using modem connections do not have an IP address. If you're on a LAN and an IP address has not been assigned to your Macintosh, you need to know what protocol your server uses to assign these numbers. The most common is MacIP for a Mac only environment, although if you are in a mixed environment you might be using DHCP or BootP. If you're connecting with a modem, you'll probably be using a protocol called PPP.

➤ *The number of your domain name server (DNS) and the hostname for modem connections*—DNS numbers are similar to IP addresses, whereas the hostname (also known as the domain name) is generally two or more words separated by periods (such as apple.com, duke.edu, or ibm.net).

➤ *Your email account and host*—The email account, incoming mail server, is where you receive mail. The host is a Simple Mail Transfer Protocol (SMTP) computer that processes outgoing mail.

If you already have an account with an ISP or if you're set up on a LAN with an older system, be sure to copy down all the information *before* installing Mac OS 8.6. Otherwise, the new system might overwrite preference files for your old connection software.

TIP
If your existing ISP requires a connect script, ask for an updated version. The utilities that ship with Mac OS 8.6 do not modify connect scripts.

ISP Referral Assistant

This is all well and good if you already have access to the Internet, but what if you don't? Never fear—the ISP Referral Assistant automates the process of selecting a

Internet Connectivity 497

new ISP, choosing a payment plan, and calibrating your system to work with the ISP. See Figure 19.6 for an example of what it's like to use Mac OS 8.6's ISP Referral Assistant.

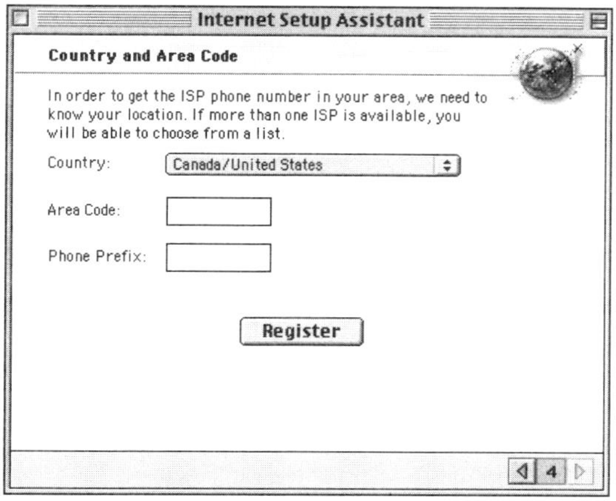

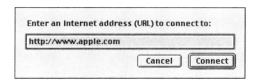

Figure 19.6 The ISP Referral Assistant automatically finds a list of the closest ISPs in your area.

After asking for some basic information (name, phone number, type of modem), the assistant automatically finds a list of local ISPs. Your modem will have to be connected to your computer when you do this, because the list of ISPs will be downloaded from the Internet. Select the ISP you wish to use, then register with the provider and choose a payment plan. After you've registered, the assistant sets the appropriate preferences on your machine.

Now that you're set up, activate the Connect To option from the Internet Access submenu of the Apple menu to connect to the Net, as shown in Figure 19.7.

Figure 19.7 With all your settings in place, you can connect to the Internet simply by typing the Uniform Resource Locator (URL).

Open Transport And Remote Access

The assistants make setting up Internet connections much easier. Most users, however, will get ever better benefits from the core software suites: Open Transport and Apple Remote Access.

What Is Open Transport?

Open Transport, the successor to MacTCP, is the part of the Mac OS that handles networking—and it's much more flexible than its predecessor. Macs using Open Transport can easily configure and switch between different types of networks or use more than one type of network at the same time. For example, Open Transport makes it possible to communicate with a network printer while using TCP/IP to connect to the Internet. Open Transport is also a lot faster than MacTCP because it's PowerPC native. When it's used with Macs that are also Internet servers (such as Web, email, and FTP servers) Open Transport can host more simultaneous connections than MacTCP.

In an earlier section of this chapter, we discussed using the Internet Editor Assistant to create several sets of connection settings. This is possible because of Open Transport. Open Transport 2.0, which ships with OS 8.6, allows users to optimize online help, so inexperienced users will be able to figure out how to use Open Transport with little outside assistance.

TIP
Older versions of Open Transport allowed you to turn it off and use MacTCP instead. With Mac OS 8.6, this is no longer possible; MacTCP is incompatible with the Internet access section of the OS.

Open Transport Components

Open Transport consists of a handful of Extensions and two Control Panels: AppleTalk and TCP/IP. If you've used the Internet Setup Assistant to configure your system, you most likely won't need to adjust these Control Panels very often unless your Mac is on a LAN, WAN, or intranet.

AppleTalk Control Panel
The AppleTalk Control Panel, shown in Figure 19.8, allows you to choose which port your AppleTalk connection uses. This port is the main avenue of communication between your Mac and network devices—printers, network modems, and so on.

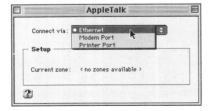

Figure 19.8 Configuring the AppleTalk Control Panel.

This Control Panel also allows you to link to a local Ethernet network and locally attached printers, which use AppleTalk to communicate with the Mac OS through a serial cable. Both the AppleTalk and the TCP/IP Control Panels allow you to set one of three levels of user configuration:

➤ Basic, for novice users

➤ Advanced, for more sophisticated users

➤ Administration, for network supervisors or parents who want to keep Junior from tampering with the settings

A good rule of thumb is to use the lowest user mode possible unless you really understand what you're doing. Figure 19.9 shows the User Mode dialog box.

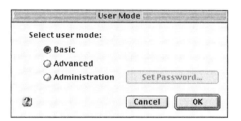

Figure 19.9 Change the AppleTalk or TCP/IP User Mode only if necessary.

TCP/IP Control Panel

The TCP/IP Control Panel controls how your Mac connects to the Internet when you use the TCP/IP protocol. Macs can connect via a direct connection over an Ethernet network, or by way of one of two dial-up networking protocols—Standard Line Interface Protocol (SLIP) or Point-to-Point Protocol (PPP). SLIP was dominant up until a couple of years ago, but PPP offers better throughput when small amounts of information are going back and forth between two computers. It's also a recognized Internet standard, whereas SLIP never achieved full recognition.

With TCP/IP, you connect using AppleTalk, Ethernet, or PPP; these options are available with the standard Mac OS 8.6 installation. You can install additional networking hardware or software that will add additional options to the TCP/IP Control Panel. AppleTalk and Ethernet are for people who are using an Ethernet adapter to connect through a dedicated network. PPP is mainly used for one computer to connect via a modem. Figure 19.10 shows the TCP/IP Control Panel.

When you connect via PPP, you can enter the IP address yourself or get it automatically from a server (the method you choose depends on your ISP). If the IP address comes from the server, it's important to find out if the server is a Boot Protocol (BootP), a Dynamic Host Configuration Protocol (DHCP), or a Reverse

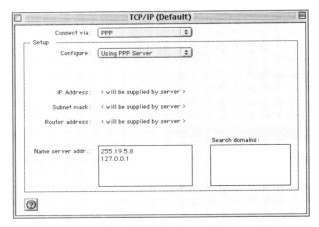

Figure 19.10 The TCP/IP Control Panel allows users to connect to the Internet via Ethernet, AppleTalk, or PPP.

Address Resolution Protocol (RARP) server. Again, someone at the ISP can answer this question; the default is the simple PPP server.

Apple Remote Access Components

Apple Remote Access 3.1 (ARA) is a complete set of technologies for networking via modem. It takes the place of two previous Apple Technologies: Open Transport/PPP and the former ARA 2.1. Three Control Panels compose the interface of ARA: the Modem Control Panel, the DialAssist Control Panel, and the Remote Access Control Panel.

Modem Control Panel

The Modem Control Panel, shown in Figure 19.11, is a simple interface for designating the modem brand, model, and port. If you chose PPP in the TCP/IP Control Panel, you'll need to set your Modem preferences in this Control Panel.

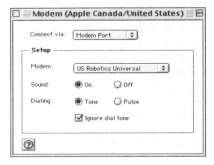

Figure 19.11 The Modem Control Panel allows users to easily make changes to their modem configuration.

Mac OS 8.6

Mac OS 8.6 supports most of the major brands and models of modems, but if yours isn't on the list, don't panic—the Apple Modem Script Generator, a tool to add new modem scripts, is available at asu.info.apple.com/swupdates.nsf/artnum/n10664. Try the Hayes-compatible modem script first, because many modems are Hayes-compatible.

The Modem Control Panel is easy to use (you're using a Mac, after all). To get started, take a look at the back of your computer to see where the modem is plugged in—the modem port or the printer port. If you have an older PowerBook, you may have only one choice, a combination modem/printer port. Next, make the appropriate port selection in the Connect Via portion of the Modem Control Panel. Then choose a modem type, whether you want the modem's sound on or off, and whether your phone line uses touch-tone or pulse. You should probably leave the Ignore Dial Tone option unchecked, because most modems need to detect the dial tone in order to function properly.

DialAssist Control Panel

When connecting via modem, you'll most likely encounter several problems and many situations in which you have to enter redundant information. To take some of the frustration out of the dialup experience, Mac OS 8.6 offers the DialAssist Control Panel. It provides a convenient place to enter information such as your area code, country, and so on. You can also put in numbers for special circumstances, such as when you have to dial 9 to get an outside line, or a calling card number if you have to dial long distance.

Remote Access

The Remote Access Control Panel lets you record information that will affect your network session. You can use the Remote Access Control Panel as a "front end" to store your user ID and password for your ISP. Figure 19.12 shows the Remote Access Control Panel.

The Options button takes you to the true core of the Control Panel. You can use this interface to modify the way that your modem connects in regard to redialing, the length of time that a connection should remain active, and the way that your dialup protocol is being used. Figure 19.12 shows some of these options. If you're using PPP (and chances are good that you are), you may want to check the box (you can see it in Figure 19.13) that says "Connect automatically when starting TCP/IP applications." This will cause the modem to automatically connect whenever you start a program that uses network connectivity. You'll probably want to leave this box unchecked if you often use a Web browser to look at files on your hard drive, however. This Control Panel, like the others we have discussed, can manage

Figure 19.12 The Remote Access Control Panel.

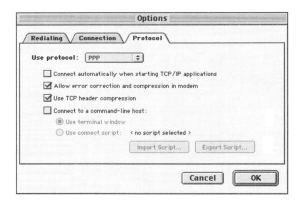

Figure 19.13 The Options within the Remote Access Control Panel.

multiple configurations, so you can easily switch all of your settings if you want to connect in a different way at a different time.

Wrapping Up

The Internet is an important part of modern life, and this chapter has shown you how the Mac OS 8.6 has taken this fact into account:

➤ You've seen how the Internet Setup Assistant can be used to modify an existing account with an ISP or LAN, and how the ISP Registration Assistant can help you set up new service.

➤ You've learned how to work with Open Transport.

➤ You've seen how ARA can be used to speed your connection to the Net.

Of course, there's more to life than Web surfing—eventually it's time to start publishing online. One of the most powerful aspects of the Macintosh is its ability to serve as a sturdy, secure Web server. Until now, third-party developers provided most of the server software. The new Mac OS changes that, bundling fast, efficient Web server software as part of the basic installation. As we'll see in the next chapter, any Mac can now be a Web server, and anyone who can use the Mac OS can be a Webmaster.

Personal Web Sharing

You've seen how easy it is to connect your Mac to the Internet—now it's time to see just how easy it is to publish on an intranet or the World Wide Web using the Mac OS. Mac OS 8.6 includes Apple's Personal Web Sharing, a fully-functional Web server designed to be used by individuals who want to share information over the Web without having to install, configure, and manage a commercial Web server. You can use the Web server to share just about anything on your Mac, including HTML documents, images, word processing documents, spreadsheets, and much more. If you can point and click a mouse, then you can be a Webmaster, thanks to the Mac OS. Take a look at Figure 20.1, which shows an example of a document that comes with the Web server; it took only one click of the mouse to publish this document using Personal Web Sharing.

This chapter will explore all the facets of how Apple's Personal Web Sharing is set up and configured, as well as a few tidbits about how the Web works and how to test your server without even being connected to the Internet.

The Web And HTML

The Web is a collection of Web servers that are accessed by Web browsers such as Netscape Navigator, Microsoft Internet Explorer, and many others. Web browsers are available for virtually every computer hardware and software platform, for handheld personal digital assistants, such as the Palm Pilot, and for mainframe computers. The Hypertext Markup Language (HTML) makes it possible for one document to be read by so many different types of computers. HTML is a low-level programming language called a markup language; it's very unsophisticated and easily implemented into existing applications and operating systems. HTML uses simple formatting instructions like this example to make portions of the document appear underlined, boldface, and centered:

Chapter 20

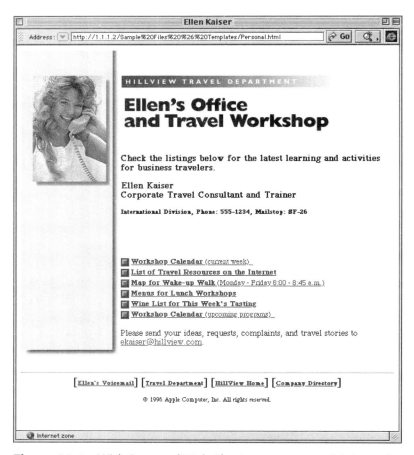

Figure 20.1 With Personal Web Sharing, you can publish on the Web with just one click of the mouse.

```
<HTML>
<HEAD>
<TITLE>HTML Example</TITLE>
<META NAME="generator" CONTENT="BBEdit 5.0">
</HEAD>
<BODY>

<P>
<CENTER>
This is an example of <U><B>underlined and bold text</B></U> in the middle
of a sentence that is centered on the page.
</CENTER>
</P>

</BODY>
</HTML>
```

Mac OS 8.6

HTML is really just a collection of commands written in easy-to-understand ASCII text that tells Web browsers how to display formatted text, insert images, and link to other pages on the Web. Figure 20.2 shows what this example looks like when served using Web Sharing.

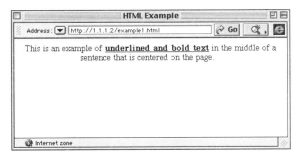

Figure 20.2 Web pages are composed of HTML code that tells Web browsers how to display text as well as images, movies, and sounds.

You'll need a good text editor if you plan to get serious about HTML, and a demo version of a great text editor called BBEdit is included on this book's companion CD-ROM. You'll probably like it for its text editing capabilities as well as for its HTML abilities. If you want to get the full version, visit the Bare Bones home page (www.barebones.com) for more information. It will be a worthwhile investment.

The availability of Web servers and the ease of HTML programming are two reasons the Web is so popular, but the *real* reason is the Mac OS! More than 60 percent of all Web sites are created and maintained using the Mac OS. Now, consider that about 10 percent of the computing population uses the Mac OS, and you can only come to one conclusion: it must be far easier to create and maintain Web sites using the Mac OS than any other platform. By including Personal Web Sharing with Mac OS 8.6, Apple has made that task even easier.

Web Server Configuration

Commercial Web servers are often expensive and come with hundreds of individual application files, plug-ins, graphics, and configuration files. Apple's Web Sharing server is not this kind of server, however. It's lean and simple to use. In fact, everything you need to get started publishing on the Web is available with Mac OS 8.6, including the following:

➤ Web Sharing server

➤ Sample HTML documents

➤ Documentation

508 Chapter 20

➤ Resources for further reading

➤ Local Web access to your own computer using a loopback interface

This last item may be a bit confusing to some readers. How can you access the Web without Internet connectivity, you ask? Easy!

Using A Loopback Interface

The Mac OS can do a really nifty networking trick called a loopback interface, which makes your Mac, Web Sharing server, and Web browser think they're on the Internet. This allows you to run the Web server and use any Web browser to test it just as if it were on the Internet or an intranet—but without being connected. Also, if you have a second Mac and can connect it to the Web server Mac using an Ethernet connection, then the second Mac can also access your Web server.

To set up your Mac to use the loopback interface, just follow these easy steps:

1. Open the TCP/IP Control Panel.

2. Choose Connect via Ethernet.

3. Choose Configure Manually.

4. Enter 1.1.1.2 in the IP Address field (see Figure 20.3).

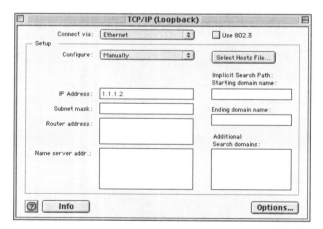

Figure 20.3 Create a loopback interface setup to test your Web server without connecting to a network.

5. Choose File|Quit (or Command+Q), and if warned, "You have not provided a subnet mask value. TCP/IP will use a default subnet mask that corresponds to your IP address class," choose Continue. The networking software is smart enough to take care of the subnet mask value, and it will work like a charm.

Mac OS 8.6

6. Finally, if you want to save these settings so that you can easily recall them without having to make the changes manually, choose File|Configurations (or Command+K), choose Duplicate, rename it Loopback (or whatever), and then choose Make Active. The next time you want to switch from your ISP to the loopback interface, just choose Command+K, select Loopback, and then Make Active, as in Figure 20.4.

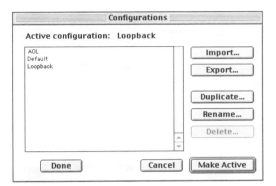

Figure 20.4 Save your loopback interface as an Open Transport configuration so you can easily recall it for future reference.

When you're ready to connect to the Internet, just go back to Open Transport and activate your previous settings.

Starting Web Sharing

When Mac OS 8.6 is first installed, the Web Sharing server isn't active by default, but starting it up is easy. Once you've configured your Mac on a network (as outlined in Chapter 18) or configured the loopback interface, you're ready to start the Web server. Just follow these steps:

1. Open the Web Sharing Control Panel, as shown in Figure 20.5.

2. Click the Start button, and the default settings, including the security settings and the location of the Web folder, will be applied.

3. The Web server will check to see if a valid network connection can be made and then it will start up, as shown in Figure 20.6.

Stopping The Web Server

Once you've started the Web server, it will continue to provide access to your Web site until you stop it. If you shut down your Mac without stopping the Web Server, access will no longer be available. Once you restart your Mac, however, users will

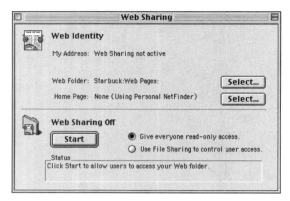

Figure 20.5 Open the Web Sharing Control Panel to start publishing with the Web server.

Figure 20.6 The Web server will use the default settings when started for the first time.

once again have access. To stop the server, therefore, you can either shut down your Mac or follow these steps:.

1. Open the Web Sharing Control Panel.
2. Click the Stop button.

The server will not be accessible again until you manually restart it using the steps detailed above.

Selecting A Web Folder

When Mac OS 8.6 is installed, the Web server and its components are installed using several default folders and documents, including a folder called Web Pages on the root of the boot volume. This is the folder the Web server uses to store your HTML documents, images, and "other content," which is known in

Webmaster-speak as the base directory, root folder, or docs folder. Because of a limitation in the Web server program, Apple recommends that if you change the location of the Web Pages folder or if you choose another folder entirely, this folder should not be located more than five levels deep on the boot volume.

To set or change the location of the Web folder, follow these steps:

1. Open the Web Sharing Control Panel.
2. Click the Select button beside the Web Folder field, shown in Figure 20.7, and select a folder less than five levels deep on the boot volume.

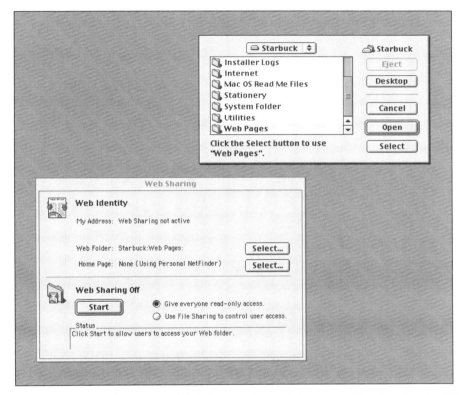

Figure 20.7 Select a new Web folder through the Web Sharing Control Panel.

3. Close the Web Sharing Control Panel by clicking the close box or by pressing Command+W.

The Web Pages folder contains many files, including documentation, instructions, and sample HTML documents and images. You should keep these on hand even if you do select another folder as home for your Web pages.

Selecting A Home Page

All Web servers have what is known as a *default* home page, which means that when you open a Uniform Resource Locator (URL) to that server without specifying a particular HTML document, the Web server gives you a document anyway. For example, when you go to www.apple.com (and you should!), the Web server gives you www.apple.com/index.html instead because *index.html* is specified as the default home page. Moreover, when you open a URL to a directory within a Web server without specifying a document, any document in that directory named index.html (or whatever you have selected) will be served by default. The names of the most common default pages include:

➤ default.html

➤ home.html

➤ index.html

Web servers on Windows-based PCs often use the extension *.htm* instead, so you might see home.htm or default.htm, for example.

The Mac OS's Web Sharing server allows you to select a home page for your Web site. By default, no document is selected, which causes the Personal NetFinder to serve as the default (more on this in just a minute), so you'll probably want to select a default document instead. To change the default home page for your Web server, follow these steps:

1. Open the Web Sharing Control Panel.
2. Click the Select button beside the Home Page field, as shown in Figure 20.8.

You can change your default home page at any time by repeating these steps.

Personal NetFinder

HTML is a limited language and lacks certain interface features that could make browsing the Web an easier process. Apple has noticed this fact and added a very cool feature to their Web server called the Personal NetFinder, which can replace the default home page to present users with what looks like the Finder in the Mac OS. In Figure 20.9, for example, the Personal NetFinder displays the contents of the base directory of the Web server on a computer running Mac OS 8.6.

The Personal NetFinder gives users a Mac-like experience by presenting the contents of the directory in a list view that lets users view the directory by:

➤ Name

➤ Size

Mac OS 8.6

Personal Web Sharing 513

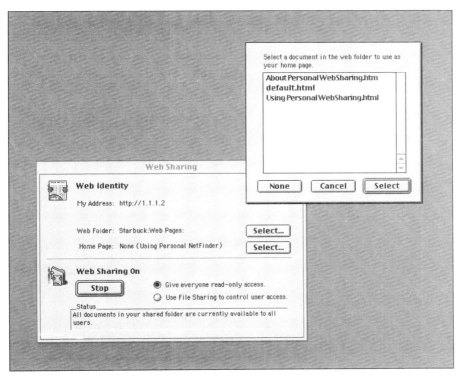

Figure 20.8 Select a default home page to replace the NetFinder.

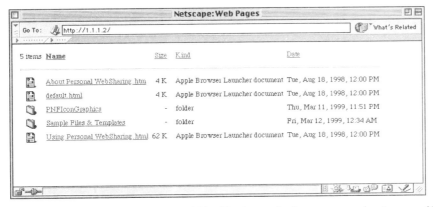

Figure 20.9 Use the Personal NetFinder to help users navigate your Web site.

➤ Kind

➤ Date Modified

Of course, it doesn't emulate the look and feel of the entire Mac OS. Instead, it mimics the Finder's ability to view the contents of a directory by the ways people

Mac OS 8.6

use most. More specifically, it emulates the Finder as it appeared in System 7. When a user clicks on the Name, Size, Kind, or Date Modified hyperlinks at the top of the page, the current window is redrawn accordingly. For example, Figure 20.10 shows the same window as in the previous example, but sorted by Kind instead of Name.

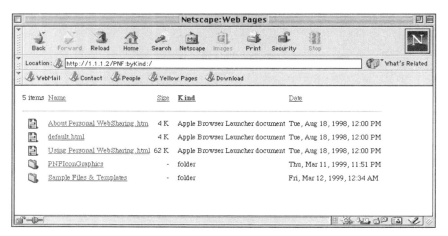

Figure 20.10 The Personal NetFinder lets visitors view the contents of folders in several ways, including by Kind.

The Personal NetFinder takes the place of the default document for a particular directory and is only usable if a directory does not contain a document entitled index.html. If index.html isn't available, Personal NetFinder will take over and display the contents of a directory. If index.html is present, it will be displayed in place of the Personal NetFinder, even if a default home page by another name has been selected, such as default.html or home.html. The filename index.html is reserved by the Web Sharing server.

TIP
If your Web site slows down, try turning off Personal NetFinder because it sometimes can't handle large folders efficiently.

Web Sharing Preferences

The Web Sharing server has several preferences (located under the Edit|Preferences menu) that you'll want to review before letting anyone know about your new server. The preferences fall into three basic categories, two of which may not be intuitive for many users. The good news, though, is that the server comes preconfigured for 95 percent of all users; chances are that if you have to tinker too much with these preferences, you'll probably end up needing the support of a commercial Web server such as WebSTAR, WebTen, or Apache. The preferences you'll want to review for Apple's Web Sharing server include:

> *Options*—This section allows you to configure several general configuration options, including logging of connections to your server, the port on which your server listens for incoming connections, file permissions, and memory allocation for the server (see Figure 20.11).

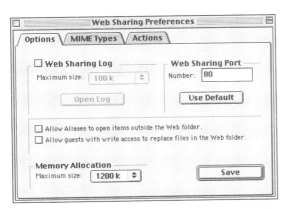

Figure 20.11 The Options tab of the Web server's configuration preferences.

> *MIME Types*—Multipurpose Internet Mail Extension (MIME) allows Web servers to deliver different kinds of data to Web browsers based upon a predetermined set of file types. There are about seven kinds of MIME files, including text documents, applications, and image files, for example. This section allows you to review, add, and delete MIME type mappings which affect how your server answers requests from browsers for HTML documents, images, or Adobe PDF documents (see Figure 20.12).

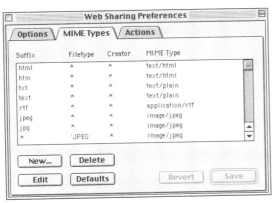

Figure 20.12 The MIME Types tab of the Web server's configuration preferences.

Mac OS 8.6

➤ *Actions*—The Web Sharing server can communicate with external applications called Common Gateway Interfaces (CGIs), and the Actions tab is where you'll go to add actions for pre- and post-processing of documents by CGIs. For example, Figure 20.13 shows the addition of an action that processes documents created in a CGI program called NetCloak before being served to a browser (so-called pre-processing).

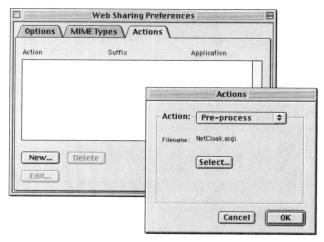

Figure 20.13 The Actions tab of the Web server's configuration preferences.

Security

Commercial Web servers provide very robust security by way of several different methods, including realms-based, per-directory, per-user, and Secure Sockets Layer security. These types of security take up valuable server resources and can become very complex, which wouldn't be appropriate for a personal Web server. Instead, Apple's Personal Web Sharing offers two levels of security for your Web server:

➤ None at all (read-only access for all visitors)

➤ File Sharing rights and restrictions

To change between these two levels of security, follow these steps:

1. Open the Web Sharing Control Panel.
2. In the lower half of the Control Panel, choose one of the radio buttons to change the level of security. The change will take effect immediately.
3. Close the Web Sharing Control Panel.

If you've selected the Give Everyone Read-Only Access radio button in the lower half of the Web Sharing Control Panel, shown in Figure 20.14, then anyone will be able to access any document on your Web server.

Mac OS 8.6

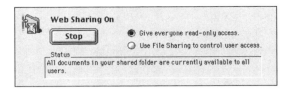

Figure 20.14 Granting everyone access to the Web server.

If you want to share access to your Web server using File Sharing rights and privileges, then select the Use File Sharing to Control User Access radio button, shown in Figure 20.15.

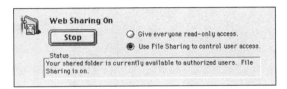

Figure 20.15 Granting access to the Web server using File Sharing.

Finally, to disable the Web server all together, select the Stop button.

Refer back to Chapter 17 for the fine details of File Sharing on the Mac OS. To configure File Sharing for the Web Pages folder, however, follow these steps:

1. Click the Web Pages folder or the alternative folder assigned in the Web Sharing Control Panel.

2. Choose File|Sharing and make any additions, deletions, or modifications to the rights associated with this folder.

3. Close the Sharing window and test access to the server.

TIP
You don't have to worry about Personal Web Sharing opening up your Mac to attacks by hackers. Apple's File Sharing rights and restrictions are also the basis for security for commercial Web servers such as WebSTAR. Web servers running on the Mac OS don't suffer from the well-documented security holes other platforms (Unix, Windows NT) do. In fact, when properly set up, they've proven to be unhackable in several well-publicized contests—despite offers of thousands of dollars in prize money and the best attempts of thousands of hackers world-wide.

You can use the Chooser on another computer on your network to test the access to your Web server; the results will be the same results you would get if you were using a Web browser. To change access rights to the Web folder so members of the

Mac OS 8.6

group called WebUsers can access its contents, a File Sharing group called WebUsers was created, shown in Figure 20.16. Members may be assigned to that group by dragging and dropping their user icons into the group window.

Next, click on the Web Pages folder, select Sharing from the File menu, and assign the group read and write access, shown in Figure 20.17.

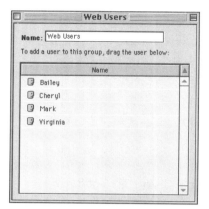

Figure 20.16   Creating a group of users to access a Web site.

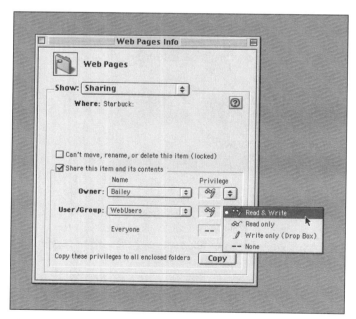

Figure 20.17   Assigning access to the folder for the group.

Next, test access to the server by using a Web browser on another computer to access the folder by entering the following URL: http://WebUser@1.1.1.2/.

Mac OS 8.6

Note that *WebUsers@* is inserted into the URL between http:// and the IP address of the server. This tells the Web server, "Hey, I want to access the server as an authenticated user named WebUsers." The Web server responds by sending a name and password dialog box for you to enter any of the usernames in the WebUsers group. Figure 20.18 shows what this looks like using the new Mac-only Web browser called iCab.

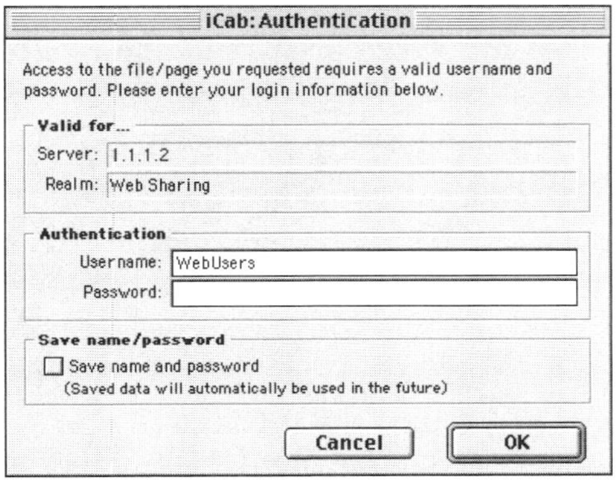

Figure 20.18 An iCab user being authenticated to access a Web site using File Sharing's Users & Groups users and groups.

TIP
Most elements of the Mac OS pertaining to Web servers are not case sensitive.

Getting Help

The Web Sharing server comes with several resources to help get you started publishing on the Web. The folks at Apple have included everything you'll need to start learning HTML and using your Web server, including:

➤ Sample Web pages that include a personal Web page, a calendar, lists created in HTML, and sample hyperlinks.

➤ Templates for creating your own personal Web page, a calendar, and different types of lists.

➤ Sample graphics.

➤ Tips for creating your own Web content.

➤ Links to resources on the Web for HTML design and tutorials.

➤ Information on how to run Common Gateway Interface (CGI) programs on your personal Web server.

One resource you may need that isn't provided is detailed information on setting up and maintaining a Mac Web server. Several books that cover this topic are available, as are the following Web sites:

➤ *WebSTAR*—www.starnine.com

➤ *WebTen*—www.tenon.com

➤ *Apache for Mac OS X*—www.apple.org

Wrapping Up

This chapter introduces the Web Sharing server included in Mac OS 8.6. You should now have a well-grounded understanding of what's involved to configure and maintain a Mac Web server. Of course, the Web server that's included is a very basic server that's capable of meeting the needs of individuals, departments, and small businesses. With the Web Sharing server, you can serve any type of HTML document and many types of images, and even password-protect your Web site. In the next chapter, we'll look at the Web browsers and other Internet software that come with the Mac OS. These Internet applications and utilities will enable you to be a power user of the Internet minutes after installing Mac OS 8.6.

Internet Applications And Utilities

As we've seen in previous chapters, the Mac OS 8.6 makes it easy to connect to a local area network (LAN), to set up an account with an Internet Service Provider (ISP), and even to set up a simple Web server. These new developments are a continuation of Apple's long tradition of making the Mac OS the easiest and most efficient operating system for networking with other computers.

So if these innovations are simply a continuation of an old tradition, what's different about the Mac OS's relationship to the Internet? Well, plenty—and most of it's in your Internet folder. Along with integrating Internet connectivity into the operating system itself, Apple has included as part of the basic installation of Mac OS 8.6 all of the major applications and utilities you'll need to master the Internet and the Web.

In this chapter, we'll look at the applications and utilities that are installed by the Mac OS, find out how they can be used to explore the Net, and examine some other programs that can enhance the online experience. Some of these programs are commercial products, but most are available as inexpensive or reduced-price shareware. We'll discuss these add-ons later in the chapter. First, let's check out what Apple has packaged with this release of the Mac OS.

Mac OS 8.6 Internet Software

During the basic installation of Mac OS 8.6, the installer leaves a few presents in the Internet folder, including Netscape Communicator, Microsoft Internet Explorer, and Microsoft Outlook Express (see Figure 21.1). In addition to these essential applications, the Mac OS also installs several plug-ins for Web browsers, and two utilities from Aladdin Systems: StuffIt Expander and DropStuff. These programs, which are wildly popular with users of other versions of the Mac OS, can help you make the most of the Internet, the Web, and—most importantly—your time. Using these applications, you can check email, browse Web pages, read newsgroups, exchange files with other users, and access popular online software libraries. Pretty nice presents, huh? Figure 21.1 shows the Internet folder, where Mac OS 8.6 installs these programs.

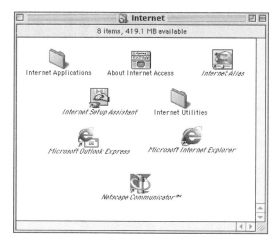

Figure 21.1 The Internet folder of Mac OS 8.6 includes a variety of popular online applications and utilities.

Several of the core components of the Mac OS are Internet-savvy as well. Sherlock, the Internet Control Panel, time server synchronization, and URL aliases are good examples of how a modern operating system like the Mac OS is designed to work with the Internet. And if that's not enough, you can download hundreds—if not thousands—of Internet applications and utilities for the Mac OS for free, as shareware, or as commercially packaged software. Let's take a look at some of the items in the Internet folder, beginning with the three applications you're likely to use the most.

Netscape Communicator

If you've ever browsed the Web, odds are you've heard of Netscape Communicator. Formerly known as Netscape Navigator, the program is the dominant browser on the Web, and its logo and name are everywhere. Navigator's influence is so strong that it has been able to drive the development of new Web features like frames, centered text, and background colors and pictures. Now Communicator, Navigator's successor, is part of the basic installation of Mac OS 8.6. Figure 21.2 shows a typical setup of Netscape Communicator, which is installed into the Internet Applications subfolder of the Internet folder on your hard drive.

But what *is* Netscape Communicator, exactly? The short answer is that it's a Web browser—an application people use to view World Wide Web pages. But it's also an email client, a Usenet news reader, and more. The basic features include:

➤ Netscape Navigator (Web browser)

➤ Netscape Messenger (email and Usenet news reader)

Internet Applications And Utilities   523

Figure 21.2   Mac OS 8.6 installs Netscape Communicator by default on your hard drive.

➤ Netscape Composer (HTML editor)
➤ Netscape Calendar (calendar application)

Netscape Navigator

Navigator, the browser component of Netscape Communicator, sports an easy-to-follow interface with well-labeled buttons and loads of help options. Figure 21.3 shows the BMW of North America Web site in a Navigator browser window. This site, and the majority of all Web sites, was created and is most likely managed using the Mac OS!

However, Navigator didn't become the single most popular online application simply because it was a good Web browser. The program's strengths lie in its ability to work with non-Web resources like File Transfer Protocol (FTP) and Gopher servers, email, and newsgroups. Navigator can use third-party programs called plug-ins to enhance its multimedia capabilities, and it allows users to build large, organized lists of favorite sites, known as bookmarks.

TIP

There are many great resources for learning more about the various components of Netscape Communicator, but none more useful than the Netscape home page (www.netscape.com).

Mac OS 8.6

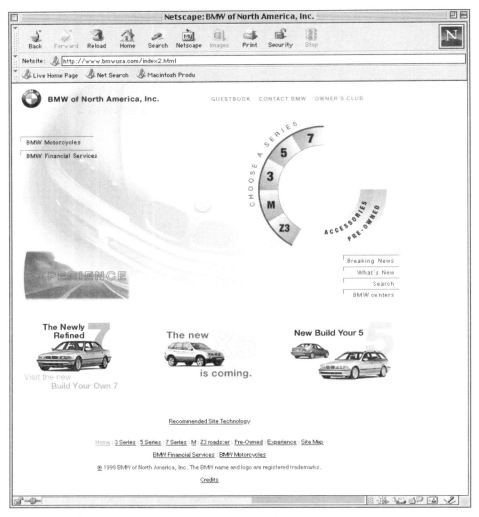

Figure 21.3 You can easily access both Web pages and FTP sites using Navigator, the browser component of Netscape Communicator.

Bookmarks

Now that setting up an account with an ISP has been reduced to clicking a button or two (see Chapter 19), the most difficult thing about starting new service is building a useful list of bookmarks. Luckily, Apple has done newbies (new users) a favor and packed the default list with loads of sites ranging from official Apple sites to publications to software developers and resellers. Of course, you can create your categories of bookmarks as well, as shown in Figure 21.4.

Internet Applications And Utilities   525

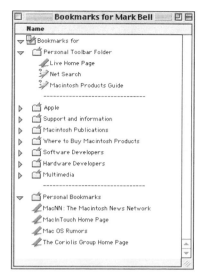

Figure 21.4 Netscape's default bookmarks are chock-full of helpful information sites, computer publications, and software developers.

Plug-ins

Over the past 10 years, many programmers have moved away from writing huge, monolithic programs that can't be extensively modified. Instead, many popular programs ship with an open architecture that allows third-party developers to write small extensions that enhance the main program's operations.

In the online world, Netscape Navigator was the most evident example of this trend. Early versions of the browser relied upon a large number of helper applications that would automatically launch when you downloaded a file of a certain type. For example, if you clicked on a movie, the file would download, and then Movie-Player or another program would launch and play the file. This process was slow and made real-time sound and video impossible.

Recent versions of Navigator have taken care of this through plug-ins. With the right additions, Navigator can now show complex graphics, play movies and sounds in real time, and even display virtual reality environments. With Mac OS 8.6, you get the following plug-ins for Netscape Communicator, shown in Figure 21.5:

➤ *Beatnik*—The Beatnik plug-in turns Netscape into a sound-ready multimedia application. Using this plug-in, browsers can play a sound file without launching an external helper, and because you're using a Macintosh, you don't need a sound card or other multimedia hardware.

➤ *Shockwave*—This plug-in is vital for sites that feature games, online animation, interactive interfaces, and other multimedia bells and whistles. Shockwave,

Mac OS 8.6

526 Chapter 21

Figure 21.5 The Mac OS 8.6 installation includes four useful plug-ins for Netscape Communicator.

created by Macromedia, allows developers to use programs like Director, Flash, and Authorware to create small, streaming presentations for their Web sites. Since its introduction, the plug-in has become ubiquitous; the player is included with Netscape Communicator and Microsoft Internet Explorer. To try out Shockwave, check out Rob Terrell's game site, The Blip Internet Playground (www.theblip.com). Be sure to try racing your baby around city streets in Perambulator GP, shown in Figure 21.6!

➤ *PDFViewer*—PDFViewer is a plug-in version of Adobe's popular Acrobat software. Acrobat creates Portable Document Format (PDF) files, which can be read on any machine on which the Acrobat Reader program has been installed. This format allows the files to be transported to a wide variety of machines without worrying about compatibility problems.

Since Acrobat allows you to include graphics, styled text, and complex information, many developers are moving toward Acrobat and away from SimpleText's limited text file for Read Me files and manuals. (We'll discuss Acrobat Reader in more detail later in this chapter.) PDFViewer allows you to read these files online without having to download the whole file to your hard drive.

TIP
Adobe's home page, www.adobe.com, offers a guide to using Acrobat Reader and information about the commercial Adobe Acrobat PDF creator.

Mac OS 8.6

Internet Applications And Utilities 527

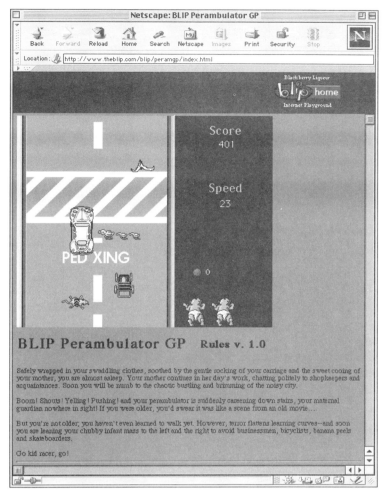

Figure 21.6 Macromedia's Shockwave plug-in allows Web browsers to play games like Perambulator GP.

➤ *QuickTime*—This plug-in allows you to view QuickTime movies and QuickTime VR documents directly in the browser window. With this plug-in, Navigator can play video, audio, animation, and even virtual reality scenes directly in a Web page. Without the plug-in, you'd have to download the file to your hard drive and play it with MoviePlayer or other software.

TIP
More information and updated versions of the QuickTime system extension and the plug-in are available at the QuickTime home page (www.apple.com/quicktime).

Mac OS 8.6

528 Chapter 21

> ➤ *Other Plug-ins*—Many more plug-ins are out there, but they're best acquired on an as-needed basis. Why chew up your RAM loading 80 additional files if you only need 1 or 2? If you run into a page that requires a plug-in you don't have, Navigator asks if you want to get it. It then takes you to Netscape's plug-in finder page, which helps match you up with an appropriate plug-in, as shown in Figure 21.7.

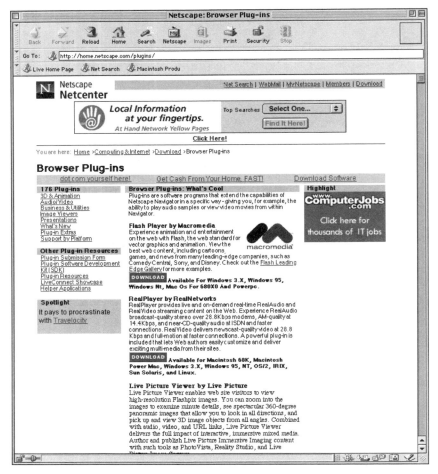

Figure 21.7 Netscape's Plug-in Finder page helps you download the appropriate plug-in for your needs.

TIP

For more information about plug-ins and Netscape Navigator, see home.netscape.com/plugins.

Mac OS 8.6

Netscape Messenger

Although the browser portion of Netscape Communicator is the main attraction, the program includes two other important features called Netscape Messenger (formerly known as Netscape News) and Netscape Mail. These two applications allow people to use Communicator as their one and only Internet application.

Email

Netscape Messenger's email client can access any mail server that supports the Post Office Protocol (POP) or Internet Message Access Protocol (IMAP). Depending on which type of server you access, your mail folder may look a bit different from the one shown in Figure 21.8. In this example, the mail boxes are at the left, messages are at the top right, and the text of the selected messages is displayed at the bottom right. Double-clicking a message will open it in its own window, which many users feel is easier to read.

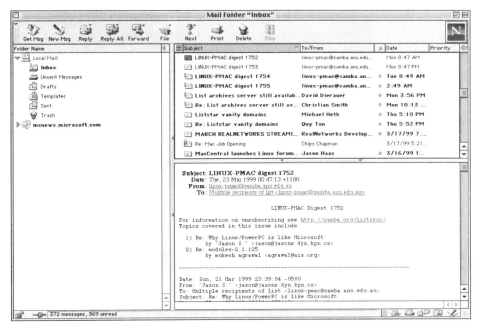

Figure 21.8 Reading email with Netscape Messenger.

The email capabilities of Netscape Messenger are very thorough and much like those of its rival browser, Microsoft Internet Explorer.

Usenet News

Some of the craziest, silliest, most controversial, and most useful information appears in Usenet newsgroups. Usenet was created in the late 1970s and early

1980s by Duke University and the University of North Carolina at Chapel Hill to facilitate communications between the two schools, which are only about 15 miles apart (and constitute possibly the greatest rivalry in college basketball—always a popular topic on Usenet!).

Usenet newsgroups are automatically updated bulletin boards where people around the world come to learn, debate, swap programs and information, or just chat. Their subjects range from the prosaic (alt.tv.seinfeld) to the profound (soc.religion.bahai), from the technical (comp.lang.fortran) to the tasteless (alt.barney.dinosaur.die.die.die).

TIP

See your local ISP for information on accessing Usenet newsgroups. There are over 20,000 groups, and chances are that your ISP will only subscribe to some of them.

Netscape Messenger allows you to burrow through the newsgroups to find subjects that match your interest. Once you find some, you can subscribe by clicking in the column marked by a checkmark (the interface needs a bit of work). Clicking on the name of the newsgroup brings up a list of posts in that group, and clicking on the title of a post brings up a copy of the post (see Figure 21.9).

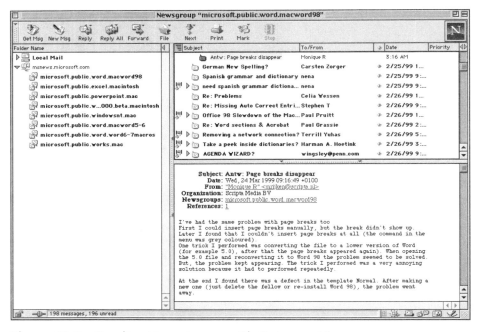

Figure 21.9 Reading Usenet news with Netscape Messenger.

On the down side, Netscape News's interface is a bit cumbersome and less powerful than some of the other newsreaders available for Macs, such as InterNews, NewsWatcher, or Yet Another NewsWatcher.

Microsoft Internet Explorer

The second Web browser that is automatically installed with Mac OS 8.6 is Microsoft Internet Explorer. It's comparable to Netscape Navigator, and you should try them both and decide which you like best. Of course, you can use both—or neither. If you use America Online as your Internet Service Provider (ISP), you might be using AOL's own version of Web browser instead. As far as Internet Explorer goes, however, it differs from Netscape Navigator in several respects:

➤ Internet Explorer is specifically a Web browser and not a Usenet news reader or an email client. Like Netscape Navigator, however, Internet Explorer also supports protocols such as FTP (File Transfer Protocol) and Gopher.

➤ Version 4.5 of Internet Explorer is faster than Netscape Navigator when it comes to things like redrawing windows and navigating between cached pages.

➤ Internet Explorer has more similarities to other applications Mac users are likely to use, such as Office 98.

Browsing the Web with Internet Explorer is pretty comparable to most other Web browsers. URLs are entered and pages are loaded just as they are with Netscape Navigator. For example, Figure 21.10 shows the Internet Explorer home page on the Microsoft Web site.

Explorer Bar

One noticeable difference in the Web browsing experience is that Internet Explorer adds what is called the Explorer Bar, which is visible in Figure 21.10 on the left side of the browser window. The Explorer Bar provides quick access to several useful resources:

➤ *Favorites*—A collection of bookmarks

➤ *History*—A log of the Web pages you've recently visited

➤ *Search*—One of several Internet search engines

➤ *Page Holder*—A temporary marker for a specific place in a Web page

You can expand or collapse the Explorer Bar by clicking once on any of the four tabs. When expanded, you can resize the Explorer Bar to make it wider or narrower by dragging it to the right or left, respectively. Figure 21.11 shows the Explorer Bar portion of the browser window with the Page Holder tab selected and linked to the

532 Chapter 21

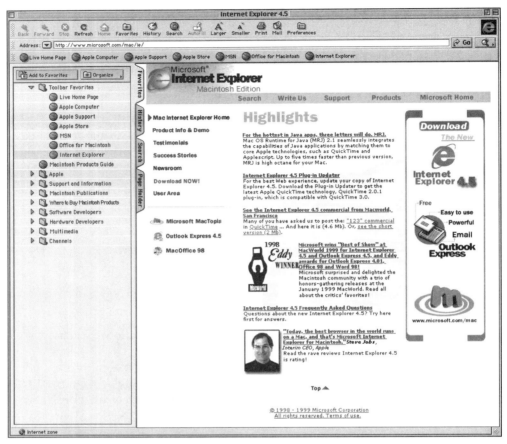

Figure 21.10 Browsing the Web with Microsoft Internet Explorer.

bookmarks for Netscape Navigator. This is one way to access Navigator's bookmarks from within Internet Explorer.

Printing Improvements

One outstanding advantage of Microsoft Internet Explorer is its ability to preview a Web page before printing. Many people never experience the need to print Web pages, but many others print pages on a regular basis and have been frustrated be the lack of control over how Web pages are printed. By choosing File|Print Preview when browsing a Web page, you can preview the page before printing as well as customize a few layout options and preview the changes before printing. Figure 21.12 shows an example of the Print Preview feature.

Experiment with the following preview options to determine the best layout configuration for your Web pages:

Mac OS 8.6

Internet Applications And Utilities 533

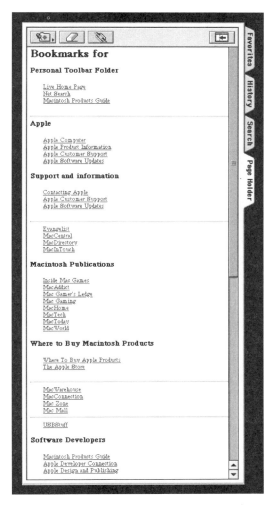

Figure 21.11 The Page Holder tab of the Explorer Bar.

➤ Headers and Footers
➤ Print Background
➤ Print Images
➤ Shrink Pages to Fit
➤ Crop Wide Pages
➤ Print Wide Pages

Once you've made your selections, choosing the Print button will open the print dialog window instead of sending the page to the printer.

Mac OS 8.6

534 Chapter 21

Figure 21.12 Internet Explorer allows you to preview a Web page before sending it to your printer.

Microsoft Outlook Express

Outlook Express is the email companion application to Internet Explorer. More accurately, Outlook Express is a less sophisticated version of Microsoft Outlook, a robust messaging application found predominantly on the Microsoft Windows platform. Outlook Express has many of the features of Microsoft Outlook; some of the missing features, such as calendaring, are present in Netscape Communicator. For the most part, Outlook Express performs all the functions of Netscape Messenger, and resembles Messenger as well. Figure 21.13 shows an example of Outlook Express.

Like Netscape Messenger, Outlook Express can use either the POP or IMAP protocol, and create multiple folders, access multiple mail accounts, manage an address book (called Contacts in Outlook Express), and read Usenet news. Other features include:

➤ Multiple signatures

➤ Screen tips

Mac OS 8.6

Internet Applications And Utilities 535

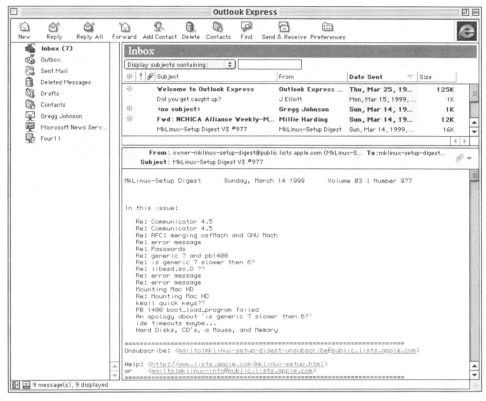

Figure 21.13 Microsoft Outlook Express.

➤ Robust attachment support

➤ Message filters

➤ Send and receive plain-text or HTML-styled messages

➤ Scheduled receipt and delivery of email

Outlook Express Contacts, shown in Figure 21.14, is one feature that users especially like. The Contacts feature is highly customizable and allows you to create and maintain contact information on individuals, as well as groups of recipients or mailing lists.

Mailing lists are very easy to create. Just choose the Mailing List button from the toolbar, or choose File|New|Mailing List and give the list a name. Then, in the Contacts window, Command+click on the users you'd like to add to the list, and drag them to the list. Figure 21.15 shows a mailing list that was created with this technique.

Mac OS 8.6

536 Chapter 21

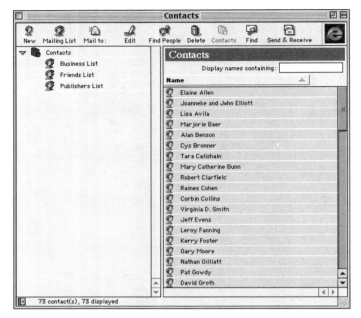

Figure 21.14 The Contacts feature of Outlook Express.

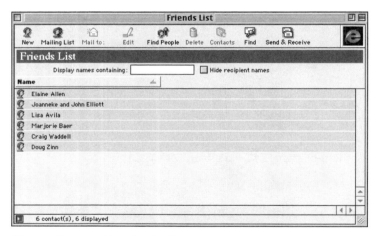

Figure 21.15 Use Outlook Express to create your own mailing lists.

TIP

To suppress the names of a list's recipients so they don't know who else is on the list, choose the Hide Recipient Names option.

Mac OS 8.6

Mac OS Internet Features And Utilities

In addition to the major Internet applications mentioned above, Mac OS 8.6 installs a few other Internet features to make communicating over the Internet easier. Hundreds of such utilities—too many, in fact, to list in this chapter—are available. For a list of the most essential Internet utilities, see the section below entitled "Must-Have Utilities." For now, however, let's take a look at the main features and utilities installed by Mac OS 8.6.

Internet Control Panel

The Mac OS has benefited in the past from Internet Config, a utility from the prodigious shareware author Peter Lewis. This utility shares information such as your name, email address, default Web browser, email client, and so on among Internet Config-aware applications. The functionality of Internet Config is now included in the Mac OS via the Internet Control Panel, shown in Figure 21.16.

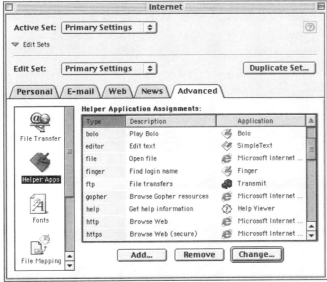

Figure 21.16 The Internet Control Panel stores information about you and your preferred Internet applications and utilities.

Use the Internet Control Panel to store information about you, your email address, default home page and search engine, Usenet news servers, and your preferred Internet applications. Figure 21.17 shows the program called Transmit selected as the preferred helper application for FTP, one of many configuration options available in the Internet Control Panel.

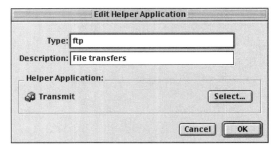

Figure 21.17 Use the Internet Control Panel to select helper applications such as Transmit.

Time Server Synchronization

Setting your Mac's internal clock has never been easier, thanks to the Date & Time Control Panel's ability to synchronize with Internet-based time servers and atomic clocks. You can schedule synchronization to take place automatically or manually. Manual synchronization is a good option if you don't go online often enough for the scheduled synchronization to take place reliably. To enable synchronization, open the Date & Time Control Panel, select Use A Network Time Server, and select the Server Options button, the result of which is shown in Figure 21.18.

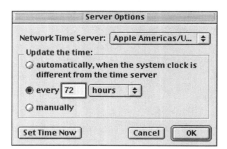

Figure 21.18 Set the time on your Mac's clock using an Internet-based time server via the Date & Time Control Panel.

Internet URL Aliases

The Mac OS is able to create Internet URL aliases from clippings (text that has been selected with the mouse) that have been dropped onto the Desktop from applications like Internet Explorer and Eudora. It does this by parsing (translating) clippings for tale-tale information such as "http://" and "mailto:" before creating the Desktop clipping. If a clipping contains the appropriate information, it will be associated by the OS to the appropriate helper application defined in the Internet Control Panel. When double-clicked, the application is opened and the URL contained in the clipping will be automatically entered into the application. Figure 21.19 shows a folder containing three different types of Internet URLs: Web, email, and FTP.

Mac OS 8.6

Figure 21.19 Three different types of Internet URLs.

StuffIt Expander And DropStuff

StuffIt Expander and DropStuff are really two sides of the same coin. In fact, both grew out of StuffIt, Aladdin Systems' popular file compression and extraction program. These programs create and read compressed and encoded files and archives. StuffIt Expander can open a variety of compressed file formats, whereas DropStuff uses a drag-and-drop interface to create new archives.

StuffIt products are the dominant force on the Mac side of the wide variety of file compression utilities out there. They're fast, they're generally bug-free, and StuffIt archives have become so common that almost every Mac user will eventually use one. But before we jump into a discussion about StuffIt Expander and DropStuff, it's important to understand why files are compressed and encoded.

Why Compress Or Encode Files?

Files are compressed for two main reasons: time and money. Since compressed files and archives are smaller, they take less time to transmit between computers or through the Internet. And because compressed files take up less space on the hard drive, some users compress rarely used files to make room for new files. Liberal use of DropStuff can help stave off the need for a new hard drive or a faster modem. Figure 21.20 shows the contents of a folder in uncompressed (Web Pages) and

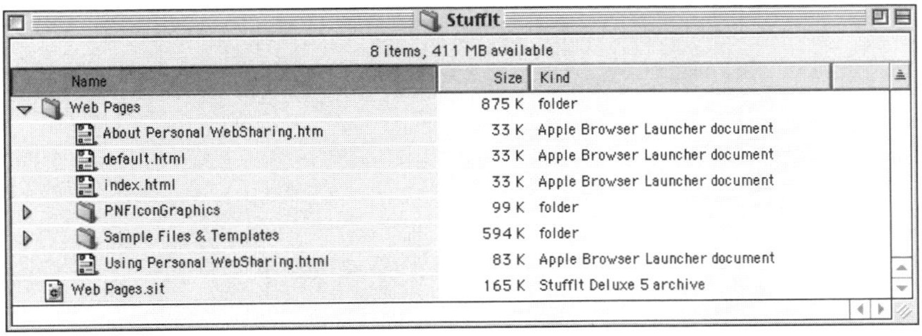

Figure 21.20 By compressing several files in a folder, you can save large amounts of disk space.

Mac OS 8.6

compressed (Web Pages.sit) formats. Notice that when compressed, the folder Web Pages.sit is approximately 25 percent the size of the uncompressed folder.

Files are also encoded for two reasons: data security and cross-platform capability. When files encoded in BinHex or MacBinary (two of the most popular encoding schemes) are transmitted, they suffer fewer problems with lost data, compatibility, and so on. If you were to pass a UUencoded file between Macintoshes via non-Macintosh computers, chances are it would be corrupted. However, even if the only Macs in a chain of 50 computers are the first and last ones, an encoded file will usually go through unscathed.

StuffIt Expander

If you're like most people, you'll receive more information from the Internet than you'll send. Therefore, you'll probably spend quite a bit of time with StuffIt Expander running in the background. Luckily, this utility is extremely simple to use and runs just fine with no tweaking.

Expander can decompress StuffIt and Compact Pro archives (files ending in .sit, .sea, and .cpt) and decode MacBinary (.bin) and BinHex (.hqx) files. It can also handle the larger, multipart BinHex files commonly found in newsgroups (like comp.binaries.mac). You can set the program to delete archives after expanding, join split archives, move the new files to a specific folder, or convert text files to Mac format (see Figure 21.21).

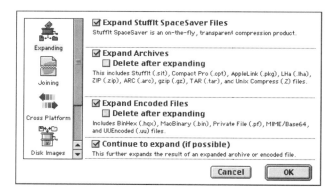

Figure 21.21 Using StuffIt Expander's preferences screen, you can determine how the program deals with compressed and encoded files.

StuffIt Expander can also "watch" a folder and expand any new files it finds (see Figure 21.22). The program periodically checks the contents of a user-specified folder for unexpanded archives or encoded files. If a new archive is found, StuffIt Expander expands it in the background. This is useful for dealing with multifile

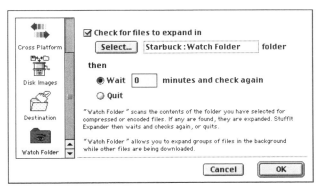

Figure 21.22 StuffIt Expander can "watch" certain specified folders for new archives and encoded files. It then expands the files in the background.

downloads from Internet sites; while new files are being downloaded, Expander can decompress others.

DropStuff

There's a kind of "chicken-and-egg" conundrum at work in the world of StuffIt programs. Expander can open compressed files, but first they have to be compressed by DropStuff. DropStuff adds to the confusion by including the StuffIt Engine, a.k.a. Expander Enhancer, an extension that adds flexibility to both programs.

Even if we don't know which one comes first, we can spend a little time getting to know DropStuff. This program was designed to allow people to create StuffIt archives quickly and efficiently through a drag-and-drop interface. To use it, simply drag folders and/or files onto the DropStuff icon. The program creates a new archive and compresses a copy of the files or folders. Simple as that. Figure 21.23 shows the compression options that are available to a user.

DropStuff is pretty simple, so there's little reason to worry about settings. However, by using DropStuff's preferences screen, you can determine how the program deals

Expander Enhancer

The basic installation of StuffIt Expander works well with Mac-based compression schemes like Compact Pro, but it can't handle non-Macintosh files like PC Zip (.zip) or UNIX Tar archives (.tar).

To deal with those files, you need to install DropStuff, the sister program of Expander. The DropStuff w/ EE 4.0 installer adds the Expander Enhancer to your system, which allows you to decompress files like ZIP and ARC archives from PCs, Unix Tar archives, Z and GZIP compressed files from Unix, AppleLink packages, and UU-encoded files. Needless to say, if you're receiving a lot of files from PC or Unix users—or if you're downloading graphics from newsgroups—this enhancement is a welcome one.

542 Chapter 21

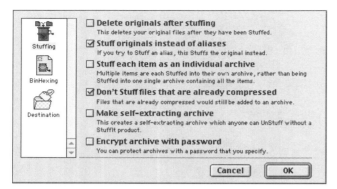

Figure 21.23   DropStuff can compress files, create password-protected and self-extracting archives, or encode files in BinHex.

with its archives. For example, if you're sending a file across the Internet, you can use DropStuff to first compress and then BinHex it. Or, if you're sending a file to someone who doesn't have StuffIt Expander, you can use DropStuff to create a self-extracting archive—an archive file that decompresses itself when double-clicked.

Must-Have Internet Utilities

As we've seen, Mac OS 8.6 makes it possible to go online and begin working mere minutes after installation. By including Netscape Communicator, Internet Explorer, Outlook Express, and the StuffIt utilities, the engineers at Apple ensured that even the most novice Internaut has the tools and applications needed to use the Net.

Of course, these are not the only Internet and Web applications available. Thousands of Mac applications have been written to work on the Net. While many of

---

A Word (Or Several) About Shareware

While the Macintosh platform hasn't traditionally had the same volume of commercial software as Wintel machines, Macs have a long and proud tradition of shareware—software uploaded to public sites and available on a use-before-you-buy basis. Generally, these programs are small, simple applications and utilities that enhance larger commercial products and add functionality to the Mac OS or are simply silly, fun activities.

The deal with shareware is simple: if, after using it for a while, you decide you can't live without it, then send payment to the author. Generally, most shareware is available for a nominal fee; some programs, called freeware, are available at no cost.

Shareware is a long-standing custom on the Internet. Many of the most popular programs began life as shareware; some of the best still are. In fact, two of the programs we discussed earlier, Internet Config and DropStuff are shareware. StuffIt Expander and Acrobat Reader are free.

Please remember that if you use shareware you have to pay for it. These programs are available on the honor system—don't mess up a good thing by not paying.

Mac OS 8.6

them are simply alternates to these popular programs, many of them are useful additions. Best of all, most of them are shareware or freeware, so you won't break the bank while stocking up.

The following utilities are essential to ensure that your Internet toolkit is complete.

Adobe Acrobat Reader

Transferring files between two computers is the essence of the Internet; unfortunately, it can also be a real pain in the neck. This is especially true for documents created by word processing and page layout programs.

Because no two computers are the same, a file that looks great on one system may look like garbage—or may not even work—when transferred to another system. Even if a file is transferred between two identical computers with all the same fonts and programs, there's no guarantee the document will look the same when it gets to its destination.

As a result of this problem, users were forced to make a choice between compatibility and design. If a file was translated into a format like plain ASCII text, it would open on most machines. However, it probably wouldn't look much like the original. If the file were to remain in the original format, other users may not be able to view it.

This situation took a turn for the better a couple of years ago when Adobe introduced Acrobat. This cross-platform (Mac, Unix, and Windows) program creates and reads Portable Document Format (PDF) files, which are platform- and application-independent files. Acrobat can also translate documents created in other programs—PageMaker, QuarkXPress, Microsoft Word—into PDF files. The new files include all the fonts, graphics, and other visual items of the original files. This feature allows users to share complex documents without worrying about maintaining their original look and feel. Totally cool.

Of course, in order to use these files, the recipient computer needs to have the ability to read PDF documents. That's where Acrobat Reader comes in. Reader is a PDF viewer that is distributed at no cost on the Internet and by user groups. It is also included on the companion CD-ROM.

Before we get into what Reader can do, let's outline what it is—and what it is not. Whereas Acrobat is an application that can be used to make new PDF files, Reader is a PDF viewer that can only read *existing* files. On the bright side, Acrobat sells for hundreds of dollars, while Reader is totally free.

So if you can't create new things with Reader, what good is it? Well, it's your only option when downloading a lot of user manuals nowadays—in fact, many of

Apple's online manuals are now in PDF form, an example of which is shown in Figure 21.24.

Reader is a lot more powerful than it first appears. Because PDF is so flexible, users have a great deal of control over how the document is displayed. Reader allows you to zoom in and out, find text, and display information as either a continuous scroll, one page at a time, or as facing pages.

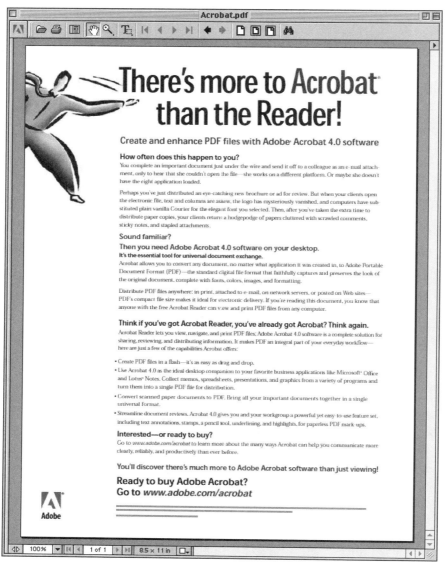

Figure 21.24 The basic Acrobat Reader window. Users can navigate around the document by using the scroll bars or the index on the left.

Internet Applications And Utilities

> **TIP**
> Adobe has more information about Reader and the full version of Acrobat at its Web site, www.adobe.com/prodindex/acrobat/main.html.

Transmit

The sole purpose of Transmit, a relatively new utility from Panic (www.panic.com), is to transfer files to and from FTP servers. It performs this task using an efficient, Mac OS-like interface backed by a PowerPC-native, multithreaded code base. According to tests performed by Panic, Transmit is the fastest FTP client available for the Mac OS. To see how Transmit works, take a look at Figure 21.25, which shows a session to the Adobe FTP site being opened from the Favorites menu.

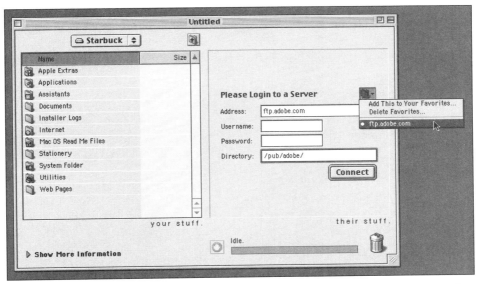

Figure 21.25 Opening an FTP session from the Favorites menu in Transmit.

Once connected, you can upload and download files, as well as synchronize folders. You can also resize the window and show more information about a connection (see Figure 21.26). To add a connection to the Favorites menu, choose File|Add Path To Favorites.

> **TIP**
> These programs and many, many other shareware applications are available at most of the large FTP libraries, including the Info-Mac Archive (ftp://hyperarchive.lcs.mit.edu/) and the University of Michigan Mac archive (ftp://mac.archive.umich.edu/mac/).

Mac OS 8.6

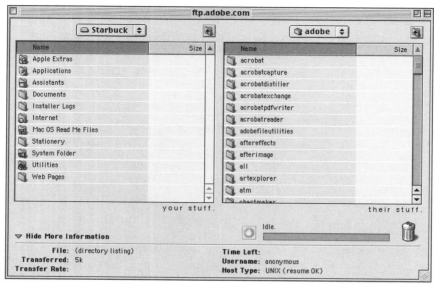

Figure 21.26 An established FTP session in Transmit.

Finally, here are some other Internet programs to check out:

▶ *Better Telnet*—Better Telnet is a freeware Telnet client from Sassy Software (www.cstone.net/~rbraun/mac/telnet/) that also has a built-in FTP server and client.

▶ *NetPresenz*—NetPresenz is a shareware FTP and Web server from Peter Lewis and Stairways Shareware (www.stairways.com) that you can easily install on your Mac to enable users to access files. It's easy to set up and is an ideal personal FTP and Web server.

▶ *Yet Another NewsWatcher*—Yet Another NewsWatcher is a good, solid newsreader that's better organized than Netscape News, and it allows you to perform complicated searches on newsgroups. Yet Another NewsWatcher is from Brian Clark (www.kagi.com/)

▶ *Disinfectant*—Disinfectant, from John Norstad (hyperarchive.lcs.mit.edu/HyperArchive/HyperArchive.html) is an anti-virus program. If you're going to wander around the Net downloading files, you're running the risk of catching a computer virus. This free application can keep your hard drive virus free.

Wrapping Up

Apple invented the first commercial personal computer 20 years ago, and Mac OS 8.6 continues to improve on the basic principle of its first operating system: make it simple, make it powerful, and most importantly, make it fun! Mac OS 8.6 implements many improvements as well as several new features to help you harness the power of the Internet and the Web as well as the personal computer itself.

I hope you find that Mac OS 8.6 meets your expectations!

PART IV

Appendixes

Appendix A
Getting Help

Getting help with the Mac OS and your favorite applications has never been easier, thanks to several powerful features provided by Mac OS 8.6. The Help Viewer application, context-sensitive help, and the ability to summarize documents are the most useful methods of getting help. Users who are familiar with earlier versions of the OS will not be disappointed, however, because all the older types of help, including Balloon Help and the Apple Guide, still exist. Some applications, such as Microsoft Word, offer their own online help viewers as well.

Help Viewer

Getting help with a particular task can sometimes be difficult when you're not sure what terms to use in a search for help. Of course, this is still a better situation than in the days prior to online help when you had to thumb through the index of the software manual and search for the topic. The latest version of Apple's Help Viewer application provides the very best tools possible to enable you to search for help about the Mac OS. Software developers are now able to incorporate Help Viewer-style assistance in their applications, as they did in years past with Balloon Help and Apple Guide. To assist you in finding important information, the Help Viewer provides several basic functions:

- Browse documents
- Search for one or more terms
- Launch AppleScripts

To try it out, go to the Finder and choose Help|Help Center, which launches the Help Viewer and opens the Help Center document, shown in Figure A.1.

Let's look at each of the main functions of the Help Viewer.

Figure A.1 The Mac OS 8.6 Help Center.

Browse Help Documents

Help Viewer allows application programmers to create help documents that may be categorized and viewed. For example, Figure A.2 shows the section of the Help Center entitled Mac OS Help, which is broken down into several subcategories.

Clicking on any of the categories in the left-hand side of the browser window brings up even more information on the right-hand side of the browser window, as illustrated by the section entitled "Internet and Networking," shown in Figure A.3.

Finally, each of these items is an individual topic that may be selected for viewing. Figure A.4, for example, shows the result of clicking on the topic entitled "Connecting to a local network."

The Help Viewer is navigated using a Web browser-style interface. To pilot your way around the Help Viewer, click the left-arrow button to return to the previous page, the right-arrow button to go to the next page (that has already been visited), or click the house button to go back to the Help Center home page (see Figure A.5).

Getting Help 553

Figure A.2 The Mac OS Help portion of the Help Center.

Figure A.3 A top-level heading of the Mac OS Help section of the Help Center.

Mac OS 8.6

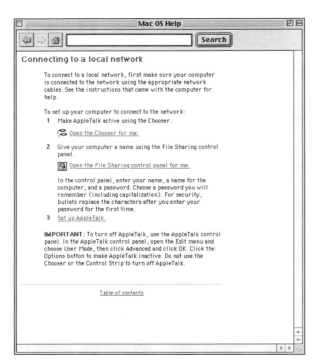

Figure A.4 An individual topic as seen through the Help Viewer.

Figure A.5 The navigational buttons in the Help Viewer.

Search Help Documents

In addition to browsing documents, the Help Viewer also allows you to search for help topics using two methods:

➤ Keyword searches

➤ Boolean searches

Only the documents in the Help folder (in your System Folder) will be searched, although you can always open Sherlock and perform a full-text search of an entire indexed volume if you want to try expanding your search to your local hard drive. Depending on what components you have installed on your computer, the contents of the Help folder may differ from the example shown in Figure A.6.

To enter a simple keyword search, just type a phrase into the search field, paying no attention to case, as in Figure A.7.

Getting Help 555

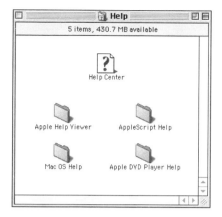

Figure A.6 The Mac OS stores all the Help Viewer's files in the Help Folder, located in the System Folder.

Figure A.7 An example of a simple keyword search.

The Help browser window displays the search results in much the same way you'd expect to see results of a Web search (see Figure A.8). For example, results are ranked according to how closely your term matches the contents of the Help Viewer's indices, and are displayed 10 results (or *hits*) at a time. In this example, 33 hits are returned over four pages of results, which you can browse using the navigational buttons.

In addition to keyword searches, you can also execute Boolean searches to further refine your searches using the criteria in Table A.1.

For example, suppose you want to search for help on creating AppleScripts with Folder Actions. You could just go to the AppleScript section of the Help Center, but you don't necessarily want to exclude the sections of the Help Center that aren't specifically about AppleScript. The answer is to create a Boolean search using *AppleScript + folder + action*, the result of which is shown in Figure A.9.

Table A.1 Boolean operators for searches with the Help Viewer.

Character	Meaning	Example
+	and	AppleScript + folder + action
|	or	DVD | CD-ROM
!	not	monitor ! sound
( )	group	(Desktop + printer) ! Chooser

Mac OS 8.6

Appendix A

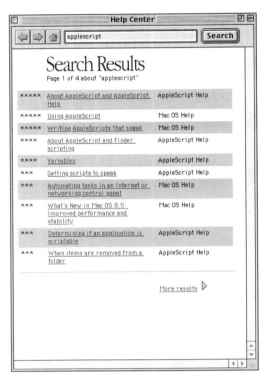

Figure A.8 The results of a simple keyword search.

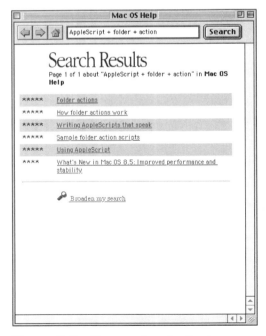

Figure A.9 The results of a Boolean search.

Getting Help 557

Finally, you can command the Help Viewer to search for related terms whenever you see the magnifying glass with the phrase "Broaden my search." The Help Viewer does this by summarizing the keywords of the result summaries and adding these terms to a new search. Apple developed and patented this summarizing technology a few years ago, and this feature of the Help Viewer is one of the first and best applications of this technology. Figure A.10 shows the result of a broadened search.

Figure A.10 The results of a broadened search.

Launch AppleScripts

Not only does the Help Viewer allow you to browse and search help documents, it also allows AppleScripts to be launched from within help documents. The chief benefit of this capability is that interactive examples can be created to lead you through the help process, not just explain it to you in a document. Of course, AppleScripts can do just about anything under Mac OS 8.6, including launch applications and accept user input. For example, Figure A.11 shows a Help document with a link to a compiled AppleScript called *OpnShrlck* that launches Sherlock to the Search Internet tab.

Mac OS 8.6

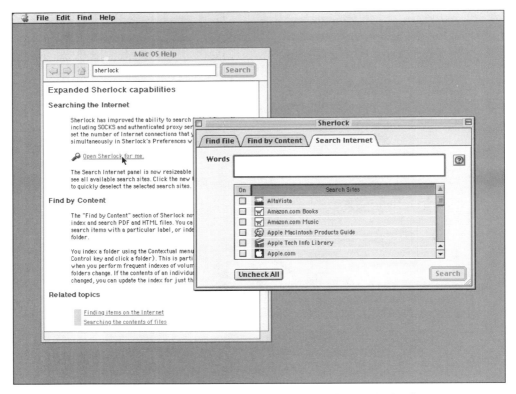

Figure A.11 The result of launching an AppleScript from a help document.

Context-Sensitive Help

Context-sensitive help, another feature of Mac OS 8.6, is the ability of the Mac OS to sense where you are in the Finder and offer immediate help on a selected item. For example, you can Control+Click a folder such as the Utilities folder and select Help from the contextual menu. The Mac OS sends information about that item to the Help Viewer and executes a broadened search (see Figure A.12). The cleverness of context-sensitive help lies in the kinds of information the Mac OS sends to the Help Viewer. For example, the Utilities folder is (A) a folder that contains (B) utilities, so the Help Viewer executes a search for "utilities folder."

Summarizing Text

Mac OS 8.6 also provides help in a way that is unique to all operating systems through its ability to summarize a document and send the summary to the Clipboard. From there, you can view or copy the information to another source, such as a word processor. To summarize a document:

Getting Help 559

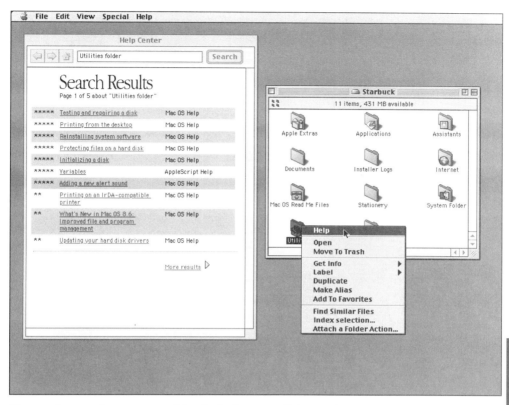

Figure A.12 Context-sensitive help is accessible via the contextual menu (Control+Click) on a selected item in the Finder.

1. Activate the contextual menu (Control+Click) on a document in the Finder.
2. Choose Summarize File to Clipboard.
3. The document summary, such as the one shown in Figure A.13, will appear in the Clipboard.

Not all documents are summarizable, however, but SimpleText, BBEdit, and Acrobat documents are among those that are.

Balloon Help

The venerable Balloon Help feature is also present in this version of the Mac OS, providing quick help for window elements and application features. Activate Balloon Help from the Help menu and position the mouse over a screen element to see if any help is available. Many applications lack Balloon Help support, however. Figure A.14 shows a balloon activated in Eudora Pro while mousing over the attachment menu.

Mac OS 8.6

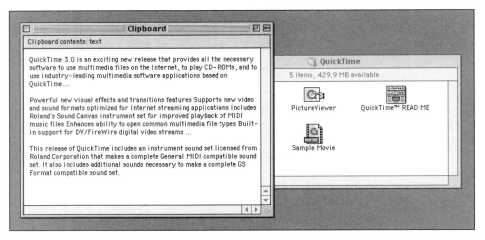

Figure A.13 The result of summarizing a document.

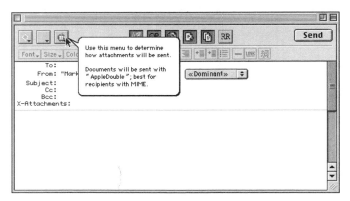

Figure A.14 An example of Balloon Help for Eudora Pro.

Apple Guide

Apple Guide is the predecessor to the new Help Viewer. It continues to be supported in Mac OS 8.6 and probably will be for some time to come while software developers adapt their products to the new help format. For those applications that have Apple Guide support, the guide documents are activated by selecting them from the Help menu. Apple Guide has been around for about 10 years, so most users will be familiar with it, including how it can lead users through a tutorial process of how to print a document, for example. Figure A.15 shows a portion of BBEdit's Apple Guide.

To use an Apple Guide, just select a topic area and then a subtopic (which may have multiple subpages). For example, Figure A.16 shows an Apple Guide stepping through the process of displaying line numbers in a BBEdit document.

Getting Help 561

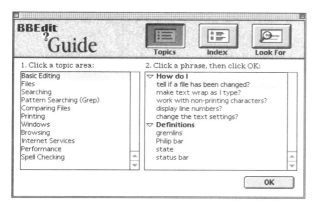

Figure A.15 An Apple Guide example.

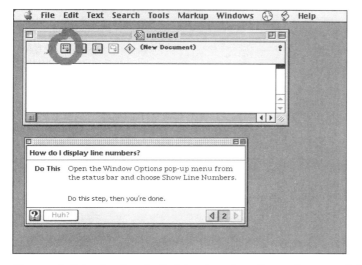

Figure A.16 An Apple Guide stepping through a tutorial process in BBEdit.

The coachmark has circled the Window Options pop-up menu, where the Show Line Numbers option resides.

Proprietary Help

Finally, users can get help in Mac OS 8.6 from proprietary online help systems provided by applications. Microsoft Word, for example, has gone to great lengths to make their help system for the Mac OS version of Word look as much like the Windows version as possible. Figure A.17 shows two versions of Microsoft Word's proprietary help system, the new Assistant (left) and the Windows-style MS Word Help viewer (right).

Mac OS 8.6

562 Appendix A

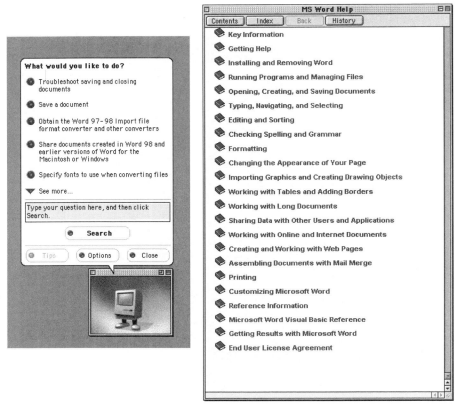

Figure A.17 Proprietary help systems from Microsoft.

Appendix B
Shortcuts

The Mac OS has always been easy to use, but some people just can't get enough of the many shortcuts that are available to help navigate the keyboard and start up and shut down the computer. For those of us who aren't satisfied by the dozens of shortcuts provided by the Mac OS, luckily several third-party applications and utilities are available to create shortcuts for virtually anything else. Programs such as KeyQuencer and QuicKeys can be lifesavers for users with repetitive-motion injuries!

Common Shortcuts

Table B.1 lists the most common shortcuts involving starting up, shutting down, working with applications, and other miscellaneous actions. When using these or any other shortcuts, be sure to press the key combination only once and release the keys once the shortcut has been activated. In the case of zapping the PRAM, release the keys once the startup chime sounds for the second time. Also, some PowerBook keyboards may abbreviate the names of the keys, so choose your keystrokes carefully.

Table B.1 Common keyboard shortcuts.

Action	Keystroke(s)
Startup, shutdown, restart	Power key
Start without Extensions or Startup Items	Shift key (while starting up)
Rebuild Desktop	Command+Option (while starting up)
Zap PRAM (parameter RAM)	Command+Option+P+R (while starting up)
Close all open Finder windows	Option (while starting up)
Boot from CD-ROM (must be bootable format)	C (while starting up)
Bypass startup disk	Command+Option+Shift+Delete
Force quit an application	Command+Option+Escape
Force a restart	Command+Control+Power key

(continued)

Table B.1 Common keyboard shortcuts *(continued)*.

Action	Keystroke(s)
Stop processing (some applications)	Command+Period
Stop processing (some applications)	Command+Escape
Switching between applications	Command+Tab
Take a screenshot of the entire screen	Command+Shift+3
Take a screenshot of a region of the screen	Command+Shift+4
Take a screenshot of a specific window	Command+Shift+Caps Lock+4
Rotate to the next keyboard layout	Command+Space
Rotate to the previous keyboard layout	Command+Option+Space

Finder Window Shortcuts

Many people use Finder window shortcuts without really thinking of them as shortcuts, and you may be surprised by how many shortcuts for moving around Finder windows exist. Table B.2 lists the Finder window shortcuts available in Mac OS 8.6.

Table B.2 Finder window shortcuts.

Action	Keystroke(s)
Close active window	Command+W
Close active window	Click close box
Close all open windows	Command+Option+W
Close all open windows	Option+Click close box
Convert pop-up window into closed, normal window	Command+Shift+W
Close all open windows and convert all pop-up windows into closed, normal windows	Command+Option+Shift+W
Open selected item and close the parent window	Command+Option+O
Open selected item and close the parent window	Option+Double-click
Expand closed subfolders one level in a list view	Click (on a closed folder triangle)
Collapse open subfolders one level in a list view	Click (on an open folder's triangle)
Expand closed subfolders one level in a list view	Command+Right arrow (on a closed folder)

(continued)

Table B.2 Finder window shortcuts *(continued)*.

Action	Keystroke(s)
Collapse open subfolders one level in a list view	Command+Left arrow (on a closed folder)
Expand all closed subfolders in a list view	Command+Option+Right arrow
Collapse all open subfolders in a list view	Command+Option+Left arrow
Open a window to its largest possible size	Option+Click (on zoom box)
Collapse window (WindowShade)	Double-click (on title bar)
Collapse window (WindowShade)	Click collapse box
Collapse all windows (WindowShade)	Option+Double-click (on title bar)
Collapse all windows (WindowShade)	Option+Click collapse box
Move down to the next item in a list view	Down arrow
Move up to the next item in a list view	Up arrow
Select an item in a list view	(Type the first letter in that item's title)
Move to the top of a list view	Home
Move to the bottom of a list view	End
Scroll up one page in a list view	Page Up
Scroll down one page in a list view	Page Down
Move up one folder level	Command+Up arrow
Open the selected item	Command+O
Open the selected item	Command+Down arrow
Locate the original of an alias	Command+R
Activate icon proxy pop-up	Command+Click (on proxy icon)
Activate icon proxy	Click (on proxy icon)
Scroll left, right, up, or down	Command+Drag mouse in window
Move an inactive window by its title bar	Command+Drag (title bar)
Select an item in an icon view	Left, Right, Up, or Down arrow
Select next item, alphabetically, in a list	Tab
Select multiple, noncontiguous items	Shift+Click
Select multiple items	Click+Drag mouse
Select everything in a window	Command+A
Copy all the filenames of a window's contents to the Clipboard	Command+A, then Command+C
Create a new folder	Command+N
Get Info for selected item(s)	Command+I
Rename	Return

(continued)

Mac OS 8.6

Table B.2 Finder window shortcuts *(continued)*.

Action	Keystroke(s)
Create an alias	Command+M
Create an alias	Command+Option+Drag
Copy	Command+D
Copy	Option+Drag
Put away	Command+Y
Move to Trash	Command+Delete

Navigational Window Shortcuts

The navigational windows in Mac OS 8.6 (the Open and Save dialog boxes, also know as Navigational Services) have many shortcuts that are similar to the Finder window shortcuts described above. However, since this is a relatively new scheme for programmers to follow when creating their own applications, not all the listings in Table B.3 will work for all applications.

Table B.3 Navigational window shortcuts.

Action	Keystroke(s)
Move down one item	Down arrow
Move up one item	Up arrow
Select an item	(Type the first letter in that item's title)
Move to the top	Home
Move to the bottom	End
Scroll up one screen	Page Up
Scroll down one screen	Page Down
Move up one folder level	Command+Up arrow
Open the selected folder	Command+Down arrow
Expand closed subfolders one level	Command+Right arrow
Collapse open subfolders one level	Command+Left arrow
Open selected item	Return
Go to the Desktop	Command+Shift+D
Close the dialog box	Esc
Close the dialog box	Command+Period
Select all openable items	Command+A
Navigate forward to a previously visited folder	Option+Right arrow
Navigate backward to a previously visited folder	Option+Left arrow

Mac OS 8.6

Appendix C
Installing Or Updating Mac OS 8.6

If you've recently purchased a new Mac, Mac OS 8.6 might already be installed. However, if you purchased your computer in the spring or early summer of 1999, it probably came with Mac OS 8.5. If this is the case, you might be entitled to a free upgrade to Mac OS 8.6. Check the Mac OS home page at www.apple.com/macos for more information. Finally, you might have a much older Mac for which you recently purchased Mac OS 8.6. In each of these cases, this appendix will cover the following steps:

- Perform a new installation of Mac OS 8.6
- Reinstall Mac OS 8.6
- Perform a *clean installation* of Mac OS 8.6

If you've never installed system software or components before, don't worry. After all, it's the Mac OS we're talking about here—it can't be too difficult!

Performing A New Installation Of Mac OS 8.6

Whether it's a new installation, a reinstallation, a custom installation, or a deinstallation, the mechanics of installing the Mac OS are all pretty much the same. The most significant difference is in performing a new installation; be careful in what you do with your existing system software so you don't accidentally lose anything important. We'll get to that in a minute, but first let's look at the steps involved in installing the software.

The first step to installing the Mac OS successfully is to reboot your Mac and quit any applications that might have been automatically launched on startup. Most software installation programs, including the Mac OS installer, require that you quit all applications prior to the installation process because the files being installed could become corrupt if another program interferes with them during the installation process.

The next step is to insert the CD-ROM containing the Mac OS installation program that launches the installer. Of course, the ideal solution would be for you to boot from the installation CD by restarting with the CD inserted and holding down the C key until bootup begins. Figure C.1, for example, shows the disk containing all the files necessary to perform an installation, including the installation application, update application, and Mac OS 8.6 documentation.

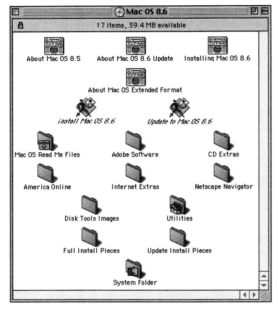

Figure C.1 A typical Mac OS 8.6 installation disc.

Once the installer has been launched, you'll need to perform four main tasks:

1. Choose a drive onto which the OS is to be installed.
2. Read the Important Information document that details known problems and incompatible hardware. This is a very important step.
3. Complete the software license agreement.
4. Choose the software to be installed.

After you've completed these four main tasks, the installation program will ensure that your hard disk is capable of containing the installation of the software, check the integrity of the disk, and begin installation. With Mac OS 8.6, the installation is like one-stop shopping: everything will be installed without requiring additional intervention on your part.

You may also deinstall portions of the Mac OS using these same steps.

Step 1: Select A Destination Disk

Selecting a destination disk is the first step. If you have multiple disk drives from which to choose, the installation program will automatically evaluate each one to determine if it has enough available space for an installation of Mac OS 8.6. Figure C.2, for example, shows the hard drive named Roswell selected for deinstallation.

Figure C.2   Select a destination disk for Mac OS 8.6.

To perform a clean installation, which creates a brand new System Folder without deleting your existing System Folder, click the Destination Options button and check the box entitled Perform Clean Installation, which is unchecked by default (see Figure C.3). If you've run into problems installing Mac OS 8.6 before, if you are doing a major upgrade from Mac OS 8.0, or if you are having persistent problems concerning system stability, you should check this box.

Figure C.3   Choose the Perform Clean Installation option to install a brand new System Folder.

Step 2: Read The Installation Notes

Without a doubt, you should read every word of the installation notes (see Figure C.4) to ensure that your hardware fully supports Mac OS 8.6. Every version of the Mac OS has known problems in relation to certain hardware platforms, so you should find out what they are now rather than later—like when your system has deleted the report that's due at the end of the day!

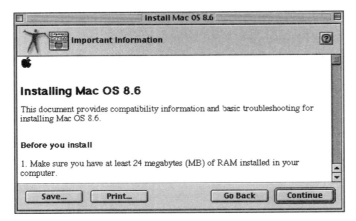

Figure C.4 Be sure to read the installation notes!

Step 3: Complete The Software License Agreement

You will not be permitted to install Mac OS 8.6 unless you agree to the terms of the license agreement (see Figure C.5). After all, you technically don't own the software; Apple is selling you a license (subject to terms, conditions, and caveats) to use a copy of it on your machine.

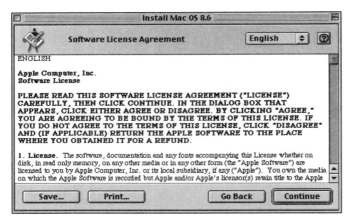

Figure C.5 The Mac OS licensing agreement.

Step 4: Choose The Software To Be Installed

The final step is to select the software you want to install. You can choose from a basic installation of Mac OS 8.6 and certain applications and utilities. Alternatively, you can perform a customized installation that includes all the software or just a single program. Figure C.6 shows a standard installation of Mac OS 8.6.

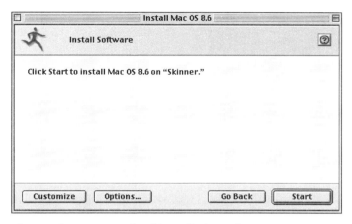

Figure C.6 A standard installation of Mac OS 8.6

At any time between Steps 1 through 4, you can click the Help icon for context-sensitive help. A window that addresses the issues presented in the current installation screen will be displayed, explaining what each option is and the consequences of each possible selection. Figure C.7 shows what a Help window looks like for the custom installation.

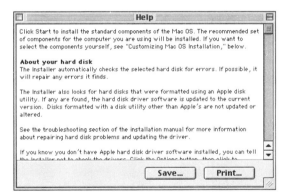

Figure C.7 Take advantage of the Help information for the Mac OS 8.6 installation process to better understand what you're about to install.

To perform a customized installation of Mac OS 8.6 or to deinstall any of its components, click the Customize button. Then click on the checkbox beside each component that you want to install or remove, as in Figure C.8, in which only the Internet Access component has been selected.

From this point, you may now customize the selected component even further by clicking on the pop-up menu shown in Figure C.9.

572 Appendix C

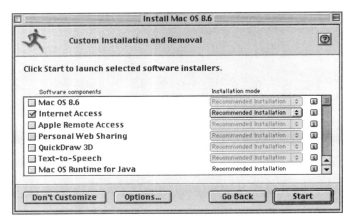

Figure C.8 Selecting a specific component to install.

Figure C.9 For each component, select from these three options to perform the recommended installation, customized installation, or customized removal.

If you select a customized installation or removal, a window like the one shown in Figure C.10 appears. In this example, the Internet Utilities portion of the Internet Access component has been chosen for installation. Figure C.11 shows a custom deinstallation for the Printing components of Mac OS 8.6.

Last but not least, review the Installation Options button. It allows you to determine whether your hard disk drivers will be updated to the latest version. You can also choose to receive an installation report of what was added, removed, or replaced during the entire installation process (see Figure C.12).

Mac OS 8.6

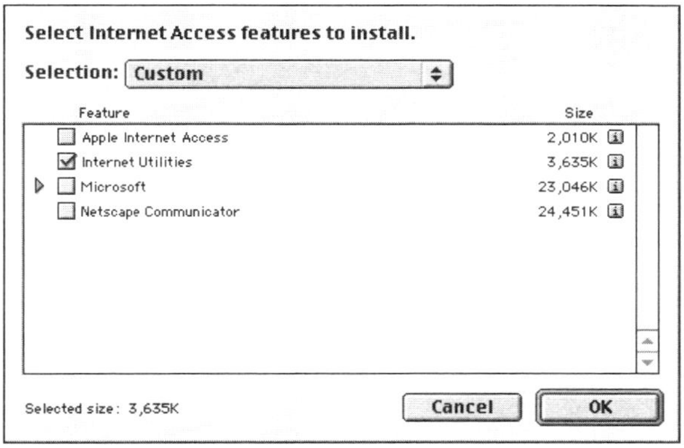

Installing Or Updating Mac OS 8.6 573

Figure C.10 A customized installation for the Internet Access component of Mac OS 8.6.

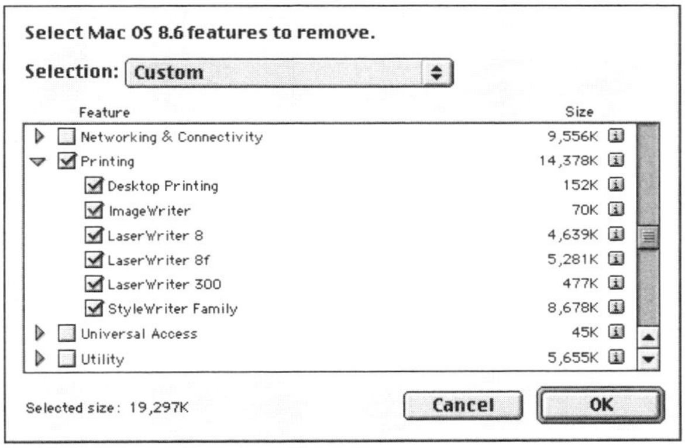

Figure C.11 A customized deinstallation for the Printing components of Mac OS 8.6.

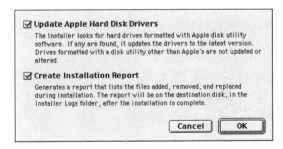

Figure C.12 The Installation Options menu.

Mac OS 8.6

Once you've selected the software to be installed, click the Start button to begin the process, which could take anywhere from just a few minutes to almost a half hour, depending on the software being installed and the speed of your computer and hard drive. Throughout the process, the installation program will display a progress window like the one shown in Figure C.13.

Figure C.13 The Installation Options menu.

Reinstalling Mac OS 8.6

If you need to reinstall Mac OS 8.6, go back to Steps 1 through 3. Pay careful attention to Step 1, in which you were asked whether or not you wanted to perform a clean installation. You may want to consider performing a clean installation if your system is behaving strangely for any reason and as long as you have enough disk space available. If you're convinced you don't have enough disk space, proceed to Step 4 and install only the software that you think is needed.

Should you select a disk that already contains a previous installation of Mac OS 8.6, the window shown in Figure C.14 will appear. The Mac OS installer will recognize that you already have Mac OS 8.6 installed and ask whether you want to reinstall the OS, add, or remove selected components. The remainder of the process is as described previously.

Figure C.14 The Mac OS installer detects which version of the OS you already have installed and presents this window if version 8.6 is already present on the selected drive.

Updating To Mac OS 8.6

Finally, if you have a previous version of Mac OS 8 on your hard drive and you want to update to version 8.6, select the application entitled *Update to Mac OS 8.6* on the installation CD-ROM. Once you've selected the appropriate destination disk, a window like the one shown in Figure C.15 will appear.

Installing Or Updating Mac OS 8.6 575

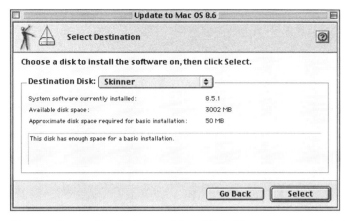

Figure C.15 Updating to Mac OS 8.6 from version 8.5.1.

Again, the process for updating to Mac OS 8.6 is parallel that described previously, except that some of the custom removal options will be unavailable because the components have not yet been installed.

Appendix D
Additional Resources On The Web

Thousands of Web sites contain relevant information about the Mac OS, Apple Computer, Mac software and hardware, and news about computers in general. Too many, in fact, to be always sure where to go for the most accurate and up-to-date information. The following categories of Web sites contain the URLs of some of the best sites available at this time, although the biggest and best Web site of all might open up for business tomorrow morning!

Apple Computer

Apple home page
www.apple.com

Apple products
www.apple.com/guide

Apple support
www.apple.com/support

Apple software updates
www.apple.com/swupdates

Apple news
www.apple.com/hotnews

Apple Store
www.apple.com/store

Apple developer
www.apple.com/developer

Apple resource locator
www.apple.com/buy

Apple And Macintosh News

MacInTouch
www.macintouch.com

iMacInTouch
www.imacintouch.com/imac.html

Macintosh News Network
www.macnn.com

Apple Insider
www.appleinsider.com

Mac OS Rumors
www.macosrumors.com

MacCentral Online
www.maccenter.com

Macinsites
www.macinsites.com

EvangeList
www.evangelist.macaddict.com

Apple And Macintosh Publications

Macworld Magazine
macworld.zdnet.com

MacAddict
www.macaddict.com

MacWEEK
www.macweek.zdnet.com

Inside MacGames Magazine
www.imgmagazine.com

Mac Gamer's Ledge
www.macledge.com

Mac Gaming
www.macgaming.com

MacHome Interactive
www.machome.com

MacTech Magazine
www.mactech.com

MacToday Magazine
www.mactoday.com

Macintosh Hardware And Software

Deal-Mac
www.deal-mac.com

Mac Trading Post
www.mactradingpost.com

MacMall
www.macmall.com

MacWarehouse
www.warehouse.com/apple

MacConnection
www.macconnection.com

MacZone
www.zones.com/mac_zone/default_mac.htm

Mostly Mac
www.mostlymac.com

USB Stuff
www.usbstuff.com

Index

A

About This Computer dialog box
  Finder menus, 64
  memory control, 245-247, 253-255
  memory and multitasking, 277-278
  virtual memory, 246
Access, remote. *See* ARA (Apple Remote Access).
Access privileges (File Sharing), 468-470, 471-476
  Copy These Privileges to All Enclosed Folders option, 468-470
  Everyone category, 474
  Inbox folders, 474
  None option, 472
  Outbox folders, 474-475
  Owner category, 473-474
  Personal Web Sharing, 516-519
  Read & Write option, 473
  Read Only option, 473
  remote volumes and, 482-483
  strategies, 474-476
  User/Group category, 474
  workgroups, 475-476
  Write Only option, 472
Acrobat Reader, Adobe, 543-545
ACTION Utilities, Open dialog boxes, 131-134
Actions tab, Personal Web Sharing, 516
Active programs, foreground and background processing, 266-267
Activity Monitor tab, File Sharing, 476-477
Add Alias to Apple Menu AppleScript, Useful Scripts set, 353, 354, 375
Additive color, ColorSync Control Panel, 317
Adobe Acrobat Reader, 543-545
Adobe Type Manager. *See* ATM.
Alert dialog box, File Sharing, 459
Alert When Folder Changes AppleScript, More Automated Tasks folder, 376
Alerts section, Monitors & Sound Control Panel, 127
Alias folders, 147-148
  launching applications from, 203

Aliases, 139-153
  Add Alias to Apple Menu AppleScript, 353, 354
  advanced concepts, 145-147
  aliasing, 145
  Apple Menu folder, 37, 38, 40
  applications, 149-150
  Control Panels folder, 44
  creating and using, 142-145
  defined, 37
  deleting, 146
  deleting original files, 146
  edition file, 342
  finding original files, 146-147
  Get Info dialog box (Finder), 111-112
  grouping, 149, 150
  hard drive, 152
  Internet URL, 538-539
  italic type, 143
  Launcher Control Panel, 206
  launching applications with, 141
  links, 144-145
  moving original files, 146
  multiple, 145
  multiple data file, 150
  network servers and, 142, 152
  organizing data files, 141
  removable cartridge maps, 151-152
  removable media and, 141, 150-151
  renaming, 143
  replacing icons, 147
  stationery document, 211
  Trash, 151
  volume, 149, 483-484
  ways to use, 141-142, 149-152
Allow Remote Program Linking check box, 489
Allow User to See All Disks feature, File Sharing, 466
Alphabetically jumping in dialog boxes, 215-216
AMICO utility, customizing Apple menu, 136-137
Anti-virus tools, 446
Appearance Control Panel, 19, 113-117
  Appearance tab, 114
  AppleScript and dictionary, 353, 354

582 Appearance Control Panel

Desktop tab, 115-116
Fonts tab, 114, 115
Options configuration tab, 116-117
Smart Scrolling feature, 116, 117
Sounds tab, 116
Themes tab, 113, 114
Appearance folder, System Folder, 35-36
Apple DVD Player, 417-419
Apple Extras folder, AppleScript, 359
Apple FM Radio application, 414
Apple menu
   About This Computer command, 64
   Add Alias to Apple Menu AppleScript, 353, 354
   AMICO utility, 136-137
   BeHierarchic utility, 137, 138
   Finder menus, 64
   GoMac utility, 134-136
   launching applications, 202, 203
   Options Control Panel, 118
   Recent commands, 64
Apple Menu folder, 36-40
   aliases, 37, 38, 40
   contents of, 36-37
   rearranging items in, 38-39
   special characters for alphabetizing files, 38-39
Apple Remote Access. *See* ARA.
Apple System Profiler
   Finder menus, 64
   troubleshooting tools, 440
Apple Video Player, 414-416
AppleCD Audio Player, 416-417
AppleEvents, 323-327. *See also* IAC (Interapplication Communication).
   AppleScript and, 356
   FileMaker suite, 325, 326
   linking programs, 326-327
   Program Linking and, 326-327, 489
   suites, 324-325
AppleGuide file, AppleScript, 359
AppleScript, 351-377
   Add Alias to Apple Menu, 353, 354
   Appearance Control Panel dictionary, 353, 354
   Apple Extras folder, 359
   AppleEvents and, 356
   AppleGuide file, 359
   AppleScriptLib extension, 358
   Application Switcher and, 120
   applications and compatibility, 199
   architecture, 355-357
   attachable level, 361-362
   Automated Tasks folder, 359
   dictionary and Appearance Control Panel, 353, 354
   dictionary and StuffIt Deluxe, 355
   encapsulation, 352
   event suites, 356-357
   extensions, 357-358

Finder and, 371, 372
Folder Actions, 372-375
Guide file, 359
Help, 361
IAC (Interapplication Communication) and, 356
inheritance, 352
Internet Suite, 372
learning resources, 376-377
levels of, 361-362
More Automated Tasks folder, 359-360, 376
new features, 357-358, 371-375
Object Model, 356
OSA (Open Scripting Architecture), 355-357
recordable level, 361
references, 356
resources, 376-377
sample scripts, 375-376
Script Editor, 359, 360, 362-369
scriptable level, 361
Scripting Additions folder, 358
scripting applications, 369-371
scripting basics, 357-362
Scripts folder, 359, 360-361
Standard Editions file, 357
statements, 352-353
StuffIt Deluxe and dictionary, 355
unit types, 371
Universal format, 353
URL Access Scripting Addition dictionary, 358
Useful Scripts set, 375-376
words, 352
AppleShare Volume icons, networks and, 482-483
Applet Runner application, 383-385. *See also* Java.
   Applet menu, 385
   File menu, 383
   firewalls and, 384
   Properties dialog box, 383-384
   proxy servers and, 384
AppleTalk, PowerBook system software, 180
AppleTalk Control Panel, 455-456. *See also* File Sharing.
   Open Transport (Internet connectivity), 498-499
Application menu, 69-71
   floating palettes, 70-71
Application pools, Memory Mapper utility, 248
Application Support folder, System Folder, 40
Application Switcher, 70-71, 118-120. *See also* Switching between applications.
   AppleScript and, 120
   AppSwitcher Control, 120, 121
   configuring, 118-120
   keyboard shortcut, 118
   tearing off, 118-119
   Zoombox, 119
Applications, 197-116
   aliasing, 149-150
   AppleScript and, 199

Desktop and, 212-214
drag and drop, 200
Edition Manager, 327-342
hiding, 272-274
IAC (Interapplication Communication), 321-327
Internet software, 521-547
launching, 8, 141, 200-207
Mac OS 8.6 compatibility, 197-200
multiple. *See* Multiple applications.
scripting, 369-371
stationery documents and, 207-212
switching between, 70-71, 118-120, 267-268
troubleshooting crashes, 432-435
viewing dictionaries, 369-371
ARA (Apple Remote Access), 500-502. *See also* Internet; Open Transport.
   DialAssist Control Panel, 501
   Modem Control Panel, 500-501
   PowerBook system software, 184
   Remote Access Control Panel, 501-502
ArcTest applet, Java VMs (Virtual Machines), 386-387
Arrange/Sort List commands, View menu, 68
Arranged options, View menu, 83-84
Arrow cursors, 14
Art Safari applet, 381, 382
ASCII, localization and character sets, 307
Assistants, Internet, 493-497
ATM (Adobe Type Manager), 294-296. *See also* Fonts.
   printer fonts and, 295-296
Attachable level, AppleScript, 361-362
Audio. *See* Sound.
Automated Tasks folder, AppleScript, 359
Automatic shutdowns, Energy Saver Control Panel, 128, 129
AutoPlay option, QuickTime, 401
AutoRemounter, PowerBook system software, 183

B

Background processing, 266-275
   copying files, 271-272
   foreground processing and, 266-267
   hiding applications, 272-274
   hiding Desktop, 274-275
   printing, 269-271
Backward button, Network Browser, 487
Backwards compatibility, operating system versions, 4
Balloon Help, 101-103
   history of, 101-102
   limitations of, 102-103
Bar Chart applet, Java VMs (Virtual Machines), 387
Battery Conservation slider, PowerBook system software, 176-177
Battery recharging, PowerBook system software, 174
Battery usage, PowerBook system software, 177-180

BBEdit, viewing application dictionaries, 370
Beatnik plug-in, Netscape Navigator, 525
BeHierarchic utility, Apple menu, 137, 138
Bitmapped fonts, 288-289
Blinking question mark at startup, troubleshooting, 424-426
Bookmarks, Netscape Navigator, 524-525
Bootable floppies, troubleshooting tools, 441
Browsers
   Font Reserve Browser utility, 302-304
   Microsoft Internet Explorer, 531-534
   Netscape Navigator, 523-528
   Network Browser, 485-487
   QuickTime and, 401-402
Buttons, viewing windows as, 84, 85

C

Caches, disk, 238-239
Cancel Publisher option, Publisher Options command (Edition Manager), 332
Cancel Subscriber option, Subscriber Options command (Edition Manager), 336
Card Test applet, "look and feel" of cross-platform programs, 390, 391
Cassidy & Green's Conflict Catcher, 47
CD-ROMs
   extended, 419-420
   QuickTime and, 405
CDs, AppleCD Audio Player, 416-417
Character sets, localization and, 306-307
Check Syntax button, Script Editor (AppleScript), 367
Checking spelling, IAC (Interapplication Communication), 322-323
Chooser, 17. *See also* Network Browser.
   background printing, 269-270
   connecting to networks with, 479-481
   printer extensions, 314-315
   printers, 310-311
CIE XYZ color standard, ColorSync Control Panel, 318
Clean Up command
   Finder, 100-101
   View menu, 68, 100-101
Clicking with cursors, 14
Clipboard
   Show Clipboard command, 24
   System Folder and, 40
   transferring data with, 21-25
Clippings
   defined, 27
   Internet URL aliases, 538-539
Collapsible windows, WindowShade, 72, 73
Collapsing and expanding lists, 89-90
Color section, Monitors & Sound Control Panel, 128

584 Colors

Colors
    Label command, 168-169
    troubleshooting, 435-436
ColorSync Control Panel, 316-319
    additive color, 317
    CIE XYZ color standard, 318
    subtractive color, 317
ColorSync Profiles folder, System Folder, 40-41
Columns
    reordering list, 92, 93
    resizing list, 91-92
Commands
    Finder menu, 64-71
    hiding applications, 272-273
    keyboard navigation (Finder), 93-95
    Publish/Subscribe (Edition Manager), 329-337
Comments, 169-171
    Script Editor (AppleScript), 368
    visibility, 171
Compatibility issues, 197-200. *See also* Cross-platform compatibility.
Components, 5-8
    Control Panels, 7
    Desk Accessories, 7-8
    Extensions, 6-7
    Finder, 5-6
    Open Transport, 6, 497-500
    printer drivers, 6
    ROM (Read-Only Memory), 6
    System suitcase, 5
Compound documents, OpenDoc, 343
Compression. *See* File compression.
Computer Names, File Sharing, 457
Conflict Catcher utility, troubleshooting tools, 444
Conflicts
    Extensions folder, 46, 47
    Font ID, 292-293
Connect dialog box, networks, 480-482
Connect to Server dialog box, Network Browser, 486
Connecting to networks with Chooser, 479-481
Connection Speed option, QuickTime, 401
Connectivity
    Internet. *See* Internet.
    Network. *See* Networks.
Context-sensitive help, 101-104
Contextual Menu Items folder, System Folder, 41, 42
Control Panels, 17-21
    Appearance, 19, 113-117, 353, 354
    AppleTalk, 455-456, 498-499
    ATM (Adobe Type Manager), 294-296
    ColorSync, 316-319
    Date & Time, 18-19, 123-124, 538
    defined, 41
    DialAssist, 501
    Editor Setup, 348
    Energy Saver, 128-130
    Extensions Manager, 47-48
    File Sharing, 456-459, 476-477, 487-489
    General Controls, 17-18, 120-123
    Internet, 402, 537-538
    Keyboard, 20
    Launcher, 204-207
    Mac OS 8.6 components, 7
    Memory, 236-239
    Modem, 500-501
    Monitors & Sound, 19, 20, 124-128
    Mouse, 19, 20
    Numbers, 21
    OpenDoc Setup, 348-349
    Password Security, 192
    Remote Access, 501-502
    Speech, 413-414
    TCP/IP, 499-500
    Text, 21
    User & Groups (File Sharing), 459-461
    Web Sharing, 509-512
Control Panels folder, 41-44
    aliases, 44
    contents of, 43-44
Control Strip
    File Sharing, 459
    PowerBook system software, 184-187
Control Strip Modules folder, System Folder, 44-45
Converting documents, MacLinkPlus, 228-229
Cooperative multitasking, 259-260
Copy These Privileges to All Enclosed Folders option, File Sharing, 468-470
Copying files in background, 271-272
Copyrights, QuickTime and, 397
Core suite, AppleEvents, 324
Create Publisher command
    edition files, 338-340
    Edition Manager, 331-332
Cross-platform compatibility, 217-234. *See also* Compatibility issues.
    Adobe Acrobat Reader, 543-545
    alternative solutions, 229-234
    File Exchange Control Panel, 220-225
    Java, 379-394
    MacLinkPlus, 225-229
    OpenDoc, 344
    sharing data, 217-225
    SoftWindows, 230-231
    SuperDrive, 219
    Virtual PC, 230-234
Cursors, 13-15
    actions of, 14-15
    arrow, 14
    clicking, 14
    double-clicking, 14
    dragging, 15
    pointing with, 14
    pressing, 15
    types of, 14

Customizing Mac OS 8.6, 113-138
    Appearance Control Panel, 113-117
    Apple Menu Options Control Panel, 118
    Applications Switcher, 118-120
    Date & Time Control Panel, 123-124
    Energy Saver Control Panel, 128-130
    features, 113-130
    General Controls Control Panel, 120-123
    Monitors & Sound Control Panel, 124-128
    third-party utilities, 130-137
Cut and paste, 22-25
    Clipboard, 22-24
    Scrapbook, 24-25

D

Data compression. *See* File compression.
Data management, 139-172
    aliasing, 139-153
    comments, 169-171
    Label command, 65, 167-169
    Sherlock search engine, 153-167
Data sharing. *See* Sharing data.
Date & Time Control Panel, 18-19
    customizing Mac OS 8.6, 123-124
    Server Options button, 124
    synchronizing time via Internet, 538
Default fonts, 299-301
Deleting. *See also* Trash.
    aliases, 146
    files from System Folder, 59
    items from Launcher Control Panel, 206
Desk Accessories, Mac OS 8.6 components, 7-8
Desktop, 212-214. *See also* Finder.
    applications and, 212-214
    dialog boxes and, 212-214
    hiding, 120-121, 274-275
    Open and Save dialog boxes, 212
    Printer Utility, 315-316
    viewing options, 88
Desktop tab, Appearance Control Panel, 115-116
DialAssist Control Panel, ARA (Apple Remote Access), 501
Dialog boxes
    Desktop and, 212-214
    GUI elements, 11-12
    jumping alphabetically, 215-216
    keyboard shortcuts, 214-216
    option types, 11
    tasks, 8
Dictionaries
    Appearance Control Panel, 353, 354
    StuffIt Deluxe and AppleScript, 355
    URL Access Scripting Addition, 358
    viewing application, 369-371
Directories, viewing via Personal NetFinder, 512-514

Disabled items, Extensions folder, 48
Disabling virtual memory, 243
Disconnecting from remote volumes, 484
Disinfectant utility, troubleshooting tools, 446
Disk caches, 238-239
Disk and file management, 4, 8
Disk First Aid utility, troubleshooting tools, 438-439
Disk formats. *See* File formats.
Disk space versus memory, 235-236
Display management, PowerBook system software, 180-182
DNS (Domain Name Servers), Internet connectivity, 496
Documents
    File Translation dialog box, 224
    OpenDoc, 344-347
    PrintMonitor Documents folder, 53
    saving Publisher, 341-342
    stationery. *See* Stationery documents.
    translating via MacLinkPlus, 225-229
    troubleshooting opening problems, 437-438
Double-clicking
    with cursors, 14
    launching applications, 201, 202, 204
Drag and drop, 22, 25-28
    applications and, 200
    Note Pad and, 28
    QuickDraw 3D and, 412
    QuickTime and, 397
    SimpleText and, 26-27
    Stickies and, 27-28
Dragging
    cursors, 15
    files between inactive windows, 95-96
    launching applications via, 202, 204
    lists, 90, 91
DrawTest applet, Java VMs (Virtual Machines), 387, 388
Drive Setup utility, troubleshooting tools, 439
Drivers, printer. *See* Printer drivers.
Droplet icons, running scripts, 366
DropStuff utility, file compression, 539, 541-542
DVD, Apple DVD Player, 417-419

E

Email
    accounts and Internet connectivity, 496
    Microsoft Outlook Express, 534-536
    Netscape Messenger, 529
Edit menu, Preferences options, 66, 67
Editing
    OpenDoc and in-place, 344
    stationery documents, 211-212
    subscribers with Edition Manager, 337
Edition files, 338-342
    aliases, 342
    linking, 338-339

586 Edition files

nested, 340-341
networks and, 340
republishing, 340
unavailable, 340
Edition Manager, 327-342. *See also* IAC (Interapplication Communication); OpenDoc.
   Create Publisher command, 331-332, 338
   editing subscribers, 337
   edition files, 338-342
   nested edition files, 340-341
   Publish/Subscribe commands, 329-337
   Publish/Subscribe feature, 327-329
   Publisher Options command, 332-334
   republishing editions, 340
   saving Publisher documents, 341-342
   Subscribe To command, 332
   Subscriber Options command, 334-337
   tips, 340-342
Editor Assistant, Internet, 494-496
Editor Setup Control Panel, OpenDoc, 348
Empty Trash command, 105
Encapsulation, AppleScript, 352
Energy Saver Control Panel, 128-130
   AutoRemounter, 183
   PowerBook system software, 175-180, 183
   Scheduled Startup & Shutdown section, 128, 129
Errors. *See* Troubleshooting.
Event suites, AppleScript, 356-357
Events, AppleEvents, 323-327
Everyone category, File Sharing, 474
Everyone option, File Sharing, 468
Expanding and collapsing lists, 89-90
Explorer Bar, Microsoft Internet Explorer, 531-532
Export/import file types, QuickTime, 399-400
Extended CD-ROMs, 419-420
Extension Manager, troubleshooting tools, 440-441
Extension Overload utility, troubleshooting tools, 444, 445
Extensions
   AppleScript, 357-358
   Mac OS 8.6 components, 6-7
Extensions folder, 45-48
   conflicts, 46, 47
   disabled items, 48
   Extensions Manager Control Panel, 47-48
   INITs, 45
   printer drivers, 45-46, 314-315
   Shift key and suppression of, 46-47
Extensions Manager Control Panel, 47-48

F

Favorites button, Network Browser, 486-487
Favorites folder
   Finder menus, 64
   launching applications, 202, 204, 205
   System Folder, 48

File Buddy utility, troubleshooting tools, 443-444
File compression, 539-542
   DropStuff utility, 539, 541-542
   QuickTime and, 403-405
   StuffIt Expander utility, 539, 540-541
File Exchange Control Panel, 220-225
   File Exchange, 222-225
   File Translation dialog box, 224
   PC Exchange, 220-222
File formats
   MacLinkPlus and, 225-228
   SuperDrive and, 219
File menu
   Applet Runner application, 383
   Label command, 65, 167-169
   Move To Trash command, 65
   Show Original command, 65-66
File Sharing, 451-477. *See also* Networks; Program Linking.
   access privileges, 468-470, 471-476
   accessing hard drives remotely, 484-485
   Activity Monitor tab, 476-477
   Alert dialog box, 459
   Allow User to See All Disks feature, 466
   AppleTalk Control Panel, 455-456, 498-499
   Computer Names, 457
   Control Panel, 456-459, 476-477, 487-489
   Control Strip, 459
   creating groups, 463-464
   creating new users, 461-464
   Everyone option, 468
   folders, 467-471
   groups, 459-461, 463-464
   Guest Preferences dialog box, 465
   icons of shared items, 470
   limits of, 453-454
   Macintosh Owner Preferences dialog box, 465-466
   monitoring, 476-477
   Owner Names, 457
   Owner Preferences dialog box, 465-466
   owners, 468
   passwords, 457, 462-463
   Personal Web Sharing, 516-519
   preparing for, 455-456
   privileges, 468-470, 471-476
   registering users and groups, 459-461
   Sharing dialog box, 460-461, 467-470
   Shutdown dialog box, 458
   Start File Sharing/Stop File Sharing AppleScript, 375
   starting, 456-459
   steps to using, 454-455
   turning off, 470-471
   User & Groups Control Panel, 459-461
   User Preferences dialog box, 462-463
   User/Group option, 468
   volumes, 467-471

Fonts folder   **587**

File synchronization, PowerBook system software, 174, 187-189
File Translation dialog box, File Exchange Control Panel, 224
FileMaker suite, AppleEvents, 325, 326
Files
    adding to System Folder, 57-58
    copying in background, 271-272
    deleting from System Folder, 59
    dragging between inactive windows, 95-96
    GUI elements, 15-16
    managing, 4, 8
    multiple, 96-97
    searching for. *See* Sherlock search engine.
Find By Contents tab, Sherlock search engine, 160-163
Find dialog box, Sherlock search engine, 161
Find File tab, Sherlock search engine, 156-159
Find Items section, Sherlock search engine, 158-159
Finder, 61-112
    advanced features, 92-101
    AppleScript and, 371, 372
    Clean Up command, 100-101
    collapsible windows and, 72, 73
    comments, 169-171
    context-sensitive help, 101-104
    Desktop window basics, 71-92
    dragging files between inactive windows, 95-96
    Get Info dialog box, 49, 107-112
    hiding, 71
    icon proxies, 99
    keyboard navigation, 92-95
    Mac OS 8.6 components, 5-6
    menus, 62-71
    multiple files and, 96-97
    Option key options, 99
    pop-up folders, 73
    Preferences menu, 73-76
    resizing windows, 99-100
    System Folder, 48-49
    tabbed folders, 73
    title bar pop-up menus, 98
    Trash, 105-106
    View menu, 78-88
Finder menus, 62-71
    About This Computer command, 64
    Apple, 64
    Apple System Profiler command, 64
    Application menu and Application Switcher, 69-71
    Arrange/Sort List commands, 68
    Clean Up command, 68, 100-101
    commands, 64-71
    Favorites folder, 64
    Help menu, 69, 70
    Label command, 65, 167-169
    Move To Trash command, 65
    pop-up windows, 66

    Preferences options, 66, 67
    Recent commands, 64
    Sherlock search engine, 64-65
    Show Original command, 65-66
    Special menu, 68-69
    View menu, 66, 68
Finder suite, AppleEvents, 325
Firewalls, Applet Runner application and, 384
Floating palettes, Application menu and Application Switcher, 70-71
Floppy disks
    formatting, 16-17
    types of, 16
FM Radio application, 414
Folder Actions, AppleScript, 372-375
Folders
    aliasing, 147-148
    File Sharing, 467-471
    GUI elements, 15-16
    icon proxies, 99
    opening with space bar, 75
    Share a Folder/Share a Folder (No Guest) AppleScript, 375
    spring-loaded option, 74-75
    stationery document, 211
    tabbed (pop-up), 73
    viewing as lists, 84-87
Font Reserve utility, 301-304
    Browser application, 302-304
    imaging models, 282
    Settings application, 301
Fonts, 288-310. *See also* Imaging models; Printing.
    adding to Fonts folder, 309
    advanced typography, 304-305
    ATM (Adobe Type Manager), 294-296
    bitmapped, 288-289
    default, 299-301
    difficulties with, 281
    Fonts folder, 49, 50, 309
    glyphs, 304-305
    ID conflicts, 292-293
    installing, 307-308
    localization and character sets, 306-307
    mixing types of, 299-301
    PostScript, 290-296
    printer. *See* Printer fonts.
    removing from Fonts folder, 310
    screen, 292-293
    suitcases, 308, 309
    tasks, 8
    text effects, 306
    TrueType, 284, 296-299
    types of, 282-283
Fonts folder
    adding fonts to, 309
    removing fonts from, 310
    System Folder, 49, 50

Fonts tab, Appearance Control Panel, 114, 115
Foreground and background processing, 266-268. *See also* Background processing; Multiple applications.
   active programs, 266-267
   switching between applications, 267-268
Formatting
   floppy disks, 16-17
   scripts (Script Editor), 367-369
Forward button, Network Browser, 487
Found Items dialog box, Sherlock search engine, 158
Foundation Classes, Java, 390-392
Fragmented memory, 246
Frames, OpenDoc, 345-346
FTP clients, Transmit, 545-546
FWB Hard Disk ToolKit, troubleshooting tools, 442

G

General Controls Control Panel, 17-18
   configurable elements, 122-123
   customizing Mac OS 8.6, 120-123
   hiding Desktop, 120-121
   Launcher Control Panel, 205, 206
General Information section (Get Info dialog box), 107-109
   Icon option, 107-108
   Locked option, 108, 109
   Stationery Pad option, 109
General tab (Preferences menu), 74-76
   grid spacing options, 76
   Simple Finder option, 74, 75
   spacing options, 76
   spring-loaded folder option, 74-75
Get Editions Now option, Subscriber Options command (Edition Manager), 336
Get Editions option, Subscriber Options command (Edition Manager), 335-336
Get Info dialog box (Finder), 107-112
   aliases, 111-112
   General Information section, 107-109
   Memory section, 110, 250-253
   "Not Enough Memory" dialog box, 253, 254
   Sharing section, 109-110
   stationery documents, 210
   Trash Info dialog box, 106, 111
   versions of, 251-252
Glyphs, 304-305. *See also* Fonts.
GoMac utility
   Apple menu, 134-136
   program bar, 134-135
Graphical User Interface. *See* GUI.
Graphics
   QuickDraw, 283-285
   QuickDraw GX, 285-287

Grid spacing options, General tab (Preferences menu), 76
Groups
   alias, 149, 150
   File Sharing, 459-461, 463-464
   Launcher Control Panel, 205-206
   User & Groups Control Panel, 459-461
Guest Preferences dialog box, File Sharing, 465
GUI (Graphical User Interface), 9-17
   cursors, 13-15
   dialog boxes, 11-12
   files and folders, 15-16
   floppy disks, 16-17
   icons, 9-10
   menus, 13, 14
   mouse and cursors, 13-15
   palettes, 12
   QuickDraw 3D, 410-411
   windows, 10-12
Guide file, AppleScript, 359

H

Hard drives
   accessing remotely, 484-485
   aliasing, 152
   troubleshooting "not recognized," 430
Hardware control, 4
Help, 101-104
   AppleScript, 361
   Balloon Help, 101-103
   contextual, 102, 103-104
   Personal Web Sharing, 519-520
Help folder, System Folder, 49
Help menu, Finder menus, 69, 70
Hide/Show Folder Sizes AppleScript, More Automated Tasks folder, 376
Hiding
   applications, 272-274
   Desktop, 120-121, 274-275
   Finder, 71
Hierarchical lists, viewing, 88-92
Home pages
   Personal NetFinder, 512-514
   Personal Web Sharing, 512
HTML (HyperText Markup Language), Personal Web Sharing, 505-507

I

IAC (Interapplication Communication), 321-327. *See also* Edition Manager; OpenDoc.
   AppleEvents, 323-327
   AppleScript and, 356
   spellchecking, 322-323

Icons
    AppleShare Volume, 482-483
    droplet (running scripts), 366
    General Information section (Get Info dialog box), 107-108
    GUI elements, 9-10
    PostScript and TrueType font, 308
    proxies, 99
    replacing alias, 147
    shared item, 470
    Sherlock search engine, 159
    View menu, 81-84
    View Options configuration window, 82-83
    viewing windows as, 81-84
    Views tab (Preferences menu), 77
Imaging models, 281-287. *See also* Fonts; Printing.
    Font Reserve utility, 282, 301-304
    QuickDraw, 283-285, 287
    QuickDraw GX, 285-287
Import/export file types, QuickTime, 399-400
In-place editing, OpenDoc, 344
Inactive windows, dragging files between, 95-96
Inbox folders, access privileges (File Sharing), 474
Index Volumes button, Sherlock search engine, 162, 163
Inheritance, AppleScript, 352
INITs. *See* Extensions; Extensions folder.
Ink attributes, QuickDraw GX, 286
Input support, PowerBook system software, 174
Installer, System Folder, 57
Installing
    fonts, 307-308
    QuickDraw 3D, 409
Interapplication Communication. *See* IAC.
Interfaces
    Graphical User. *See* GUI.
    loopback, 508-509
International languages, localization and character sets, 306-307
Internet, 491-547
    ARA (Apple Remote Access), 500-502
    assistants, 493-497
    DNS (Domain Name Servers), 496
    email accounts, 496
    Editor Assistant, 494-496
    Explorer. *See* Microsoft Internet Explorer.
    IP addresses, 496
    ISP Referral Assistant, 496-497
    ISPs (Internet Service Providers), 491-492
    LANs (Local Area Networks) and, 491-492
    modems and, 492, 495-496
    Open Transport, 6, 497-500
    Personal Web Sharing, 505-520
    Setup Assistant, 493-494
    Setup folder, 493
    Sherlock search engine, 163-164
    software, 521-547
    troubleshooting connections, 430-431
    URL aliases, 538-539
    utilities, 542-546
Internet Control Panel, 537-538
    QuickTime, 402
Internet Search Sites folder, Sherlock search engine, 50, 51, 64-65
Internet software, 521-547
    Date & Time Control Panel, 538
    file compression, 539-542
    Internet Control Panel, 537-538
    Microsoft Internet Explorer, 531-534
    Microsoft Outlook Express, 534-536
    Netscape Communicator, 522-531
    utilities. *See* Internet utilities.
Internet Suite, AppleScript, 372
Internet utilities, 542-546
    Adobe Acrobat Reader, 543-545
    shareware, 542
    Transmit FTP client, 545-546
IP addresses, Internet connectivity, 496
ISPs (Internet Service Providers), 491-492
    Referral Assistant, 496-497
Italic type, aliases and, 143
Items Found window, Sherlock search engine, 157

J

Java, 379-394
    Applet Runner application, 383-385
    applets, 380
    Art Safari applet, 381, 382
    features, 380-381
    Foundation Classes, 390-392
    "look and feel" of cross-platform programs, 389-393
    MRJ (Macintosh Runtime Java), 381, 382
    Pluggable Look and Feel, 392-393
    running applets, 383-385
Java VMs (Virtual Machines), 385-389
    ArcTest applet, 386-387
    Bar Chart applet, 387
    DrawTest applet, 387, 388
    LED applet, 387, 388
    Metrowerks, 385
    Neon Sign applet, 387, 389
    Pythagorean Theorem applet, 389, 390
    Roaster, 385
    Symantec, 385
    Voltage applet, 388, 389

K

Kaleidoscope utility, 130-131, 132
    Scheme Settings tab, 131

Keep Arranged options, View menu, 83-84
Keyboard Control Panel, 20
Keyboard navigation (Finder), 92-95
　commands, 93-95
Keyboard problems, troubleshooting, 431-432
Keyboard shortcuts
　Application Switcher, 118
　dialog box, 214-216

L

Label command, 167-169
　assigning labels, 169
　colors, 168-169
　configuring labels, 167-168
　File menu, 65
　ways to use, 168-169, 170
Labels tab, Preferences menu, 78
Languages, localization and character sets, 306-307
LANs (Local Area Networks), Internet connectivity, 491-492
Laptops. See PowerBook system software.
Launcher Control Panel, 204-207
　adding items to, 205
　aliases, 206
　deleting items from, 206
　General Controls Control Panel, 205, 206
　groups, 205-206
　opening, 205
Launcher Items folder, System Folder, 50, 51
Launching applications, 8, 200-207
　alias folders, 203
　aliases, 141
　Apple menu, 202, 203
　double-clicking, 201, 202, 204
　dragging, 202, 204
　Favorites folder, 202, 204, 205
　Launcher Control Panel, 204-207
　methods of, 203-204
　Recent commands, 202
　Startup Items folder, 202
　stationery documents, 202
　utilities, 200-201
　ways of, 201-202
LED applet, Java VMs (Virtual Machines), 387, 388
Linking
　aliases, 144-145
　AppleEvents and programs, 326-327
　edition files, 338-339
　Program, 487-489
Lists
　dragging, 90, 91
　expanding and collapsing, 89-90
　reordering columns, 92, 93
　resizing columns, 91-92

Sort List/Arrange commands, 68
View menu, 84-87
viewing folders as, 84-87
viewing hierarchical, 88-92
Local Area Networks (LANs), Internet connectivity, 491-492
Localization, international character sets and, 306-307
Location Manager, PowerBook system software, 189-191
Locked items, Sherlock search engine, 159
Locked option, General Information section (Get Info dialog box), 108, 109
"Look and feel" of cross-platform programs, 389-393
　Card Test applet, 390, 391
　JFC (Java Foundation Classes) and, 390-393
　Pluggable Look and Feel, 392-393
Loopback interface, Personal Web Sharing, 508-509

M

Mac OS 8.6, 3-29
　AppleScript, 351-377
　applications, 197-116
　backwards compatibility, 4
　basic operations, 9-28
　common software elements, 4
　compatibility, 197-200, 217-234
　components, 5-8
　cross-platform compatibility, 217-234
　customizing, 113-138
　data management, 139-172
　disk and file management, 4
　Edition Manager, 327-342
　File Sharing, 451-477
　Finder, 61-112
　Finder menus, 62-71
　fonts, 288-310
　freezing at startup problem, 427-428
　freezing during use problem, 428-429
　GUI (Graphical User Interface), 9-17
　hardware control, 4
　IAC (Interapplication Communication), 321-327
　imaging models, 281-287
　Internet, 491-547
　Internet software, 521-547
　Java, 379-394
　memory management, 235-257
　multimedia, 395-421
　multiple applications, 259-279
　networks, 479-489
　OpenDoc, 342-349
　PCs and. See Cross-platform compatibility.
　PowerBook system software, 173-194
　printing, 310-319
　QuickDraw, 283-285
　QuickDraw GX, 285-287

Multimedia 591

QuickDraw 3D, 408-412
QuickTime, 396-408
System Folder, 31-59
tasks, 3-5, 8-9
Themes Web site, 117
transferring data, 21-28
troubleshooting, 423-447
utilities, 17-21
Mac OS Purge, memory utilities, 250
Mac OS X Server, multitasking, 264
Macintosh Desktop, Finder, 61-112
Macintosh Owner Preferences dialog box, File Sharing, 465-466
Macintosh Runtime Java (MRJ), 381, 382. *See also* Java.
MacLinkPlus, 225-229. *See also* Cross-platform compatibility.
   converting documents, 228-229
   file formats, 225-228
MacsBug utility, troubleshooting tools, 441
MacTCP DNR file, System Folder, 51
Mapping memory, Memory Mapper utility, 248-249
Marquee selections, Finder and multiple files, 96-97
Memory, 235-257
   About This Computer dialog box, 245-247, 253-255
   controlling, 245-257
   disk caches, 238-239
   disk space comparison, 235-236
   fragmented, 246
   Get Info dialog box, 110, 250-253
   Memory Control Panel, 236-245
   Memory Mapper utility, 248-249
   MultiFinder and, 262
   multitasking and, 277-279
   out-of-memory alert box, 246
   Sherlock search engine requirements, 155
   storage comparison, 235-236
   32-bit addressing, 243
   troubleshooting application crashes, 432-435
   utilities, 248-250
   virtual, 239-243, 255-256
Memory Control Panel, 236-245
   disk caches, 238-239
   Modern Memory Manager and, 244
   32-bit addressing, 243
   tips, 244-245
   virtual memory, 239-243
Memory Mapper utility, 248-249
   application pools, 248
   System Heap, 248-249
Memory utilities, 248-250
   Mac OS Purge, 250
   Memory Mapper, 248-249
Menus
   AMICO utility, 136-137
   Apple. *See* Apple menu.
   Finder, 62-71

GUI elements, 13, 14
OpenDoc, 347
title bar pop-up, 98
types of, 13, 14
MetaFile format, QuickDraw 3D, 409-410
Metrowerks, Java VMs (Virtual Machines), 385
Microsoft Internet Explorer, 531-534. *See also* Internet software; Netscape Communicator.
   Explorer Bar, 531-532
   MS Preference Panels folder, 52
   printing with, 532-534
Microsoft Outlook Express, email, 534-536
MIME Types tab, Personal Web Sharing, 515
Mirroring, video, 181-182
Miscellaneous suite, AppleEvents, 325
Modeling with QuickDraw 3D, 411-412
Modem Control Panel, ARA (Apple Remote Access), 500-501
Modems, Internet connectivity, 492, 495-496
Modern Memory Manager, Memory Control Panel and, 244
Monitors, quality features, 126
Monitors & Sound Control Panel, 19, 20, 124-128
   Alerts section, 127
   Color section, 128
   Monitor section, 124-126
   PowerBook system software, 181-182
   Sound section, 126-127
   VRAM (Video RAM), 124-125
MooV file type, QuickTime, 398
More Automated Tasks folder, AppleScript, 359-360, 376
Mouse
   Control Panel, 19, 20
   cursors and, 13-15
   cut and paste, 22-25
   drag and drop, 22, 25-28
   troubleshooting problems, 431-432
Move To Trash command, Finder menus, 65
MoviePlayer, QuickTime, 406
Movies, QuickTime, 396-408
MPEG 3 players, 420-421
MPEG standard, QuickTime, 397
MRJ (Macintosh Runtime Java), 381, 382. *See also* Java.
MS Preference Panels folder, System Folder, 52
MultiFinder, 259, 262-263. *See also* Finder.
   complexity of, 263
   insufficient memory and, 262
   negative reputation of, 262
Multimedia, 395-421
   Apple DVD Player, 417-419
   Apple FM Radio application, 414
   Apple Video Player, 414-416
   AppleCD Audio Player, 416-417
   extended CD-ROMs, 419-420
   MPEG 3 players, 420-421
   QuickDraw 3D, 408-412

592 Multimedia

QuickTime, 396-408
speech generation, 413
text-to-speech, 413-414
Multiple aliases, 145
    data file, 150
Multiple applications, 259-279
    background printing, 269-271
    background processing, 266-269
    copying files in background, 271-272
    foreground and background processing, 266-268
    hiding applications, 272-274
    hiding Desktop, 274-275
    MultiFinder, 259, 262-263
    multitasking, 259, 260-262, 263-264, 276-279
Multiple documents, stationery documents, 211
Multiple files, Finder and, 96-97
Multitasking, 260-262, 263-264
    benefits of, 261-262
    cooperative, 259-260
    history of, 263-264
    Mac OS X Server, 264
    memory and, 277-279
    OpenDoc architecture, 264, 344
    preemptive, 259-260
    Thread Manager, 263-264
    time slices, 259
    tips, 276-277
    types of, 259-260

N

Names
    Computer and Owner, 457
    Domain Servers (DNS), 496
    PostScript font, 292
    PostScript font conflicts, 293
    Sherlock search engine criteria, 156
Neon Sign applet, Java VMs (Virtual Machines), 387, 389
Nested edition files, 340-341
Netscape Communicator, 522-531. *See also* Internet software; Microsoft Internet Explorer.
    Messenger, 529-531
    Navigator, 523-528
Netscape Messenger, 529-531
    email, 529
    Usenet newsgroups, 529-531
Netscape Navigator, 523-528
    Beatnik plug-in, 525
    bookmarks, 524-525
    PDFViewer plug-in, 526
    Plug-in Finder page, 528
    plug-ins, 525-528
    QuickTime plug-in, 527
    Shockwave plug-in, 525-526, 527

Network Browser, 485-487. *See also* Chooser.
    Backward and Forward buttons, 487
    Connect to Server dialog box, 486
    Favorites button, 486-487
    Recent button, 487
    Shortcuts button, 486
Networks, 479-489. *See also* File Sharing; Internet; Program Linking.
    accessing hard drives remotely, 484-485
    accessing volumes, 479-485
    aliases and servers, 142, 152
    AppleShare Volume icons, 482-483
    Connect dialog box, 480-482
    connecting with Chooser, 479-481
    disconnecting from remote volumes, 484
    edition files and, 340
    local area (LANs) and Internet connectivity, 491-492
    Network Browser, 485-487
    Program Linking, 487-489
    remote volumes and access privileges, 482-483
    selecting specific volumes, 481-482
    servers and aliases, 142, 152
    Sharing command, 483
    sharing data, 217-218
    tasks, 9
    troubleshooting connections, 430-431
    volume aliases, 483-484
Newsgroups, Netscape Messenger, 529-531
NFNT, PostScript fonts and ID conflicts, 292-293
None option, access privileges (File Sharing), 472
Norton AntiVirus, troubleshooting tools, 446
Norton Utilities, troubleshooting tools, 442, 443
"Not Enough Memory" dialog box, Get Info dialog box (Finder), 253, 254
Note Pad, 28
Numbers Control Panel, 21

O

Object Model, AppleScript, 356
O'Grady Web site, PowerBooks, 175, 176
Open command, stationery documents, 211
Open dialog box
    ACTION Utilities, 131-134
    Desktop and, 212
    keyboard shortcuts, 214-216
Open Publisher option, Subscriber Options command (Edition Manager), 336-337
Open Scripting Architecture (OSA), AppleScript, 355-357
Open Transport (Internet connectivity), 497-500. *See also* ARA (Apple Remote Access); Internet.
    AppleTalk Control Panel, 498-499
    components, 498-500
    Mac OS 8.6 components, 6
    TCP/IP Control Panel, 499-500

OpenDoc, 342-349. *See also* Edition Manager; IAC (Interapplication Communication).
   benefits of, 343-344
   compound documents, 343
   consistency of, 344
   Control Panels, 348-349
   cross-platform compatibility, 344
   documents and parts, 344-347
   Editor Setup Control Panel, 348
   frames, 345-346
   in-place editing, 344
   menus, 347
   multitasking, 264, 344
   part handlers, 345-347
   Setup Control Panel, 348-349
   storing compound documents, 346-347
Opening
   folders with space bar, 75
   Launcher Control Panel, 205
Operating system. *See* Mac OS 8.6.
Option key
   options, 99
   Sherlock search engine and, 159-160
Options configuration tab, Appearance Control Panel, 116-117
OSA (Open Scripting Architecture), AppleScript, 355-357
Out-of-memory alert box, fragmented memory, 246
Outbox folders, access privileges (File Sharing), 474-475
Outlook Express, Microsoft, 534-536
Owner category, access privileges (File Sharing), 473-474
Owner Names, File Sharing, 457
Owner Preferences dialog box, File Sharing, 465-466
Owners, File Sharing, 468

P

Page formatting, Print dialog box, 312-313
Palettes
   floating, 70-71
   GUI elements, 12
Part handlers, OpenDoc, 345-347
Parts, OpenDoc, 344-347
Password Security Control Panel, PowerBook system software, 192
Passwords, File Sharing, 457, 462-463
PC Exchange. *See also* Cross-platform compatibility.
   File Exchange Control Panel, 220-222
PDF files, Adobe Acrobat Reader, 543-545
PDFViewer plug-in, Netscape Navigator, 526
Personal NetFinder, viewing home pages and directories via, 512-514
Personal Web Sharing (Web server), 505-520. *See also* Internet.
   access privileges, 516-519
   Actions tab, 516

   configuring Web servers, 507-508
   File Sharing, 516-519
   help, 519-520
   home pages, 512
   HTML (HyperText Markup Language), 505-507
   loopback interface, 508-509
   MIME Types tab, 515
   Options tab, 515
   Personal NetFinder, 512-514
   preferences, 514-516
   security, 516-519
   starting/stopping Web Sharing, 509-510
   Web Pages folder, 510-511
   Web Sharing Control Panel, 509-512
PictureViewer, QuickTime, 407
Placeholders, stationery document, 208, 209
Plug-in Finder page, Netscape Navigator, 528
Plug-ins
   Netscape Navigator, 525-528
   QuickTime, 396-408
Pluggable Look and Feel, Java, 392-393
Pointing with cursors, 14
Pop-up folders, Finder, 73
Pop-up menus, title bar, 98
Pop-up windows
   Finder menus, 66
   View menu, 80-81
Poster images, QuickTime, 400
PostScript fonts, 290-296
   ATM (Adobe Type Manager), 294-296
   difficulties with, 291-293
   Font ID conflicts, 292-293
   icons, 308
   name conflicts, 293
   names of, 292
   non-PostScript fonts and, 291
   printer font availability, 292
   printing, 294
   QuickDraw and, 284
   screen font availability, 291-292
   TrueType fonts and, 297, 299-301
   Type 1 format, 293
PowerBook system software, 173-194
   AppleTalk, 180
   ARA (Apple Remote Access), 184
   AutoRemounter, 183
   Battery Conservation slider, 176-177
   battery recharging, 174
   battery usage, 177-180
   Control Strip, 184-187
   display management, 180-182
   Energy Saver Control Panel, 175-180, 183
   file synchronization, 174, 187-189
   input support, 174
   issues, 173-175
   Location Manager, 189-191

Monitors & Sound Control Panel, 181-182
O'Grady Web site, 175, 176
Password Security Control Panel, 192
power/performance management, 175-180
presentation services, 174
processor cycling, 179, 181
remote access, 174
remounting servers, 183
SCSI disk mode, 182
security, 191-193
sleep mode, 179, 181
spooling print jobs, 174
video mirroring, 181-182
Preemptive multitasking, 259-260
Preferences folder, System Folder, 52
Preferences menu, 73-76
General tab, 74-76
Labels tab, 78
Views tab, 76-78
Preferences options, Edit menu, 66, 67
Presentation services, PowerBook system software, 174
Previewing printing, Microsoft Internet Explorer, 532-534
Previews, QuickTime, 400
Print dialog box, 311-313
page formatting, 312-313
Printer drivers
Extensions folder, 45-46, 314-315
Mac OS 8.6 components, 6
Printer fonts
ATM (Adobe Type Manager) and, 295-296
availability of, 292
System Folder, 57
TrueType, 298-299
Printers, 314-316
Chooser and, 310-311
Chooser extensions, 45-46, 314-315
Desktop Printer Utility, 315-316
Printing, 310-319. *See also* Fonts; Imaging models.
background, 269-271
Chooser and, 310-311
ColorSync Control Panel, 316-319
Microsoft Internet Explorer, 532-534
PostScript fonts, 294
Print dialog box, 311-313
QuickDraw and, 287
spooler, 174, 313-314
tasks, 9
troubleshooting, 436-437
PrintMonitor Documents folder, System Folder, 53
Privileges, File Sharing. *See* Access privileges.
Processor cycling, PowerBook system software, 179, 181
Program bar, GoMac utility, 134-135
Program Linking, 487-489. *See also* File Sharing; Networks.
Allow Remote Program Linking check box, 489
AppleEvents and, 326-327, 489
User Options dialog box, 488

Properties dialog box, Applet Runner application, 383-384
Proportional thumbs, Smart Scrolling feature, 116, 117
Proxies, icon, 99
Proxy servers, Applet Runner application and, 384
Publish/Subscribe commands, Edition Manager, 329-330
Publish/Subscribe feature, Edition Manager, 327-329
Publisher documents, saving, 341-342
Publisher Options command, Edition Manager, 332-334
Pythagorean Theorem applet, Java VMs (Virtual Machines), 389, 390

Q

Question mark at startup, troubleshooting, 424-426
Queues, print. *See* Spooling print jobs.
QuickDraw, 283-285, 408-412
Graphics suite and AppleEvents, 324-325
PostScript and, 284
printing and, 287
text effects, 306
TrueType fonts and, 284
QuickDraw GX, 285-287
attributes, 286
capabilities incorporated into Mac OS 8.6, 285-286
QuickDraw 3D, 408-412
drag and drop, 412
installing, 409
MetaFile format, 409-410
modeling with, 411-412
text and, 411-412
3DMF files, 409-410
user interface, 410-411
QuickTime, 396-408. *See also* Multimedia.
AutoPlay option, 401
browsers and, 401-402
CD-ROMs and, 405
configuring, 401-402
Connection Speed option, 401
copyrights and, 397
drag and drop, 397
file compression and, 403-405
import/export file types, 399-400
Internet Control Panel, 402
MooV file type, 398
MoviePlayer, 406
MPEG standard, 397
Netscape Navigator and, 527
new features, 397-398
PictureViewer, 407
poster images, 400
previews, 400
size of files, 404-405
sprites, 398
versions comparison, 396-397
viewing movies, 405-406
VR movies, 407, 408

R

Radio application, Apple FM, 414
RAM. *See* Memory.
Read & Write option, access privileges (File Sharing), 473
Read Only option, access privileges (File Sharing), 473
Recent button, Network Browser, 487
Recent commands
    Finder menus, 64
    launching applications, 202
Recording AppleScripts, 362-363
    Recordable level, 361
References, AppleScript, 356
Remote access
    Apple. *See* ARA.
    PowerBook system software, 174
Remote volumes
    access privileges and, 482-483
    disconnecting from, 484
Remounting servers, PowerBook system software, 183
Removable cartridge maps, aliases and, 151-152
Removable media, aliases and, 141, 150-151
Renaming aliases, 143
Republishing edition files, 340
Required suite, AppleEvents, 324
Resizing
    list columns, 91-92
    windows, 99-100
Roaster, Java VMs (Virtual Machines), 385
ROM (Read-Only Memory), Mac OS 8.6 components, 6

S

Save dialog box
    Desktop and, 212
    keyboard shortcuts, 214-216
    stationery documents, 210, 211
Saving
    AppleScripts, 363-365
    OpenDoc compound documents, 346-347
    Publisher documents, 341-342
    Sherlock search engine criteria, 165-166
Scheduled Startup & Shutdown section, Energy Saver Control Panel, 128, 129
Scheme Settings tab, Kaleidoscope, 131
Scrapbook file
    cut and paste, 24-25
    System Folder, 53
Screen display, tasks, 9
Screen font availability, PostScript fonts, 291-292
Script Editor (AppleScript), 359, 360, 362-369. *See also* AppleScript.
    Check Syntax button, 367
    comments, 368
    droplet icons, 366
    formatting scripts, 367-369
    modifying scripts, 366-369
    recording scripts, 362-363
    running scripts, 365-366
    saving scripts, 363-365
Scriptable level, AppleScript, 361
Scripting Additions folder
    AppleScript, 358
    System Folder, 53
Scripts folder
    AppleScript, 359, 360-361
    System Folder, 53-54
Scrolling, Smart Scrolling feature, 116, 117
SCSI disk mode, PowerBook system software, 182
Search engine. *See* Sherlock search engine.
Security
    Personal Web Sharing, 516-519
    PowerBook system software, 191-193
Send Editions Now option, Publisher Options command (Edition Manager), 332
Send Editions option, Publisher Options command (Edition Manager), 332
Server Options button, Date & Time Control Panel, 124
Servers
    aliases and network, 142, 152
    remounting with PowerBook system software, 183
    Web. *See* Personal Web Sharing.
Settings application, Font Reserve utility, 301
Setup Assistant, Internet, 493-494
Setup folder, Internet, 493
Share a Folder/Share a Folder (No Guest) AppleScript, Useful Scripts set, 375
Shareware, Internet utilities, 542
Sharing command, remote volumes and access privileges, 483
Sharing data, 217-225. *See also* Cross-platform compatibility; File Sharing.
    File Exchange Control Panel, 220-225
    networked computers, 217-218
    SuperDrive, 219
    TCP/IP and, 218
Sharing dialog box, File Sharing, 460-461, 467-470
Sharing section, Get Info dialog box (Finder), 109-110
Sherlock search engine, 153-167
    advanced searches, 159-160
    custom icons, 159
    file searching, 156-159
    Find By Contents tab, 160-163
    Find dialog box, 161
    Find File tab, 156-159
    Finder menus, 64-65
    Found Items dialog box, 158
    icons, 159
    Index Volumes button, 162, 163
    Internet, 163-164
    Internet Search Sites folder, 50, 51
    Items Found window, 157

locked items, 159
memory requirements, 155
name criteria, 156
Option key and, 159-160
Preferences option, 164-165
saving search criteria, 165-166
search types, 155
tips for effective searches, 166-167
visibility and, 159
Web sites, 163-164
Shift key, suppressing Extensions, 46-47
Shockwave plug-in, Netscape Navigator, 525-526, 527
Shortcuts, keyboard. *See* Keyboard shortcuts.
Shortcuts button, Network Browser, 486
Show Clipboard command, 24
Show Original command, File menu, 65-66
Shutdown, troubleshooting problems, 429-430
Shutdown dialog box, File Sharing, 458
Shutdown Items folder, System Folder, 54
Simple Finder option, General tab (Preferences menu), 74, 75
SimpleText, drag and drop and, 26-27
Sleep mode, PowerBook system software, 179, 181
Smart Scrolling feature, Appearance Control Panel, 116, 117
SoftWindows, cross-platform compatibility, 230-231
Sort List/Arrange commands, View menu, 68
Sound
    Appearance Control Panel, 116
    AppleCD Audio Player, 416-417
    "Mac OS 8.6 Themes" Web site, 117
    Monitors & Sound Control Panel, 19, 126-127
    MPEG 3 players, 420-421
Soundset Constructor application, 117
Space bar, opening folders with, 75
Spacing options, General tab (Preferences menu), 76
Special characters for alphabetizing files, Apple Menu folder, 38-39
Special menu, Finder menus, 68-69
Speech Control Panel, text-to-speech, 413-414
Speech generation, 413
Spellchecking, IAC (Interapplication Communication), 322-323
Spooling print jobs, 313-314
    PowerBook system software, 174
Spring-loaded folder option, General tab (Preferences menu), 74-75
Sprites, QuickTime, 398
Standard Editions file, AppleScript, 357
Start File Sharing/Stop File Sharing AppleScript, Useful Scripts set, 375
Startup
    Personal Web Sharing, 509
    tasks, 8
    troubleshooting problems, 423-428

Startup Items folder
    launching applications, 202
    System Folder, 54-55
Stationery documents, 207-212
    aliases, 211
    creating, 207-210
    editing, 211-212
    folder, 211
    Get Info dialog box, 210
    launching applications, 202
    multiple documents, 211
    Open command, 211
    placeholders, 208, 209
    Save dialog box, 210, 211
    tips, 210, 211-212
    using, 210-211
Stationery Pad option, General Information section (Get Info dialog box), 109
Stickies, note reminders, 27-28
Storage versus memory, 235-236
Storing compound documents, OpenDoc, 346-347
StuffIt Expander, file compression, 539, 540-541
Style attributes, QuickDraw GX, 286
Subfolders, System Folder, 32-35
Subscribe To command, Edition Manager, 332
Subscriber Options command, Edition Manager, 334-337
Subscribers
    editing Edition Manager, 337
    edition files, 338-340
Subtractive color, ColorSync Control Panel, 317
Suitcases
    installing fonts, 308, 309
    System, 5, 55-56
Suites
    AppleEvent, 324-325
    AppleScript event, 356-357
SuperDrive, sharing data, 219
Swing. *See* JFC (Java Foundation Classes)
Switching between applications, 267-268. *See also* Application Switcher.
Symantec, Java VMs (Virtual Machines), 385
Synchronization, PowerBook system software, 174, 187-189
Synchronize Folders AppleScript, More Automated Tasks folder, 376
Synchronizing time via Internet, Date & Time Control Panel, 538
SysErrors utility, troubleshooting tools, 444-446
System Folder, 31-59
    adding files to, 57-58
    Appearance folder, 35-36
    Apple Menu folder, 36-40
    Application Support folder, 40
    Clipboard, 40
    ColorSync Profiles folder, 40-41

Contextual Menu Items folder, 41, 42
Control Panels folder, 41-44
Control Strip Modules folder, 44-45
deleting files from, 59
Extensions folder, 45-48
Favorites folder, 48, 64, 202, 204, 205
Finder, 48-49
Fonts folder, 49, 50, 309-310
Help folder, 49
Installer, 57
Internet Search Sites folder, 50, 51
Launcher Items folder, 50, 51
MacTCP DNR file, 51
miscellaneous files, 56
modifying, 56-57
MS Preference Panels folder, 52
Preferences folder, 52
printer fonts, 57
PrintMonitor Documents folder, 53
Scrapbook file, 53
Scripting Additions folder, 53, 358
Scripts folder, 53-54, 359, 360-361
Sherlock Internet search engine, 50, 51, 64-65
Shutdown Items folder, 54
Startup Items folder, 54-55
subfolders, 32-35
System suitcase, 5, 55-56
Text Encodings folder, 56
System Heap, Memory Mapper utility, 248-249
System suitcase
    Mac OS 8.6 components, 5
    System Folder, 55-56

T

Tabbed folders, Finder, 73
Table suite, AppleEvents, 325
Tasks, 3-5, 8-9
    application launching, 8
    common software elements, 4
    disk and file management, 4, 8
    fonts, 8
    hardware control, 4
    networking, 9
    printing, 9
    screen display, 9
    start-up, 8
    windows and dialog boxes, 8
TCP/IP, sharing data and, 218
TCP/IP Control Panel, Open Transport (Internet connectivity), 499-500
TechTool Pro, troubleshooting tools, 442, 443
Templates. *See* Stationery documents.
Text Control Panel, 21

Text effects, 306. *See also* Fonts.
    3D via QuickDraw 3D, 411-412
Text Encodings folder, System Folder, 56
Text suite, AppleEvents, 324
Text-to-speech, Speech Control Panel, 413-414
Themes
    Kaleidoscope utility, 130-131, 132
    "Mac OS 8.6 Themes" Web site, 117
Themes tab, Appearance Control Panel, 113, 114
32-bit addressing, 243. *See also* Memory.
Thread Manager, multitasking, 263-264
3DMF files, QuickDraw 3D, 409-410
Time
    Date & Time Control Panel, 18-19, 123-124, 538
    synchronizing via Internet, 538
Time slices, multitasking, 259
Title bar pop-up menus, 98
Transferring data, 21-28
    Clipboard, 21-25
    cut and paste, 22-25
    drag and drop, 22, 25-28
Transform attributes, QuickDraw GX, 286
Translations
    File Translation dialog box, 224
    MacLinkPlus, 225-229
Transmit FTP client, 545-546
Trash, 105-106. *See also* Deleting.
    aliasing, 151
    Empty Trash command, 105
Trash Info dialog box, Get Info dialog box (Finder), 106, 111
Troubleshooting, 423-447
    application crashes, 432-435
    blinking question mark at startup, 424-426
    colors, 435-436
    common problems, 423-438
    documents not opening, 437-438
    hard drives not recognized, 430
    Internet connections, 430-431
    keyboard problems, 431-432
    Mac OS 8.6 freezes at startup, 427-428
    Mac OS 8.6 freezes during use, 428-429
    mouse problems, 431-432
    network connections, 430-431
    preventing problems, 447
    printing, 436-437
    shutdown problems, 429-430
    startup problems, 423-428
Troubleshooting tools, 438-446
    Apple System Profiler, 440
    bootable floppies, 441
    Conflict Catcher utility, 444
    Disinfectant utility, 446
    Disk First Aid utility, 438-439
    Drive Setup utility, 439

598 Troubleshooting tools

Extension Manager, 440-441
Extension Overload utility, 444, 445
File Buddy utility, 443-444
FWB Hard Disk ToolKit, 442
MacsBug utility, 441
Norton AntiVirus, 446
Norton Utilities, 442, 443
SysErrors utility, 444-446
TechTool Pro, 442, 443
Virex utility, 446
TrueType fonts, 296-299
    glyphs, 304
    GX extension, 297
    icons, 308
    PostScript fonts and, 297, 299-301
    printers and, 298-299
    QuickDraw and, 284
    technology of, 298-299
Type 1 format, PostScript fonts, 293
Typefaces. *See* Fonts.

U

Unit types, AppleScript, 371
Universal format, AppleScript, 353
URL Access Scripting Addition dictionary,
   AppleScript, 358
URL aliases, Internet, 538-539
Useful Scripts set, AppleScript, 375-376
Usenet newsgroups, Netscape Messenger, 529-531
User & Groups Control Panel, File Sharing, 459-461
User Options dialog box, Program Linking, 488
User Preferences dialog box, File Sharing, 462-463
User/Group category, File Sharing, 474
User/Group option, File Sharing, 468
Utilities, 17-21, 130-137
    ACTION, 131-134
    AMICO, 136-137
    BeHierarchic, 137, 138
    Chooser, 17
    Control Panels, 17-21
    customizing Mac OS 8.6 with, 130-137
    GoMac, 134-136
    Internet, 542-546
    Kaleidoscope, 130-131, 132
    launching applications with, 200-201
    memory, 248-250

V

Video. *See also* QuickTime.
    Apple Video Player, 414-416
Video mirroring, PowerBook system software, 181-182

View menu, 78-88
    Arrange/Sort List commands, 68
    Arranged options, 83-84
    buttons, 84, 85
    Clean Up command, 68, 100-101
    Desktop, 88
    Finder menus, 66, 68, 78-88
    icons, 81-84
    Keep Arranged options, 83-84
    lists, 84-87
    pop-up windows, 80-81
    window types, 79
    window viewing options, 79
Viewing
    application dictionaries, 369-371
    directories via Personal NetFinder, 512-514
    folders as lists, 84-87
    hierarchical lists, 88-92
    QuickTime movies, 405-406
    windows as buttons, 84, 85
    windows as icons, 81-84
Views tab (Preferences menu), 76-78
    icons, 77
    windows, 77-78
Virex utility, troubleshooting tools, 446
Virtual Machines. *See* Java VMs.
Virtual memory, 239-243, 255-256
    About This Computer dialog box, 246
    disabling, 243
    drawbacks to, 240
    enabling, 240-242
    performance tips, 242-243
    requirements, 255-256
Virtual PC utility, cross-platform compatibility, 230-234
Virus tools, 446
Visibility
    comments, 171
    Sherlock search engine, 159
Voltage applet, Java VMs (Virtual Machines), 388, 389
Volumes
    access privileges and remote, 482-483
    accessing network, 479-485
    aliasing, 149, 483-484
    AppleShare icons, 482-483
    File Sharing, 467-471
    Index button (Sherlock search engine), 162, 163
    remote, 482-483, 484
VR movies, QuickTime, 407, 408
VRAM (Video RAM), Monitors & Sound Control
   Panel, 124-125

W

Web Pages folder, Personal Web Sharing, 510-511
Web servers. *See* Personal Web Sharing.

Web Sharing Control Panel, Personal Web Sharing, 509-512
Web sites, Sherlock search engine, 163-164
Windows
    collapsible, 72, 73
    cross-platform compatibility, 217-234
    dragging files between inactive, 95-96
    Finder, 71-92
    GUI elements, 10-12
    palettes, 12
    pop-up, 66, 80-81
    resizing, 99-100
    tasks, 8
    View menu, 78-88
    viewing as buttons, 84, 85
    viewing as icons, 81-84
    Views tab (Preferences menu), 77-78
WindowShade, collapsible windows, 72, 73
Words, AppleScript, 352
Workgroups, File Sharing, 475-476
WorldScript, localization and character sets, 307
Write Only option, File Sharing, 472

Z

Zoombox, Application Switcher, 119

What's On The CD-ROM

The Mac OS 8.6 Book's companion CD-ROM contains applications and utilities specifically selected to enhance the usefulness of this book, including:

- *BBEdit*—A fully functional version of BBEdit Lite 4.1 as well as a demo version of BBEdit 5.0.2 are included, along with other utilities and plug-ins. BBEdit is an essential text and HTML editor used by professional Web designers.
- *Default Folder*—A demo version of Default Folder, a must-have utility used to enhance Open and Save dialog boxes.
- *Kaleidoscope*—A demo version of Kaleidoscope 2.1.2. Kaleidoscope is a wildly popular utility that is used to change the way the Mac OS draws windows, menu bars, dialog boxes, and icons.
- *GraphicConverter*—A trial version of GraphicConverter 3.6.1. GraphicConverter is a shareware image editing tool used by amateurs and professional graphic designers to create and manipulate images. All the figures in this book were created using GraphicConverter.
- *SoundApp*—A fully functional version of SoundApp, a freeware sound editing program used to record and edit sounds in all the most popular file formats for Mac, PC, and Unix.

System Requirements

Software:
- Your operating system must be Mac OS 8.6.

Hardware:
- A PowerPC processor is required.
- 24MB of RAM is the minimum requirement.